Inside the
secondary classroom

Inside the secondary classroom

Sara Delamont and Maurice Galton

Routledge & Kegan Paul
London and New York

W 32448 /15.95 1.87

First published in 1986 by
Routledge & Kegan Paul Ltd
11 New Fetter Lane, London EC4P 4EE

Set in 10/11 pt Times
by Inforum Ltd, Portsmouth
and printed in Great Britain
by Billing and Sons Ltd
Worcester

British Library Cataloguing in Publication Data

Delamont, Sara
Inside the secondary classroom.
1. Students, Transfer of—England
2. Education, Elementary—England
3. Education, Secondary—England
I. Title II. Galton, Maurice
373.12'914'0942   LB3064

ISBN 0–7102–0933–9

Contents

Acknowledgments   ix

1   Introduction: the ORACLE project   1

2   Ready, steady, panic? Preparation for transfer in the
        ORACLE schools   15

3   First days in the new school   43

4   Danger! schooling in progress: Physical and social
        dangers in the new schools   64

5   The Luton Airport Syndrome: Movement and immobility
        in the new schools   91

6   Speed merchants and slow coaches: Time in the
        new schools   127

7   What group are you in? Formal grouping arrangements
        in the new schools   155

8   One big family? The home and the school   182

9   Help from my friends? The staffroom and the peer
        groups   209

10 Conclusions   240

Contents

Appendix 1   Lists of participants   244

Appendix 2   Follow-up data   252

**Bibliography of publications from the ORACLE
   project**   267

Bibliography of works cited in the text   270

Index of authors   280

Index of participants   283

Index of subjects   288

vi

Tables and figures

	Tables	*page*
1.1	Main characteristics of the six transfer schools	12
2.1	Friends, siblings and cousins at new school	20
2.2	Mean anxiety scores through transfer by school	41
7.1	Craft groups at Guy Mannering	163
7.2	Guy Mannering band placements by lower school attended	167
7.3	Band placements at Guy Mannering. Guy Mannering Lower School versus other schools	167
7.4	Fourth year credits earned for St Stephen's by form	169
A2.1	Upper schools visited in follow-up phase	253
A2.2	Pen portraits of pupils followed up	255
A2.3	Fida and Karena's fifth year reports	260
A2.4	Leaving reports of Harry, Sinclair and Greg	261
A2.5	Number of girls doing science 14–16	263
A2.6	Number of boys doing a foreign language at 14–16	263
A2.7	Number of pupils staying into the sixth forms	264
A2.8	Destinations of fifth year leavers from observed classes known to schools	264
A2.9	Number of 16–year-olds recorded as truants	265
A2.10	Number of pupils gaining categories of qualifications at 16+, from Sanditon, Melin Court and Waverly	266

	Figures	
6.1	Melin Court timetable of form 1M	134

Acknowledgments

The SSRC funded the ORACLE project at the School of Education, University of Leicester, from 1975–1980, and thus enabled this work to be carried out. We are grateful to Professor Brian Simon, the co-director with Professor Galton, for his enthusiasm and support with this phase of the research and its presentation.

The three central members of the ORACLE team, John Willcocks, Paul Croll and Anne Jasman, have all made a substantial contribution to this phase of the ORACLE work. The data were gathered by John Willcocks, Paul Croll, Margaret Greig, Janice Lea, and Sarah Tann and we are indebted to them for their hard work and commitment.

Diana Stroud was the ORACLE secretary throughout the project, and has therefore carried a major burden with unfailing cheerfulness and skill. Jaya Katariya, Sheila Spencer, Val Dobie, Myrtle Robins, Cynthia Diggins and Lyndsey Nicholas all typed parts of the book or its constituent material, and we are very much in their debt.

We wish to thank the schools, teachers and pupils in 'Coalthorpe', 'Bridgehampton' and 'Ashburton' who cooperated so fully with the project. We were received with great tolerance by very busy people, and owe them an enormous debt. All these schools, teachers and pupils are protected by pseudonyms in this volume, as in our other publications.

Finally, we wish to thank Professor Gerald Bernbaum, Director of the School of Education during the life of the project, for his support, encouragement and enthusiasm.

Acknowledgements

CHAPTER I

Introduction:
the ORACLE project

The ORACLE Project was funded by the Social Science Research Council (now Economic and Social Research Council) at the University of Leicester from 1975 to 1980. A series of interrelated studies was mounted, which have been published as *Inside the Primary Classroom* (Galton, Simon and Croll, 1980); *Progress and Performance in the Primary Classroom* (Galton and Simon, 1980); *Research and Practice in the Primary Classroom* (Simon and Willcocks, 1981); *Moving from the Primary Classroom* (Galton and Willcocks, 1983) and various articles which are listed in the ORACLE Bibliography in this volume. This volume differs in several ways from the four previous ORACLE books, although it also shows continuities with them. This introductory chapter discusses the contents of this book, and shows how they differ from the previous ORACLE volumes.

The main focus of the ORACLE programme was teaching and learning in primary classrooms. However because of the way the project was designed, it also gave an opportunity to study both transfer at different ages (9, 11 and 12) *and* to compare three different types of middle school (8–12, 9–13, 11–14). Some of the relevant material on these issues has already appeared in Galton and Willcocks (1983), and although this book can be read in isolation, the reader will find it more illuminating to read *Moving from the Primary Classroom* as well. The Galton and Willcocks volume dealt with the previous literature on transfer between schools, with the systematic observation data on pupils' adaptations to the teaching styles they met in the transfer schools, with pupils' academic performance in their new schools, and with how the data on transfer related to the findings presented in the earlier volumes

1

in the series. In addition, the Galton and Willcocks book included some of the material gathered by means of ethnographic observation in the six transfer schools. It is this ethnographic material which forms the main subject matter of this book, where a whole volume allows the range, depth and variety of those data to be fully explored. The book is therefore, not only a further instalment in the presentation of findings from the SSRC ORACLE project, but also a contribution to the rich British literature on the ethnography of schooling. There are also stylistic differences between this volume and the others. The reader will notice that this book is more ethnographic, more sociological and more grounded in the contemporary educational literature, than the earlier volumes. These three features are associated: the transfer studies were based on ethnographic fieldwork, used more ideas from the literature of the sociology of education, and therefore were grounded in the debates current among other researchers in school ethnography. This volume looks more towards the tradition of Hargreaves (1967), Lacey (1970), Woods (1979), Ball (1981), and Turner (1983) than it does to the work of Neville Bennett (1976, 1980) and Rutter *et al*. (1979). However the ORACLE work differs from most of the contemporary British school ethnographies (detailed in Hammersley, 1980 and 1982) in a variety of ways.

While ethnographic studies of schools and classrooms have become more common in the last decade, most have been done by one observer in one school. (Curriculum evaluation scholars are the exception here.) Comparing the ORACLE ethnography with the 'Mainstream' schools studies in Britain we spent less time, and cannot claim the same depth of experience as Stephen Ball (1981), Peter Woods (1979) or Lynn Davies (1984). However, we have gained two kinds of comparative ethnographic data. We studied six schools in three cities, to find out how they socialized new entrants. We have placed three observers in each school, and every observer worked in at least two of the six schools. Sara Delamont worked throughout the whole of September 1977 in the two 9–13 schools, and in the two 12–18 schools in 1978. Maurice Galton, John Willcocks, Sarah Tann, Margaret Greig and Janice Lea worked in two or more schools for shorter periods during the Septembers, and visited 'their' schools later in the year. Team-based ethnographic research is rare in Britain outside the big evaluation projects, and in ORACLE we had a precious chance to engage in such research. The ORACLE transfer studies are an important venture in team ethnography, and in comparative ethnography.

In addition to being an exercise in comparative, team ethnography, the ORACLE transfer studies gathered data on five aspects of school life which are the central themes of the book. These five themes are all relatively neglected in the published work on schooling for the 9–16 age range in Britain, and this volume therefore goes some way towards redressing the balance of the research tradition. These five themes are:

1 Initial encounters between pupils and teachers.
2 Mixed ability teaching in the secondary age range.
3 The whole range of the secondary curriculum.
4 Material which challenges the familiarity of the classroom.
5 Data on the long term schooling outcomes of the target pupils.

1 Initial encounters

Much of the ethnography of schools and classrooms has been conducted on teacher-pupil relationships which were already established.

Initial encounters between teachers and pupils have been largely neglected by classroom researchers (Delamont, 1983a). The only research in Britain has been done by Ball (1980) and Beynon (Beynon and Atkinson, 1984). ORACLE has a large body of data on initial encounters, because the research team were in the schools most intensively during the first six weeks of the school year. The material presented in chapter 3 is particularly concerned with initial encounters, and adds to our knowledge of how teachers establish themselves. This important aspect of schooling was addressed briefly in chapter 7 of Galton and Willcocks (1983), and is expanded upon and thoroughly investigated here.

2 Mixed ability teaching

The introduction of mixed ability teaching in the secondary age range has been controversial (Newbold, 1977; Ball, 1981; Davies *et al.*, 1985). ORACLE was able to study several different grouping systems, and these data are presented. We also have material on many kinds of groups which are created in the school, from sports teams to academic classes; and groups which pupils arrange for themselves. These findings are the main subject matter of chapters 7 and 9, and these contain informative work on how complex the internal organization of contemporary secondary schooling is.

3 The whole range of the curriculum

As Delamont (1981) has argued, too much classroom research has been focused upon maths, English, science and French compared to other areas of the curriculum. Too many projects ignore *all* the practical subjects in the school curriculum – we have studied it 'in

3

the round'. Thus data are presented on such subjects as woodwork and PE, and the emphasis is placed on the totality of the pupils' experiences, rather than just on a few' academic lessons. Such insights into the full range of the curriculum are spread throughout the chapters in this volume, and go some way towards giving research attention to 'practical' subjects.

4 Making the familiar strange

Much classroom research suffers from a failure to make the familiar strange (Delamont, 1981). In this volume we have deliberately arranged the material in such a way as to make the classroom unfamiliar, so that the reader sees teacher-pupil interaction from a fresh perspective. The chapters therefore focus on such issues as 'danger', and 'time' rather than covering the school subject by subject, or via conventional categories. Additionally, there has been a self-conscious attempt to draw comparisons and contrasts with non-school settings. In this regard the material from the ORACLE transfer data are presented in a different manner from Galton and Willcocks (1983).

5 Schooling outcomes

The ORACLE transfer studies are also unusual among school ethnographies in that the pupils studied have been followed up over eight years. In 1977 and 1978 the sample pupils transferred from first to middle school or from 8–12 middle school to upper school. In 1983 the sample pupils were followed up, to discover what their secondary-school careers were like. We visited the 13–18 upper schools in Ashburton (Local Authority A) whence children from Gryll Grange and Guy Mannering had gone, and in Bridgehampton (Local Authority B) the 14–18 upper school to which our Maid Marion and Kenilworth pupils had moved. In Coalthorpe (Local Authority C) we revisited Waverly and Melin Court to see how our sample had fared. Some of these data are integrated with our findings throughout the book, but the main body of our work here forms appendix 2. The rest of this chapter outlines how we conducted the ORACLE transfer studies, deals with the way in which we have allocated pseudonyms and ensured confidentiality, introduces the three cities and their schools, and describes the structure of the book.

Managing the ORACLE ethnography

The transfer studies were conducted in six schools in three local authorities, over two successive years. In 1977 the ORACLE target pupils in Local Authority A – Ashburton – moved from their 5–9 first schools into 9–13 middle schools, and we carried out an ethnographic study of that change in two contrasting schools, one organized on primary school lines (Gryll Grange, APT) and one on secondary school lines (Guy Mannering, AST). The timetable of the ethnographic research allowed us to use the study of the 9–13 schools, in September 1977, as a pilot study for 1978, when the pupils transferred into the 11–14 and 12–18 schools in the other two local authorities (Bridgehampton and Coalthorpe). Sara Delamont and Maurice Galton were involved in both years, the others only worked in one year, but some of the lessons learnt during the 1977 transfer study were carried forward to 1978.

We never believed that ethnographers enter the field open-minded. In the 1977 study of the two 9–13 schools we had a short list of 'foreshadowed problems' derived from our reading of other school studies. These were of two kinds: some tentative 'theoretical' ideas we had derived from the literature, and some 'common-sense' ideas derived more from our 'members' knowledge'. Among the more 'theoretical' ideas we were interested in utilizing Basil Bernstein's (1971, 1974) ideas on classification and framing and visible and invisible pedagogies; the beginnings of labelling, and the notion of 'coping strategies' (Pollard, 1985). More concretely, we asked all observers to look carefully at pupils' 'adjustments' to the new schools, sibling comparisons, staffroom discussions of pupils, bullying and the schools' responses to it, and to compare 'theory' and 'practice' in such areas as curriculum balance, pupil groupings, allocation of teachers to classes and so on. For example in Local Authority A (Ashburton) we found that allocation of children to teaching bands at Guy Mannering School (AST) was more closely related to primary school attended than ability or head's reports (see chapter 7 for more details of this finding). Once such an insight had been made, we were able to build it into the design of the second year's work into transfer. Thus by 1978 we had a fistful of ideas from the 1977 study which we could use as 'foreshadowed problems' or 'sensitizing concepts' in Local Authorities B (Bridge-hampton) and C (Coalthorpe), and so we asked the observers in Local Authorities B and C to examine band allocation, class allocation and so forth. How far the observers took any notice of these 'foreshadowed problems' is, in retrospect, unclear – because of the diverse nature of the observers.

The observers used had very different academic backgrounds. Sara Delamont was the only experienced ethnographer, but all the other observers had been trained and were experienced as class-room observers with the Teacher and Pupil Records. Maurice Galton had previously done systematic observations with the Science Teacher Observation Schedule. In each town there were regular meetings among the observers to discuss their 'findings'. No systematic attempts were made to harmonize fieldnotes or diary-taking, and the resulting documents vary enormously in length, depth, social scientific language-use and the extent to which judgments are explicitly made. While there cannot be inter-observer reliability in ethnography of the kind demanded by the Teacher and Pupil Records, we found surprising similarities in our accounts of the same classrooms. Sara Delamont had been concerned that a series of incompatible and unrelated accounts would result. However, in practice the big problem was the one mentioned by Howard Becker (1971) – observers who found the school day too familiar to be able to write much about it. Some of the observers including Maurice Galton handed over everything they wrote to the ORACLE secretaries for typing and circulation, while others handed in only an edited account. Sara Delamont had her diary typed, but not her field-notes. Once the fieldnotes were gathered all of those taken by five of the six observers were handed over to Delamont, who has analyzed them and written up the material. This was considered to be the only practical course, but also has the effect of giving a coherence and common focus to the resulting account which may be exaggerated.

The management of team research is always problematic. We are confident that the material gathered is worth reading, providing as it does an unusual perspective on schooling. The authors have written an account of researching the ORACLE transfer studies (Galton and Delamont, 1985) and interested readers can consult that paper for more details of our difficulties. Our successes can be found in this volume.

Confidentiality and pseudonyms

Throughout chapters 4 to 9 use is made of three kinds of data: interviews, observations without a schedule, and pupil essays. Each kind of data is clearly indicated. The material reproduced from the 'fieldnotes' taken by ourselves is given with the name of the school. All the schools, teachers, pupils and observers are unidentifiable. The observers have been left anonymous, as at least three different people worked in each school, and data collected by each of them have been used.

The presentation of a comparative ethnography of six very different schools is complicated. We have talked as far as possible of *feeder schools*, and *transfer schools*, except where this hinders clarity. As in the previous volumes, the teachers are generally referred to as female and the pupils as male except where specific examples are quoted.

The schools, teachers and pupils are all disguised. All the schools at the centre of our analysis (middle and upper schools) have names from novels, while the lower schools in all three local authorities have names of cricket grounds used in the 1979 Prudential World Cup. Where pupils moved on to an upper school (in Local Authorities A and B) these have names from Jane Austen novels. Pseudonyms also replace the initials used for the schools in Galton and Willcocks (1983). Those schools in Galton and Willcocks called 'PT' (for primary type) are here given names from the novels of Thomas Love Peacock: Gryll Grange (9–13), Maid Marion (11–14) and Melin Court (12–18), but they are referred to in the earlier chapters as 'Gryll Grange 9–13 APT' to enable the reader to become familiar with the name, age-range, and type of school. Those schools called 'ST' (for secondary type) are here called after novels by Sir Walter Scott: Guy Mannering (9–13), Kenilworth (11–14), and Waverly (12–18), and have the AST, BST, CST added for the first few chapters.

The teachers referred to only by initials in that volume are also given pseudonyms here, in the belief it helps the reader identify and remember their characteristics. The pupils' pseudonyms in this volume are the same as those used in Galton and Willcocks (1983). Naming the pupils for these two volumes was an intricate task, which was carried through in the following way. Many pupils were observed during the project (at least 300 pupils are described in the ethnographic fieldnotes from the six schools) and a substantial number are mentioned in the texts of this and the previous (Galton and Willcocks, 1983) volume. Each pupil has been given a pseudonym which is unique, and is not the real name of any child in his or her own class. Accordingly, in some cases the pupils' names may strike the reader as 'exotic'. In fact no name given in this book is unimaginable in these schools, just a little more unusual. Where a pupil had a striking name, such as Gianetta, a pseudonym such as Estelle was given, where a name was straightforward, such as John, a plain pseudonym such as Dick was used. As Delamont (1980a) has observed elsewhere, girls' names are more varied and unusual than boys', and this has been echoed in their pseudonyms. Every pupil studied in the six transfer schools has been given a unique name, but for boys this has sometimes been achieved by assigning different spellings and diminutives of the same name to different boys. That is Martyn, Martin and Marten are three separate individuals, as are

Rob, Bob, Bobby and Robert. In real classes many boys and girls have the same name – there may be four Pauls, three Johns, two Darrens and two Waynes – but for this book no names are duplicated. Where a name indicates an ethnic group – such as Antonio, Achilles or Ibrahim – these have been preserved in the pseudonym.

To help the reader keep track of three LEAs, six schools, and numerous teachers and pupils, appendix 1 contains a complete list of the pseudonyms of all the schools, teachers and pupils mentioned in the text. We hope in this way to avoid the problems caused by authors such as James Macpherson (1983) who used code numbers, and made his text difficult to follow. Appendix 1 also lists the names of one or two pupils who appeared in Galton and Willcocks (1983) with a mistaken pseudonym due to author error. Thus Jessamine, in class 10 at Maid Marion, appears in Galton and Willcocks as Jasmine by mistake. Any hawk-eyed reader who spots these few mislabelled pupils in Galton and Willcocks should consult the appendix. Overall, pupils in this book have the same names that they were given for all the other publications, so that Davina in Gryll Grange is always the same girl.

Having described our policy over confidentiality and pseudonyms we turn to a brief description of the three cities and their schools, and the six transfer schools in particular.

The cities and their schools

Ashburton: Local Authority A

Ashburton is a city in the English Midlands, in existence since Norman times, prosperous in the nineteenth century and now expanding rapidly. The old centre built in Victorian red brick, also boasts a new glass and concrete shopping precinct; and the whole town is today ringed with new housing estates both council and private. Ashburton has grown rapidly due to 'overspill': large numbers of people rehoused from the larger Midlands connurbations and from London. An article on Ashburton in a news magazine (which we are not including in the references to protect its anonymity) described it as follows:

> A new traffic scheme shunts us round the town centre, difficult to get at . . .
> A thriving cattle market . . . a thumping great . . . brewery dominates the
> town . . . Despite unemployment, relative prosperity is reflected in the new
> shopping precinct, and the bowling alley now converted into a mammoth
> discount store. . . . the image of bustling industriousness, of people making
> good. They come to the midlands for the jobs and the better material life. On
> the outskirts, the relentless march of the new Ashburton proceeds across the
> open countryside. It is Saturday afternoon, and migrants from the slums of

Introduction: the ORACLE project

Birmingham and London are moving treasured belongings into the new
villages in their sector and a new life.

New houses are completed every week and consequently new children
arrive in the Ashburton schools all the time. The new estates have been
provided with new schools; indeed primary schools are a central feature of
the kind of town planning that has designed the 'new' Ashburton. As the
news magazine wrote 'almost all new town and overspill plans organize
residential groups around the primary school. About 1,200 households will
support the usual school . . . these are to be within five minutes' walking time
of the school . . . necessary to build between twelve and sixteen houses to the
acre.

Later in the article the author suggested that the growth of
Ashburton, and the location of open space and of industry had been
much less artificial than the plans of many more famous new towns
such as Milton Keynes. Whether or not this is true, the new areas
looked raw when our fieldwork was going on, and despite the
school-building programme the two schools in which we worked
were severely overcrowded. The education system of Ashburton
and its surrounding country is a three-tier one. Children go to lower
schools until they are 9, when they transfer to 9–13 middle schools,
from which in turn they go to an upper school from 13–18 years.
Some of the upper schools were based in the old technical or
grammar schools, while some of the former secondary modern
schools were reincarnated as 9–13 middle schools. One of our two
sample schools, Guy Mannering (AST), was chosen for the research as a traditional school with a house system, uniforms,
streaming, and a conventional curriculum. Gryll Grange (APT) was
deliberately chosen as a contrast. It was a purpose-built show
school, opened in 1972, and run on 'progressive lines' with mixed
ability groups, an integrated day and individualized curriculum. A
summary table (1.1) shows how all six transfer schools compared on
a variety of key indicators.

Guy Mannering (AST) School had gone through a series of
metamorphoses from elementary school, through girls' secondary
modern school, to 9–13 middle school. This was a sequence which
could be seen all over the city centre. Thus in one area of the old city
the visitor can see St Bridget's Middle School in a set of Victorian
buildings, where notices still hang reading 'St Bridget's Secondary
Modern School for Girls', and the twin arches over the gates still
bear the legends 'Boys' and 'Girls and Infants' carved in the stone
when the building was erected in 1870. Similarly in the very centre
of the city there still stands, where Linenmarket Street joins
Cheesemonger Row, the original 1770 building which once housed
Josiah Martlet and Obadiah Heap's SPCK elementary school. This
was an elementary school until at least 1945, and today it is a

pre-school playgroup. Guy Mannering, unlike St Bridget's, had been given a new building and been moved from the red brick terraces of Balaclava Road to a site surrounded by new estates, but its previous manifestations were still visible in the school library, its cookery facilities and so forth.

Bridgehampton: Local Authority B

Bridgehampton is a similar Midlands city to Ashburton, founded by the Romans, and in continuous occupation since. Prosperous in Victorian times, the unemployment of the 1970s has hit it hard. Our two (11–14) schools Maid Marion (BPT) and Kenilworth (BST) are located in a suburb, which was largely built in the 1950s and 1960s. The suburb included a golf course, and Bridgehampton race course, surrounded by private housing in all price ranges and council estates. Bridgehampton people came out to this suburb to shop, because it had been chosen by Sainsburys, Woolco and so forth as a prime location for hypermarkets. The city has a university and a polytechnic, is a county town with a famous cricket ground, and a first division football team, but the impact of these facilities in the suburb where our two schools are located was muted.

The county of which Bridgehampton is the county town was a pioneer of comprehensive schooling, adopting a pattern of primary schools, 11–14 middle schools based in the secondary moderns, and 14–18 upper schools or community colleges based in the old grammar schools. Kenilworth (BST) had been built as a secondary modern school, and still had the specialist facilities. Maid Marion (BPT) had been purpose-built as an 11–14 middle school when the population of the suburb grew rapidly and a new middle school was needed. Pupils from both Kenilworth and Maid Marion transferred to the same upper school – Sanditon Community College, which was located on the same campus. This site has mature trees, and most of the pupils walk to their schools from their homes.

Coalthorpe: Local Authority C

Coalthorpe is a product of the industrial revolution. A town that grew and grew rich on coal and wool in the nineteenth century, it has been plunged into depression in the last fifteen years. The two schools we studied served an area of terraced and modern council housing with boarded up shops and visible poverty. Indeed these two schools, Melin Court (CPT) and Waverly (CST), were dealing with pupils who looked worse fed, worse shod and more shabbily dressed than those in Ashburton and Bridgehampton. The city was prosperous in the last century, when ample municipal buildings, a university, and an art gallery were established by local industrialists. Today there is a polytechnic, a famous theatre, and first division football. The energetic city council is trying to build a new prosperity on tourism and bureaucracy, to replace the lost industrial jobs. The educational policy is regarded as innovative and imaginative, although many of the schools serve pupils from dilapidated housing and visibly rundown streets. The city has been comprehensive for over fifteen years, and runs a three-tier system. There are lower schools for pupils aged 5–8, middle schools for the 8–12s, and upper schools for the 12–18s. We studied transfer into two 12–18 upper schools, Melin Court (CPT) and Waverly (CST) located about 3 miles apart on the outskirts of Coalthorpe.

Waverly (CST) was established in 1960, and opened its sixth form in 1974. The buildings dated from throughout that period, and the school also used an old primary school two miles away as a craft annexe. Melin Court (CPT) was opened in 1956, and also had a modern extension built in the 1970s. Both these schools were large, Waverly having 1,200 and Melin Court 960 pupils. The distinction between 'primary' and 'secondary' type was least obvious between these two schools, both of which were already facing the problems of youth unemployment in 1978. Much emphasis in Coalthorpe was being placed on improving the schools' training for working life and vocational curricula.

The six schools compared

Galton and Willcocks (1983: 11–14) includes a comparison of the six schools, which is briefly reproduced here. Table 1.1 summarizes the main criteria on which the two types of school were differentiated.

Gryll Grange (APT) 9–13 Middle School had been purpose-built on the same campus as a technical college, across a road from a 5–9 lower school and a 13–18 upper school called Woodhouse to which many of the ORACLE sample transferred at 13. Gryll Grange had a central core with the hall/gym, the dining room, the staffroom, the library, and the art, cookery, and science rooms, and then four base areas each containing four classrooms and a cloakroom. Our sample occupied three out of the four classrooms in one area, and the three class teachers, Mr Valentine, Miss Tweed, and Mrs Hind, shared the teaching of the three forms between them for much of the timetable. When we chose the school it did not have a uniform, but the new head, Mr Judge, who started as we began our research, had introduced one.

Guy Mannering (AST) 9–13 Middle School was in the same buildings that had housed Guy Mannering Girls' Secondary Modern School, and the staff were still largely women. The school was two-storey, with specialist rooms for all subjects, and the children

11

Table 1.1 Main characteristics of the six transfer schools

Local authority: School name and type:	A – Ashburton		B – Bridgehampton		C – Coalthorpe	
	Secondary type Guy Mannering (AST)	Primary type Gryll Grange (APT)	Secondary type Kenilworth (BST)	Primary type Maid Marion (BPT)	Secondary type Waverly (CST)	Primary type Melin Court (CPT)
Age-range of pupils:	9–13	9–13	11–14	11–14	12–18	12–18
First year base	No	Yes	No	Yes	No	No
First year playground	No	Yes	No	Yes	Yes	Yes
First year assembly	No	Yes	No	Yes	No	Yes
Most lessons taught by class teachers	No	Yes	No	Yes	No	No
House system	Yes	No	Yes	No	No	No
Banding/setting/streaming in academic subjects	Yes	No	Yes	No	Yes	No
Stars/conduct marks	Yes	No	No	No	No	No

moved from one room and its teacher to another every time the bells rang. Uniform was strictly enforced, there were houses called by saints' names, credits for good work, and debits for bad conduct. Pupils were placed in two bands on entry which received very different treatment as we show later in the book.

Kenilworth (BST) 11–14 Middle School in Bridgehampton had a regime very similar to Guy Mannering's, but its architecture was different because it had been purpose-built for coeducation. Kenilworth had a system of streams labelled with Greek letters within two broad bands, and a house system. Pupils moved from one specialist teacher to another, and the top stream actually started Latin.

Maid Marion (BPT) 11–14 Middle School was in a similar building to Kenilworth's, but operated with a system of a first year base with its own playground. Some subjects were taught by specialists, but they came to the first year area. The pupils therefore saw a small group of teachers whose own base was the first year area. The atmosphere at Maid Marion was more like Gryll Grange than Kenilworth.

It is harder to distinguish Melin Court (CPT) and Waverly (CST), the two 12–18 schools. Both were mainly concerned to prepare pupils for CSEs and O levels. However Melin Court did not stream or set pupils, and taught all crafts to both sexes; while Waverly quickly put pupils into sets for languages, English, maths, history and geography, and taught wood and metalwork only to boys. Waverly made more attempt to get pupils into uniform than Melin Court, but otherwise the schools were fairly similar.

Throughout this volume we have woven material from the six schools together to illustrate our themes, and it is not essential for the reader to keep them distinct in her head to follow our arguments about school transfer.

To conclude this chapter, the structure of the book is outlined.

The structure of this volume

This volume is structured rather differently from the others in the ORACLE series, partly because it has been written by two people from data collected by six. The material is organized in two ways. Chapters 2 and 3 present data in a chronological way, while the rest are thematic. Chapter 2 deals with an important issue in pastoral care: how the feeder schools and transfer schools organize informing pupils and parents about the transfer schools in the summer before the pupils move. Chapter 3 deals with the first days of the new school year in the transfer school, and reveals how pupils meet the features of school life, such as danger and grouping, which form the subject matter of chapters 4 through to 9. Appendix 2 presents the follow-up data, on how the pupils had fared five and six years later. Chapters 4 to 9 are organized thematically, and form the heart of the book. They cover the material gathered on everyday life in the transfer schools and make a self-conscious attempt to present it in a novel way. The chapters focus on danger (physical and social), movement, time, formal groupings and informal associations, and attempt to highlight some taken-for-granted features of school life. Finally chapter 10 presents our conclusions and our thoughts on the implication of the work for educational policy.

CHAPTER 2

Ready, steady, panic?
Preparation for transfer
in the ORACLE schools

At the end of their first year the pupils in the 11–14 schools wrote for the ORACLE researchers an essay reflecting on their first impressions of, likes and dislikes about, and experiences in, their schools. The four quotes given below – with the children's spelling retained – show the effects of the pre-transfer programmes which are the subject of this chapter.

> Jessica wrote: The large kitchen was the first thing which caught my eye . . .
> At dinner time I had a salad and milkshake which was delicious but I thought
> that it might be a special dinner put on to make us think the dinners were that
> good all the time.

> Odette wrote: When I first came to Maid Marion I thought it was a very large
> school and that I would find it hard to find my way a round . . . I was looking
> foreward to Maths and P.E.

> Dan wrote: I remember the first time i came up to maid marion it semd very
> lonly and the school semd very big.

> Harry wrote: The day we came up to see what the school was like I thought it
> was great.

Here we see 11-year-olds coming warily towards a new experience. Jessica fears that the new school is putting on a false face to lull them into a false sense of anticipation. Odette and Dan are struck by the larger building and fear getting lost. Harry on the other hand, merely says he was eager to come.

In this chapter we look at how six schools prepared new pupils and their parents for the transfer, and examine pupil expectations and fears. The chapter opens with a discussion of transitions between different sectors of the education system in Britain and offers a perspective for studying them. We then characterize five distinct arrangements for preparing pupils to transfer, examine pupils' fears and fantasies about their new schools, and compare the effectiveness of the five options in reducing pupil anxiety. The chapter ends with the pupils and their perspectives on school transfer.

Social science approaches to transitions

Pupils in contemporary British schools make a variety of transitions in and out of the school system and between sectors within it. If pupils between the ages of 3 and 19 are considered there are many different patterns of transitions between the one from home to education, and the final transfer out of education into the world of work. Different children experience some of the following possible transfers:

Home to pre-school
Home to infant school
Pre-school to infant school
Infant to primary school
First to middle school
Primary to secondary school
Middle to upper school
Secondary/upper school to work
Secondary/upper school to FE/tertiary or sixth form college
Secondary/upper school to higher education

Research on transitions has not proceeded uniformly. Some of these transfers have received attention, others have not. However, it is clear from the extant research that common themes emerge from all the transitions studied, which are fully applicable to this book's emphasis on transfer in and out of middle school. The pattern of transfers has altered over time with social changes. Blatchford *et al.* (1982) show that 74 per cent of children now make the transfer from home to pre-school and *thence* to school – so that it is now a minority of 5-year-olds who go from home to school 'cold'. Similarly at the other end of the system fewer teenagers move from school to work, as more and more of them experience the intermediate stage of a 'scheme' (Rees and Atkinson, 1982). However, there are common social science themes in all such transfers, and before addressing the detail of the material from the ORACLE research, the common themes of all the transfer research can be outlined.

School transitions are a variety of *status passage* (Glaser and Strauss, 1965): a term used in anthropology, sociology and social psychology to categorize the process of changing from one status to another. Thus pregnancy and childbirth are the status passage into motherhood (Oakley, 1979), medical school is the lengthy status passage from student to doctor (Becker *et al.* 1961; Coombs, 1978; Atkinson, 1981), and courtship and engagement the status passage from the single to the married state (Leonard, 1980). Many status passages are marked by ceremonies or rituals, religious and or secular. Special clothes may be worn, special food prepared and eaten, and special words said in special buildings. Thus 'the wedding' marks the final stage of the status passage from 'single' to 'married' (Leonard, 1980; Delamont, 1983c), the *bar mitzvah* marks the entry to adulthood of the Jewish male (Bullivant, 1978) and the coronation puts the monarch legitimately upon her throne. British state education is lacking in rituals to mark status passages. Those completing higher education *can* take part in a graduation ceremony, and ritualize their status passage from student to adult. In the USA there are similar ceremonies for those graduating from high school, and even leaving junior high schools. British schools have not generally engaged in such rituals, and although the pupils, their parents and their teachers may regard the transfer from middle to upper school as significant status passages, they do not mark them with rituals.

Researchers have not collected very much data on how participants see these status passages, but it is clear from the studies we do have that certain key perspectives are common across all transitions from home to school up to leaving education. As British culture has become more child-centred more care has been exercised to ease transitions and prepare pupils for them. Thus the project on entry to infant school by Cleave *et al.* (1982: 121–2) focuses extensively on ways to minimize pupils' anxieties when they start their full-time education. All the six ORACLE schools were concerned to reduce pupils' fears before transfer, and we can compare the relative effectiveness of their strategies. To do this we present accounts of how our six schools tried to ease the transition. Our six 'destination schools' offered the following methods of introducing new pupils and their parents to their buildings and staff:

Option 1:
Teachers from the 'destination schools' come to the feeder school and give talks and answer questions. (They may bring a few pupils from their school on the visit.)

This option was used by Kenilworth (BST) 11–14 School and Maid Marion (BPT) 11–14 School, and followed option 2 in most of the feeder schools. The option was also used by Waverly (CST) 12–18 School.

Option 2:
Children go in parties from their feeder schools (with or without their class teacher) on a short visit to their destination school.

This option was used at Kenilworth, Gryll Grange (APT) 9–13 School, Guy Mannering (AST) 9–13 School, Melin Court (CPT) 12–18 School, and Waverly (CST) 12–18 School, and was the commonest option in the ORACLE project.

Option 3:
Parents (with or without their children) visit the destination school for an open evening.

This option was offered by Waverly, Melin Court, Gryll Grange, Guy Mannering and Maid Marion, but was mainly aimed at parents rather than pupils.

Option 4:
Children come from feeder schools to spend a whole working day in their destination school, having lessons, lunch, assembly and break. (Usually a whole year group in the school are sent on a trip to clear space for the visitors.)

This was the practice at Maid Marion (BPT) 11–14 School.

Option 5:
Teachers from the destination school actually teach at the feeder schools on a regular basis, and get to know some of their future pupils over a long period.

This was done by a French master from Waverly, who taught at a middle school where there were no French staff, but was done for reasons of curriculum continuity, rather than anxiety reduction. As the above list shows, all the ORACLE pupils were scheduled to experience one of these visits and some of our children experienced more than one of these options. A handful of children missed out on any pre-transfer visits due to illness, holidays, moving house, etc., and they were the most apprehensive of all, so there is evidence that each of the five options reduces anxiety levels. However one of the five is noticeably the most successful, and when we have examined what fears pupils suffer, we will discuss the relative efficacy of the five options in reducing them.

The pupils' fears, fantasies and phobias
There are now several studies on pupils' anxieties (e.g., Bryant, 1980; Measor and Woods, 1983) but little material on how they can be reduced or on which signs and symbols of school transfer are

important to the pupils. Measor and Woods (1983) have some data on this, but it has been a neglected research area, like much else in children's folklore (Bauman, 1982). There is a good deal of consensus in the accounts of fears that pupils and students have concerning transfer to new educational institutions, and our findings from the ORACLE sample are in general agreement with those in the literature. The anxieties we discovered among the ORACLE pupils can be categorized into four groups, according to their focus, as follows:

(1) fellow pupils;
(2) school buildings and facilities;
(3) teachers;
(4) the curriculum.

We have several sources of data bearing upon these issues. Sometimes the researcher who accompanied the pupils on a school visit returned with them to their lower school and collected immediate impressions. More systematically, however, we collected interview data and/or essays from the children after the transfer in which they recalled their reactions to the impending move. Here we use data from several sources to illustrate the main points children made about their expectations. First, it is important to note that many pupils already know pupils at the transfer school, because they have friends, cousins and siblings who already attend them.

A sample of pupils was interviewed at five of the six schools. Many of them were not forced to rely on their visit(s) to the school for information, because they knew someone already there. Table 2.1 shows the number of pupils *interviewed* in the five schools who had siblings, friends or cousins already at the new school. This table reveals that of 96 children interviewed, 36 had one or more siblings at the school, 11 had a friend or friends there, and 7 had one or more cousins. One boy at Waverly, Gordon, had two sisters and three cousins at the school already! What information did such pupils get? Some pupils had received little or no information from teenagers already there, some had been told 'horror' stories, while some had been reassured. The interview quotes show this range of information.

Ellis (Melin Court) had heard from a cousin who was already there that it 'was O.K.' This noncommittal type of comment may or may not be reassuring to pupils, but it was quite commonly reported. Thus Peggy's (Waverly) sister 'didn't tell me much' and Keith's (Waverly) cousins had said 'it was a big place, that if he got lost he should ask a teacher, and that if you were late you got a detention.' None of these are likely to cause panic, but neither do they lavish praise on the school.

Table 2.1   Friends, siblings and cousins at new school

School	Friends	Siblings	Cousins	Total interviewed
Guy Mannering (9–13)	1	7	0	22
Gryll Grange (9–13)	0	6	0	11
Maid Marion (11–14)	0	9	0	32
Melin Court (12–18)	6	7	2	15
Waverly (12–18)	4	7	5	16
Totals	11	36	7	96

Some people had been told favourable things. Mervyn's brother had told him about Melin Court and said 'it were great'. Similarly Joscelin's cousin at Melin Court said 'it was good'. However she had also heard a rumour about children being beaten up. This was not the only 'horror' story the prospective pupils had heard. Bart described Ashwood Bank Lower School as 'great' and had really enjoyed it there. He 'were bothered about coming here, Miss' (to Waverly) because 'friends had told me it were bad. They said you got beat up a lot.' Ellen's sister in the fourth year had told her 'horrible stories' but this was said with a laugh and the interviewer assumed Ellen had known her sister was teasing. Merle's brother at Maid Marion had got the cane 'dozens of times' and the only reason she could think of was that he had been cheeky. Denzil at Waverly knew people in the 3rd and 5th years who had told him 'you have to clean the toilets out if they flood, Miss.' Gordon's three cousins and two sisters had said 'it was O.K. but the exams were horrible.'

From these interviews we can see several of the worries already outlined: about the other pupils, about the buildings, about the teachers and about the curriculum. Some of these concerns are more likely to be the subject of pupils' folklore and mythology than others: bullying and the cane are more the subject of 'horror stories' than learning English, losing one's friends, or simply getting lost on the way from maths to dinner. While our data are neither as rich nor as extensive as those gathered by Measor and Woods (1983, 1984) it is worth comparing our findings with theirs.

We examine each area of concern with some quotations from the pupils' interviews and essays, and from fieldnotes taken by the researchers. The children's anxieties about their fellow pupils at the destination school were of two main types: fears about friendship and about bullying. Pupils were anxious about whether they would

20

be separated from their existing friends, and whether they would be able to meet new ones. For example, two boys, Josh and Luke, transferring to Maid Marion (BPT) School (11–14) in Bridgehampton, told the ORACLE interviewer:

> they had been very worried about finding new friends here and were very scared that they would not make friends easily and get very left out.

In fact the two boys admitted that:

> once they arrived here they did in fact make friends very quickly!

Eunice, a girl making the same transfer, wrote in an essay for us:

> I was very nervous . . . everybody seemed to know their names and they all had lots of friends. I soon got settled in, though, and made many friends.

Bryant (1980) found similar themes in the essays written by transferring pupils:

> One thing I won't like is leaving all my old friends who are going to different schools
>
> I don't really like leaving because in this school . . . all my friends and people I know are here.

Fears about bullying have been reported by Measor and Woods (1983 and 1984) and were certainly widespread in our sample. For example, among the children going to Waverly (CST) and Melin Court (CPT) 12–18 Schools in Coalthorpe, Joscelin had heard a rumour about children being beaten up, while Bart said he:

> were bothered about coming here, Miss, (because) friends had told me it were bad. They said you got beat up a lot!

Dawn had been frightened by rumours that on the first day 'You got kicked in, Miss.' As one anonymous pupil at Maid Marion (BPT) 11–14 School told us:

> On the first day I was very nervous, afraid of being bullied by older children.

Alongside their anxieties about other pupils – friends and bullies – are the children's concerns about the new school buildings.

The ORACLE children's anxieties about their destination school's buildings and facilities were mainly general – the new institutions were so much bigger they feared getting lost. However, some children were scared of specific facilities, especially showers. Two girls going to Maid Marion (BPT) 11–14 School, Karena and Fida, had specific fears. Fida was afraid of showering after PE and Karena had seen the school's four-storey 'tower' block and as she was afraid of heights, this had alarmed her. In general, though, children apprehensive about their new school were alarmed by its vast size. As children going to Maid Marion (11–14) School wrote for us in essays:

> Daphne wrote: When I first came to Maid Marion I thought it was a large school with many classes. I found it difficult to find my way round.
>
> Greg wrote: Maid Marion was a lot bigger than I expected, my sister had been here in previous years but I didn't think it was as big as she told me.
>
> Heather: When I came to Maid Marion, on intake day, I was amazed at the size of the whole place. The teacher who was taking us around speed round saying 'Now this is the . . . '

This can be paralleled by the child who told Bryant (1980):

> I've seen my new school and its very big there's corridors everywhere you look and an endless supply of classrooms and its very easy to get lost in a school like this.

The teachers also figured in the children's fears. There were anxieties about how fierce and strict the staff would be, and concern that there were so many different teachers that it would be impossible to sort them out, remember their names and adapt to them. As Gail, a pupil at Maid Marion recollected:

> On my first day I was very scared when I met all the new people. My worst thing was when I met all the teachers.

Similarly Eunice wrote:

> I was very nervous when I saw all the teachers . . . I also dreaded my teacher with a name like Mr Slaughter. [actually Salter].

Royston commented:

> When I first came I was shown round by Mr Salter. My first impressions were that it was a huge school with a much stricter set of teachers than Whitteck [first school] where I had come from.

George, who entered Kenilworth (BST) 11–14 School, also reflects this anxiety:

> When I first came I thought all the teachers would be stricked (*sic*) and tell you off if you got something wrong but they did not . . .

Apart from teachers being numerous, and possibly strict and fierce, Measor and Woods (1983, 1984) report one further fear about staff which we did not. Woods and Measor found a persistent myth that one of the male teachers was a homosexual and had to be avoided. This became added to as the school year progressed, in that boys began to warn each other about 'poufters' in their own age range, as well as a 'queer' teacher. The authors see these myths relating to the boys' own emerging sexuality, and the need to define this unambiguously in the new school.

The larger number of teachers is directly linked with the wider curriculum the chidren know they have to meet. Here again there are two classes of fear: about the work being too hard, and about particular subjects. As Clyde, who went to Kenilworth (BST) 11–14 School, summarized these:

> When I first came to Kenilworth it seemed easier than I expected . . . The lesson that I was most nervous about was French, but it hasn't been too bad.

And his classmate Gilbert agreed:

> One subject I thought I wouldn't be any good at is French but I think I'm quite good at it.

Similarly Eunice (at Maid Marion) was 'dreading maths' and other pupils feared science, PE, craft, English and cooking.

Not all our children had anxieties, of course. Some were totally unworried about their moves to larger schools. However, many pupils had some fears, as did those studied by Measor and Woods (1983, 1984). As part of their ethnographic study of transfer, Measor and Woods focused both on the pre-transfer programme, and, with particular originality, on the teenagers' folklore, or mythology of transfer. Their findings on this mythology are worthy of particular attention from schools trying to design pre-transfer programmes to reduce anxiety, and have therefore been presented in some detail here.

Measor and Woods studied a cohort of pupils transferring *from* a 9–13 middle school into a large (2,000 plus) upper school. They found that all the transferring pupils *knew* a set of myths about the upper school, although only boys recounted them. One 'typical' myth was that 'You get yer' 'ead flushed down the loo on yer birthday in that school,' which has been reported by other researchers from all over Great Britain over the last thirty years at least. In the USA, too, the 'restrooms' are seen as a dangerous area for pupils, and Judith L. Hanna (1982) reports similar, and more unpleasant stories – leaving unclear in her account whether she is reporting actual harassment and attacks, or merely myths. Measor and Woods report that the myths told and retold among the pupils fell into three broad categories:

(1) Myths concerning 'new forms of knowledge and work which involves both girls and boys'.

(2) Myths concerning 'new situations and activities' where both the official and the unofficial culture of the school deman- ded male toughness and 'hardness'.

(3) Myths concerning developing sexuality.

The first category of myth was the only type recounted by both boys and girls. The example collected by Measor and Woods which had widest currency was that in science 'everyone' had to dissect a rat, a prospect which boys claimed to relish and girls to fear. (In fact, the teacher did the dissection and a boy fainted!)

The second category, retold by boys only, and referring only to boys' futures, included the lavatory myth, and stories about bully- ing, getting 'the slipper', exhausting cross-country runs and being thrown into the showers fully clothed. The Welsh Boys Compre- hensive studied by John Beynon was actually characterized by all these events taking place, so it is not the case that pupil folklore is always mistaken (Beynon and Delamont, 1984). Measor and Woods argue that these myths carry the messages that the upper school is a more impersonal place, where the boys will be the youngest, weakest and most vulnerable pupils. Personal status was to be gained by being brave and tough, and also by not volunteering personal information – if you are in danger on your birthday, you do not reveal when it is. The third category included the supposedly homosexual master we have already mentioned, and stories about effeminacy among the male pupils themselves.

We have divided our data on pupil fears in a somewhat different way, but the reader will recognize similar themes underlying vari- ous questions and comments made by pupils (such as Denzil) we have quoted earlier. Here we want to offer our data on boys' views about the third theme Measor and Woods highlight, developing sexuality. At the end of their first year at Kenilworth and Maid Marion pupils wrote essays for the project team reflecting on the previous year. The developing sexuality comes through in some of these, especially those written anonymously.

Kenilworth (BST) – anonymous boy
I have been out with a nice girl (not mentioning any names) . . . Sometimes I

wish I wasn't at this school because you have to wear uniform. A boy in 1 alpha 1 is sex mad. My best subject is history . . .

Maid Marion (BPT) – Irving
The thing I don't like about Maid Marion are the dinners because I don't think they're worth 25p. Having to wear school uniforms because you look a puff.

Maid Marion – Jerome
Having to wear a school uniform is another thing I dislike because we look like 'BOFFS'.

Kenilworth – anonymous boy
I have begun to look at girls and most men do this if a woman is nice. I have improved my knowledge considerably. My faivorite subject is games. I play football for the school and enjoy it. I have made a lot of friends some of them girls.

There is no evidence that teachers recognized that pupils' queries about ties and blazers were actually masking fears about looking like 'Boffs' – and it is unclear how a school could dispell such fears even if they were recognized.

Apart from the common fears we have now covered, we also found some pupils who had individual or idiosyncratic worries. Miles was a bit worried that he was going to be called names when he got to Maid Marion like 'dumbo' because he was 'such a dunce'. Karena and Fida found that most of their friends were going to Kenilworth but they were going to Maid Marion. They thought that they would not do much work at Maid Marion and it would be very lazy and 'very unstrict' and that they would not get on very well. However these two at least had each other for support. Those children who had been facing the transfer alone, because other children from their lower school were going elsewhere, and those who had missed the visits and open evenings, seem to have been especially apprehensive.

Elmer had missed the visit to Maid Marion at the end of the summer term because he had been on holiday. He had been very worried when he came that he would get lost. Bryony knew no one at Melin Court before she came. She came from Villebourne School and came with her mother to meet Mr Stackpole but not to an open day. She was very frightened on the first day. Delia had a brother and a sister who were both at Waverly but she said this was so long ago that the school was completely new to her. She was very apprehensive about coming on the first morning because she only knew one other girl and two boys who were going to be in her class. Dawn had a sister at Coalthorpe High School, and she had been put down for that. When she was refused there she was also too late for

rt where her lower school friends were going. She had felt
 own on that first day and had been very frightened
 he had heard a rumour that on the first day 'You get
 Miss.'

 viously important to know at least two things about these
fears: whether the school visits before transfer allayed or increased
them, and whether they die away after transfer in the Autumn term.
It should also be stressed that many children were looking forward
to the change, and expressed no anxiety about it.

The rapid dissolution of fears has been reported by previous
researchers (e.g. Youngman and Lunzer, 1977; Bryant, 1980;
Blatchford *et al*. 1982; Cleave *et al*. 1982) who also report similar
foci of concern. For example the anticipatory dislike of showers by
our 9-, 11- and 12-year-olds is paralleled by Blatchford *et al*'s (1982)
finding that nursery school children feared being forced to do PE in
their vests. Indeed the anxieties of reception class infants in Cleave
et al. (1982) are strikingly similar to those Cohen (1972) reports
from 'new boys' at the Harvard Business School. In the following
sections we have focused on how pupils responded to the five
options, and then on how quickly their anxieties left them in the
autumn. First, the efficacy of the five options is compared.

Five pre-transfer programmes compared

The ostensible purpose of the five types of pre-transfer visit we
found is to inform parents and pupils about the destination school,
and thus allay some of the fears pupils have. The five options used
by our six schools were:

> Option 1:
> Teacher visits to the feeder schools.
> Option 2:
> Pupil tours of the destination school.
> Option 3:
> Parents' evenings at the destination school.
> Option 4:
> Pupils spent a whole working day at the destination school.
> Option 5:
> Teachers from destination school teach at feeder schools.

We were not, unfortunately, allowed by Maid Marion to observe
our sample pupils experiencing option 4, which at the time we did
not realize was such a successful option in reducing anxiety.

The test data on changes in pupil anxiety before and after transfer
were presented in Galton and Willcocks (1983:173). From these
data also shown at the end of the chapter, Maid Marion (BPT) was
clearly the school whose pre-transfer arrangements produced the

least anxious pupils, while Guy Mannering's generated the most. The Maid Marion pupils *were* anxious, as their interviews and essays showed, but less so than the pupils due to go to any of the other schools. We have therefore concluded that four of the five types were relatively ineffective, and only the 'full working day' plan (option 4) reduced anxiety to a significant extent. When we examine the typical features of options 1, 2, 3 and 5, their relative ineffectiveness at reducing anxiety will become clearer.

The first option used by some of our schools was a visit by teachers from the destination school to a feeder school to talk to the pupils facing transfer. This was used by both Kenilworth and Maid Marion (11–14) Schools in Bridgehampton, and ORACLE researchers saw visits to two different feeder schools, Mitchell Butler and Kenilworth Warden. In mid-June, two teachers, one male and one female, came from Kenilworth (BST) 11–14 School to Mitchell Butler Lower School to see pupils who had already paid a visit to Kenilworth. Those pupils going to Kenilworth were brought into the hall and:

> divided into two groups: boys and girls. The girls went to one end of the hall to talk to the female teacher and the boys went to the other end of the hall to talk to the male teacher. They were then each invited to ask any questions of the teacher with them to clear up any points which might have arisen from the visit they had already made.

Mrs Appleyard spent time with the girls explaining what would happen on their first day at Kenilworth in some detail, and reassured them about finding their way round, and avoiding older children.

> She began by saying that it would be best to arrive between 8.30 and 8.45. 'Come in the front entrance from the main road.' She explained that there would only be first years there on the first morning so there was no need for them to worry about being bossed about by the older children. The second and third years would only be coming to school after lunch. This was so that the first years could have the school to themselves to get used to finding their way about without the others there. She kept re-assuring the children that if they got lost, 'do not worry just ask where you want to go and there is bound to be someone to help you.'

The questions which girls raised were about games, cookery, French and Latin. Mrs Appleyard stressed that these would be manageable, and how similar most of the subjects would be to their current work (e.g. English). The questioning moved on to jewellery, the tuckshop, and the assembly. Then girls again raised more questions about all the different teachers, which, the observer commented, 'was obviously causing quite a lot of concern amongst the children'.

The boys at the other end of the hall with Mr Southern were discussing discipline, games kit, sports teams, breaktime, trips and excursions, theft, lost property, punctuality, science and dissections, streaming, and remedial teaching. The observer noted:

> The boys at the other end of the hall with Mr Southern were having a very different conversation. Mr Southern began by inviting the boys to ask questions. The first one was 'will we be treated as babies or will we be bossed about?' Mr Southern was very surprised and hastened to assure them that they would not be treated as babies and also went into the explanation that the first years would be there, for their first day, on their own in the morning so that they wouldn't be bossed about by anybody else and he assured them anyway that such things did not happen.
>
> Many of the subsequent questions concerned games kit, the teams, the different sports, what competitions were held, what kind of games they could play at play time, what kind of trips and excursions they could go on and also whether they could play with the Maid Marion children during break as it was on the next-door site. Mr Southern said 'no', otherwise there would just be too many children, it would be safer to keep them separate. However there was plenty of time to play with them after school.
>
> Another topic which concerned the boys was punishment. They wanted to know what would be done. Mr Southern said 'Oh well, we don't need to punish children but it is usually written work.' He then asked the boys what kind of punishments they thought would occur. There were various suggestions, like the cane, slippers, etc. He assured them that none of those happened at all, it was mostly written work. Another boy was concerned whether they could carry knives in school. Mr Southern said 'no'.
>
> Another question concerned whether there were high and low classes. Mr Southern said 'No, there were different classes so that each child was in the class that was best suited to it.' He did say, however, that there were tests and that they allotted to different classes on the basis of that.
>
> Another boy asked what they actually did in science, would they do any dissections? Mr Southern said 'Sometimes, but not directly after lunch,' which the boys all found apparently funny.

These extracts from the visit by Mrs Appleyard and Mr Southern to Mitchell Butler Lower School give a flavour of such occasions. They show teachers trying hard to allay fears, and using both reassurance and humour. For the equivalent visit from Maid Marion to Kenilworth Warden Lower School the pupils were not sex-segregated, the three visiting staff were all men, and they brought a boy and girl pupil with them, but the agenda was similar. That is, staff reassured pupils that they would not get lost, would soon get to know teachers, would not be bullied, and would find the work manageable. Among the issues raised by pupils was uniform.

> Gareth also asked if boys had to wear ties. Mr Seed said 'yes certainly' to help

make them look tidier and feel more comfortable if they were all wearing the same kind of clothes. Gareth did not take kindly to that. Donna asked if girls had to wear blazers. She was obviously rather dreading the idea and the girl exhibit (a pupil visiting from Maid Marion with Mr Seed) assured her that it wasn't compulsory, although many people did because they were nice and warm and had lots of handy pockets.

Later in their talk, Mr Welsh and Mr Blundell raised the topic of bullying.

Mr Welsh assured all the children the stories they were bound to have heard about all the bullying and batterings that go on were quite unfounded and that there was no bullying of any kind at all. He then appealed to the two exhibits who had come along, they nodded their heads vigorously in agreement. Mr Blundell then said behind his hands so that they all could hear: 'I'll give you your 50p afterwards for saying that.' There was general laughter.

The adults involved in option 1 clearly intended it to be reassuring to pupils. We found, however, that it was not very effective because pupils even as young as 9 were cynical. They believed that only nice teachers are assigned to make such propaganda visits, that staff on visits are probably putting on an act, and that the whole purpose of the exercise is to lull them into a false sense of security. As a supplement to option 4 we would not condemn option 1, but alone it does not alleviate pupils' deepest fears.

Option 2 is the most common arrangement, where pupils visit their destination school for a short time. Typically they are harangued by a senior teacher in a large space (e.g. the hall or gym) and then taken on a 'whistle-stop' tour of the school by a teacher or senior pupil. For example, when pupils from Stourbridge Road and Wellington Lower Schools visited Melin Court (CPT) 12–18 School in Coalthorpe, they were put in the hall and addressed by Mrs Hallows, the head of the first year. Mrs Hallows explained what would happen on the first day of term, procedure for lunches, what clothes they were to wear, and reassured them that there was no truth in stories about heads being pushed down toilets. Then fourth-year pupils arrived and took small groups around the school. The observer wrote:

It is very uninformed. The pupils just take you past doors in a rush and say 'This is the geography room; this is an English room' . . . Indeed we seemed to pass the same room on 3 or 4 occasions as we went round and round the school. It just gave me an added impression of its size and confused me all the more . . . we arrive back in the hall without having seen the special first year complex or the first year yard which was talked about.

When the observer went back to Stourbridge Road School s/he talked to the pupils. The girls reported that they had not liked being taken around by boys on the school tour, and they all felt the school was 'so big'. Their main worries were the size and the bullying, and all children had wanted to see inside classrooms and the first year area. Such tours confused our observers, as well as the pupils. For example at Waverly (CST) 12–18 School:

> I joined a group of 6 girls being shown around by a 6th form girl. We did not go inside many of the rooms but went up and down several staircases, being told that some were only to be used for going up and others for going down, all of which was rather confusing. To add to this our guide, although very friendly and helpful, spoke in a very quiet voice and much of what she said was lost to all but the front two girls. After a while the others made no attempt to hear but just followed along looking rather overawed. Everyone brightened up as we passed a chocolate vending machine at the foot of one of the staircases – but I doubt whether anyone could have found their way back to it (including me!).'

After this visit the observer wrote:

> The children then began to leave, as subdued as when they came, seeming to bear out Mrs Ackrill's comments that they were 'scared to death' about coming to the school and would ask lots of questions when they returned to Ashwood Bank School.

These pupils were rising 12, and both Waverly and Melin Court were large and complicated buildings. However the accounts of visits to Guy Mannering (AST) 9–13 School, which was quite a small building, show a similar pattern. In the afternoon, children from the feeder schools came to Guy Mannering, and were gathered in the hall, where the head, Miss Tyree, addressed them:

> She welcomed them rather formally, thanking the teachers for bringing them, and talking to them as if she were making a speech to the parents. Most of what she said was about the first day. About how they would come to the school, ten minutes to nine was a good time, not 8.30 a.m. and not 9 o'clock and that they should come without their parents. They should also come in their nice new uniforms looking smart. They could have school lunches. She asked for a show of hands for those who would be bringing sandwiches, saying beforehand 'I hope there will not be many of you doing this.' She then said that she would answer any of their questions adding 'providing that they are sensible questions.' It was, therefore, remarkable that a number of children still put their hands up following this aside. The children asked questions such as 'How many teachers do we have?' 'How many teachers are there in the school?' and were clearly surprised at her answer of 30 and that they would probably see at least 10 of those in their first year. Some children asked about games and there was an interesting exchange about swimming. Miss Tyree said that they could not always go swimming because there were

only four periods a week for them at the baths and there would be six classes. She then went on 'There's an interesting maths problem for you. If there are four periods and six classes, how often would your class miss swimming?' She then went on to say that she hoped they liked maths and that she would be taking some maths, not that she could do maths but she did know her tables and she hoped they knew theirs!

The organization of the visit round the school was then passed over to one of the male teachers (whose name I did not get). For the visits the pupils were broken down into groups of four and taken round by senior pupils, (that is those in their final year who were about to go to the upper school). Many of these wore sashes indicating that they were prefects or had some positions in the form. Naturally, the tour was fairly perfunctory. For the group I went with it consisted of pupils opening doors and saying 'This is the French room' or 'This is where you do maths' or 'This is where you do PE.'

There was little questioning between the two groups although the children taking the visiting pupils round were polite they were not very chatty about the school itself. One nice point was when the lower school children were crossing the playground. They held hands as no doubt they had done as they walked up to the school. The children from Guy Mannering who were having their break called out and jeered at them particularly the holding of hands part. By the time they had left the playground therefore none of the children were holding hands anymore.

When the primary children did visit a classroom where the teacher was teaching the situation could be regarded as one of mutual embarrassment on both sides. The teacher would call them in and ask them the standard question 'Are you coming here next year? Well I don't think I will be teaching you but I will sometime. Do you like maths/French, etc.?' To all these questions the children would answer 'Yes' or 'No'.

However, when we reassembled in the hall and Miss Tyree asked them whether they had enjoyed their visit they all shouted enthusiastically that they had. As most of the children live locally, they were then dismissed and allowed to find their own way home.

Another observer accompanied one group of four girls on their tour, and recorded the following comments. She felt that the four 'Spent a bewildered twenty minutes hurrying after the prefect.' They were shown very few of the classrooms because the majority were locked. In the science lab, 'the prefect showed them a dissected rabbit and the human skeleton.' In the gym, '3rd form girls in immaculate leotards were practising cartwheels.' Then the tour looked at tennis courts and hockey pitches and the prefect claimed 'We run round several times before games – just for a warm up, you know.' The observer commented 'The smaller girls were duly impressed.'

Teachers obviously intend these visits to be informative and reassuring. However, they suffer from the same drawback as option 1, which is that the children are aware of the transitory nature of their exposure, and are cynical about the things they are shown. Pupils suspect that the staff who address them are showing their best side and/or have been chosen to be reassuring. The 'really' fierce and strict staff that they hear of in rumours are, they believe, kept well away from them. The tours fail to reduce anxiety because they are too perfunctory and superficial, and hence bewildering. As an observer in Ashburton wrote:

> Having closely observed children's reactions when let loose in a school for the first time the priorities in children's minds . . . (were) where to put things, i.e. a desk or a drawer which *belonged* to them, a peg also exclusively theirs, and to explore the toilets!

These needs are not met on the short visits and therefore they are not sufficient to calm apprehension. A short visit which was planned to take account of pupils' folklore, and thus included meeting the legendary fierce teacher, seeing the showers and lavatories, and even walking the mythical 'ten mile' cross-country running course, might reduce anxieties, but adult-centred ones do little to calm the children's fears.

The third option we found in the ORACLE schools was an evening visit. Some of the schools arranged parents' evenings, to which children were not invited, but others allowed pupils to come. These usually took a similar form to pupils' visits, and the children were again cynical about the 'best behaviour' they saw displayed by staff and pupils. A typical example of such an evening at Melin Court (CPT) 12–18 School Coalthorpe follows:

> On the evening of 4th July 1978, Maurice Galton and I attended the Open Evening given by Melin Court School for the parents of children transferring to the school in September. At the start of the meeting there were approximately 100 parents and chidren present, but most of the empty seats were filled by late arrivals during the first half hour.
>
> Mr Stackpole, the headmaster, introduced himself and Mrs Hallows the first year tutor, and welcomed everyone to the meeting. He made reference to a similar meeting the previous December when parents had first been offered choices of schools, and said that the purpose of the present meeting was, now that the choices had been made, to give any final information they might need to set their children's minds at rest. He referred to letters which all the parents should have received from the school, containing all the relevant information. He went on to say that Melin Court was of 'middling' size as secondary schools go, but still large compared with the middle schools, with over 900 children and 50 staff. The year group was 270 children, but they would only have contact with 6 or 8 staff who would know them very well. Mrs Hallows would also get to know them very well and parents should contact her in the first instance if any problems arose. He emphasized that no formal appointments were necessary. Parents could 'take pot luck – we'll be happy to see you' or make appointments, as it suited them.
>
> Mr Stackpole went on to describe the course they would follow. In the 1st year this consists of a common course with a full range of subjects, with no selections or decisions necessary. Those needing extra help in reading and

maths would be given this. In the 2nd year parents would be asked to make certain choices and in the 3rd year they would be asked 'much harder questions' about whether their child would take a full range of examinations. At the end of this they could go into the 6th form or leave for further education or employment. They would be encouraged to take 'O' levels if they were capable but, again, that would be decided later. Perhaps parents would be asking 'if my child goes to your school, what are the chances of him leaving with a job?' Mr Stackpole was fairly optimistic on this and quoted that out of 210 leaving in the last year only 6 were still unemployed. He finished with the hope that the results of education should be a 'happy and fulfilled adult life.'

At this point, Mr Stackpole handed over to Mrs Hallows to give information about the first day, sensible clothing and so on. This Parents' Evening followed pupils' visits to the school, and one observer noted:

Mrs Hallows, who makes the same speech that she made to the pupils when I visited the school before: 'On the 3rd September, you are in for a time because your child won't be sleeping but I want you to know that there will be 269 others who will not be also. They are to get here for 8.45 where they will be introduced to their group tutor in the hall. They will be with pupils from their school and whether they will be with their best friend will depend whether they waste their time. 1M is no better than 1R academically. After their tutors they go to their classrooms where they register . . . '

When Mrs Hallows had finished her piece, Mr Stackpole asked if anyone had any questions before they dispersed to tour the building. Among the public questions from parents were:

Question: 'If I buy a blazer, then I have to buy a coat to cover it. Can I get by with an outside jacket?'
Answer: 'I will be frank. We do insist on comfortable clothing suitable for school, but we don't insist on a blazer, a dark sports jacket will do. But we don't want them competing with special clothes. You must have them dressed for the job.' (A very political answer, since he has not answered the question at all).

Question: 'Can they try school dinner for a week and then change?'
Answer: 'I'm not hard and fast on this. If you decide, you can write and tell us that you want to change. After all, "rules are made for men and not men for rules".'

Question: 'If there are holidays inside term do you need a special form?'
Answer: 'No, just a letter.'

Question: 'Do they need a tie?'
Answer: 'Yes, but if September is sunny, we will have summer dress, but start in December on the assumption that it is winter.'

Question: 'Is there any homework?'

Answer: 'Yes, good question. In the first year it consists of finishing off tasks set in class. In the third year you will get a homework timetable and in the fourth year they will get quite a lot to do.'

Question: 'Textbooks, do they bring them all home?'
Answer: 'We don't have desks, but we do have lockers, so they don't need to bring all books home everyday.'

Mr Stackpole then thanked everyone for coming and divided the audience into two parties to start their tour of the building. One observer wrote:

It was rather reminiscent of being dismissed from assembly. We saw displays in all the departments of the school. The science laboratories had experiments laid out with sixth formers explaining them. The domestic science department was a great attraction, with pupils in the process of baking, and the delicious smells encouraged the purchase of what had been made. The gym was very popular with both parents and children. Many of the children were showing their parents around and as this was their second visit, presumably they were beginning to find their way about in the buildings.

These evenings may well be informative for parents, and may give them the means to calm their children's fears about some issues. When pupils are allowed to attend these events, though, it is clear from the interviews with pupils that they are equally cynical about what they are shown on these flying visits. Children believe that the school is putting on its most welcoming face – as, of course it is. At Melin Court (CPT) 12–18 School the observer noted:

It was clear that the school had had a good clean since I had been there last week.

This observer had attended the parallel event at Waverly (CST) 12–18 School, who s/he felt had made an even greater effort to impress parents and future pupils:

One gets the feeling that the staff have made far less effort here than at Waverly where the whole school was geared to presenting itself on parents' night to the best possible advantage. Pupils here lounge about and fool around and have come in their out-of-school clothes, whereas at Waverly everyone was blazered. In the science laboratories the equipment, although similar to that at Waverly, is not so expensive and there is far less effort made to interest the parents in the work.

The pupils are, therefore, quite correct in believing that during options 1, 2 and 3, the destination schools are presenting themselves in a favourable light. The problem with these three arrangements is that children do not actually experience the things they already fear, and in some cases they meet new things that add to their anxieties, in a threatening way. Being *told* that there will not be any bullying is no substitute for experiencing a special first year playground with the head on duty, stopping fierce third years from stealing your crisps, football or comic.

Option 5 (destination school staff teaching regularly in feeder schools) was not widely used in our six transfer schools as a device to calm pupils, although there were teacher visits to discuss curriculum continuity, an issue discussed in Stillman and Maychell (1984). This option probably suffers from the same disadvantage, in that cynical pupils will never believe that the dangerous staff would be the ones sent to meet them before transfer, and this programme does nothing to help with fears about fellow pupils or the building. The one option which does begin to tackle all the pupils' fears is option 4, the full working day in the transfer school, which Maid Marion alone employed. In restrospect we should have tried harder to arrange observation of it. We were less successful in negotiating access than Measor and Woods in their ethnography of transfer. Measor and Woods (1984) followed a cohort of pupils from Hayes Middle School to Old Town Upper School, and their research also included observation of the pre-transfer programme. Old Town had designed their pre-transfer programme on the lines proposed by Hamblin (1978). Pupils from a feeder school had two visits to Old Town, one lasting a full day (option 4) plus one of a half day (option 2), plus a parents' evening (option 3). Measor and Woods were given access to all three phases of the programme, and their verdict is that the Old Town induction scheme was successful for pupils and parents. Unfortunately our data are less complete than Measor and Woods' because we were unable to attend the option 4 full day at Maid Marion (BPT) 11–14 School.

This chapter has outlined the main fears about transfer expressed by the pupils (friends and bullies, the building, the staff, and the new curriculum), and compared these with the data on myths collected by Measor and Woods (1983). It has then outlined five options in pre-transfer arrangements used by the ORACLE schools to reduce anxieties, and suggested why some are more successful than others. The next part of the chapter deals with two aspects of reassurance in the pre-transfer programmes: teachers' jokes, and attempts to address fears pupils are thought to have. Staff can only deal with apprehensions that they are aware of, or are asked about, and some of the issues that concerned the ORACLE pupils were never voiced in some of the schools, while others were never raised in any of the programmes. While we have argued that *organizationally*, the 'full day' spent in the transfer school is the most reassuring, we do want to stress that all our schools tried hard to reduce pupils' fears in their homilies and question and answer sessions. If they were unsuccessful, it was usually because they addressed 'wrong' topics (i.e. those pupils were not scared about) or failed to tackle the issues pupils had secret worries about. For example, some boys are convinced that wearing school uniform makes them look effeminate but no boy actually *voiced* this anxiety in public, and no teacher addressed it in a speech – probably because they had no idea such a piece of folklore existed. A more detailed examination of the issues raised and avoided by staff therefore follows.

Mr Washbrook, the retiring head of Gryll Grange (APT) 9–13 School described the aim of pupil visits as one of reassurance. They were 'to make sure we haven't got fangs'. One way in which staff tried to show that they were friendly was to tell jokes.

Teachers' pre-transfer jokes

A typical teacher joke during a pre-transfer visit occurred when Mrs Hallows talked to prospective pupils at Melin Court (CPT) 12–18 School about the uniform:

> Girls are to wear blouses and skirts and sensible shoes. They can wear trousers after October but again not jeans. She tells the boys that if they think that is unfair they can all wear skirts and there is laughter.

It is not clear how far such jokes serve mainly to relieve tension during the actual homily or meeting, or actually reduce longer-term anxieties. It is certain that they are a common part of such teacher talk. The literature on school humour (Walker and Adelman, 1976; Walker and Goodson, 1977; Woods, 1979) has mainly focused on classroom interaction among those who know each other, or jokes in the staffroom. Situations of the kind we are discussing here, where a strange teacher is trying to appear friendly, have not been studied before. It is noticeable that while the jokes and puns seemed to amuse the children, the observers were less enthusiastic, as in the aside about not doing dissection after lunch quoted above (p.28) from Mr Southern's visit to Mitchell Butler Lower School in Bridgehampton. The observers were unimpressed by the following two 'jokes'. At Gryll Grange (APT) 9–13 School, Mr Washbrook, the retiring head, told children who had come from Banbury Lower (a school where the head was called Mr Jolly) that the incoming head at Gryll Grange was called Mr Judge. He added that now they had had a jolly time with Mr Jolly it was time to be judged by Mr Judge. At Melin Court (CPT) Mrs Hallows told the pupils they would do all crafts irrespective of sex and

'We've had no girls cutting their hands off or boys dying of food poisoning yet.'

The observer noted 'the childern enjoyed this.' A similar observer view is reported in Measor and Woods (1984:32) when the head told pupils

'I'm known high and low as "the boss" and other things as well, but not to my face.' *This amused the pupils greatly* (emphasis ours).

Such jokes do not impress researchers, but do seem to release tension in pupils.

The other strategy teachers used was to address the specific fears they thought pupils had, which sometimes misfired because they created new anxieties in place of those they alleviated.

Allaying specific fears

Apart from the jokes, there were straightforward reassurances on many of the topics where pupils had fears, such as friendship and bullying, getting lost and so on. For example at Waverly (CST) Mr Bronte explicitly told the children that they would be shown round the school again next term by their new teacher, and that if they became lost they must ask someone for help. At Kenilworth (BST) the teacher leading the tour stressed that children would have a plan so that they would not get lost, and showed them the way into the school they would use on the first day so they would think 'Ah yes, I have done this before' and they would not feel at all nervous. When the Maid Marion (BPT) staff visited Kenilworth Warden Junior School Mr Blundell brought two children, a boy and a girl who were ex-pupils of Kenilworth Warden who had 'already survived' the first year at Maid Marion. Then Mr Seed took over, and told the children that the first years had most of their lessons in a special complex at the side of the main hall.

From the observers' perspective, such reassurances were often wide of the mark. For example, only one teacher actually took pupils into the shower room. When the children visited Kenilworth (BST) 11–14 School, Miss Chichester showed her group the PE facilities.

As we passed the changing room she allowed the boys to go into the boys' changing room and the girls to go into the girls' changing room to have a look at the showers and the other facilities there. She told them that they would have a couple of lessons of PE a week, and that they must always remember to bring their sports kit. A boy asked her what would happen if they didn't, and she said they would get into trouble . . .

hichester's school tour was quite unusual, in that pupils
y entered changing rooms. Few tours included visits to
ng rooms or toilets, and we would recommend that they
l, because otherwise myths about what 'showers' or toilets are
actually like can continue unchecked. No school tour let the pupils
inspect the lavatories.

Staff were also careful to reassure pupils about their new staff,
and new curriculum. However, sometimes this, too, appeared to
the observers to 'backfire'. The visit we have already quoted by Mrs
Appleyard of Kenilworth (BST) School to Mitchell Butler included
one such 'own goal'. When Mrs Appleyard asked if there were
questions:

> Some of the girls again brought up the question about separate teachers, for
> different subjects. She realized that this was quite an area of concern for them
> and said that they would very soon get used to it and they would very soon
> learn the different teachers' names, but the important thing is to remember to
> bring the right books. This meant that they had to very carefully pack their
> bags at the beginning of the day because they would be moving around many
> different classrooms before they had a chance to return to their home base to
> get any other books they might have forgotten. This was obviously causing
> quite a lot of concern amongst the children.

Here the teacher replaces a fear about the number of staff with a
new one – forgetting your books!

In general, the concern about the number of staff was closely
related to concern about the curriculum. Before concluding this
section, it is necessary to point out that none of our six schools
explicitly said that there were no strict teachers, or tried to explode
pupil myths about fierce staff. (And, of course, no school said that
all the male staff were heterosexual.) In one case, the observer felt
that pupils' fears about fierce teachers may even have been amplified. After the pupils' tours of Kenilworth (BST), they were all led
back to the hall where:

> Miss Chichester asked in quite a loud voice if she could have a bit of hush.
> The children's chatter continued, and then, with a volume of noise that would
> not have disgraced Krakatoa she bellowed (with a sizeable pause between
> each pair of words) 'I said can I have a bit of hush. I am not accustomed to
> asking twice and I have no intention of starting this afternoon.' I think it
> reasonable to suppose that this outburst might have given many of the
> newcomers a nasty fright; it certainly did not do my metabolic rate any good.

Similarly, giving children the classlists of the particular form they
will enter in their new school is only reassuring for those who are
with their friends. For those separated from them, anxiety is
heightened: a theme we return to in chapter 9. While these specific

reassurances are well meant, they leave several fears unspoken, heighten others, and may even create new ones. When the data on the pupils' views of the process are examined, it is clear that neither the jokes nor the specific reassurances are sufficient. Overall, the data gathered during the ORACLE ethnography suggest that schools should operate both a spoken reassurance *and* an experiential one, and should try to cover all the spoken and unspoken fears that pupils have. That is, a senior teacher should say that bullying is not allowed, and then this should be demonstrated by showing pupils their special first year yard, the lavatories and the shower room. Similarly, telling pupils that the maths they will do is similar to the sums they are currently doing should be reinforced by doing some simple maths. Clearly staff do not want to suggest that there are no strict teachers, but an emphasis on fairness and the appearance of the most dreaded teachers in person could be organized.

In the absence of experiencing a day in their destination school, pupils 'hear' comments such as the following as empty rhetoric, on which, at best they suspend judgment. A typical teacher promise was observed when Mrs Hallows of Melin Court (CPT) met the Stourbridge Road and Wellington Lower Schools' children, she tackled fears of bullying by explaining that second years (12-year-old new pupils) had a special yard separate from the older pupils.

'No-one is going to beat you to a pulp, or any other stories you hear,' she said. She then attempted to reassure them about stories of bullying by saying that she knows they will have heard that new boys get rolled off banks and get their heads pushed down the toilets, but it is not true. 'I don't say nothing will happen. Someone might say "Oh, first years". But you have got a year tutor and he will be there to look after you.'

For pupils to believe this, they need to *see* their year tutor looking after them, their special yard, and find that if someone *does* try to roll you down a bank, a teacher will intervene. Verbal assurances in all areas need to be supported by experiential ones if the pupils are to rest easy in the summer holidays.

The final topic to be addressed is the pupils' reactions to their pre-transfer programmes.

Pupil responses to the five options

As one might expect the pupils differed in their responses to the school visits. At the beginning of the chapter we saw pupils comment on their expectations in essays, and the points made in the interviews are similarly divided. Nathan was pleased he had been on a visit and seen everything (at Maid Marion) for himself. He was glad he had seen the actual rooms he was going to work in and his teachers and he felt perfectly happy with what he had seen. Vincent had a brother already at Melin Court who said it was 'all right sometimes'. He came on a visit from Burton Upton but did not get much from it because 'They showed you round too quick.' Fenella also came on a school visit to Melin Court when they were shown around by prefects. She felt she did not get a lot from it because there was too much to see in too short a time. She felt the open evening was better when they could find their own way round. Coming on visits certainly does not always calm fears. Sandra came to have a look round Waverly on a visit from Pickwick but her family did not come to an open evening. She said 'I was scared before I came, Miss, but its all right now.' Delia came to Waverly with her mum and dad to the open night but she was very apprehensive about coming. Peggy was very nervous before she came to Waverly and the visit from Ashwood Bank with her class and teacher 'didn't make me feel any better.' Gordon came to Waverly and had a look round on a visit from Pickwick and his main fear was about the size of the building. 'I felt terrible, Miss, on the first morning.'

The observers who accompanied pupils on pre-transfer visits (option 2) were unenthusiastic about them, and felt they did not calm children's fears. One researcher returned to Stourbridge Road Lower School after a visit to Melin Court.

> Coalthorpe 28/6/78
> Afterwards I went back to Stourbridge Road and talked to the pupils who had been there. The girls, in particular, were perhaps apprehensive and very quiet. It emerged in our conversation that (a) they hadn't liked being taken around by boys on the school tour, (b) they felt it was so big (this was spontaneous comment). When asked what they were worried about they said it was the size and the bullying. They said they were told that the boys tended to pull or flick your ears.
> When asked what they would like about going to the new school one girl said the work because there were lots of things to do. The boys in particular commented on the metalwork and the woodwork opportunities. All the children would have liked to have seen inside the classrooms and to have seen the first year area in more detail.

Similar observer comments have been threaded through the chapter so far. However, even these who were anxious soon found their fears vanished once the new term began in the autumn. For example:

> My first day was terrifying . . . but I soon settled in and I had some friends . . . I have got lost about twice, one with the whole class and one on my own, but the teachers don't mind unless you're a second or third year so first years get away with it.
>
> (anonymous boy, Kenilworth)

I expected Kenilworth to be a strict horrible school. But I think its the
school I've been to yet. The teachers I suppose are all right but sometin
they get on to you. One subject I thought I wouldn't be any good at is F
but I think I'm quite good at it. I thought the 3rd year boys would pick o
but gradually I found they won't if you learn to stand up to them . . . I
surprised myself by getting in the rugby team.

(Gilbert)

At first when I came to this school I was frightened because I thought
everyone would bully me, but I was wrong. This school is GREAT and so are
the teachers.

(Emily)

Similar pupil comments will be quoted throughout the rest of this book, but these give a perfect flavour of the typical pupil's reaction to transfer. Once you get there, friends *are* made, bullies can be avoided, no one gets lost, teachers are just teachers, and new subjects are no more impossible or incomprehensible than familiar ones. School is still school, even in a larger building.

To conclude this chapter, the project's test data on anxiety is reproduced from Galton and Willcocks (1983:173). The pupils were tested for anxiety three times during the transfer period, in the June before transfer, in November in their new schools, and in June at the end of their first year at the new school. Table 2.2 shows the mean anxiety scores as a percentage of the maximum possible. Three main features are apparent from Table 2.2 Pre-transfer anxiety is lower in the 'primary type' schools: Gryll Grange, Maid Marion and Melin Court, than in the 'secondary type': Guy Mannering, Kenilworth, Waverly. After transfer pupils generally become less anxious, as they find their feet in the new schools. However by the end of their first year, among the younger pupils (9 and 11) tension rises during the year.

Table 2.2   Mean anxiety scores through transfer by school

| | Ages and schools | | | | | |
| | 9+ | | 11+ | | 12+ | |
	GM	GG	K	MM	W	MC
Anxiety scores as % of maximum possible						
June pre-transfer	57.4	45.4	47.1	43.9	48.6	44.5
November post-transfer	55.4	48.6	46.9	41.3	45.1	42.6
June post-transfer	50.3	49.2	45.2	46.7	47.8	41.6
n =	38	39	16	15	10	15

Table 2.2 shows that the Maid Marion pupils were the least anxious before transfer, and their anxiety rose during the second half of the school year. In contrast Guy Mannering pupils became less worried as the year progressed. The numbers here are small, and do not in themselves offer schools clear guidelines on organizing a pre-transfer programme. However taken with the other kinds of data, our conclusion is that Maid Marion had the most successful pre-transfer arrangements, and, endorsed by Measor and Woods' (1984) findings, those we recommend to schools. The subsequent changes in pupils' anxieties must be due to their experiences in the schools, and it is to these that this book now turns.

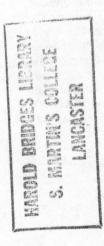

CHAPTER 3

First days in the new school

Postern of Fate, the Desert Gate, Disaster's Cavern, Fort of Fear
The Portal of Bagdad am I . . .
Pass not beneath, O Caravan, or pass not singing. Have you heard
That silence where the birds are dead yet something pipeth
Like a bird?

(Gates of Damascus, J.E. Flecker)

Flecker's poem refers to the East Gate of Damascus, that into the desert where a high proportion of travellers perished *en route* to Bagdad. For many of our sample the school gate on the first day of the autumn term loomed as menacingly as the desert gate of Damascus. Few of them felt like singing as they passed through the school entrance into what they feared might indeed be 'disaster's cavern'.

Once inside, and caught up in their new schools' routines, these fears soon vanished, and this chapter examines how the routines were established. This chapter presents data collected in the first few weeks of the new school year in the six schools studied intensively. These were two 9–13 middle schools (Guy Mannering and Gryll Grange) in Ashburton (Local Authority A); two 11–14 high schools (Kenilworth and Maid Marion) in Bridgehampton (Local Authority B); and two 12–18 comprehensive schools (Waverly and Melin Court) in Coalthorpe (Local Authority C). The previous chapter has described how the parents and pupils were introduced to their new schools before the transfer and their reactions to the introductions. Here we use ethnographic data to describe the period of adjustment to the new schools, and to introduce our analytic themes which are expanded in the succeeding five chapters.

We have briefly addressed the topic of initial encounters in the six

43

First days in the new school

ORACLE schools in two previous accounts. In these we focused on how teachers introduce their rules to new pupils (Delamont, 1983b: 119–34) and on how contrasting pairs of pupils responded to their new environments. In Galton and Delamont (1980) we contrasted how Dudley and Davina reacted to starting Gryll Grange (9–13) school, and in Delamont (1983b) how Rex and Wayne started out at Waverly (12–18) and Melin Court (12–18) schools. This volume takes a rather different perspective on starting school, and explaining that view is a major purpose of the chapter. However, before the introduction of the five themes, we address the issue of initial encounters, and the ways in which teachers establish order when faced with new pupils. The chapter ends with data on how pupils set about testing their teachers' regimes, and an example of a successfully negotiated shared meaning.

Initial encounters

When a teacher faces a new class for the first time, both parties have ideas about what classroom life is like in general, but new rules have to be established for the particular new relationship. This *initial encounter* can be contrasted with a routine meeting between a teacher and a class who know each other. In the routine situation some rules are known, and negotiations take account of earlier encounters, as the 'strawberries' incident made famous by Walker and Adelman (1976) shows. Wragg and Wood (1984) comment that:

> a common response to a request to be allowed to watch lessons in early September is for the teacher to say, 'Would you mind coming in a fortnight when things have settled down?'

Wragg and Wood therefore deliberately observed experienced teachers' initial encounters, to compare them with student teachers' first meetings with classes. Researchers need to gather data on both initial and routine encounters, while recognizing that each type has its own problems for observer and observed.

In many ways it should be easier for researchers to gather data during initial encounters because the investigator is in the same knowledge state as the participants. Rules, norms and procedures are more likely to be made explicit. The routine encounter, because it draws on previous meetings between that teacher and that class, has many implicit features which are less accessible to researchers. In practice, there are many published studies of routine encounters but few initial ones because the first meeting of a teacher and class is problematic for the staff and observers rarely gain access to it. The main source of material on initial encounters is that vigorous tradition of educational writing: the autobiography or 'non-fiction novel' popularized by Blishen. This *genre* is discussed by Whiteside and Mathieson (1971) and is used by Hargreaves (1972) to illustrate the establishment and maintenance of order. Bream (1970) is an example from New Zealand which has been used by Delamont (1983a) to illustrate the establishment of negotiated order. Research on the process is rare, but the ORACLE team were privileged to enter five of the six schools on the first day of the school year, and all six were visited regularly from the first week onwards. We thus have unusual data on initial encounters between teachers and pupils.

Studies by David Hamilton (1977, reprinted in Delamont, 1984) and by Mary Willes (1981) have focused on how very young children first learn the pupil role. Many features of classrooms occupied by older children which are taken for granted are seen, through the eyes of 5-year-olds, as problematic. For example, Hamilton (1977:45) shows a teacher explicitly teaching children how to say 'Good morning, Mrs Robertson' in chorus: something learnt within the first week of school. As more and more research is done by practising teachers (Nixon, 1980), more data on initial encounters will become available. Analyses are needed of how different schools try to socialize new pupils, and how the protagonists in classrooms come to construct shared meanings, establish rules, and learn to live together in a joint world. The ORACLE project allows us to compare the process across six schools, and we relate our data to research on beginnings in a variety of settings.

Stephen Ball (1980) provides a framework for analysing initial encounters between teachers and strange classes. He accepts that teachers are often reluctant to have researchers around during the earliest days of the school year and then goes on:

> but the reasons for the teacher's reluctance are exactly the reasons why the researcher should be there. These early encounters are of crucial significance not only for understanding what comes later but in actually providing for what comes later.

Ball then focuses on what he terms the 'process of establishment' which he defines as:

> an exploratory interaction process involving teacher and pupils during their initial encounters in the classroom through which a more or less permanent, repeated and highly predictable pattern of relationships and interaction emerges.

Ball analyses two sets of data on the process of establishment: some from a comprehensive school introducing mixed ability teaching and some from student teachers on school practice. These data reveal two stages in the pupils' treatment of strange teachers:

> The first is a passive, and in a sense, purely observational stage . . . After this the second stage is embarked upon, which usually involves at least some pupils in being 'real horrible' . . .

In other words, the pupils first make observations to get a series of hypotheses about the kind of teacher they are facing, and then test their hypotheses. Ball argues that pupils use the results of these testing sessions to guide their future attitudes and behaviours. For the rest of their careers with that teacher they will face a multitude of decisions about whether to obey each instruction, command or order the teacher issues or not, and they can only make these decisions if they can predict how the teacher will react. Ball says that the pupils' anticipation of the teacher's likely response enables them:

> to weigh up the amount of satisfaction to be obtained from the commission of a 'deviant' act against the dissatisfaction likely to be involved in the teacher's response to it, if any. This may in fact account for pupils' often stated preference for 'strict' teachers. Strictness usually provides for a highly structured and therefore a highly predictable situational definition.

A broadly similar framework characterizes Measor and Woods' (1984) account of a cohort of pupils entering 'Old Town' Comprehensive, where they talk of a 'honeymoon phase' followed by a period of 'coming out'. The second (testing) stage, the pupils' decisions, and the part played by violence in the establishment process are the subjects of two papers by John Beynon (Beynon and Delamont, 1984; Beynon and Atkinson, 1984), to which we make reference in this chapter. Beynon's data are from a boys' comprehensive in South Wales where the pupils and teachers used aggression and violence in the testing and establishment process. Our data, like Measor and Woods', show less violence than Beynon's but the processes are similar. The teachers work hard to establish order.

Establishing order

The establishment of order is a central task for a school faced with new pupils and the ORACLE team concentrated on how order was brought about. Wragg and Dooley (1984) point out that apprehension about establishing and maintaining order is characteristic of student teachers, and studies of experienced staff show a need for order to be common among them. There is, however, little research on how discipline, control and order are established and maintained either by experienced or novice teachers. Wragg and Dooley (1984) report one study of student teachers, and Wragg and Wood (1984) one of experienced teachers compared to novices. The experienced teachers had a clearly articulated position on how their initial encounters with new classes were to be handled:

> The experienced teachers were able to describe events with considerable precision and certainty. For them . . . first lessons were part of a taken-for-granted set of routines during which they established varying degrees of dominance by restricting pupils' movement, taking up a central position, clearly being 'in charge', and making use of their eyes.

One teacher summarized her position with the statement, 'my rules, for my room, for my area!' The researchers stress the way in which experienced teachers began by exaggerating themselves, and being 'larger than life'.

Equally important, the experienced teachers regarded the *content* of their first lesson with a new group as less relevant than its success as a management task. There had to be some content, some task, but its importance was to establish the teacher's regime, not an intrinsic one. These points, which reinforce those we made in our first report (Delamont, 1983b: 119–34) of the ORACLE transfer study, will again be apparent in the rest of this chapter. We described in the previous ORACLE volume how the class teacher, and later other staff, spend a good deal of time *locating* the pupils in time and space; giving them the rules for using new and familiar objects; explaining how the authority structure and the curricular system function. Here too we present data on how pupils are oriented to the school's time and space, to the use of objects and to authority, but we have structured the material differently and used previously unpublished illustrations from our fieldwork. Our themes here are those of the whole volume: danger (both physical and social), movement and immobility, time and pacing, formal groupings, and unofficial memberships. All these features of life in secondary schools are presented to the pupils, and accepted or rejected by them, from the first days of the new school year. We end the chapter with a comparison between our data and Beynon's, and our example of one successful establishment process: a shared class joke like Walker and Adelman's (1976) 'strawberries'. The chapter is organized so that we present a detailed account of a 'typical' first day, and then elaborate on some themes which arise during it.

First days in the new school

Through the postern of fate

The very first day in the new school is an anxious one for all pupils. Peter Cohen (1973) captures the anxieties when describing his first day at the Harvard Business School:

> Questions begin to cloud the mind's horizon. What kind of people are these? Who do they really want here? . . . The feeling of apprehension. The strange faces. Not knowing what lies in front of you. Everybody is starting from a common denominator which is uncertainty. (pp.13–14)

We have seen in the previous chapter how schools try to alleviate these feelings in pupils before they come. The very first day at the new school is also carefully designed to reassure the pupils about it. We have presented, below, a detailed account of the first half-day at Waverly (12–18) School, but it is essentially similar to those at the other five schools. The day opens with all the children, and the observer, in the school hall with the head of first year, Mr Bronte.

> Monday September 4th, 1978, 8.50 a.m.
> Children directed in to the main hall. Very quiet and subdued. All look 'well-scrubbed'. Mr Bronte welcomed them briefly then got down to information on school rules, etc. 'When you come in here again for assembly, you will come without your coats, and in silence.' Importance of uniform. Also 'politeness will get you a lot.' The children should walk on the right-hand side of corridors. Also some stairs were for going up, others for coming down. Very important to be on time, everyone who was late got a detention. Anyone thinking of playing truant should know that there were two attendance officers who were sent to visit their homes if anything was suspected – so in case of genuine absence parents should phone or send a letter. Main thing to remember – although he knew about all of them, their teachers didn't, so they could start 'with a clean slate'.

This opening session is clearly control-oriented. The school is represented as being in charge of noise, of space, of time, of clothing, and even has a right to send an offical to the pupils' homes. The overall message of Mr Bronte's opening speech is clearly one of strictness and rule-governed order. Then two senior teachers took the stage.

> Mr Spencer (assistant headmaster) spoke briefly about rules. Families had them and 'as we are a big family' it was important to have them. They should be clean, tidy, well-behaved and work hard – and if they did 'you won't cross us.' (!)
> Mrs Osbaldeston (senior mistress) again stressed uniform. 'You have chosen to come to a school which has uniform . . . you must obey our rules.' Girls especially should not try to introduce fashion ideas.
> Mr Bronte then read out each class in turn, and each filed out with their teacher.

48

First days in the new school

Mr Bronte's initial message is reinforced here by two senior teachers, each emphasizing the school's control over the pupils. Then the children are put into *classes*, allocated to a teacher, and thus divided up for the first time into their new groups. The observer's focus then shifts to one form-room, as the pupils' does.

> 9.30 a.m. with Mr Bronte in 1BE.
> (This is not one of the target classes, but I had not met the two teachers involved – Miss Lawrence and Mrs Bobbin and so could not observe in their rooms yet.) Children filed in and sat where they liked. As far as I could see this was with class mates (from their middle schools). Register checked for dates of birth, addresses, phone numbers. Mr Bronte has to pick several children up for not saying 'Sir'. Others soon get message. He tells them 'There are lots of things for you to remember today – assemblies on Tuesdays and Thursdays – you go straight in after the bell. On wet days, have "wet breaks", signalled by four bells. You can't go out and get soaked. In afternoons – no break if wet, school finished 10 minutes early.'

The observer followed the teacher already known to the research team, because it is not feasible to follow a teacher one has not met, who has not given permission. Mr Bronte's first concern is to identify the pupils, but he is also insisting that they address him 'properly'. He then reverts to control messages, about movement, time and demeanour. Then the pupils get their first task, copying their new timetable.

> Mr Bronte explains that for most of their lessons they will be taught as a class except for English, German and French. Then he puts up timetable on board for class to copy. Twenty minutes pass. Several need new pieces of paper and have to start again because they have 'made horrible mess of them'. Question from boy. 'Sir, do we go to any lessons today?' 'Yes, this afternoon.'
> Mr Bronte: aside to me, 'panic, panic!'

Pupils are given a timetable both because of the information it contains, *and* as a task that will absorb them. It also reveals for the form teacher which pupils cannot read, write poorly, or fail to follow simple instructions.

Mr Bronte, as head of first year, has several administrative responsibilities for the year as a whole, and his next act was to call on three girls (including Simone, one of our targets) from Ashwood Bank Middle School to take copies of two official letters to the other classes nearby. These letters were then distributed to pupils in his own room.

> Letter 1: Asking parents about dinner arrangements. 'Take it home, get your parents to sign it and bring it back. Do it neatly.'
> They were not allowed to go and buy things and eat them in the street – 'and

49

if you do you'll get bashed, won't you Royce?' 'Yes Sir.' (Royce a small child
sitting at front has been spotted out already as a 'character'.)
Letter 2: Second letter requests information about pupils for the school, e.g.
where parents can be contacted, etc. 'Bring these back as soon as possible,
which means tomorrow. Don't leave them to fester in your pocket tonight.'

Such letters, requesting parents to supply details about where they
work, what the child will do at lunchtime and so forth, are a routine
part of the opening term at all six schools. Here the school is further
establishing its right to organize where pupils go at lunchtime and
what they eat. Mr Bronte then returns to everyday school organization, turning to how pupils enter and leave the first year block
before school, and after breaks.

Mr Bronte explains that when there is no assembly, or at the beginning of the
afternoon the class should line up outside with the other first year classes and
wait to come in. They all go outside and practise.

Once the class has practised lining up and coming into their class,
Mr Bronte turns to uniform.

Jewellery – 'No big dangly earrings or big knuckle dusters.'
Finally, Mr Bronte reassured them that while they were bound to lose their
way in the next few weeks, they must always ask the way. Once they settled
down and made a few friends they would be all right.

At this point the bell rang for break. The class had spent one and a
half hours listening to rules, and copying down a timetable. This is a
typical first segment of the opening day in a new school. The
observer writes:

10.30 Break. Mr Parkin (headmaster) always does this break duty in yard by
first year buildings. Had coffee in staff room. Met one of the attendance
officers.

The first year pupils at Waverly had a special playground patrolled
by Mr Parkin, to prevent bullying, and it is noticeable that even on
the first day of the year, he was there, as he had promised them on
their pre-transfer visits.
    After break, when 1BE were back in their room, they met
another teacher.

10.50 Mr Bronte busy. Mr Harpole takes us all on a very good tour of the
school. Only one question asked by children – this re school dinners.

Such tours, repeats of these taken during pre-transfer visits, are frequent features of induction days. They are particularly necessary when lessons start after lunch.

> 4th lesson. Mr Oakley (woodwork teacher) takes over while Mr Bronte is busy. Gives out paper. 'Always use a margin down left hand side of paper in pencil.' Pupils must put their name and the date, then write about 'yourselves, family, interests, etc.' One boy writing in red biro – 'you must write in blue from now on.' Another boy (worried) 'Is black all right, Sir?' 'Yes.'
> Mr Oakley walks round room and notices one boy's home address – chats about his older brother who has just left.

In this lesson we see the first rules about how work is to be presented, a theme examined in our earlier volume (Delamont, 1983b: 119–34). There is also the first mention of siblings, an issue we address in detail in chapter 8. Essays about 'Yourself' are frequently found in the early days of secondary schooling, presumably because it is considered to be a topic on which everyone can write something. Thus the morning passes.

> 11.38 Mr Bronte returns. Hands out forms which are used to check attendance. Children fill in information and dates on them {. . .}
> 12.00 Bell for lunch. This week the girls on the first sitting for lunch.
> Afternoon. Registration, then I go to lesson 5 and 6 with Miss Lawrence's class 1LE. They have physics with Mr Rutherford. He has a word with them outside the lab – they come in in silence. He takes an attendance register.

The pupils therefore start 'a lesson' after lunch, and we will leave them there. They have completed a further form, and been divided by sex for the first time to eat their lunch. School life has begun.

Analysing and interpreting the opening days of the new school year is more important than merely describing it. Indeed the reader would find detailed description uninspiring, because the situation is a familiar one. Instead of repeating the points made in our earlier work (Galton and Delamont, 1980; Delamont, 1983b) we wish here to show how our five analytic themes (danger, movement, timing, formal grouping, and informal groupings of two types) are relevant right from the opening day of the school year. Thus the rest of this chapter introduces the central themes of the book while providing accounts of the first days of schooling from all six schools. Our first theme is danger.

Danger

A new school is a dangerous environment for the pupils, and a new intake of pupils can also pose a threat to their teachers (Beynon and Delamont, 1984). Three kinds of danger are considered in chapter

4, all of which are apparent in the first few days of the school year. These are: physical dangers present in the strange environment which new pupils must face, physical dangers from teachers and pupils which pupils believe lie ahead, and threats to the self-esteem and *amour propre* of both staff and children. All three types of danger are apparent in the first days of schooling, and the morning at Waverly has already made this clear. Many of the environments in the new schools were potentially dangerous to the pupils, whether they knew this or not. A typical first lesson in such environments focuses on the dangers and how pupils are to behave safely. For example, an observer at Maid Marion (11–14) school wrote:

> 1I science, Mr Salter
> The first lesson, which I did not observe, had been given over to explaining some of the more common dangers of working in a laboratory. The children had been given a picture of a lab in which various children were carrying out some experiments and in the picture were at least 20 different mistakes which the children were asked to identify.

The observer attended the second lesson, in which the pupils handled apparatus for the first time. Mr Salter told them:

> How to heat a can of water. He then also explained that it would be unsafe to put a can of water straight onto the tripod as it might slip over, so a gauze mat was needed and an asbestos mat underneath the tripod and bunsen burner so that it wouldn't heat the bench.

This is a typical introduction to a potentially hazardous location, and we examine such locations and how they are 'tamed' in chapter 4. A second source of danger, taken equally seriously by pupils, is physical force used against them by staff or fellow pupils. As chapter 2 showed, pupils transferring from one school to another are apprehensive about the strictness of the teachers, and whether their fellow pupils will bully them. Beynon and Delamont (1984) report an incident from a boys' comprehensive in South Wales which illustrates these twin dangers from the first week of term.

> The form were queueing up outside the French room. There was a lot of movement between classes and boys were milling around. David King was using his weight to barge other boys out of his way. Suddenly Mr Changeable (the head of the Lower School) shot across the hall . . . and manhandled King, then smacked him loudly over the head with a book. 'I've told you about barging before boy!' he shouted, 'don't fool around with me! I'm more than a little tired of your ignorant behaviour, King!' There was absolute silence throughout the hall, boys quickly disappearing into their classes.

Here we see one boy barging others and a master hitting a pupil. The new pupil does not know which other children are dangerous, or which teachers hit you and which do not. The ways in which these physical dangers are discovered and handled are analysed in chapter 4. None of the ORACLE schools was as violent as that studied by Beynon, so although pupils had feared bullying and strict teachers, they soon found their apprehensions groundless.

Finally, there are threats to self-esteem. In the first weeks of a new school year, both teachers and pupils are vulnerable to attacks on their self-esteem. Pupils are scared that they will be 'shown up' by teachers (Woods, 1979); teachers also have to guard against being 'shown up' by new classes of pupils who may be to noisy or even uncontrollable (Denscombe, 1980). The way in which a pupil can be humiliated is shown in the following extract from an early science lesson on measurement with Miss Fern at Melin Court:

> There is at once a good example of discouraging questions. She wants to tell them to round off to the nearest decimal place because:
> Miss F: We are lazy and we don't want to work out in full so we use?
> Girl: Digit numbers.
> Miss F: Digit numbers? She does not mean digit numbers she means?
> Boy: Ditto marks.
> Miss F: Yes (and so as to rub it in further) What did the young lady mean then when she said digit?
> Boy: (smugly) A number, Miss.
> Miss F: Yes.
> Thereafter it is noticeable that the 'young lady' takes little part in answering further questions.

Many pupils are extremely concerned about risking such incidents, although others are not subdued by them, and continue to participate, even if rebuked or 'shown up'.

Teachers, especially new recruits to a school, are vulnerable too. A master, Mr Woolfe, at Guy Mannering (9–13) school had been redeployed to the school, to teach, among other things, art. He was, because of the redeployment, labelled as incompetent by his new colleagues, and was especially prone to revealing his weaknesses to other teachers, as this incident shows:

> Meanwhile I have gone back to Mr Woolfe's lesson. He hasn't finished in time to pick out the best piece of work so he asks the children to hold up their pictures and 'show our visitor'. I must stay out of his class in future otherwise he is going to involve me in very curious ways. He is clearly very nervous and keeps on nagging at the children to leave the room tidy. I suspect that someone has been at him about its state in a previous class. As a result of the tidying up, the children arrive late for the last period before lunch which is mathematics with Mrs Forrest.

> She is appalled. 'You are messy. You've got paint all over you. You look like Red Indians.' {. . .}
>
> Clearly Mr Woolfe is going to be in trouble. It emerges that all the toilets in the art and craft area are kept locked so they couldn't go in there to wash their hands and that there were no aprons available. Mrs Forrest gives up at this and concludes, 'Well I had better come along next week and see what you are doing.'

Here Mr Woolfe had, unwittingly, revealed to Mrs Forrest that he was unable to organize an art lesson so that the children arrive clean, tidy and on time at their next lesson. In chapter 4 we examine how teachers may be particularly in danger of this type of exposure to their colleagues in the early weeks of the school year.

These, then, are three kinds of dangers that can be studied during initial encounters. The issue of movement and immobility, the second theme, is also clearly apparent during the first days in the schools.

Movement and immobility

Teachers at the six schools we studied believed that one of the biggest changes facing children moving to secondary and upper schools is the demand for immobility. It is believed that pupils at first and primary schools can and do move freely around the room, and even come and go at will. In the secondary and upper schools, movement is curtailed, and the pupils are no longer allowed to go to the lavatory, or even leave their seats, without permission. 'Movement and immobility' is the subject of chapter 5, illustrated here with an example from the earliest days of the new school year. Gryll Grange (9–13) School was the only one to allow pupils freedom of movement, the other five curtailed it. At Maid Marion (11–14) School, one of the observers had watched the children in their lower schools too, and commented in her field diary:

> Maid Marion
> The main difference from the children's point of view (apart from the size which they seemed to get over very easily) was the fact that every lesson was class taught and that very few teachers allowed any talking and none allowed any movement around the classroom. Mr Barrell was the only exception.

As well as movement around the room being curtailed, all the schools except Gryll Grange prevented children leaving the classroom to go to the lavatory during lessons. For example in:

> Science with Mr Pardoe at Kenilworth
> A boy wanted to go to the lavatory, and Mr Pardoe said that if it was very urgent he could, but it would be highly irregular. He would rather that the boy waited if he could.

First days in the new school

Being expected to plan lavatory visits to coincide with breaks and lunch is a new experience for many children. Another aspect of control over the children's movement concerns their use of space outside the individual classrooms – in playgrounds, corridors, assembly halls and so on, which we also examine in chapter 5. Rules for the use of space figured largely in the first day at Waverly (12–18) School already described. Chapter 5 also focuses on those places and times when movement is wanted, organized and demanded by teachers such as drama, PE and games. Discovering that they have to make certain movements can be as much of a shock to newcomers as having to stay still, as the myth of the '10 mile run' (Measor and Woods, 1984) shows.

Movement and immobility are closely related to our third organizing theme: time and speed. However, in chapter 6 we relate speed not so much to physical movement but to *productivity* – to the pressures on teachers and pupils to get through the work (Ball *et al.*, 1984).

Speed merchants and slow coaches

The speed at which work has to be done is another of our major organizing themes, and is developed at length in chapter 6. The management of the pupils' workrate is an issue even in the first days of the new school year, as is their use of time. The chapter focuses upon the various cycles of 'school time', the year, the term, the week and the day, comparing each with divisions of time, and cycles, in non-school settings. In the account of the first morning at Waverly (12–18) School it is clear that pupils are told not to be late, to attend regularly, how the week is organized, how to spend their lunch hour, *and* that the copying of the timetable is the first exercise of 'lock step' class work where their work rate is under scrutiny. The introduction of lock step class work brings us to our penultimate theme – formal groupings.

Formal groupings

Philip Jackson (1968) pointed out that school children have to learn to be alone in a crowd. The relationships between solitude, couples, groups and crowds in school form the subject matter of chapter 7, and are foreshadowed here. In the first week of the secondary school pupils are expected to start both cooperating with previously unknown classmates for group work, and to work alone, ignoring them, depending on the teachers' instructions. They are also organized into a myriad set of groups: teams, clubs, choirs, pairs, quartets, year-groups, sexes, and so forth. In the first days of the new year the pupils are organized into many different groups. Thus, on the first day at Maid Marion (11–14) School the pupils are put into *forms*; as the observer noted:

> The first year in-take has been divided into seven classes, each class takes one letter from the school name Maid Marion and hence they are named – 1M, 1A, 1I, 1D, 1R, 1O and 1N. The two classes which we are watching are 1I Mr Salter's class and 1O Miss Square's class. The seven classes are divided into two blocks: firstly, 1M, A, I, D and secondly 1R, O and N. There appears to be a different set of teachers for each of these two blocks. However, there is obviously a lot of collaboration between the two blocks across subjects as well as within them. Thus the maths lesson for 1O is exactly the same as the maths lesson for 1I in terms of content and materials used. This goes for social studies, English and all the other lessons as well.
>
> There are occasional opportunities for contact across classes, for instance in social studies two classes are scheduled to have the subject at the same time and although they have different classrooms they do sometimes meet together in the lecture theatre for a slide show. Design is another subject area where the whole of one block M, A, I and D, or R, O and N meet together. The classes are then divided up into many different groups which then alternate between two of the design subjects. At half term each group's two subjects will be changed so that they have experienced all the main areas during the first three terms.

Thus, in the first days of the school year, children entering Maid Marion found they were in a year group, a class, a block, *and* a smaller craft group. The contemporary comprehensive school enrols pupils in an enormous variety of formal groupings, making it genuinely difficult for a pupil to sort out which she is in, and providing many opportunities for pupils to create 'trouble' by appearing for the wrong class at the wrong time.

Family and friends

In addition to the formal groupings which are the subject of chapter 7, pupils also belong to a variety of informal groups and groups stretching beyond school such as the family. Chapter 8 examines how the pupils' families (and to a small extent the teachers'), though not physically present in the school, are invoked and referred to during the school day. The pupils' siblings are also discussed as a feature of school life which has been largely neglected. Finally chapter 8 compares the two types of 'symbolic family' which are regularly mentioned or conjured up in schools: the image of the school itself as a family, and the mythical Judaeo-Christian idealized family which appears in textbooks, homilies and classroom talk. The family and the school, and 'the family in the school' are the focus of chapter 8, and its theme, too, is apparent in the first days of the new year. In the Waverly extract, the pupils' families were being

asked to complete forms, and make school-related decisions, while
a boy is asked about his brother.

In the following extract from the first days at Maid Marion the
theme of chapter 9 becomes apparent – friendship, both among the
pupils and among the staff – and its opposite – quarrels and
opposing factions. When pupils arrive in their new schools the
influence of their old friends from their former lower schools was
apparent:

> As the children came into the room for the first day they were allowed to sit
> wherever they chose. This in fact meant that the children from Mitchell
> Butler sat together and children from Kenilworth Warden sat together, etc.
> Not only did they sit together school by school they also sat together class by
> class in that Mr B's children from Kenilworth sat together and Mr X's
> children sat together. There were obviously a few exceptions to this: in 1I Fay
> from Kenilworth Warden has left her friends and sits in a pair with a girl
> called Eunice who is new from London. Daphne from King's Heath left her
> two other King's Heath friends who were obviously very close buddies and do
> everything together and she has joined the remaining children from
> Kenilworth Warden. The Mitchell Butler children so far have stuck together.
> Amongst the boys there is one from Dorridge and one from Whitteck sitting
> together. The rest are in larger groups from Kenilworth Warden and Mitchell
> Butler and they too stick together in their previous own class and school
> bases.
> In Miss Square's class a similar pattern follows, each school, each class
> keeps itself to itself. The one girl from Knowle Park, Althea, has joined the
> Kenilworth Warden children and Trudie from Lichfield Lane has joined the
> Mitchell Butler children. Two boys from King's Heath, Miles and Lester, are
> very close buddies.

In chapter 9 we examine not only the pupils' informal groupings,
but those of the teachers as well, and how the staff judge, and try to
influence their pupils' choices and associations.

These then are the five analytic themes (danger, movement,
speed, formal and informal groupings) with which we bring the first
weeks of the school year into an unusual focus. Before we leave the
period of the initial encounter, however, we wish to compare our
data with that of Beynon from South Wales (Beynon and Delamont, 1984; Beynon and Atkinson, 1984). That is, we examine the
opening stages in the pupils' campaign to find out how soft or hard
their new teachers are.

The pupil as novice: learning the ropes
Stephen Ball (1980), Beynon and Delamont (1984) and Measor and
Woods (1983, 1984) have all written on the ways in which pupils
view the transfer to new schools, and how they study new teachers.
Ball argues that the typical pupil observes new teachers fairly

passively for a bit, and then begins to test them. Some pupils are active in the testing process, issuing challenges to the staff, while others are content to watch the challengers, form an interaction set (Furlong, 1976) with them, and do their testing more passively. While the teachers are being 'sussed', the other pupils are also being 'sized up'. This process is a central preoccupation of the first weeks in a new school or even a new class. Beynon and Delamont (1984) show how new boys entering Victoria Road School in South Wales used violence as a testing strategy on the staff and on each other. The boys were quite explicit about this period of hypothesis-testing. For example, Robert Bright told John Beynon how he and David King had tested Mr New:

> . . . in that first week we were messing around like anything and he took us back behind {the building} after a lesson and we knew that if he was soft that he would just tell us off, and if he was hard he'd hit us, and he hit us! He smacked Kingsy against the wall and kicked us both up the backside . . . that's how we found out about Mr New.

Similarly – Mark Dark told John Beynon

> At first you don't know the teachers and you have to judge them by their reactions. Some give lines, some whack you or tell you off, and others throw you outside. You just got to see how they act. You got to suss them out – there's no other way.

Beynon found that this was true of all the boys, whether conformers to school rules or those who resented and rebelled against them. Those who were conformists were more likely to watch the 'rebels' doing the testing for them, while the 'rebels' took pride in being the frontiersmen, who took the risks and bore the glory when they won and the punishment when they lost. A ringleader of the rebels, David King, explained his active strategy to John Beynon as follows: 'You've got to see if they'll come out and hit you and all that.' In our six schools we found some boys, and a few girls, deliberately testing the teachers in the same ways as David King. We are also convinced that other pupils were watching the testing to see where the lines were to be drawn by their new staff. Elsewhere (Delamont, 1983b: 146–53) we have briefly described one boy at Melin Court, Wayne Douglas Patel, who was very active in testing the staff in the same way as David King at Victoria Road. Wayne's speciality was turning up to the wrong lessons – a good test of the strictness of the regime – and we have described this in more detail in chapter 7. However he clearly set out to challenge the regime in other subjects too, and broke the rules from day one. Wayne can be seen as Melin Court's less aggressive equivalent to David King. The reaction of the staff at Melin Court, and at our other five schools, was much less violent than Victoria Road, where some of the staff behaved violently to the boys even in front of John Beynon. Mr Changeable, the head, thumped and shook the boys in Beynon's presence from the beginning of term. Mr Megaphone, the deputy, hit a boy with a slipper for misbehaviour after the cross-country run:

> When we arrived back in the yard, Mr Megaphone gathered 1Y around him whilst he dressed down Ginger for running on the road and racing across the junction without looking on the way back from Seaview Park. 'It's the dap for you, twit!' he said, 'and for any other idiots like you!' He then let the class into the changing rooms. Here he produced what he termed his 'size 11', ceremoniously bent Ginger over, and walloped him half a dozen times. Ginger hopped around smiling and rubbing his backside. 'Anyone else want a sore bum?' asked Mr Megaphone. There was a chorus of 'No thanks' and laughter. 'You'll listen to what I tell you next time,' Mr Megaphone said to Ginger, 'or I'll really make it hurt.'

He also threatened violence from the first days of the school year – for example, when he saw a boy misbehaving he yelled:

> 'You! It'll take me just seven strides to get to you across the hall, Seven Strides! I won't tell you what I'll do when I get there, but it'll hurt a lot!'

To an outsider, these events from Victoria Road may seem like brutal attacks. However, from the boys' viewpoint it was a teacher's duty to hit boys. A teacher who did not use physical force was 'soft', and a soft teacher had classes which messed around and therefore no work got done. As Ginger told Beynon:

> Teachers got a right to hit, mind you, because we're here to learn and they're here to teach us and they get paid for keeping us quiet and learning us and telling us what to do and not be noisy. I think that the only good teachers are the ones who smash you around because you'll learn in time 'cos the more they hit you, the more you'll learn to shut up.

It is possible that Wayne felt the staff of Melin Court were too soft, though we lack the type of data to be sure of this. The data on deliberately provocative pupils we have offered so far has been about two boys, Dudley (Galton and Delamont, 1980) and Wayne (Delamont, 1983b), but girls can also set out from day one to test where the teachers' limits are set. One such girl was Annabel, in class 1.6 at Guy Mannering (9–13) School. Annabel was in the 'B' band, and she specialized in 'dumb insolence'. She always sat in a sprawled slumped way, looked bored, and fidgeted endlessly. She habitually pushed her desk forwards to barge other children, tipped her chair and rocked her desk up and down. All her postural and gestural cues were expressively hostile to school. The following extracts will reveal how, over the first weeks of the autumn term, Annabel tested the disciplinary regimes of her new teachers.

> History, 1.6 with Mrs Macauley
> Annabel keeps lifting the desk lid, and swinging the desk and her chair. Mrs Macauley bawls her out – offers her the chance to go outside the door if she is bored. It doesn't stop Annabel . . . The bell goes, and Annabel who was fidgeting and yawning says 'Oh good'. Mrs Macauley tells them not to pack up. Tells off Annabel, reminding her that she is Arlene's sister and 'She behaves much better than you.'

Annabel was unimpressed by this comparison. Her behaviour, and that of a boy called Dirk, was so disruptive that it coloured the staff's reactions to their form. Within a fortnight of the start of the school year, one of us wrote:

> . . . At break it is clear that 1.6 are already the most unpopular form (which is tough for Miss O'Hara their form mistress), and that Dirk and Annabel are unpopular already.

This class, 1.6, had two or even three teachers for basic subjects, and for English they were taught both by Miss O'Hara and by the deputy head, Mrs Evans (whose husband taught the 'A' band form we studied). Annabel was not, however, overawed by Mrs Evans.

> {Mrs Evans is asking them to tell her things about themselves and their families preparatory to writing an autobiographical essay}. It is very noticeable that the class do not sit still even for the deputy head. They swing in the chairs, and Annabel, at the back, is pushing a desk into the back of the boy in front.

The consequences of behaving badly are soon apparent. The next extract shows how, once labelled a disciplinary problem, Annabel began to miss out on the rewards the school offers.

> English with Miss O'Hara
> They are told to get out their spelling books (for a test) and if they get 10 they will get a credit. They start the test . . . The words are: 'screaming, noise, tired, bright, light. . . ' The children cannot keep up and every so often someone calls out to ask 'What was No.27' or 'Number 3' or whatever. Annabel has been made to stand up. I don't know why, but every time she begins to half sit, Miss O'Hara calls out 'Stand up, Annabel.' . . . 14 get 10 out of 10, and they are told to write 'credit' on the back . . . Interestingly she tells anyone to stand up who got two more marks than the last time, and Paula and Annabel stand. Paula gets a credit, but not Annabel. Presumably because Miss O'Hara thought she was standing anyway.
> After the spelling test they start some RE . . . There is a whistling in the room and Annabel is shouted at and told to get outside. She leaves the class

with what can only be termed as a 'grin of triumph'. The rest of the class are told to finish off Jacob and draw a picture of Jacob's dream . . . Annabel is brought back in and told to sit down and to make no more stupid . . . Lionel sits and sucks his pen. In between attending to Dirk, Miss O'Hara has to keep on coming across and urging him to get on. 'I can't find myself' replies Lionel. Annabel is whistling again and she is told to stay behind after the lesson. At break Miss O'Hara tells me that if I hadn't been there she would have throttled Annabel.

Annabel could, occasionally, behave in a less challenging way. When 1.6 were promised a trip to the Gas Board showroom as part of their cookery course, her behaviour was a curious mixture of challenge and acquiescence.

Cookery trip to the Gas Board: preparation
We begin the period in Mrs Bird's class. Dirk and Benedict sit together, Crispin is sitting by himself and Annabel comes in late. She is reasonably behaved for a change. Next week they are to visit the Gas showrooms and to see a demonstration of cooking in gas. 'If you are well behaved, you get what the lady cooks.' Mrs B says, 'We want you to be smart, to look your best so that we can be proud of you. You must be clean, there should be no talking, you should stand quietly in twos.' The other teacher who is joining her comes in and tells them what they are going to do and how long they will have to wait and that they must bring 10p for the bus. The class seems very pleased and Mrs B again exorts them to be smart on the day. There is some irony in this because 1.6 unlike 1.5, are a very badly dressed lot. Most of the boys have their shirts out of their trousers, the girls have their stockings round their ankles.

The following week, the same observer made a point of going on the trip to the Gas Board.

Monday 17/10/77 – Gas Board trip
I arrive in time to find two lost boys who fasten on to me and ask me where they hand in their 10p for the trip to the Gas Board. We gradually get organized and under Mrs Bird's eagle eye we are inspected to make certain that we are clean and that our clothes are tidy. We then file out quietly to the bus which is waiting outside. It is interesting that as we go down the corridor the children begin to talk and chatter but as we come round the corner past Miss Tyree's office there is spontaneous shhshhhshhhh from one to another and we pass by in total silence!
On the bus they are very well behaved indeed and I sit next to the little Hassan boy who tells me about life in Uganda before he came to England. We are ushered through the Gas showroom and into their lecture hall where two quite attractive young girls are introduced to us as the demonstrators. She begins by asking them whether they know the safety points of using the gas cooker. Lots of hands go up and give all the answers pit pat. (It occurs to me that they have been briefed last week in the Wednesday craft class.) Mrs Bird has told me that only Annabel and Dirk didn't bring their 10p. Annabel is in trouble straight away because as we file into the showroom she inches forward and tries to bag a seat at the front. Mrs Bird hauls her out and makes

her stand at the back so that she will be last and sit next to her! She also makes certain that she has Dirk just in front of her. Halfway during the demonstration Annabel who has been fidgeting throughout asks to go to the lavatory and much to Mrs Bird's annoyance has to be taken out.

The demonstration is received very well in spite of the fact that the children at my end of the row cannot see in the mirror hanging above the workbench. They then file round to get chocolate crispies and orange while we have a cup of coffee. They are then shown the gas cooker, bit by bit. Annabel, who has remained totally silent throughout, spends at least five minutes talking to the demonstrator about the gas cooker, long after all the others are sitting down and munching their crispies. This one small moment she behaves very responsibly but as soon as she is back under Mrs Bird's eye, she reverts to her usual performance so that when we are asked to clap the lady demonstrators she sits there on her hands and refuses to do so. She is in trouble again while waiting for the bus because we are all told to keep our feet well behind the kerb edge and Annabel of course has hers sticking over. On the way back on the bus there is some spontaneous singing but Mrs Bird stops it.

Annabel, and her classmate Dirk, behaved so badly over the next few weeks that their whole class was punished. They were, for example, stopped from going swimming, because they were too rowdy on the bus.

These extracts from the first five to six weeks of the school year show Annabel behaving as badly as any 9-year-old could, and testing several of her teachers to the limits of their tolerance and endurance. While she is never physically punished, she has found the school's limits as surely as David King did at Victoria Road. Appendix 2 contains data on how Annabel (and Wayne, Dudley, Rex, and others) fared over the next six years of their school lives. While Annabel cannot be equated with Beynon's respondent, King, she serves well as an example of a pupil who is unwilling to abide by the rules which teachers are announcing and trying to enforce.

In contrast to the Waynes, Dudleys and Annabels are many pupils whose reactions to their first weeks of a new school are predominantly relief that the school gate did not lead them into 'disaster's cavern' or the 'fort of fear' after all, but only into a school. For such pupils the early weeks of the school year are the time when they and their new teachers begin to build shared meanings.

Building shared meanings: Horace rises

Walker and Adelman's (1976) decoding of the joke about 'strawberries' has become well known. In Miss Tweed's class at Gryll Grange, we saw such a joke beginning. One of us recorded how:

During the morning Miss Tweed has referred to 'Horace' on several occasions and each time the children have laughed. She says, for example, 'There's Horace at the window again.' One little girl's (stuffed toy) mouse is called Horace. Everyone giggles when it is mentioned. During the break Miss Tweed tells the girl, Yvette, to tell me why it's called Horace. The girl laughs, and Miss Tweed then explains that when she was writing on the first day Yvette spelled 'horse' as 'Horace' and another child called out: 'Look! There's a Horace outside the window eating the grass.' Then when she made a mouse in needlework Yvette called it Horace. There is much giggling from the listening children at this explanation of the joke.

Later in the fieldwork, the observer wrote:

> Anyone who mis-spells anything is referred to as Horace. For example, Miss Tweed says, 'It's like that Horace looking through the window' to another girl who has mis-spelt a word in her writing, or 'take it away and alter it – we don't allow anyone else to have a Horace in here.'

A few days later, Miss Tweed explained to the researcher why she was particularly supportive of Yvette.

> She tells me more about the little girl with the Horace joke. Her parents are split up and she now lives with her Gran. She was very nervous when she came in and is more settled now.

All three of the observers visiting 1T recorded how Miss Tweed encouraged Yvette to paint her special pictures (sometimes even when other pupils were doing academic tasks), and how Yvette became a big fan of Miss Tweed. When Miss Tweed read aloud to the class, Yvette would move her chair next to the teacher's desk, and when praised she blossomed. For the whole class the 'Horace' joke is a sign that the initial encounter is over, and routine class-room life is in progress.

Conclusion

In this chapter we have discussed how initial encounters can be understood, described a typical first day of the autumn term, and analysed how pupils set about testing their new teachers. Our five analytic themes have been introduced, and in the next chapter we turn to the first of these: the dangers beyond the postern of fate.

CHAPTER 4

Danger! Schooling in progress: physical and social dangers in the new schools

In the course of one school day a child might conduct a scientific experiment using corrosive acid, climb up to the top of the wall-bars in the gym, use solvents in the craft workshop and bake a cake in a hot oven.

(*Good Housekeeping*, August 1983, p.99)

Girl Dies
A 13 year-old girl whose skull was pierced by a javelin at her school sports day has died in hospital. Samantha Atherton never regained consciousness after the accident at Wirral Grammar School for Girls, Bebington, Merseyside. An investigation into the accident has begun and its findings will be reported to Wirral Borough Council.

(*TES*, 12 August 1983)

Three types of danger are focused upon in this chapter. We look at the physical dangers children face once they enter school buildings with specialist facilities (e.g. metalwork rooms) and specialist equipment (e.g. trampolines), we look at the threats to self-esteem of both teachers and pupils, and we look at the dangers of physical attack from staff and from other pupils. We not only look at the dangers which face teachers and pupils, but at strategies for dealing with them. In particular we examine how teachers attempt to get children to behave safely in dangerous environments by enforcing *precision* – detailed attention to behaving in precisely defined careful ways.

Dangerous environments

The transfer schools had more locations which contained equipment potentially hazardous to pupils than the lower schools from

64

Physical and social dangers in the new schools

which the pupils had come. Cookery areas had sharp knives and hot stoves; needlework rooms had electric sewing machines, pins, needles and scissors; science labs had heat and gas and poisons. Teachers of wood and metalwork, pottery and even technical drawing all have to accustom pupils to using new equipment which could damage them. Being a secondary school pupil is a hazardous experience, like working in many adult, particularly adult male occupations. There are clear parallels between learning how to study in many areas of a secondary school, and learning how to work successfully in dangerous trades. For example, Orbach's (1977: 28–9) study of tuna fishermen working out of San Diego points out that:

> Almost everything about tuna fishing is dangerous . . . Working around heavy equipment, especially heavy running rigging, is also dangerous . . . it is obvious to everyone on board that the *potential* for serious injury is always present.

It would be hysterical to overstate the physical dangers of schoolings. The Health and Safety Executive have yet to produce up to date national statistics on precisely how dangerous schools are, but in 1981, in Hereford and Worcester, there were 31 serious school accidents in a population of 41,500 secondary pupils. This is a much lower incidence of accidents than in male manual work, such as American building trades. In the USA, the average injury rate is 8.5 per 100 workers, while in construction it is 15.7. Schools are clearly much safer than building sites which, as Applebaum's (1981:77) research on construction workers points out:

> The construction industry has the highest incidence of accidents and deaths of any industry in the United States . . . In 1978, there were 628,000 injuries and illnesses due to construction work . . . (which) accounted for 20% of all deaths in industry but employs only 5% of the total number of employees.

Applebaum recounts several cases of accidents which befell men on the construction sites he studied, for example: 'I once saw a man get his eyes burned because an oil hose burst while he was operating a new backhoe' (p.83).

It is to avoid the educational equivalent of this that teachers stress safety with pupils. For example Shone and Atkinson (1982: 12–13) studied two industrial training units for slow learners in a FE college; they found the staff putting great emphasis on safety in the use of industrial equipment. For example, on one occasion the observer noticed the manager hurrying over to where one boy, Dennis, was using a circular saw.

He switched off the main power and called everybody to 'gather round'. He said something to Dennis which I couldn't hear[1] and then he asked if anyone would put their hand on the bench while he picked up a piece of wood and waved it up and down aggressively. Someone replied 'No', then the manager said 'Why not?' I was at the rear of the assembled group and as I shuffled forward I saw that it was Tina who was replying to the questions. 'Well, this saw blade is travelling at 120 mph and it cuts this wood. What do you think it could do to your fingers?' (Rhetorically). The telephone rang and then the manager asked another lecturer to take over and to 'show them the other display.'

He moved over to the edge planer machine and selected a long length of wood about 6 feet and said something to the effect that 'imagine this was a finger.' He then pushed it against the rotating cylindrical blade of the planer, and in a matter of a few seconds it was reduced to about 18 inches in length. Stuart said 'You've proved your point' (sarcastically). The lecturer then said that the saw travels at 120 mph 'the same speed as the high-speed train' . . .

The lecturer then pointed out that putting their hands near the unguarded saw was as dangerous as standing in front of the high speed train. Then the students were directed back to work. The impression here is of a well-established 'routine' to make the safety point: and the point was certainly well made.

The teachers at the six schools which we studied during the ORACLE project were meticulous in their endeavours to train pupils to behave safely and recognize the hazards of specific environments – such as science laboratories – where dangers lurked. The following examples from our ethnography make this clear:

> After break I go to see 1.6 with Mrs Bird. They have spent the morning writing out the rules of working in the kitchen:
> Never carry a knife with the blade out.
> Never leave a cupboard door open.
> If the oven doesn't work, tell the teacher.
> Children are told that they will have to use a stove other than the one they use at home so that if they have gas at home they use electricity here. However, most children appear to have gas at home and there are not enough electric stoves. She warns them yet again about the dangers of using gas and of playing around with the equipment. On the whole she is very firm and strict with them but there is a surprising amount of noise allowed while they are working. It will be interesting to see whether this goes on once they are actually cooking rather than sorting out equipment.
> (Guy Mannering (AST) 9–13)

> Waverly (CST) 12–18, cookery – Mrs Sutcliffe
> Girls must not wear rings for cooking.
> 'Today we are going to learn where things are kept and refresh our memories

---

1 The observer was later told that the manager was seeking the boy's permission to use the incident as a teaching example.

on how a cooker works . . . Now we'll have a little lesson on how to plug in because I don't want anyone to have an electric shock.' Gives out textbooks and spends some time going through items of kitchen safety.

Maid Marion (BPT) 11–14, design Mr Brett (metalwork and head of design) told them to take their blazers off and to put their bags well away from the workbenches. He began by saying 'I'm not going to tell you hundreds of rules of how to work in here but just remember two basic things: don't touch anything without permission and don't rush about.' He showed them how to operate the blowtorch – the group seemed to be somewhat subdued by the noise and the rather dramatic way in which the blowtorch operated and were very wary about going anywhere near it.

Maid Marion, PE (boys) – Mr Weir
Mr Weir then gave a little talk about safety, and said it was the main thing we always think about.
   He told off some boys very strictly for vaulting without having other children to stand by and support them. Again he emphasized the importance of safety precautions.

Kenilworth (BST) 11–14, pottery with Mr Mauss
He asked the children how many had aprons. Those who hadn't definitely must get something.
Pottery is very messy –
Showed the children potter's wheel – (adults at evening class only) – Pugmill – he is only person to use it.
Told children he would show them kiln tomorrow – a sink in the kiln room and he will tell children when they may use it.
He also showed the wire cutters which are called harps, and emphasized that the children must be careful when using them because they are expensive to replace.

Kenilworth – woodwork with Mr Moore
Mr Moore told the children that making a key ring would let them get used to the way in which you *have to work in a workshop*.

The above extracts show teachers of cookery, PE, metalwork and pottery introducing new pupils to dangerous, or potentially danger-ous, rooms and equipment. In Galton and Willcocks (1983:125) we give our examples of such teacher introductions to hazardous environments. Among such environments are science laboratories which are typically introduced to pupils in the following way, which comes from Beynon's (1985) study of new pupils entering Victoria Road Boy's School. In their first science lesson, Mr Bunsen warned them:

> Now in here you can see at the moment that this is not a normal type of classroom. In fact it is probably, ah, completely different to all the rest of the rooms in this school with the exception of the art room. This is a laboratory, and a laboratory is the most dangerous room in the school.

Physical and social dangers in the new schools

Mr Bunsen spent the first science lesson going over the rules of laboratory safety. Among these were:

> Mr Bunsen:
> Number 4, I think we've got to. Don't distract anybody at any time. (Checks comprehension of 'distract') . . .
> Concentration right. Now I can speak from personal experience. I was once doing an experiment and it involved sucking sulphuric acid in a tube and somebody distracted my attention at just the wrong moment and I ended up with a mouthful of acid.

Teachers frequently use such 'horror stories' to illustrate what can happen if a rule is breached. However, it is also the case that in retelling such a story, the teacher admits to breaching a different laboratory rule, about not tasting, smelling, or putting equipment near the face, by describing himself 'sucking sulphuric acid' without explaining the difference between an expert's attitude to rules, and those that are typically required of novices. An experienced scientist would 'get the point' of this story, the novice pupil may 'hear' that science involves 'sucking acid'. The contrasting strictness of the adherence to rules of safety between the high-status expert and the low-status novice (the master can suck up acid, the pupils must not) is an interesting parallel with Julius Roth's (1978) material on the observation or neglect of protective clothing by staff in TB sanatoria. Roth found that the higher status staff (e.g. doctors) rarely wore masks or gowns when seeing patients in their rooms, while low-status aides usually did. As Roth puts it 'The people of higher rank seem to have the privilege of taking the greater risks.' This seems to be true of the science teachers, but it is not clear how far pupils realize this.

Mr Bunsen was observed by Beynon (1985) but his key points on laboratory safety are similar to those recorded in the ORACLE schools. For example at Maid Marion we can see safety as a recurrent motif in these four lessons.

> (1) Class 10 – science – Mrs Rumsey
> Bunsen
> She gave very precise instructions about how they were to line up on the left, light their taper from her light, return to their place from the right so that they wouldn't bump into each other.

> (2) Science – Mr Salter
> Evap. salt
> Mr Salter warned the children in rather a casual way not to lean too close over the evaporating basin, because it might spit and he did not want them to get splashed with boiling salt solution – did not want children to taste the salt.
> This produced anxious snickers all around because children had been tasting it already – the teacher has enough authority for there to be no irresponsible messing about.

(3) Mrs Rumsey (really maths teacher)
Same science as above
She gave out goggles to all the children, and even gave a pair to me saying: 'If you want to go round and look at them afterwards, I'm afraid you'll have to have some too.'
She emphasized that the children must all put on their goggles before they heated anything.

She told the children not to taste the salt. It was not clean and therefore not fit for tasting.

(4) Science – Mr Salter
Condenser
He urged the children to be careful because he did not want anybody burned in the lesson . . . no turning around . . . wandering about . . . that's how accidents happen.

During the experiment Heather and Fern managed to knock over a flask of water and flooded their desk . . . Mr Salter said 'good job the water wasn't hot' and pointing the moral once again that it pays to be careful. During his lessons he frequently mentioned the importance of safety and reasons why care must be taken when making experiments in the labs.

On several occasion through the practical lesson, Dan got up to many pranks . . . On one occasion (Mr Salter) came over and speaks rather fiercely to Dan to bring him back to order.

The slightly older pupils entering Waverly School met the same concern from their science teachers as the extracts from the following four lessons show:

(1) Chemistry – Mrs Wheel
There is a great emphasis on safety factors. Girls with long hair must tie it back with elastic band; all bags must be out of the way so no one can trip over them. She shows them some rock salt. Tells them that they mustn't taste anything which is the rule she gave them last time.

(2) Chemistry – Mrs Wheel
Goes through work done in previous lesson – rules of labs . . . 'Now you must always listen very carefully to what I tell you . . . When I'm not using a Bunsen, I must always turn it to a luminous flame. Why?' A boy answers: 'So that people can see it.'

(3) Chemistry – Mr Darwin
He gets the class round the front bench . . . explains how to heat the solution gently to avoid spitting. He then asks them about the lab rules – when doing an experiment, must move books and stools out of the way, share the work out, and don't argue . . . 'Listen to me and keep quiet, otherwise it could result in an accident' . . .
Also reminds them of the importance of not tasting anything in chemistry.

(4) Physics – Mr Rutherford's class
He is away – senior chem. master taking it. They go back to the work. There is a little note passing between some of the girls and the boys and when a ruler is thrown across the table he reacts sharply.
Teacher: 'Who did that?'

Pupil: 'It were him, sir.'
Teacher: 'In a lab you pass things otherwise I might have to throw you around.'

This sharpness from the senior chemistry teacher is considered reasonable by all parties, because it is several weeks into term and pupils are expected to know how to behave. This firm reminder about the rules is paralleled by incidents from the industrial training units studied by Shone and Atkinson (1982:12–13):

> At the completion phases of the clearing-up operation, a lecturer turned around and spotted Colin blowing sawdust from his clothes with the airline, which was normally used for cleaning metal dust and sawdust from machinery. He called everybody together and proceeded to instruct them on the dangers of using the airline to clean themselves down. He said to Colin 'You could have slipped with that and blown it in your eye. It would have taken your eye out with the pressure from that.
>
> At this point another lecturer began adjusting valves on the airline feed in order to direct the pressure to a release valve. Several of the kids began to make grumbling noises, oh no, etc., and some started to put their fingers in their ears. After making these adjustments the lecturer opened the release valve, and a sort of booming noise, like a car repeatedly backfiring, only several times more loudly, occurred. During the noise most of the kids were covering their ears and complaining. However, their complaints were more like signals of the impressiveness of the noise or their appreciation of the pressure they had just been told about.
>
> The lecturer then said 'This pressure produced by the airline nozzle is even greater than that, because it's a smaller hole,' – or words to that effect – 'So you can go now.'

Several issues arise from this stress by science teachers on safety. For example, do children behave 'responsibly' in the dangerous rooms? Are lessons conducted safely? Do pupils even remember the exhortations about safety the teachers make? Does the stress on safety and danger cause girls to fear and shun science and heavy craft?

These questions cannot be answered definitively from the ORACLE data, and deserve further study. It is clear that the different science and craft teachers had different standards of safety. Some insisted on goggles, while others did not. Some ensured that pupils wore overalls, others let them work in their own clothes. The fieldnotes on laboratory and craft-room behaviour suggest that most pupils do not *remember* the safety rules; but they have internalized them so thoroughly that they behave properly in the danger zones. The question of danger and girls (discussed thoroughly by Kelly, 1985) has become a major research topic, and so those data we have are presented next.

Physical and social dangers in the new schools

Girls' reactions to science and craft

Measor (1984) has recently discussed the controversy surrounding girls' attitudes to science in her report of male and female pupils' reactions to their first science lessons at a comprehensive school. Measor found that all but two girls were repelled by the danger, the smells, the dirt, the manipulation of equipment, and the safety precautions (goggles, tying hair back) of physics and chemistry. The only boy who disliked science was stigmatized as a 'poofter' and despised by everyone. Among Measor's sample of girls were Ros (too scared of the Bunsen to light it or do any experiments), Amy (who refused to wear the safety goggles), and Rebecca (who was scared to boil water).

We had completed our data gathering before the debate on girls and science (Kelly, 1981 and 1985; GIST, 1984) had focused our attention on this potential problem. However we did interview a small number of the pupils, and these were asked about which subjects they liked and disliked in their new schools. These interviews included the following comments on science from girls:

At Waverly
Delia: particularly likes chemistry.
Ellen: likes most lessons, particularly biology and maths.
Laura: likes the science subjects which are new to her (only boys at Ashwood Bank did science).
Dawn: expressed a liking for chemistry and cooking.

Maid Marion
Vaudine and Merle: both girls enjoyed French and they also enjoyed science and PE. They thought the apparatus was good and they also thought lighting the Bunsen burners was 'very good'.
Althea and Trudie: Althea said that she did not like science because they had such a bad teacher in her other school and she never thought she would be able to understand it at MM.

Melin Court
Fenella: likes most subjects particularly science, Diene maths, and PE.
Natalie: she enjoys the swimming – a lot of fun – likes Diene maths and science. They did some science at Burton Upton but couldn't do any experiments.
Colette: science isn't bad – she likes doing the experiments.
Yvonne: she likes woodwork, swimming, PE and science – although they are doing work they have already done at Fordhouse.

Science and heavy craft do not seem to be particularly salient for the ORACLE girls, and their interviews and our fieldnotes do not show the exaggerated 'hyper-feminine delicacy' Measor (1984) found. However it is also important to recognize that pupils, especially girls, are also warned of the dangers of non-science environments.

For example during the pre-transfer programmes both Mrs Hallows from Waverly and Mrs Appleyard from Kenilworth used safety as an explanation about the school uniform rules:

> Mrs Hallows: At the end of the talk several questions were asked. One girl asked what jewellery could be worn. 'Very good, that's a sensible question' said Mrs Hallows and went on to describe what was allowed, mainly for reasons of safety. Another was asked on footwear . . . 'something sensible,' then this led on to a brief account of PE equipment.

> Mrs Appleyard: A few of the girls were concerned about the rule of jewellery. They wanted to know if they could wear earrings. Mrs Appleyard, who herself wore very large earrings, said that 'yes' you could wear earrings as long as they were sleepers or studs. It wasn't safe to wear any others in case they got caught up in gymnastic equipment. She told some lurid stories about what had happened to a couple of kids in another school in which she had taught.

Thus it would be an oversimplification to say that only science labs and the heavy craft rooms are dangerous. The metalwork master at Kenilworth, Mr Flanigan, may say 'You can kill yourself a dozen different ways' in a workshop, but the pupils are told that many other places are equally dangerous. Apart from the classrooms, the schools and their surroundings are also potentially hazardous.

Dangers beyond the classroom

One specific danger which teachers have to prepare children for is fire. Schools rarely burn down in daylight, but pupils have to be drilled so they know *how* to leave the building if a fire alarm sounds. The ORACLE observers were lucky enough to see this training taking place at Kenilworth. The observer was with Miss Stephenson's class:

> She told them about the firedrill that the whole school would be involved in later that morning. She told the class to 'do what the teacher tells you.' They must be quick and quiet so that they could hear instructions and warned them which way they would usually go out of the building. In the event of a real fire that might be altered, hence the need for quietness so that new instructions might be given.

The fire drill did not go well, and so in assembly the following week, Mr Leach (the deputy head) made an announcement:

> Last week's fire drill was 'an absolute shambles' – so today there would be another fire drill for half the school. They were to follow their teacher's instructions, and lead out in a quiet and orderly manner.

Mr Leach then read out a list of which classes were to rehearse the new fire drill that day. Later in the morning the observer was with 1 zeta when Miss Airdale was teaching them English:

> The bell went for the fire drill and some children leapt up to go to it. Miss Airdale told them that the bell did not concern them. Some children looked very confused and she asked them if they had not heard the notice in assembly.

The new arrangements, rehearsed by the rest of the school the following day, were a success. The material on fire drills leads us on to other dangerous environments. Classrooms may be dangerous, but there are also hazards elsewhere in the school. As Mary Metz (1978: 144) points out:

> Students inhabit not just classrooms but corridors, cafeterias and washrooms. The problem of maintaining order and safety in these contexts is more severe than in the classroom.

A similar point is made by Judith Hanna (1982: 332) from her ethnography of Pacesetter School who found that aggressive incidents between pupils occurred: 'in the classroom, in the lunch line, on the playground and in the restroom.' The dangers that face new pupils in these spaces are the focus of this section. Our first concern is the hazards that can face pupils in the corridors. For example, at Guy Mannering:

> When the bell goes and the class streams out and converge towards the door in the corridor. By this time it is joined by a number of other classes, some coming in the opposite direction and a real scrum ensues around the corridor. Some of the little children are getting pushed quite badly and staff have to appear from their rooms in order to get some order. When we reach the art and craft area there is further chaos as no one seems to know what they are doing for that day. Eventually everything is sorted out and 1.5 go off to do art with Mr Woolfe. 1.6 are mainly with Mrs Bird doing cookery.

There are also potential dangers in the playground; and when children come to and from school. Again the assembly at Maid Marion made this clear:

> Mr Seed was giving the new pupils the rules, including: not to take short cuts over the grass or by the wall along the hallway when there was another class in the hall as it distracted them. He then reminded the children of the playground boundaries and that the bicycle shed was out of bounds. This he explained was because if anything had got stolen or broken the children who were found in the shed during the break time would be the obvious suspects.

The senior mistress at Melin Court made a similar point in an assembly there:

Mrs Marks is giving an homily on 'responsibility'. She quotes another
example nearer home of having the door in the corridor slammed in one's
face. 'You are responsible when you pass through a door of making sure that
it doesn't harm the next person.'

To make sure that disturbance and danger in the corridors are
minimized, many schools not only make rules, but operate systems
of policing such spaces. Rules for behaviour in corridors were
stressed to our sample in their early days in their transfer schools –
as in this example from Maid Marion:

Assembly – Mr Seed (acting HM)
Apologised for the 101 rules that the children must be hearing about on their
first few days but he then added a couple more. Mainly, 'Don't rush in the
corridors.'

Mr Seed returned to this rule later in the week in an assembly for
first years:

Mr Seed
The next point concerned running in the corridors. He said that enthusiasm to
get to one's next lesson is highly commendable but there must be no running.
He gave two or three anecdotal examples of dire misfortunes which had
befallen children who had head-on collisions with other children, the sharp
edges of doors, etc.

Crossing the road was also covered in one assembly:

Mr Seed told the children that if they cross Station Road they must use the
traffic patrol. Mr Pollit, the traffic patrol officer, is a very pleasant man and
they must be friendly to him. They should say 'hello' and be polite and
pleasant to him, but they must always obey his instructions very carefully.
    A lorry driver phoned the school last week because some children are
crossing the bypass without using the crossing . . . If the children try to be
grown up and cross the bypass and at places other than the crossing they are
asking for trouble. The rule is for their own safety and the safety of their
families.
    Mr Welsh took over – 3,000 children arriving and departing at campus –
hence crossing patrol. Should use it.

Here we see the senior staff of a school stressing both the dangers of
the school's environment, and how to deal with them. The material
on movement in the school, presented in chapter 5, amplifies the
ways in which such dangers are contained. When *Good Housekeeping* ran an article on 'School Safety Rules, OK' in August 1983
(p.99) they concentrated on physical safety, of the kinds we have
been discussing so far in this chapter. They warned about the
'horrendous' list of accidents reported to LEAs:

Physical and social dangers in the new schools

Mishaps in science laboratories include bites from gerbils and mice; burns from acid, alkali or hot tripods; cuts from scalpels; injuries caused by slipping on wet floors; hair-singeing; eye damage from broken glass particles or copper sulphaté crystals. In the metalwork shop, . . . accidents include cuts from circular saws; shocks from faulty electrical equipment; poisoning from toxic fumes. In the art room, hot wax and caustic chemicals . . . cause some incidents, and in the rural science department, pesticide poisoning and injuries inflicted by garden tools . . .

These are physical hazards, which the caring parent is urged to fear. We know, too, that some pupils do, indeed, fear these dangers. As the paragraph makes clear, phsyical dangers were differentially distributed around the school – some areas offered no physical threat or hazardous equipment, others were very dangerous. In this way secondary schools are not unitary environments but varied ones, with different working conditions in different rooms. Thus they aṛe like the factories and other workplaces studied by Blackburn and Mann (1979: 50–60). That is within any one workplace there are dangerous areas and safe ones, quiet and noisy, busy and slack, dirty and clean and so on. Ethnographies of workplaces (e.g. Applebaum, 1981; Gamst, 1980; Orbach, 1977) rarely miss the differential atmosphere of various sub-locations, and their various degrees of physical danger. The social atmosphere of a workplace may also vary, as Blackburn and Mann (1979:53) describe it in a food processing plant where:

The atmosphere varied considerably between sections. The cooking areas were environmentally unpleasant, in the bottling/canning areas the pace of work was somewhat pressurised by the speed of the machines, but in the large warehouses there was an easy, friendly working atmosphere which permitted quite extensive card-playing.

Sociologists of education have been rather remiss in differentiating the equivalent areas of the school. A secondary school is *not* a single environment, but a multifaceted one. The metalwork room is an intensely 'masculine' environment – noisy, dirty and dangerous. The language laboratory is clean, noisy and physically safer, the standard classroom may be noisy or quiet, clean or dirty, but contains few physical dangers. This aspect of schools has been relatively under-explored by ethnographers, just as researchers into medical socialization have been relatively insensitive to the teaching hospital as a highly segmented environment (Atkinson, 1983). Just as Furlong (1976) was right to point out that pupils' peer groups were not always fixed in membership and the more fluid notion of interaction sets could help explain how some lessons were disrupted while others were orderly, so too the various locations of

75

classes are an important variable in understanding them. Beynon's (1985) boys were more disruptive in the drama classes (a sissy subject) than with a tough man in the masculine gym. So too, Willis' (1977) lads probably responded better to schooling in heavy craft rooms than in French lessons, although he does not explore such subtleties in his ethnography. Certainly the ORACLE ethnography reveals that even the simplest school, Gryll Grange, contained a wider variety of learning environments than pupils had met previously, where both physical dangers, and their more pervasive social counterparts were differentially distributed. It is to the second type of danger – danger of *humiliation*, of being 'shown up' that we now turn.

Showing people up – the dangers of humiliation

Both staff and pupils are constantly under potential threats of exposure to humiliation – pupils can be 'shown up' in front of their peers, teachers can be 'shown up' in front of their classes, and, perhaps worse, in front of their professional colleagues. We deal first with threats to the self-esteem of teachers, and then to those facing pupils. There is no systematic sociological literature on how staff may be shamed in front of their colleagues, or in front of the pupils, or both. Isolated incidents are reported from several ethnographies, but the subject deserves greater attention. Beynon (1985) found senior masters humiliating the drama teacher; Woods (1979) a headmaster embarrassing a young man he perceived as a deviant teacher; and Denscombe (1980) has produced a sensitive account of how colleagues judge each other by the amount of noise emanating from their rooms, so uproar can shame a teacher. There is no doubt from such accounts that observing a teacher 'shown up' by children, or by colleagues, is one of the most uncomfortable experiences for the ethnographer. Teachers who laid themselves open to being humiliated were rare in the ORACLE schools, but those few examples we had are revealing about both the degree of control, and the norms and values of the staffroom, in our six schools. Analysing how some teachers are humiliated also provides an insight into how routine classroom encounters are always potentially open to disruption.

Showing up the teacher

Pupils can show up a teacher, either to his or her colleagues, or during research, to the researcher. For example: at Melin Court the observers found that music lessons with Mr Eggleston sometimes resulted in his embarrassment.

They have become much more confident and clever in their indiscipline. Now the boys shout and some deliberately sing out of tune and it is clear that they know they are doing it since there is a lot of nudging and winking going on behind the singing books . . .

So the pattern for the rest of lesson is established. As long as he doesn't play the tune while they sing but stands over the boys the song is correctly sung. As soon as he returns to the piano however the boys ham it up for all they are worth.

There is a clear indication in these fieldnotes that the boys in this class were deliberately misbehaving to 'show up' their master in front of the observer, or for their own satisfaction. Such lessons are mercifully rare for researchers, but one maths master at Waverly was humiliated by his pupils in front of one observer. The master never succeeded in getting order in the lesson and soon:

The lesson is now out of control totally and I am embarrassed . . . The quiz goes on . . . Some boys are now definitely singing. It is hopeless and embarrassing . . .

This master asked the observer if the pupils were always as badly behaved when under observation, and the answer had to be that they were not. The same pupils had been well-behaved and worked hard in chemistry the previous lesson, and sang lustily for their music master in the next. They appeared, however, to enjoy 'showing up' their maths teacher in front of an audience. Such events can only happen if the teacher is vulnerable already, as in the case of Mr Woolfe at Guy Mannering, who was revealed as incompetent to both the observer and his new colleagues, during his first weeks in the school, to which he had been redeployed.

Mr Woolfe begins for apologizing for his lateness. He is very tentative, 'I've got to do something at the front (dinner money) so you are going to have to get on with something too.' He begins. He asks them why artists can see more than others. There is general puzzlement at this question but Howard says its because they are good at imagining. There are no other offerings so Mr Woolfe says, 'Well, we must get on so you will have to think about that question' and doesn't answer it. He then goes on to ask them about trees changing their dress and this time there is a much more animated response. He tells them that trees are different shapes not like those that their young brothers draw which are like upside-down dish mops (laughter).

Here he allows them to call out without putting up their hands, something that the more experienced teachers would never allow here at Guy Mannering. He is clearly very frightened about messing up the art room. They are warned about not taking too much water, about not spoiling the brushes. He tells them that if they had time they could go out and look at trees and see what the different shapes were like. Eventually he tells them that why an artist sees sometimes more than ordinary people is because they notice things and that when he paints flowers for half a day he begins to see

77

more in each flower. Again, and again, he apologises to them. 'As I say, I haven't had time to prepare this lesson, so I will need some help from you.'

He asks who the form captain is. Barry isn't in this group and so isn't available. Instead, Mr Woolfe then asks which boy is best at art and then says out loud, 'I shouldn't do this.' He goes round and distributes jobs. 'You're not making a fuss, you're sensible, give out the paper, give out the palettes, etc.'

Eventually, all the children have a brush, a sheet of paper, a stick of charcoal and a palette and then they are all given a painting board. There is quite a lot of noise while they are organizing their equipment (something that Mr Evans would not allow).

One of his worries is how they will handle the water. So he is only going to allow four people to share one pot. Four are to come out at a time and collect the equipment and fill up the water pot. He gives a signal to say who will come out first but fails then to nominate the second group. Consequently they are all bent double as if in a race to ensure that they will be the next group. By this time we have had a whole period and they still haven't started painting.

To spare his embarrassment I leave his classroom and go to see Mr Bradshaw who is doing craft and woodwork.

The observer spent twenty minutes in Mr Bradshaw's woodwork room, and after break went to cookery. This observer wrote 'I must stay out of his class in future.' This researcher noted:

He is clearly very nervous and keeps on nagging at the children to leave the room tidy. I suspect that someone has been at him about its state . . .

Mr Woolfe proceeded to reveal himself as incompetent to his new colleagues. Among his errors are making the pupils late for their next class and not getting them cleaned up. Thus he let 1.5 return to their form for maths with Mrs Forrest both late and 'covered' in paint. The researcher who saw this event wrote:

Clearly Mr Woolfe is going to be in trouble. It emerges that all the toilets in the art and craft area are kept locked and that there were no aprons available. Mrs Forrest concludes 'Well I had better come along next week and see what you are doing.'

Later that same day the observer saw Mr Woolfe default on school norms again, and wrote:

Mr Woolfe appears to be in trouble again for he has taken some of them out running and they got back late. Mr Evans comes back his face set in a grim look. 'If you want this and that and the other from other members of staff you don't take it out of *MY TIME*.'

The following week the observer did not go to the whole art lesson, but dropped in towards the end of double period:

Physical and social dangers in the new schools

I go straight to 1.5. They have been doing finger painting and their hands are filthy. I wonder what Mrs Forrest is going to say after her threat last week? The class are very happy and relaxed and have obviously enjoyed the session. When the bell goes, some of them are still working and so Mr Woolfe offers to do the tidying up for them when they have gone. He says he will put some colour on the faces they have been painting. {. . .}

When the class get back to their form-room Mrs Forrest inspects their hands:

She pretends to be incredulous about them painting with their fingers and says 'Whatever will you do next?' I imagine she will be having a word with Mr Woolfe later.

By half-term, Mr Woolfe had revealed himself to the pupils, the researchers and his new colleagues as unable to plan lessons, keep order, run a tidy art room or keep to the school timetable. Such teachers are routinely humiliated by everyday school of life. Everyday life in schools can also be humiliating for some pupils, and the danger of being 'shown up' looms larger in their minds than the physical hazards of their environment. Woods (1979) has demonstrated how much teenagers detest being humiliated in front of their coevals, and how fear of such humiliation is a controlling tactic used by some staff.

Showing up pupils

The argument thus far has been that schools are dangerous environments; both physically hazardous and potentially shaming. While schools are not, as we have argued, unitary, undifferentiated environments, it is arguable that pupils are threatened with humiliation – potentially – throughout the school day, from arrival to departure. However, different pupils may be more at risk in some areas than others. The unathletic may be most 'at risk' in PE, the clumsy in woodwork, the thick in academic subjects. The argument of David Hargreaves (1982:63) is pertinent here:

I was not successful, during my schooldays, at woodwork. Slowly I grew to dislike and then to hate the subject . . . Soon I was the target of teacher criticism. 'Everyone stop work' the teacher would announce, 'and look at Hargreaves.' I knew I was going to be the examplar of what not to be doing.

Hargreaves goes on to argue that, for him, school would have been a nightmare if the physical-manual skills had been the most valued:

In this nightmare my secondary school's timetable is dominated by compulsory woodwork and metalwork, gymnastics, football and cricket, drawing and painting, technical drawing, swimming and cross-country running. (p.64)

Hargreaves' point is that for an academic pupil, such a curriculum would be *dangerous*: for every class would be potentially humiliating. Peter Woods (1975, 1979) has probably discussed the pupils' view of humiliation more sensitively than any other researcher. In doing so, he clearly espouses the pupils' view of schooling and neglects the teachers'. For this, he has been quite unreasonably attacked by MacNamara (1980), who fails to grasp that Woods' viewpoint is that of the adolescent, and they dislike being humiliated. The relationship between discipline, protection and humiliation is a complex one. The position of the teacher who may have to organize pupils in a particular way for their own safety, is paralleled by the role of the lifeguards on the Californian urban beach studied by Edgerton (1979: 38–9, 42–8). The lifeguards, all white, mainly male, and many highly educated, face a control problem of a particularly sensitive kind with Chicano and Negro beach users:

> Who lack even rudimentary knowledge of the ocean or swimming. Lifeguards agree that such persons make them very nervous, not only because they are in danger but also because they may misinterpret a lifeguard's concern for their safety as an unwarranted show of 'Anglo' authority . . .
>
> Ironic as it may seem, many swimmers are embarrassed when a lifeguard swims out to 'save' them, feeling that their ability as swimmers is being challenged.

Teachers face the same problems as lifeguards – they have to keep order, but to do so may find they are humiliating their charges. Indeed Jacquetta Hill Burnett (1973) has located much of the disciplinary trouble in urban Chicago schools in the refusal of Chicano males to accept any discipline or control from women high school teachers. Burnett does not differentiate between control problems for the female staff in ordinary classrooms and in hazardous environments, but the teacher's problems would be worse in the latter because, like the beach for the lifeguards, the discipline has to be imposed whatever the cost to the *amour propre* of the clients.

The two types of danger may be found together – a cookery teacher may also have a savage tongue and rely on humiliation – but they may be spatially quite distinct in the school. Whereas the chalk-and-talk lesson in a conventional classroom presents few physical dangers, it may be the *locale* of endless humiliations. French classes are conducted in physically safe environments, yet offer great danger to pupils – especially boys. This was noticed and recorded by one observer at Melin Court watching 1M having French with Mr Haydon:

> In French everybody sits quietly. The teacher has a good command and no

discipline problems. Part of the strength of French is that trouble makers can be picked upon and requested to speak out and answer in the language. Melvyn, for example, who clearly has no interest in French and so is too embarrassed to even attempt an answer to a simple question keeps silent all the time in case he is picked upon to answer the next question.

The four boys who sit at the back were the most disruptive in the music lesson but here they keep their heads down and remain silent. Typical of their treatment is what happens to Selwyn. He fails to answer a question which has already been answered by one of the girls. Teacher, 'Come and sit up here at the front. You must be unable to hear there.'

The fear of humiliation was noted in several other oral lessons:

Melin Court – French – Mrs Zeldin
The lesson consists of conversation. Mrs Zeldin giving instructions and the children carrying them out: e.g. point to the door, touch the desk, etc. The children are generally reluctant to respond if they are asked to do so in spoken French.

Melin Court – Mrs Zeldin's class taught by Mr Clift
Towards the end of the lesson teacher asked a girl to stand at the front of the class. He asks her to question someone else. They then take it in turns. There is a lot of giggling and embarrassment.

Waverly – French – Mr Mowbray
Last 5 minutes of lesson spent 'playing a game of French' – girls and boys asking each other questions. Children rather reluctant and need a lot of prompting.

French – Mr Baden
Settles the class down, then questions and answers in French – names, colours, numbers . . . When children's attention wanders the teacher is quick to pick it up and ask them questions.

In this atmosphere, pupils who wish to avoid humiliation stay silent and do not misbehave. Several of the pupils said in their interviews that they found language lessons embarrassing. Among the Maid Marion pupils Fida:

Fida obviously feels that she gets more than her share of the questions, and, being a shy girl, she doesn't like to have to answer in front of the class.

Similarly, Althea and Trudie:

Althea said she did not like French. Trudie agreed and they said it was because they did not like being laughed at when they tried to speak French. The teacher was always asking them questions and this showed them up in front of the others. Althea said 'I always mind if I do things wrong' . . .

French is not the only subject in which such shame may be felt. For

example in Miss Lawrence's English class at Waverly; the class were supposed to read out essays they had written.

> On the board there are 3 items; one about early memories has been written about by Cherie. She tells of an unlucky thing that happened when she fell down the stairs. As soon as she has finished the teacher asks the other pupils for comments:
> 'Too short'
> 'Not interesting'
> 'Doesn't tell us how you feel'
> There is an element of condemnation in all these remarks and in the face of this criticism Cherie is reluctant to participate. But gradually as the other children make jokes about her accident she becomes aware that they are laughing at her but that she is the object of attention and she begins to join in.

Then in maths at Guy Mannering three different pupils were 'shown up':

> The class are doing the 24 hour clock.
> Carter Pilch is new, so Mrs Forrest asks Carter:
> 'Have you ever done the 24 hour clock?'
> Carter: 'No'
> Mrs F: 'Well, let's give you a little lesson. Can anyone tell Carter why we use the 24 hour clock?'
> Shelly does so.
> Mrs F: 'That was good Shelly. Carter should be able to follow that.'
> The work from last Friday is still on the board. They were given a number of times to convert them into 24 hour clock version. They are going to mark their own but before she does this she asks Carter to go through it in front of the class to see if he understands about the clock.
> He is obviously very nervous and the rest don't help.

On another occasion Mrs Forrest used the same strategy on Rhoda and Derrick. She appears to be using shame as a punishment for Rhoda because she had not been listening in a previous lesson. The lesson topic was elementary algebra and fractions. The class began with Mrs Forrest handing back the marked homework books.

> Rhoda has to sit by herself because she can't have been listening in class which is why her work was very bad. Two or three other people made lots of mistakes and therefore couldn't have listened very carefully – 'especially Rhoda'.

Here we see a pupil being moved as a punishment, a theme we address in chapter 5, and see the first use of public shame.

> Mrs Forrest works through the sums on the board (Half of fourteen?; half of p is five, what is p?) Rhoda, who has already been mentioned twice, is still

not ready. Mrs Forrest is irritated and says, quite sharply, 'Buck up! Listen to me!' and forces Rhoda to pay attention while she goes through the examples a second time. This time Rhoda is paying attention and gets them right, but when they go on to new examples she gets them wrong again.

This failure on Rhoda's part is now annoying her classmates, for 1.5 is an academic, striving class.

> The class get very impatient when Rhoda can't answer these new questions and there are lots of 'ooohhs' and 'aahhhs' while the children raise their arms and try frantically to attract Mrs Forrest's attention. Eventually Rhoda gets it correct and thereafter she seems more prepared to join in . . .
> The newcomer Derrick has lots of difficulty. When eventually he gets one of the sums right the rest of the class claps somewhat sarcastically. Mrs Forrest dosen't stop them.

One way in which teachers can humiliate pupils is to force them to sit next to, or worse still, work with, a peer of the opposite sex. It is not clear how far teachers are aware that doing this is a humiliation for the pupils concerned. The boy in the following incident was deeply ashamed, but it is not clear that Mr Rutherford meant to shame him:

> Physics with Mr Rutherford – Waverly
> The pupils are about to do some work on measurement in pairs. The Asian girl and one boy haven't partners for work in pairs. Their tables want to put the boy and girl together – the boy is horrified. Master finally hears, 'Sir he hasn't got a partner' and puts him with Asian girl (Gita) . . .
> (Later) Asian girl and boy partner are doing nothing.

Some staff used the potential shame of being beaten by pupils of the opposite sex as a motivator, or as a disciplinary measure. For example in Miss Tweed's class at Gryll Grange:

> Miss Tweed announces, 'I'm still waiting for most of the boys to do that measuring' . . . (Later) Yvette has finished measuring work sheet. Miss Tweed says, 'Another girl finished' . . . Later when Tammy and Stephanie are up, Miss Tweed says, 'Only seven girls to go.' Someone asks how many boys and the answer is 'lots' . . . Later when Kenneth is up for marking Miss Tweed says, 'Only five girls to go now. How many boys? Nearly all of them.'

Similar comments were heard at Guy Mannering too, as when in Mrs Bird's cookery lesson, she called out:

> '*Boys* – is it boys who are making so much noise or is it a group of girls? . . . Be careful boys that you get your tables all nice and straight.'

A number of further incidents will show how, typically sex separation is used as discipline, as motivation and as control.

> Communal singing in the hall. Two teachers and all six first year classes (180 pupils). Towards the end of the lesson they sing *There's a Hole in my Bucket* with the sexes divided. Boys are told to 'pretend to be a bit gormless. I know you're not.'

By getting the boys and girls to sing the two parts of the song, the teacher hoped to spur each side on, and be ashamed to mutter, stay silent, or avoid singing in any other way. Similarly at Gryll Grange:

> Music with Mr Vaughan. Has pupils clapping rhythms – has two girls doing it alone, then two boys. After playing part of *Peter and the Wolf* has scale singing – competing boys versus girls.

Very similar incidents were recorded with the 11- and 12-year-old pupils. For example early on at Melin Court:

> Before the first lesson in Mrs Wordsworth's class, Mrs Wordsworth gives them the rules for how to spend the time before registration . . . Does locker-labelling. Girls first, with the first use of the girl monitor for this week – Elaine – sellotaping labels after pupils have stuck them on doors. Girls have the lockers in the top row . . . The girls lead out first – Wayne ridiculed *for moving with the girls*.

Disciplining boys by comparing them, unfavourably, with girls can hardly be good for either gender. Teachers in the two 11–14 schools also resorted to gender comparisons to try and motivate boys. For example at Kenilworth in the top form's French lesson with Mrs Stockton there was an oral, informal vocabulary drill. The observer noted:

> The girls particularly seemed to enjoy this and to have remembered the vocabulary . . . This provoked a comment from Mrs Stockton to the effect that 'Are the girls the only brainy ones?'

At Waverly, too, teachers tried to motivate boys by comparing them to girls. In music we recorded that Mr Fawlty:

> Makes the boys sing, then the girls. Then he comments 'Well, boys it was better, wasn't it?'

Ten months later the same man was using the same strategy. The observer recorded:

> Mr Fawlty: 'Oh dear, where are the boys now when we need them?'

(Reference to the fact that all the boys were about to answer the previous question, but no girls.) This time only girls have put up their hands. This kind of boy/girl rivalry is often used at Waverly.

This 'aside' from the observer was based on incidents with other Waverly teachers. For example one class were in the school library with Mrs Southey, one of the English staff. We recorded:

Most of the girls have chosen to take books out. The teacher says: 'All the girls are taking out books, but not one boy yet. Can't the boys read in this class?'
A few boys take books out.

It is unclear whether such exhortations actually motivate pupils, but they certainly shame them to some extent. We also recorded one example of a pupil being shown up because of his race, when Miss Tweed marked Kenneth's maths book:

. . . Kenneth has made 82 + 47 equal over 300. Held up for public ridicule, told he should be the Chancellor of the Exchequer and that 'Scotsmen don't usually make mistakes over money.'

There is evidence elsewhere (Woods, 1975, 1979; Measor and Woods, 1984) that pupils resent such humiliations, and that they only 'work' if the status of the pupil is such that the rest of the class read the correct message from the humiliation. For example the strategy of having a test where all the pupils stand until they get an answer right, so that the stupidest pupils are left standing conveys a very different message from one where the pupil can 'escape' by getting a wrong answer and the last pupil standing is the cleverest.

Measor and Woods (1984) report that those teachers who regularly used humiliation were seen as unfair by pupils, and it is therefore a risky strategy for the teacher. Sensitivity to the pupils, with the use of shame only as a punishment for a clear breach of a known rule, can work. Mr Barrell an English master at Maid Marion seemed to have developed a regime that 'worked'.

In this lesson the class were going to read *Danny the Champion of the World*. Mr Barrell said they must not be afraid that they would be forced into reading out loud if they were shy . . . He asked various children to read and if they were shy he would try genial coaxing. 'Aren't you going to have a go? That little paragraph there? No? You then?' After some have read aloud he gets children to read to each other in pairs. The only time he insisted on a child's reading when the child did not want to was with John. This was because he had been chattering and laughing with the boy next to him . . .

Reading in a pair, to a friend, is less embarrassing than reading to the whole class, and Mr Barrell was seen by pupils as fair.

Thus pupils can be humiliated by teachers by being forced to perform in front of their peers, by being made to sit next to or work with a pupil of the opposite sex, or by being compared to the opposite sex. Fear of being humiliated can help a teacher keep control, but it is a risky strategy for the staff member because it can result in being seen as unfair if used too often, or against pupils who have not broken the rules of the class. Mrs Forrest could use shame in 1.5 because its general tone was competitively academic, and Rhoda had not been working. Mr Barrel could use it because his normal regime was supportive and protected pupils' self-esteem. In less skilled hands, it can merely strengthen a deviant peer group, or sour the teacher-pupil relationship.

Pupils have to face both physical dangers and threats to their self-esteem inside lessons. Outside the classroom, in the cloakrooms, corridors and yards, they may also face a third danger – bullying, and it is this hazard that concludes the chapter.

Danger: other pupils about?

Bullying has already been discussed briefly in Delamont (1983b: 141–6), where the strenuous efforts made by all six schools to prevent intimidation starting, and nip it in the bud if it occurred, were discussed. The schools reassured pupils before transfer that bullying was not allowed, and that they would be protected, and did their best to stop any that they were aware of once the new pupils arrived. Most of the pupils interviewed after transfer reported that, indeed, bullying was prevented, and the few incidents that occurred had been brief and relatively painless. A typical example of a school reacting strongly against bullying occurred at Guy Mannering on September 27th:

> For the afternoon 1.5 have English with Mr Evans. There is a boy in the classroom who has obviously been sent to Mr Evans and is in trouble.
> Mr Evans: 'What did I have you for last time?'
> Boy: 'Stone throwing'.
> Mr Evans: 'Stand there. At the front.'
> (Turning to the class) 'Don't pay any attention to him. Ignore him. He's trouble.'

Mr Evans was the senior master, and teachers often sent discipline problems to him. On this occasion he sent this miscreant off to fetch his co-offender, and then:

> He begins to harangue the two boys for bullying. It appears that the object of

their attention was Mitchell Gardiner in this class. Mitchell is called out, and
Mr Evans asks the two offenders 'What has he ever done to you?'
They reply that they don't even know his name, and that they have done
nothing.
Mr Evans: 'Well I'll tell you. Its Mitchell Gardiner. I'm not going to repeat
the other name you have used about him. When you upset him – and you
have upset him – you upset me. Is that clear?'
He then tells the two boys to go outside with Mitchell, and he leaves with
them. From inside one can hear his voice rise as he deals with the situation.

Mitchell Gardiner was a quiet boy, who had an older brother higher
up the school with a bad reputation. The trouble in the yard had
been two older boys walking behind him calling him 'Big Ears' and
flicking his ears, until in desperation he had gone and told the
teacher on yard duty, who in turn had sent the offenders to Mr
Evans. Mr Evans had reacted strongly to the incident, forced the
older boys to apologize to Mitchell, and punished them. Similar
firm responses to incipient intimidation were reported from Gryll
Grange and Maid Marion in Delamont (1983b: 144–5). As we
reported in that volume, we saw very little fighting, and no serious
bullying, but could not claim that meant none took place. The issue
is however an emotive one, and has attracted media attention.

There is considerable public concern about bullying and intimidation in schools. In recent years both *Women's Realm* (19/4/80) and
Woman (29/1/83) have run major articles on the dangers that lie in
wait for school children, and how, at the extreme, a victim may be
driven to a suicide attempt. Our own pre-transfer data showed that
fears about bullying are present in many children before they enter
their transfer schools. Yet it is all to easy to interpret all the physical
aggression that takes place in schools as 'bullying'. The reality is
more complex. As John Beynon's research (1983, 1985; Beynon
and Atkinson, 1984; Beynon and Delamont, 1984) shows vividly,
for some pupils (mostly boys) 'fighting', 'scrapping', 'mucking', and
generally 'rough housing' are an important way of finding out what
the other pupils are like. Boys, particularly those who are anti-
school, value prowess at fighting very highly, and get *pleasure* from
it, as well as using it as a discovery process to establish their pecking
order. This is both a problem for those who want an orderly school
(such as dinner ladies, teachers, parents) and a distressing social
fact for those pupils who do not want to be part of the system and
those who end up at the bottom of the heap. Observers can also be
puzzled by the phenomenon:

> During lunch I watch the children play out on the grass. There is only minimal
> supervision and quite a lot of fighting and bullying. A big boy pushes a small
> boy. The small boy attempts to push back which means that the big boy now

87

attacks him, kicks him, etc. Eventually the dinner lady spots it and intervenes. It is amazing how the little kids seem to accept all this and put up with it, for immediately the disturbance is over the little kid goes back and joins the group with the big boy. In a few moments one sees the big boy with his arm around the little boy.

The corridors, playgrounds, lavatories and even the classrooms can be both an arena for the pupils' research into who is 'hard', and a frightening place for those who do not want to be involved in such fighting. Metz (1978: 149) argues that: 'The spaces outside the classroom also provide opportunities for hostile and predatory activities. Children . . . get into physical fights.' Such spaces could seem terrifying to the ORACLE observers, as well as the pre-transfer pupils, during their school visits. The observer who visited Guy Mannering with children from Orton Water wrote after following four small girls on their tour guided by a 13-year-old prefect:

> Just as we were ascending the stairs, the bell for break rang, and many larger children surged downwards. The four small girls, alternately biting their fingernails and holding hands with their partner, were somewhat unnerved by this . . .

There can also be considerable differences between children who like fighting and those who do not. Judith Hanna (1982) did an ethnography of an integrated school in Texas, and concluded that the black children, both boys and girls, had a *positive* attitude towards fighting, and believed that the white children only disliked fighting because they were bad at it, and scared of challenging black children. The white children felt the blacks were 'nasty', and did not, for the most part, want places in the aggression hierarchy. Similar sub-cultural clashes could be found in the ORACLE schools. Some boys wanted to fight and sort out a hierarchy of toughness, others did not. Even if the playgrounds are age-specific, those boys who want to fight may terrorize those who prefer not to. When the playspace is occupied by pupils of several different ages and sizes, these problems become more acute. Two boys at Maid Marion, Elmer and Gerard, reported that playtime was boring, and they 'just walked around in circles'. Elmer added that they 'couldn't do much' because of the bigger children: 'It's like being a small ant with jumbo jets running around you.' When there is a size imbalance even pupils who are not interested in fighting you or intimidating you can be menacing just because they are larger, 'own' the space, and are senior to you in the school. There are also sex differences in the use of playspace which can lead to boys dominating girls, and this is discussed in chapter 5. Girls may also become frightened of bullying when they see boys scrapping in a rule-governed manner, because they may not be any better at distinguishing unwilling victims from cheerful challengers than staff or observers. (Jessamine and Lavinia's terror about the playground at Maid Marion, reported in Delamont (1983b: 143) and the next chapter may well be understood best in this way.)

The proper role of the school in controlling, channelling or destroying peer group cultures among the pupils is an issue which divides different types of school. Leila Sussman (1977) argued that the more 'progressive' a school is, the more of the norms of the peer group become dominant, and fill the vacuum left by the withdrawal of staff authority. Her enthnography of several 'progressive' schools in the USA includes accounts of bullying and aggression in their playgrounds, accentuated by racist and sexist abuse and attacks. No comparable research has been done in Britain, and our data were not gathered with such issues in mind. However it does appear from the fieldnotes, essays and interviews that the three 'primary type' schools – Gryll Grange, Maid Marion, Melin Court – had less control over their playgrounds, and more pupils who said that fighting and bullying went on. In all three, the staff could usefully have paid more attention to separating those who wanted to scrap from those who did not, *and* ensuring the former establish their hierarchies without undue damage to each other.

The senior staff in these three schools, when interviewed in the summer term after transfer, saw adjustment to their new peers as one of the main criteria of successful adaption to the destination schools. Their opposite numbers at Guy Mannering, Kenilworth and Waverly did not give peer adjustment any priority in discussing whether our sample had settled in. It appears that the amount of fighting and quarrelling in the group were of more concern at the three 'primary type' schools. In chapter 9 the lengths to which staff at Maid Marion went to intervene in a class where the peer relations were felt to be poor are described in detail. These staff, like their equivalents at Gryll Grange and Melin Court, were perturbed by fighting. At Gryll Grange and Melin Court the head of year used associating with pupils outside the year group as an indication of poor adjustment, and a behaviour liable to lead to trouble. Mrs Hallows, at Melin Court, characterized poorly adjusted pupils (mainly boys) as those who were: 'loners, have few friends, tended to hang around with older boys . . . {and} appeared to seek attention by fighting, challenging older boys to fight.' Such judgments are based on a misunderstanding, or a negation, of what peer adjustment can mean for certain boys. The school may not like it, but for some boys, challenging others to fight is an essential part of peer group life.

The 'danger' some pupils face from their peers is not, therefore, simple to describe or understand. While the two boys who were tormenting Mitchell Gardiner *were* a danger to him, for others scrapping is one of the best ways to spend lunchtime.

Conclusions

This chapter has focused on three types of danger which face both staff and pupils in the schools. Physical dangers, such as electric sewing machines and hot ovens, face pupils: and staff have to ensure that their professional reputations are not harmed by pupils having accidents in their rooms. Threats to self-esteem are even more prevalent, and teachers and pupils can be humiliated at any time, on any day, in any location. Finally, while pupils may fear being bullied before they transfer, in their destination schools most discover that it is a rare phenomenon, quickly suppressed by staff. From our data it is clear that the biggest danger most pupils face is being forced to sit next to a child of the opposite sex and share a textbook; not being scalded in cookery or being half-strangled in the yard.

CHAPTER 5

The Luton Airport Syndrome: movement and immobility in the new schools

The most basic problem of order in school is the result of placing large numbers of active young people in very small spaces. Junior high school students are physically active and usually sociably inclined. But from the time the bell rings for classes to start in the morning until the last bell rings in the afternoon, students must sit reasonably still and pay attention to planned work for 320 minutes, while they may move about and talk for 75.

(Metz, 1978:148)

Introduction

Mary Metz (1978) has drawn attention to one of the most central features of school life. Pupils are not allowed to choose whether to move or be still – teachers decide whether movement is legitimate or not. In this chapter we examine how the pupils' movements are controlled by the staff of our schools in six sections. After the title of the chapter has been explained, the material on pupils' activity is presented in the following order. The first section presents material on how pupils' behaviour in playgrounds is organized, along with the immediate neighbourhood of the school. Then we scrutinize the control exercised in corridors, and then analyse how teachers organize getting pupils in and out of their classrooms. All these aspects of staff control over pupil movement are important elements in the maintenance of school-wide discipline, according to Metz (1978), and are therefore worth more attention than they habitually receive. The fourth section focuses upon those areas of the curriculum where movement is *de rigueur*, such as drama. The fifth section examines how staff use movement as a punishment for pupil misbehaviour. Finally, the chapter concludes with a sceptical look at the belief that pupils have freedom of movement in primary and middle schools, while being denied it in upper schools.

It is, perhaps, artificial to deal with movement separately from timetabling, because most of the pupils' movement is legitimized by timetabling – break, lunch, PE and changing from one class to another. Indeed our whole idea of a school is a building where movement is organized, and there are 'moving' times and 'stationary' times. We do, however, expect children of school age to want to move, and we expect to see movement around schools. Compare, for example, any school and its neighbourhood in Britain or the USA with the following:

> Fun City . . . is nestled in a warm valley, about ninety miles southeast of a large metropolitan area . . . The city itself is organised around wide, well-kept streets that are remarkable in several ways: . . . there are few cars driven on them . . . they are all lined with sidewalks that no one walks on; and all of the city's streets and sidewalks can be observed at any time of the day or night in the same state of eerie desolation.
>
> (Jacobs, 1974: 1)

This city is quite unlike any school – and its nature is probably apparent from the lack of any schools in it. Fun City is an American Retirement Community in Arizona, and as Jacobs describes the place, its major characteristic is a *lack* of movement. The streets, the pools, the golf course, the shopping centre are mostly empty and still. This chapter looks at those parts of the six schools where *movement* took place, and those where, like Fun City, stillness ruled.

The chapter is called the 'Luton Airport syndrome', a term coined by David Hargreaves (1982: 89) as part of his commentary on the British comprehensive school. Hargreaves suggested that pupils may be suffering a loss of corporate identity from the organizational arrangement whereby they move from one lesson to another. He created an evocative term 'the Paddington Station effect' to characterize this.

> In many schools today it is the teachers who 'own' the classrooms and the pupils who move round the school. This is not merely an important loss of corporate territory for each class, but it guarantees the Paddington Station effect every forty minutes; the bell rings and hordes of pupils pack into the narrow corridors . . .

Even worse, Hargreaves suggests, are those schools where pupils cannot leave their belongings in desks or lockers, but have to carry them about – creating 'the Luton Airport effect': 'the children stream round the building, but are now armed with huge cases,

bags, carriers, hold-alls in which all their belongings are kept.' One
example of the problems Hargreaves outlines can be seen from one
observer's report on a day at Guy Mannering.

> A story in the staffroom illustrates how moving around creates problems.
> One little girl had lost her packed lunch. Apparently she brought it to school
> in one of three carrier bags containing books, lunch, leotard and PE kit, etc.
> She forgot in which room she had put it. Since it is the policy to lock all rooms
> at lunchtime, the staff concerned had to go round finding keys to all the doors
> of all the rooms she had been in to locate where she had mislaid the one bag
> which had her lunch in.

Five of our six schools were characterized by either the Paddington
Station or the Luton Airport syndrome, with considerable pupil
movement between lessons. The data on those movements is
examined later in this chapter, after a scrutiny of the material on
movement in the playgrounds of our six schools.

Neighbourhoods, yards and playgrounds

Educational research has paid less attention to neighbourhoods,
yards and playgrounds than to classrooms. Yet as Mary Metz (1978:
147) points out, such spaces are part of the teachers' sphere of
responsibility:

> The school staff are responsible for their students in the halls, cafeteria, yards
> and even on the streets leading to and from the school, just as they are in the
> classrooms. Ebullience or hostility can lead to injury in these contexts. And
> noisy excitement generated there does not necessarily disappear when the
> students walk through the classroom door.

Metz captures the ambivalence in the proper use of school playgrounds: on the one hand pupils should move, 'let off steam' even
be 'free', but on the other, the staff are still responsible for them and
what they do has consequences for the classroom. Consequently,
movement in breaktimes, at lunchtime, before and after school
when they arrive and leave the campuses, and how and when pupils
leave lessons, is carefully rule-governed. Pupils are told early in
their school lives where they can and cannot go, and how to behave
in certain spaces. Lightfoot (1983: 89), for example, shows how one
of the biggest problems facing John F. Kennedy High School in
Riverdale, New York is the route some pupils take to school:

> Every weekday morning two thousand Black and Brown students ride from
> West Harlem to Riverdale on the Broadway subway. At 8:00, they pour out
> of the subway and walk the several blocks to school . . . The community the
> students pass through is a blue-collar, largely Irish community known as
> Marblehead. Last year battles erupted between the Marblehead residents and

the school when the locals claimed that the students were destroying their property and threatening their neighbourhood.

The School Principal got the local authority to build a new pavement, and organized the pupils so that they all walked along that side of the road. The Principal regarded his students' conduct in the road as an element in the reputation of his school, and the very fact that he was able to ensure which side of the road they walked on showed what strong discipline the school had.

The staff of our six schools also tried to control pupils' movements both for the sake of an orderly school, and for its reputation in the neighbourhood. For example, when pupils at Maid Marion were interviewed we found that they had learnt the following constraints upon·their movements. Luke and Josh told the interviewer that the only school rules they remembered were having to be out of the first year complex by 1.15 and not being able to go behind the bike sheds or across Kenilworth Road which formed the playground boundaries. Dan, in the same class, told the interviewer that the school rules were 'keeping out of the complex after 1.15 and not going on the grass area in front of the complex which is Kenilworth's territory.' Such limitations on the pupils' movements at break and lunchtime had been emphasized by staff. For example, in assembly on the first Friday of the year, Mr Seed, the acting head, had told the children 'of the playground boundaries and that the bicycle sheds were out of bounds.' This was a reiteration of what they had been told on their first day, and was gone over again at the beginning of the second week of term. Children learnt the rules, but did not necessarily agree with them. As one anonymous child wrote in an 'end of year' essay: 'At break I think we ought to be allowed to go out of the gates. We ought to be able to have more room on the field.'

Maid Marion was not alone in controlling pupils' territorial behaviour at break and lunchtimes. At Melin Court, for example, we saw Mrs Zeldin giving her form a test on the school rules which included:

Rule 3: All first years to use first year yard only.
Rule 4: Not allowed to go out of school at lunchtime unless going home to lunch.
Rule 9: Keep off the grass and trees.

One ORACLE observer wrote about morning break at Melin Court:

Break is in a special yard and there is a teacher out on yard duty. So there is reasonable order and little fighting. At the end of break they line up on the whistle into forms and march off back into the school.

On another day, the same observer spent another break in the first year yard and wrote:

> In the first year playground there are no seats, so the pupils have to sit on the wall. They invent a game whereby they stand on the concrete bollards and try to push each other off. (That is one child stands on the bollard while others try to push them off.) After a time this becomes quite violent and eventually the master on playground duty comes over and clears them away.

Waverly had no special yard for new first years, but Mr Parkin, the headmaster, always did break duty in the yard near his own office and the first year complex, to control the pupils' movement. Supervision of yards by senior staff is reported by other researchers. In the Australian Orthodox Jewish School he observed, Bullivant (1978: 56–7) described the principal's 'periodic visits to the playground' and his 'commanding physical presence in black rabbinical garb'. Mr Parkin's visible position in the playground served a similar function, though not in rabbinical dress. Mary Metz (1978: 152) summarizes the purpose of adult supervision even in the yard: 'Supervision by adults helps to enforce rules and encourage decorum.' Mr Parkin's presence in the playground at Waverly certainly went some way towards that.

One restriction on pupils' freedom of movement in the playground, then, is rules about where to go, and a second is the presence of teachers supervising their behaviour. A third restriction is the weather. All our six schools had rules about pupils staying indoors when the weather was considered *by staff* to be too wet to go out. Pupils' views of these rules did not always coincide with staff's. For example, George at Kenilworth told us:

> If it is nice we are aloud (sic) to go on the field and we usually play soccer but if it is not fine we have to sit in the classroom if it is raining. If it has been raining but it has stopped we are aloud (sic) to go on the playground.

George found sitting in the classroom unpleasant, as did Trudie at Maid Marion who said:

> Also I like it when you can play anywhere in the school. I don't like it when you have to stay in at dinner and break. I think we should be able to go out.

Observers from ORACLE were present during some wet breaks at some schools. At Melin Court an observer was in RE with Mrs Durrant when the signal for a 'wet break' was rung. Mrs Durrant explained that they had to stay in the formroom they are in until the next period: 'Wet break means that you stay in this room. If you want to go to the toilet you come back here.'

At Waverly one afternoon an observer was in the class before the break when:

> Five minutes before the end of the lesson the bell rings four times to signify a wet break. It is not raining, but the weather is blustery. There is no break, lessons continue as per the timetable and school ends ten minutes early.

The observer commented that this arrangement is 'a fiendish device' because the teacher of the last lesson of the afternoon has the pupils 'stale, tired and very fidgety'.

We have discussed what children do in the playground in some detail in chapter 4, so here we merely contrast the occupation of three boys at Maid Marion who were interviewed together, with that of four girls there. Rolf, Madoc and Dermot told us that they 'usually mucked about in the yard kicking a football around' or 'just wandered about getting bored'. Their most 'anti-social' occupation was 'sometimes they knocked into the third year girls and annoyed them until the girls ran after them.' In contrast two girls, Jessamine and Lavinia, were so scared of bullying that they very rarely went outside at break or lunchtime. They reported that some of the 'big lads' came up to boys in their form and 'half-strangled them' and that no one helped the victims because 'they dare not'. Jessamine and Lavinia preferred to stay inside during the lunchhour and at break they often hid in the lavatories to avoid going outside. Another duo, Wanda and Petunia, disliked breaktimes both mid-morning and lunchtime. They preferred to stay inside, and had arranged several legitimate ways to do so. On Mondays at break-time they had arranged to tidy up the French boxes, and on Wednesdays they had volunteered to be in charge of the library. These gave them legitimate excuses to extend the period when they could be indoors. Both girls said not that they were frightened to go out, but that it was boring 'just wandering around' and the only outdoor activity they had was talking to the lollipop man.

Another strategy for staying indoors at break had been 'discovered' by some girls at Guy Mannering, where one observer was taking morning coffee with the home economics staff and saw:

> Annabel and Paula come into the housecraft flat also to collect Miss Tyree's coffee. This is made by one of the home economics staff and put on a tray to be taken to her office by a couple of pupils.

We neglected to enquire if the pupils were always girls, though it seems likely. Certainly the literature would suggest that girls are more likely to devise strategies like Petunia and Wanda's to stay indoors. Meyenn (1980) reports on a group of four girls at a Midlands Middle School who had opted to be science monitors.

> Most of their spare time was spent in the science lab as the officially designated science monitors. This involved the care and feeding of the laboratory animals.

These girls were academically successful, and interested in boys and fashion. They managed to amalgamate their interests on one occasion when:

> They combined school duties with pleasure and their interest in animals and boys . . . when they were able to persuade several boys to dig worms for them in the lunch hour to provide food for the toads! Normally these boys were passionately involved in lunchtime football games.

Of these two male activities, soccer was a common pursuit at our six schools, but we observed no digging for worms! There are two issues raised here which deserve further attention: sex differences and whether pupils are free to go out *or* stay in. Our schools varied in whether pupils were allowed to stay in at breaktimes. Some of them forced everyone outdoors, others let children choose. Gryll Grange allowed children to choose, and many of Miss Tweed's class stayed indoors even in a warm and sunny September. One observer wrote:

> I commented to Miss Tweed on how many of her class like to stay in at break. She says 'Yes a lot do,' and did last year too. She explains it with 'If they don't like rushing about playing football it is nicer to stay in and do colouring, elastic band pictures or games.'

Miss Tweed had many activities available to children who chose to stay in her room, and during morning break usually stayed there herself. This tolerance of pupils' choice at Gryll Grange was not popular with the 'dinner ladies', however. One day an observer was at Gryll Grange and:

> I have lunch, talk to the supply teacher and then come back to 1T to write up some notes. Kenneth and Oliver are put outside by the dinner lady . . . Tuesdays means gym club which includes Davina, Priscilla and Karel (who often spend the lunch hour in here) and cross country which seems to appeal to a lot of them. Girls come in to tell dinner lady there are boys fighting – including Kenneth, Oliver and Nigel.
> . . . I put Savlon on Oliver's leg which is badly grazed. He is tearful and resentful . . . Dinner lady says she'd like a clear ruling on whether children

were to be in or out. She says she hoped the new boss (Mr Judge) would say everybody had to go out, but he didn't. He ruled that pupils could stay in and do 'something which was worthwhile'. She finds that a difficult ruling to enforce.

As Metz (1978: 151) points out, rules about pupils are designed to:

> Forbid activities which may breed disorder, thus preventing it before it starts . . . Thus, in Chauncey, children are not allowed inside the school for more than 15 minutes before and after school unless they are directly supervised by a teacher . . . During the lunch period they must stay outside the academic buildings in certain designated areas after they leave the cafeteria.

The situation at Gryll Grange is in one way typical. Most of the available play space is occupied by boys fighting and playing soccer. As Wolpe (1977: 38–9) was one of the first to point out, there are clear sexual divisions in the use of the playground which reflect sexual differences in space usage outside the school (e.g. Hart, 1979). Wolpe says that, compared to boys:

> The girls are relatively inactive in their general behaviour. They are not rowdy . . . Consider the whole role of football within the school context. This is one of the main ways in which boys express themselves in an overt, physical activity . . . For girls there is no means of expressing themselves in overt physical fashion. They walk around, or sit around either demurely or as spectators.

Wolpe had studied a comprehensive school in 1973, which had two playgrounds, one mixed and the other, in an inner courtyard, for girls only. She characterized the former as follows:

> in the mixed playground . . . the boys monopolise almost the total area by playing football, while the girls sit around on benches or wander round the periphery.

The girls'-only playground was described by the female pupils as 'boring' and one reason for this was that ball games were forbidden. Wolpe argues that the school structured girls into passive behaviour, because when, outside school, girls were offered the chance to be active and aggressive, they were. Mahony (1985: 25–8) presents similar conclusions based on photographs in another London school taken in 1984.

Ironically, this description of sex differences in playground behaviour is a perfect replica of accounts of girls' play in the mid nineteenth century. Wolpe's inner city school in 1973 has clear echoes with the two schools overlooked by Herbert Spencer (1911) in the 1850s. In a famous passage he contrasted a boys' school, which had a large garden with 'ample scope for games' and the neighbourhood was regularly aware of the boys shouting and laughing, with one for girls. The Establishment for Young Ladies 'affords no sign of any provision for juvenile recreation.' The girls were never seen to play, or run, and never heard to laugh. Thus in the 1850s education did not expect girls to move about, play energetically or run. Wolpe's surprise and outrage is a very modern phenomenon, and is the product of the campaigns waged by nineteenth-century feminists (Atkinson, 1978, 1985) to get girls access to sport, games, and physical fitness. When the feminists opened girls' schools, their pupils had physical freedom, which has been lost again in co-educational schools.

The yards and playgrounds in our six schools showed similar sex segregation to those studied by Wolpe and Mahony. For example, at Melin Court one observer noted:

> The first year space is very empty but there are more in the second year's where there are benches. Mostly it is girls chatting or reading love magazines. For a time some staff come out and wander around just to supervise.

In the other yard, the boys fought and kicked footballs.

Sex differences in pupils' movements in their playgrounds are not the only ones which have been observed. There are also racial variations. Judith Hanna (1982) has described differences between black and white children in playground behaviour at a desegregated school in Dallas, and Christine Finnan (1982) observed variations in play patterns between Anglo-Americans and Vietnamese children in elementary schools in the USA. Thus pupils' movements in their playgrounds vary with sex and race, and with the rules that the teachers make about how the space is to be utilized. We now turn to school corridors and how movement in them is controlled.

Corridors

Children's access to, and use of, non-classroom spaces inside the school also have to be policed. In the two schools studied by Mary Metz (1978: 151–2) children were not allowed to

> be in the hallways during class periods without a pass : . . (both schools) . . . had one-way halls and staircases to facilitate traffic flow . . . Adults are assigned to supervise in crowded areas before and after school, at lunchtime, and between classes.

In this section we deal with how our six schools organized their staircases and corridors to prevent noise, fights and other forms of 'trouble'. In well-run schools, staff exercise control over the spaces outside classrooms. The Junior High School, Harold Spence, studied by Everhart (1983: 323) had a principal, Mr Edwards, who took care to control space in his school:

> Edwards stressed the physical maintenance of the building and student discipline as two key indices of a well-run school . . . Almost every day he was in the lunch-room, directing students to pick up paper. After school he was in front of the building, directing the bus loading, and general student conduct around the bus loading area . . . He was constantly stressing to teachers the necessity of close student supervision between classes, during lunch and before and after school.

A similar attitude was prevalent in most of our six schools. For example, at Guy Mannering, very early in the autumn term, an observer wrote:

> The corridors at Guy Mannering are very big and are quite noisy so that when children go up and down to change classes there are lots of laughings and bumpings into each other, etc. Clearly it is important for the staff to stop this as soon as possible and make certain that the transition from class to class is done as quietly and effortlessly as possible . . . Whenever there is noise, staff come out of their doors quickly to tell the children off and to organize them to the correct waiting positions. Children here are supposed to:
> (1)   Wait outside rooms until you are told to come in.
> (2)   Queue on the left of the door, in a double row so that you allow space for the next class and don't overlap onto stairways.

Early in the school year staff control of the corridors had not been imposed, and so we saw a certain amount of disorder. For example on October 10th:

> When the bell goes the class streams out and converges towards the door in the corridor. By the time it reaches the fire door it is joined by a number of other classes, some coming in the opposite direction, and a real scrum ensues around the corridor. Some of the little children are getting pushed quite badly and staff have to appear from their rooms to shout in order to get some order.

One of the observers had been to Guy Mannering the previous summer, and noticed the difference in the corridor behaviour: 'As we go along the corridor there is a fair crush and yet there is not the same careful movement that was observed when we visited the school last summer.' Apart from staff control of corridors, Guy Mannering also tried to avoid the fire doors causing bottlenecks and accidents by stationing pupils to open them at certain particularly busy times in the school day. The level of pupil conduct at Guy Mannering was 'good' enough too, for pupils who noticed staff approaching doors to open them for their teachers. The crowding in the corridors at our other schools was similarly striking, for example: 'My main impression of just one day in Kenilworth was one of milling crowds in the corridor, everyone moves to a different place every lesson.'

Kenilworth and Guy Mannering were typical of those schools which expected pupils to move from room to room between lessons. For example, at Maid Marion pupils were given rules for using the corridors. Dan told us that: 'He had to walk on the left-hand side of the corridor and that you weren't allowed to run.' These directions about using the corridors had been given in assembly by Mr Seed the acting head, and are quoted in chapter 4. Melin Court also had these two rules for using the corridors, so when Mrs Zeldin's class had a test on the school rules, the first two were:

(1) Always walk on the left-hand side.
(2) No running – always go quietly.

Melin Court was overcrowded and one observer wrote:

> The corridors are jam-packed and there are very silly fire-doors which restrict flow of people – staff are involved in a lot of 'traffic-policing' at all breaks, etc., and corridors jam up completely.

Typical incidents of staff policing the corridors were:

> On the way to geography, Mr Yardley tells them off for running in the corridor. Sends them back to walk . . .

> During a double period of English with Mrs Wordsworth the bell goes. Mrs Wordsworth goes out into the corridor because of the noise – not excessive but disturbing.

Melin Court also had rules about the routes pupils could take around the school, and these were enforced:

> As we go out for break the senior pupils are on the corridor doors at the entrances to prevent pupils walking through the school. They have to walk all round the outside to get to their playground.

> The next lesson is music with Mrs Altham. Her room is in the new building so we have a very long walk from the last lesson. It turns out that the children have come around the wrong side of the building to get to her room so the teacher begins by telling them off.

Waverly organized its pupils in a similar way. On their first morning, Mr Bronte told them that: 'The children should walk on the right hand side of the corridor. Also some stairs were only for going up, while others were only for coming down.' Note that Waverly and Melin Court had opted to put pupils on opposite sides of the corridor. One of the ORACLE pupils, Brent, spent a week at Melin Court, and then transferred to Waverly. We can only hope he managed to find the correct side of the corridor! At Waverly, we saw pupils' behaviour in the corridors monitored by teachers, as in the following incidents:

> We go to art with Mr Palet. He gives the rules for coming to his room. 'Wait in the outside stairwell, not blocking the art area. While waiting for a teacher, keep the corridor clear. Line up sensibly.'

Waverly had its own rules about pupils' routes around the campus, for instance: 'The girls go round by the tower block, and are sent back to go round by art block instead.'

In these ways, schools control the use of corridors and other public spaces. Before we leave the use of corridors it is important to point out that corridors are yet another place where teachers may be judged by their colleagues. If a form behaves badly in the corridors it can reflect on their form teacher. This was made very clear to us at Guy Mannering where one of our classes, 1.6, was a 'bad' form. The observer was present when:

> An interesting discussion takes place between Miss O'Hara and 1.6. It appears that they aren't going in line very well when they go down from their form room to the morning assembly. She asks them for suggestions as to how they can get their lines straight. 'Go up and down and hit us with a ruler if we are crooked.'
> 'Keep us in to do extra work.'
> Miss O'Hara is doubtful. 'Well, I could do that.' But in the end she settles on something simpler. 'If you are straight next time you will all get a credit.'
> She then gets three children out in front and shows the rest of the class how if they get their feet in the right place they must be in a straight line and they practise this until the bell goes.

The observer doubted whether Miss O'Hara was herself concerned about straight lines, and suggested that some of the older staff had noticed and their criticism had forced Miss O'Hara to try and do something about it.

If teachers are judged by the way their form behaves in the corridors, their control is also apparent in how groups enter and leave their lessons. We now turn to the ways in which teachers control the pupils' exits and entrances from the classroom.

Getting in and out of class

Our next theme is how teachers organize marshalling pupils in and out of their rooms. Metz (1978: 165) suggests that pupils did not understand why teachers tried to control this because: 'They were not responsible for getting classes into a working mood or integrating late comers into a task already explained and started.' Teachers, in contrast, understand only too well how important for classroom order controlling entry is, and for corridor control ensuring orderly exits. We examine how teachers in our six schools organized entries first, and then look at exits. In Gryll Grange the problem rarely arose because the pupils stayed in their form room most of the time, but in the five schools which asked pupils to move from room to room, teachers had different rules about whether pupils could enter their rooms on arrival without a teacher present, about how, if at all, pupils were to line up, whether they could sit down until told to do so and so on. In none of our schools was there a consistent policy across *all* teachers on any of these issues. As we shall see later in this section, children could be confused by the differences between their teachers. First, we examine how various teachers organize pupil entry when they were present as the pupils arrived. A variety of entrances were observed:

> Guy Mannering – Class 1.5 go to Miss Pink's room. They enter, and are made to stand up behind their desks and have to say 'Good morning, Miss Pink' in chorus before they can sit.

At Melin Court, one RE teacher, Mrs Durrant, sorted out how she wanted pupils to enter her room very early in the year:

> Mrs Durrant came out into the passage, and says to the children that she wants quiet lines, one of girls, and one of boys. When they have formed these she lets them in, the girls first in one line, and then the boys.

During that lesson Mrs Durrant explained why she wanted them to enter quietly. In a subsequent lesson, she praised them for coming into her room in the way she liked 'as if everyone mattered', with no pushing or shoving. The majority of pupils had remembered what to do, and she had 'enjoyed' it. Other staff stressed that demeanour was important for an appropriate entrance, as in the following science lesson at Melin Court with Miss Fern:

> Class arrive with a lot of noise. Miss Fern says she knows that they may get lost, but there is no need to fuss when they arrive and shout as if they were in the yard.

Several schools laid down rules and procedures for entrances early in the school year, as at Waverly:

Waverly – Assembly on the first morning in the hall
Mr Bronte tells the first year, 'When you come in here again for assembly you will come in without your coats and in silence.'

Waverly – Mr Bronte's class, day 1
Mr Bronte tells them that when there is no assembly, or in the afternoon, the class should line up outside with the other first year classes and wait to come in. They all go outside and practise.

Pupils quickly learnt that some staff were concerned about how they behaved while waiting to enter lessons, as this extract shows:

Waverly – physics with Mr Rutherford
Pupils line up for the lab. When I first attended this lesson the pupils made so much noise that a teacher came out and shouted at them and made them line up again. Now, although there is fooling, it is carefully controlled so that it doesn't attract attention from the staff behind the closed doors of the labs and the prep room. They still have to line up along the wall beside the door. As each boy goes to the end of the queue, he runs the gauntlet of others who attempt to trip him up. But it is all done in silence.

Sensible form teachers ensure that they despatch their forms off to lessons in an orderly manner – at Melin Court for example, Mrs Wordsworth always insisted that 1M were quiet before she let them leave for their lessons. At Waverly, the modern language rooms were near the headmaster's office and the staffroom, so classes soon learnt that it was wise to wait for the teacher in the prescribed way – parallel single-sex lines, both relatively silent.

Our schools and teachers varied over how they expected pupils to enter classrooms. At Waverly the English staff we observed had agreed that children should line up outside rooms, come in and stand until told to sit; for example:

English with Mrs Southey
Class came in noisily and sit down. Teacher has to remind them all to stand up.

English with Miss Lawrence
A lot of noise on returning to the classroom. The teacher has to remind them to stand until they are told to sit.

This pattern was shared by the modern language staff, so when a class went to the language lab for French with Mr Mowbray:

Mr Mowbray directs children to fill up the desks at the front.
'When we come in we don't sit down, we stand behind our chairs and greet each other.' They do so in French.

There were, however, inconsistencies between staff in some of our schools. For example, at Melin Court 1M had French with Mr Haydon, and at their first lesson:

> They crowd door. He tells them off for crowding the door and says in future they do not have to wait outside for him. They can come in and sit down in his room. They cannot enter workshops or labs or some ordinary classrooms without a teacher, but his room they can enter.

However, three weeks later, Mr Haydon was absent, and:

> There is chaos for the next lesson, which is French, because of a change in classroom. Mrs Marks (senior mistress) supervises the move to the drama studio. Some pupils go straight into the drama studio when they arrive. Mrs Marks yells 'Don't you dare go in there! You know you are not allowed in there without a teacher! GET OUT!'

The pupils here appeared genuinely muddled about whether to go in or not. In general, orderly entry to classes was accompanied by orderly exit. We can show this with an entry and exit from Miss Airdale's English class at Kenilworth, which will take us on to organizing exits in all six schools.

> Miss Airdale's English
> Miss Airdale had the children line up outside and somewhat stridently insisted on quiet before they went in. Once in the classroom, the children were allowed to sit where they liked.

At the end of the lesson:

> When the bell went, she told the children to put their books away quietly and sit very still. She said they would stay there until they were very quiet. She then said that children could go when she could remember their names. She then called out the children's names, as she did so they were allowed to leave.

Here Miss Airdale displays one strategy for ensuring an orderly retreat. Miss Airdale was the only teacher who combined learning pupils' names with organizing a controlled exit. Other teachers had other strategies. During a boys' PE lesson in the gym at Kenilworth, the two masters closed the class by throwing a ball at the boys. As each boy was hit he was to leave the gym to get changed. One very common strategy was to separate the sexes, so that either boys or girls left first. For example:

> Art lesson at Waverly Annex with Mr Brearly
> When all are seated after cleaning up, Mr Brearly checks on tidiness and cleanliness. 'Right, girls get your bags.' Girls fetch their belongings from the

side and come back to their seats. 'Right, well if you tidy up like that every week, I see we'll have no problems.' Lets the girls leave first.

Maths at Waverly – Mr Astill
'Right, now let's have an orderly retreat.' Says the quietest row can pack away. (Girls) Then the next row. (Girls)

Science at Melin Court – Miss Fern
Sends them back to their bench places. Tells one boy to collect the books. She is coming round to check each bench to see if they have cleared up, not left any rubbish, and handed in all the equipment. Norman is asked to put some more rubbish in the bin. As each bench is checked they can go.

As each bench is single-sex this segregates the leaving groups.

Art at Melin Court – Mrs Madder
Told to pack away. One girl collects work. Sends two girls to deliver her stuff back to her room. When they are silent they can go, table by table.

One other strategy is to allow pupils to leave as they finish their work:

French at Melin Court – Mrs Zeldin
The bell goes for lunch.
Teacher: 'When you have finished what's on the board, you may go.'
There is a sudden burst of concentration and work.

All these teacher strategies for controlling exits and entrances ensure corridor safety and maintain the teacher's own discipline, and status with their colleagues. Many, however, also serve to segregate the sexes and/or reinforce those segregations that pupils have already adopted, an issue discussed elsewhere (Delamont, 1983d).

The chapter has, so far, examined how pupils are organized to move in ways approved by staff in the neighbourhood of the school, in the yard, in the corridors, and as they enter and leave rooms. In five of our six schools the pupils had to enter and leave rooms, and move round the school, between every subject, because they travel to their teachers in what Hargreaves (1982) terms the Paddington Station and Luton Airport phenomena. Before the focus shifts to the ways in which movement is controlled *inside* classrooms, it is worth analysing how far David Hargreaves' condemnation of the Paddington Station effect is shared by the pupils. Hargreaves believes that pupils have lost a sense of territorial identity, and certainly our pupils realized that this would be one of the new experiences they would find in their destination schools. Our essay and interview data can be used to see how they reacted to the regular travelling.

Movement and immobility in the new schools

Pupils' views of Paddington

It is clear from the studies of chidren before transfer (Bryant, 1980; Measor and Woods, 1984) that they know that they will have to travel from one teacher to another. Before transfer, some pupils fear this movement, partly because they believe they will get lost. Bryant (1980) did a content analysis of 310 pupils' essays on 'My thoughts on changing schools' written before they moved schools; and a further 310 on 'My thoughts on my new school' done at Christmas after transfer. The pre-transfer essays contained apprehension about moving, and the post-transfer essays suggest that many of the pupils were still not reconciled to the Paddington Station effect.

> Chester High School is a very big place. Sometimes you get lost and sometimes you're late for your lesson.
>
> I dislike the way the stairs are one way because if you lose something on the stairs you only have a small chance of getting back to it.
>
> I don't like it when you change lessons because when you go up the stairs you get squashed.
>
> I've got used to it now (changing lessons) and I know all the teachers that take me for lessons quite well.
>
> The half hour lessons which we have are daft because some teachers tell you off for being late when you have come from a mobile or the games field and you have to go to the top floor.

Bryant did not ask specific questions but left the pupils free to write about any aspect of the transfer. The ORACLE pupils interviewed, and some of those who wrote essays also, raised movement in their responses, and we present the data we have below. The movement between classes struck the ORACLE observers themselves, and one wrote from Guy Mannering after three weeks there:

> Talking to the children they still do not like moving from class to class and find it confusing. At different times today two children (outside 1.5 and 1.6) stopped me in the corridor at the change of lessons to ask me whether it was morning, whether it was playtime.

However the essays written for us by pupils at Kenilworth and Maid Marion revealed some pupils who stated that they *liked* 'the Paddington Station effect'. Forty-seven Maid Marion pupils wrote us essays, and 10 mentioned enjoying moving between lessons; 2 people disliked it, 1 was neutral, while 34 failed to mention the issue at all. Those who mentioned moving favourably said things like:

> I like Maid Marion because we don't keep the same teachers and classrooms.
> I think swopping is a good idea. (Sally)

> I like the idea of bells ringing for the change of lessons. The times are just
> right. I like changing rooms for different subjects, otherwise staying in the
> same room would be boring. (Jessamine)

> Being able to move about from lesson to lesson is a good idea. (Karena)

> What I like about Maid Marion is being able to move around to each lesson
> and have different teachers. (Anon)

> Here are some things I like. I like the idea of changing classrooms for
> different lessons because you get to know the school better. (Trudie)

Similarly in interviews Wanda and Petunia told the researcher they
like Maid Marion because:

> They liked being able to change subjects at the end of each hour – they also
> liked being able to change rooms, and far from fearing that they would get
> lost they enjoyed a change of scene, and a change of teacher and a change of
> topic.

Similarly Magnus at Guy Mannering:

> Spontaneously said that he likes the school because you have to travel around
> different classes. 'I like to be on the move.'

Only 2 pupils out of 47 at Maid Marion said they disliked moving
from class to class. Richard listed it as a 'bad thing about Maid
Marion' and, 'having to walk to different lessons', and Gerard
wrote: 'I don't like moving round the school. You have to carry your
books with you.' Thus insofar as the ORACLE pupils had views on
moving from teacher to teacher, there was a majority in favour.
Hargreaves (1982) may well be correct in diagnosing the Paddington Station effect as a source of malaise in the comprehensive
school, but it does not cause conscious distress to the ORACLE
sample. Having examined movement around the school buildings in
some detail, the chapter now focuses on movement and immobility
inside classrooms, comparing those where it is prescribed with those
where it might be proscribed. There is, therefore, a section on
specialist areas where pupil movement is believed to be common,
such as gymnasia, and then a section on conventional classrooms,
where pupil immobility might be expected. Between the two there
is a brief discussion of how staff may use movement as a punish-

ment, which highlights how the appropriateness or otherwise of any movement is teacher-defined and situationally specific.

Specialist rooms and arenas

In this section we look at movement and immobility in specialist areas of the school – gymnasia and drama studios for example, where particular rules about movement apply. Let us first look at a lesson where movement was demanded by the teacher:

Maid Marion – drama with class 10 – Mr Barrell
The children had already had one drama lesson and as it had been so successful Mr Barrell invited me specially to come along and watch them on the second occasion.

We went over to the drama studio which is rather like an old nissen hut very darkly painted inside with a lot of spotlights from the roof. The children were thoroughly excited with the whole idea of having to give a show and were at first rather giggly and silly. Mr Barrell reprimanded them and they began again.

The music provided had been taped from a radio series some ten years earlier which Mr Barrell had thought very good. The commentary on the tape asked the children to use their imagination in the movements which they did in response to the music. They were asked first of all to move to some drumming music and to pretend the drums were all over the walls, floors and ceiling and to use any part of their bodies to beat the drums with. Later they were asked to sit down and to imagine their hands getting first smaller and smaller and smaller and then bigger and bigger and bigger and larger. Then they were asked to get into small groups and listen to a piece of music and to mime a story to it which each group then did in turn. This was greeted with great enthusiasm and the children were very very involved in the show which they gave. Mr Barrell felt that whatever the standard of what they finally gave was, the actual level of involvement justified the whole exercise.

I was surprised how generally well the boys reacted to this kind of exercise. They could so easily have become very silly and been much too embarrassed to have joined in. At first this was true particularly of Jerome, Edward, Richard and John who always do everything together. But in the group activity when they could mime an actual play and have some sense of purpose to their movements they really went to town and were very pleased with their effort. However the star of the show was definitely Dermot who was extremely good; Mr Barrell singled him out to me. Their group was voted the best by all the other children as well. Of the girls Myra and Chantel seemed to enjoy this kind of work very much. Two usually very shy girls Fida and Karena suddenly came out of their shells and really seemed to participate in a much more enthusiastic way. Normally in class these two avoid any teacher contact and are very silent wherever possible but in the drama room they really moved with much greater confidence than I had expected from them.

The children really enjoyed making up the little mime sequences and became very excited but also behaved very sensibly during the whole programme. The two boys who find most of the classwork difficult, Miles and Lester, also seemed to enjoy this opportunity of being able to express themselves by movement and mime rather than writing which was still a painful experience for both of them. Lester had been particularly keen for me to come to this lesson so that I could watch him. Mr Barrell was very pleased with them all and said that he felt most exhilarated to see how excited they had become and how well they had worked.

In this lesson a pupil who was immobile and failed to move would be deviant and Mr Barrell would have been entitled to discipline him or her. The same is true of PE, as we can see in the following extract from a boys' gym lesson at Kenilworth.

> 1 zeta (and two other forms) with Mr Pompey and Mr Cowell
> Mr Pompey and Mr Cowell took the boys into the gym. The gym was very bright and airy and smelling of polish. The boys were dressed in a variety of different coloured T-shirts. Mr Cowell said they would start with a game to warm up. The boys with blue shirts would be on and they will try and catch everyone else. When you were caught you had to stand still with your hands on your head. Philip came wandering in barefoot with his gym shoes tied together by their laces. Mr Cowell tried for a long time to untangle them, but this was interfering with what he was trying to do. He caught my eye and then tossed the gym shoes to me so that I could untangle them.

Note here that PE does not involve continual movement. Pupils are sometimes expected to move and sometimes to stand still – it is not permissable for boys in blue shirts to stay still, or the rest to move once they have been caught. Nor are pupils expected to take part at all until they are properly dressed. This pattern is repeated once apparatus is brought out.

> Mr Cowell then began to demonstrate the use of the apparatus. He chose Brett to help slot the beams in position. He emphasized how the beam should be wedged into place. I was impressed by Mr Cowell's rather gentle amiable manner. He explained the apparatus very clearly.
> Next various other bits of apparatus were got out. Edmond and Blair did most of the helping, although Brett and Kevin also helped to some extent. When all the apparatus was out Mr Cowell asked the boys to try and remember what the bits of apparatus were called. He asked some children by name, always using their surnames. It was noteworthy that the boys he chose were in general the large athletic looking ones. Presumably their names have stuck in his mind most quickly. Boys in white shirts (9 in all) had to sit out while the rest of the children were allocated to various bits of apparatus. They had to go around the gym in a circuit using each piece of apparatus in turn. No particular instructions were given, except that they should see what they could do with the apparatus. They were told to take their time and work to the best of their ability. While they were doing this Mr Pompey and Mr Cowell helped one or two of the clumsier children over the apparatus. Edmond was particularly active and agile throughout all this. After some time the boys who had been using the apparatus had to sit out while the children in white shirts had a go.

This is noticeable as an early PE lesson, because boys are free to use the apparatus in any way they choose, and they have to be taught how to erect it. Later in the year boys would be expected to get out apparatus safely themselves, and frequently particular exercises would 'belong' with specific pieces of equipment. Again, some boys are expected to be still while others move. Early PE lessons have less controlled movements in some ways, but more controlled in others.

> After that everyone sat round the edges while the two teachers chose various boys to show what they had done on various bits of apparatus. He asked Edmond to demonstrate a roll and Arnold to demonstrate a vault. They did these activities very competently. Mr Cowell then said it was nearly the end of the lesson. They did not seem to have had very long because they had spent time putting out the apparatus, but partly because the boys had been a long time getting changed. In future they must try and do it a bit more quickly.
>
> They finished by playing a game where the two teachers threw a soft football at the children who were milling about. As soon as a child was hit by the ball he had to go off to the changing room to get changed. There was no fuss about getting changed, and no insistence that anyone should take a shower.

Several features of the gym lesson are noteworthy, but may be taken-for-granted. It is a lesson for boys only – the only single-sex subject at Kenilworth. There is a variety of movement expected – by all boys, by small groups, and by designated individuals, and all of it is teacher controlled. There are individual differences in ability, signalled by the teachers, and an emphasis on *efficient* use of time. Similar themes are apparent in games lessons.

Physical education out of doors is equally characterized by teacher control over pupils' movements. One observer went to a games lesson at Guy Mannering:

> All the staff are in very flash track suits. The boys are practising soccer skills and the girls are doing hockey and netball.

Note that boys and girls are separated, and their physical activities are different.

> After half the time the boys are organized into two football games. There are about 80 boys so 40 on a pitch, 20 to a team. They just rush after the ball and the area is so crowded that there is little room for anyone to practise the skills that they were using in the first half of the lesson.

Here we see a familiar theme in specialist areas – too many pupils crowded into spaces that are inadequate and/or supervised by too few staff. In these circumstances pupils' movements may be more tightly controlled to prevent accidents, or may be undersupervised. In all our six schools we found teachers struggling to 'manage' in crowded spaces. At Guy Mannering, which had been a girls' secondary modern, there were adequate numbers of women PE teachers, but a shortage of PE *masters*. The observer commented:

> Too many children and too few staff. I talked about this to one of the masters, Mr Sturgess-Jones. He tells me that he has often thought of splitting them again but if he does that some of them don't play at all because he cannot be with two groups at once. The boys generally rush around and exhaust themselves.

Here Mr Sturgess-Jones describes a problem. Either 40 boys can have an unskilled, if energetic game, or 22 boys can have a skilful match while 18 boys cannot play at all. (A parallel problem for the craft teachers at Guy Mannering is outlined in chapter 7.) The girls' games were much more disciplined:

> Hockey and netball groups don't actually play but practise skills such as stick control.

Finally, the observer at Guy Mannering wrote:

> Only 1 or 2 boys are not doing the games.

And this final comment on the double lesson reminds us of the minority who legitimately *avoid* movement in PE lessons – by being 'ill'/asthmatic, etc. In every class in every school where movement is expected, some pupils will be allowed to remain immobile. It is also clear that outdoor PE requires specific items of clothing, and a child without the correct shirt, socks, footwear or shorts may also be allowed, or forced, to sit still. Thus at Gryll Grange:

> 1.40
> The boys get one of the specialist PE masters. He tells me later that he does not know quite how to handle it because he was never taught in the first year before. He is helped out by the first year male teacher, Mr Valentine, the probationer. Changing rooms are very small and some of the children change outside. Some don't have football socks, a few don't have the boots. They practise football skills and interestingly Raymond is probably one of the best. He uses both feet.
> Over with the girls the netball is much more organized. Miss Tweed shouts at them when they don't do it properly and makes them do it again. They are trying to practise throwing overarm and many of them still keep on doing it underarm. 'I'd like to slap some of your bottoms' says Miss T after the third attempt to do it properly. One or two children haven't done PE because they did not bring their equipment. No-one seems to make an issue of this although it would be interesting to see what happens later on in the year.

In the early weeks, anyway, lacking kit is a way of escaping PE.

Drama studies and gymnasia are places where pupils and teachers may expect movement. In contrast are craft rooms and the science lab, where – as we have shown in chapter 4 – pupils are told that movement has to be *controlled* and minimal. Beynon's (1985) data on the first weeks of the school year at Victoria Road Boys' Comprehensive in South Wales contains a typical introduction to a science lab:

> Mr Bunsen first got all satchels and bags stowed under the benches, then (told them about safety) . . .
> Mr Bunsen: 'Point no. two is never run in the laboratory. Why should I say never run in the laboratory? Why is it important that we walk everywhere? . . . I should see every hand up now. Why should we never run in here?'
> Pupil: 'In case you fall over.'
> Mr Bunsen: 'In case you fall over. Right. That's one reason, you might fall over. What's another reason? Something that could occur if you were running.'
> Pupil: 'Might bump into someone.'

Similarly the science master at Maid Marion, Mr Salter, had laid down rules about stillness, and told pupils:

> He wanted nobody turning round to see what other people were up to, and he wanted nobody wandering around the room without good reason because that's how accidents happen.

Pupils have to master these various rules for movement, and most of them quickly do so. Nathan, at Maid Marion, told his interviewer that:

> There are some rules that special teachers invent inside their own classroom. The science teacher, Mr Salter, says we can't run around in the science lab.

When pupils forget, break or ignore these rules, they are quickly reminded of them, as in this comment by Mrs Rumsey at Maid Marion:

> Mrs Rumsey said she was not impressed by the way they went about practical work. They wander about, get their apparatus as slowly as possible, and chatter about it all the time.

Note here that Mrs Rumsey links *wrong* movement ('wandering about'), with correct movement at the wrong speed (slowly instead of expeditiously) and with noise (chatter). Similar comments about immobility and controlled movement were made in all the potentially 'dangerous' areas of the school, as chapter 4 showed. Yet it would be quite wrong to see PE as an arena for untramelled freedom of movement and the woodwork room as a place of controlled stillness. When a teacher is present, pupils do not have freedom of movement in either area. This showed most vividly in the gym at Gryll Grange. The architect had designed the school with a central hall/gym, which was near the library, the offices, many classrooms, and the music/dining room. Gym had, therefore, to be done in silence. On one occasion Mr Valentine stopped a lesson halfway through and sent the pupils back to their classroom because they were noisy in the gym. When a teacher says 'jump' pupils must move, and when s/he says 'freeze' they must stop in all types of classroom. The pupil who does not move in the teacher-approved fashion incurs staff wrath, and may suffer another prescribed form of movement – the punishment detail.

Moving as punishment

Moving pupils is one way teachers have of punishing them. If one or more pupils appear to be concentrating more on their neighbours than the lesson, and there are spare desks/seats, shifting a child is a common sanction. For example:

> Melin Court, French – Mr Haydon
> Wayne reprimanded for disturbing Eamonn. Mr Haydon moves Wayne to the back of the room to sit on the bench.

> Melin Court, French – Mrs Zeldin
> One boy is being very silly. Mrs Zeldin moves him to the front. The class is very fidgety – Liam and Mervyn are fighting. Mrs Zeldin tells them off.

> Melin Court, History – Mrs Newbolt
> Three boys (Lloyd, Melvyn and Wayne) are fidgeting. Eventually she moves Melvyn to sit near her.

> Melin Court, French – Mr Haydon
> Typical of the treatment meted out to disruptive pupils is Selwyn's fate. He fails to answer a question which has already been answered by one of the girls.
> Mr Haydon: 'Come and sit up here at the front. You must be unable to hear there.'

Such moves not only happen in the classroom, but could be used by teachers to control pupils when outside school. For example when class 1.6 at Guy Mannering went on a trip to the Gas Board Showroom for a cookery demonstration:

> Annabel is in trouble straight away, because as we file into the showroom she inches forward and tries to bag a seat at the front. Mrs Bird hauls her out and makes her stand at the back so she will be last and will sit next to her!

Sometimes teachers use the threat of a seat change as a 'desist' (Kounin, 1967). At Waverly, for example, Miss Lawrence one of the English teachers, on one occasion focused on an inattentive boy: 'Are you listening, Ivor? Otherwise I might have to move you to another desk.' And in a later lesson she 'threatened to move Donald from his partner for not working'. A teacher may also keep specific pupils apart for disciplinary reasons, for example:

> At Kenilworth when Mr Gordon arrived ten minutes late to teach 1 zeta English, saying that he was sorry, the children filed in and sat down. Arnold and Kevin sat together, and Mr Gordon separated them telling them that he had already told them not to sit together.

Similarly, Mrs Forrest at Guy Mannering at one stage made Rhoda sit on her own because 'she can't have been listening in class which is why her homework was very bad'. In this case, the strategy failed, because moving Rhoda away from other children was not effective in getting her to focus on the maths task.

One variation on the use of punishment by movement was observed when Miss O'Hara taught her own form, 1.6, at Guy Mannering. This class included two particularly difficult pupils, Dirk and Annabel. One observer attended an English lesson including a spelling test:

> Dirk is still sitting by himself in the front. Annabel has been made to stand up. I don't know why, but every time she begins to half-sit, Miss O'Hara calls out 'Stand up, Annabel.'

The class are given a ten-item spelling test, and when they have changed papers and marked the test, Miss O'Hara announces that anyone who got 10 out of 10 gets a credit. The observer commented:

> Interestingly, she tells anyone who got two more marks than the last time to stand up. Paula and Annabel both did, and stand. Paula gets a credit but Annabel does not, presumably because Miss O'Hara thought she was standing anyway.

Annabel was not the only 'difficult' child in 1.6, and on another occasion Miss O'Hara used movement as a punishment. Again the occasion was a spelling test, but this time oral not written:

> It is the sit-down game, you sit down when you get one wrong . . . Lionel is turning round and fooling. Miss O'Hara says to him 'What did he say?' {i.e. the answer just given by another boy}. When Lionel can't answer she tells him to sit down.
> Lionel: 'That's not fair.'
> Miss O'Hara: 'It is, you were talking.'

115

The use of standing up or sitting down as a visible form of competition has already been discussed in chapter 4 – but here *sitting down*, not for answering wrong but as a punishment, is only usable because the class are standing up. More active movement than merely standing or changing seats is sometimes used as a form of punishment. Two examples from Guy Mannering will illustrate the point. During boys' football with Mr Sturgess-Jones the observer wrote:

> The boys in the other game are fooling around while the teams are being picked. Mr Sturgess-Jones sends them off for two laps round the field to 'cool themselves off' before starting the (soccer) game.

Guy Mannering also used movement as a punishment for boys who were caught fighting. When we interviewed Amos, a pupil in the ORACLE sample, he was asked if he was keen on sport. He replied that he was 'a bit keen, not when it's cold.' When asked what school rules and punishments there were Amos gave as one rule: 'You must not fight in the changing rooms,' and as one punishment: 'You have to run round the park.'

Ashburton has several parks, and Guy Mannering middle and lower schools are set on one edge of Castle Park, which contained the ruins of the medieval castle, the town museum, and a small lake. The interviewer thought it unlikely that 9-year-olds would be punished this way, and:

> I queried this, and he said it happened the day before the interview. Some boys were fighting in the changing rooms and so all the boys had to run round the park. I asked Amos how he felt about having to run when he had not been fighting, and he said he felt 'horrible'.

Long-distance runs are part of the mythology of transfer for boys (Measor and Woods, 1983), either as a routine or as a punishment they are seen as a way of testing 'toughness':

> Many boys repeated with some alarm that . . . you were frequently expected to go on long distance runs, especially if there was snow on the ground. Mark said 'and they say you have to run to Brookfield (a village about five miles away from the school). I didn't fancy running to Brookfield and back – it's nearly five miles!'

Running can also be punishment for the ethnographer. John Beynon's (1983) research at Victoria Road Boys' School, found that cross country runs were the 'mark of a man'. By running himself Beynon managed to prove to the PE master, Mr Megaphone, that he was no seven-stone weakling:

116

Movement and immobility in the new schools

I carried through my pledge to accompany 1X through all their contacts with
teachers . . . even if this meant going swimming . . . and running a cross
country each week! After one tortuous cross country I was sitting in the
staffroom . . . clearly the worse for wear. Mr Megaphone shouted across the
room: 'Look at old Beynon there, dripping sweat everywhere! He's just run a
few miles and learnt what a PE teacher's life is like!'

Beynon managed to turn this into a classic staffroom joke, by
retorting: 'It was carrying you on my back did it.' This established
rapport with Mr Megaphone, who said to Beynon later that:

'It was going to the baths and on cross countries that did it . . . even if that
meant slogging through the mud in Seaview Park. It was that which tipped the
scales in your favour.'

The relationship between punishment and sport is discussed in
Delamont (1980a), focusing both on pupils and researchers in boys'
schools. However it is not only male researchers who may be forced
to play games as a price of ethnographic access, for Llewellyn (1980)
was put onto the hockey pitch at the girls' secondary modern she
studied. It is important to recognize that movement and immobility
can both be forms of punishment, for pupils or observers, and both
deserve attention. Not all pupils like the movements expected of
them in PE. Lester, the boy with brain damage in Maid Marion, told
the interviewer that he did not like PE, which he finds very hard.
The researcher commented that 'I don't think he is very well
co-ordinated.' Lester went on that 'he does not like the master, Mr
Weir, who also, he feels, shouts at him.' Other pupils, of course,
value the opportunities for learning particular skilled movements in
PE very highly. In Lester's class this reaction was reported by
Gerard who wrote:

I think the PE lessons should be longer . . . The things I like are the PE
lessons because there are better fersilitis (sic). You also learn better ways to
play the sports.

A similar viewpoint was expressed by Julia, a girl in their class, who
enjoyed PE.

Before leaving movement as punishment, we need to examine
errands. There is no systematic data available on how teachers and
pupils see running errands. Some participants may see running an
errand as an example of teacher favouritism, others as a form of
punishment. When Miss Tweed at Gryll Grange sent Davina to the
school office with attendance numbers and dinner money it is clear
that she intends it as a mark of favour, and Davina saw it that way.
Other examples we have are less clear.

117

Movement and immobility in the new schools

At Maid Marion, going on errands was apparently seen by staff as a sign of teacher favour. For when staff wanted to change the behaviour of some boys who had made a bad start, one strategy was 'giving them responsibility'. So the science master, Mr Salter now sends Harry and Greg on special errands to fetch things or do things for him.'

In contrast, at Guy Mannering, it appears that at least some pupils saw being asked to run errands as a negative experience. At the end of January (four full months after transfer) an observer was watching Mr Evans teach 1.5 English:

> Mr Evans asks Gavin Radice to take Mr Black a note. 'You know where Mr Black's room is.' 'No' says Gavin and is clearly reluctant to go. Others put their hands up and with a gesture of disbelief at Gavin. Mr Evans gives the note to someone else.

Meanwhile in 1.6, Mrs Evans was sending Crispin on errands for her as a mark of favour, to try and improve his behaviour. There is a gap in our knowledge here which further systematic study could usefully address.

The chapter so far has dealt with movement and immobility in the playground, in corridors, in special classrooms where it is enjoined, and as a form of punishment. The data reveal that there are sex differences in playground use, ability differences in PE, and that controlling pupil movement is an important task for staff. The chapter now turns to the persistent belief that primary and middle school classrooms are full of uncontrolled movement, while in secondary or upper schools pupils are required to sit still.

Transfer to immobility

Teachers in the six transfer schools, like their colleagues in other 'secondary' schools, believe that children in infant, first and junior schools have freedom of movement, which they lose when they transfer to secondary or upper schools. Thus Mr Salter, a science teacher at Maid Marion, told the observer one of the things he felt that the children found most difficult was to adjust to the fact that no movement was allowed in a science lab, or certainly very little. Mr Salter felt that the children were very used to being allowed to move around their junior class, but this could not be so in a science lab, because of the safety factor. Mr Salter is not alone either in his belief that lower schools allow pupils unlimited movement, or in his determination to curtail it in his class. Stillman and Maychell (1984: 96) report that on the Isle of Wight, secondary school teachers had a 'stereotyped image of middle school teaching (which) portrays a scene of noisy classrooms, with children freely wandering around'. These secondary teachers believe that 'the pupils have to be trained to sit still and concentrate in high school lessons'. In fact, Stillman and Maychell maintain, classroom practices in the top of middle schools and the bottom of high schools are essentially similar, and the secondary teachers have no basis for their vision – which is 'a demeaning stereotype' of the middle school. Indeed, in many ways the secondary school allows *more* pupil movement, because children get up and go at the end of each lesson, rather than being fixed in one room all day. As we unveil the detailed analysis of movement and immobility in various locations in the ORACLE schools' subjects and time zones around the school, the simplistic idea that middle schools allow less movement than first schools, or upper schools less than middle schools, will be dispelled.

To scrutinize the myths about movement and immobility we have to do two things. It is necessary to show how much legitimated and illicit pupil movement actually takes place in 'primary type' classes, and to see how much goes on in the 'secondary type' classrooms where it is supposed to be non-existent. When this comparison is made it transpires that the amount of licit and illicit movement by pupils in classrooms across our six schools varies from one teacher to another, *not* from one school type to another. That is, pupils are allowed to move in one lesson and not in another within one school – and there are staff too weak to stop pupil movement in all types of school.

It is also crucial to realise that both movement and immobility are culturally and situationally specific. What is normal in one culture, or in one location within a culture, may be deviant in another culture, or another location. Wylie (1974), an American, did an ethnography of a French village, and commented on the stillness of French children compared with American ones. In a subsequent work the same point was made by Zeldin (1983: 41) as follows:

> The French seem to be in control of their muscles in a way relaxed Americans are incapable of achieving. Traditional French chairs are straight and uncomfortable, as though they are made for people who can hold themselves straight when they sit.

The British cultural assumption about a lesson in an ordinary classroom (i.e. not a gym or a pottery room) is that children will be relatively stationary, movement is under the teacher's control, and that learning is accomplished best in stillness. Thus for example at St Luke's, the expensive, academic, Scottish girls' school studied by Delamont (1983a: 11), a Greek lesson was described as follows:

Movement and immobility in the new schools

It is very quiet. No one in the room moves or speaks, though occasional shouts can be heard from outside. Three teenage girls are sitting bent over their books, while an elderly spinster sits facing them, intent on her work.

The three girls were academically successful, and they spent many hours silent and still, because that is how 'learning' is done. Yet even within Britain there are two types of school where learning is associated with movement: Jewish and Islamic schools. In both traditions, learning involves both chanting, and movement. Koranic memorization has been studied by Eickelman (1978), and Australian Chassidic Judaism by Bullivant (1978: 110–13).

Learning is also highly physical. In strict rabbinical tradition, learning new knowledge is achieved by vocalizing aloud . . . The strong kinesthetic component in learning is evident in the ubiquitous body swaying that accompanies reading, whether aloud or silently. Even if a person reads silently, his lips move, and he sways in time with the rhythm of the words . . . The intellectual hub of the school is the *Yeshivah Gedolah* . . . Students study individually rocking backwards and forwards in their seats . . .

Thus the Islamic and the Chassidic scholarly traditions associate successful scholarship with both movement and noise: with rocking and chanting. The signs of a successful Koranic class would be seen as symptoms of a failure of discipline in the British school. The regulation of pupils' movements by their teachers is therefore a culturally specific phenomenon, not a universal one.

The stereotyped view of the transfer from lower to upper school in Britain is one of a shift from classrooms where movement is allowed to those where it is not. At first glance our observations support this, so that after a few days in Maid Marion one of the observers commented that 'every lesson was class taught and very few teachers allowed any talking and none allowed any movement around the classroom except Mr Barrel.' The stereotyped view, held for example by the secondary teachers studied by Stillman and Maychell (1984), would lead us to expect that Gryll Grange (APT), the only purpose-built middle school, would be the only one where freedom of movement was encouraged. Certainly two of our three sample teachers at Gryll Grange did allow a good deal of movement as we show below, but it would be quite erroneous to suppose that, when examined in detail, there is not a great deal of movement in the classrooms of the five transfer schools which officially discouraged it. Certainly, all six schools are quite unlike St Luke's, the girls' public school studied by Delamont (1983a), where pupils actually sat immobile for 40-minute lessons. In our six schools there are all kinds of movement routinely going on in most lessons. Visitors come and go, pupils enter and leave, teachers organize the pupils into different kinds of movement, and the adolescents themselves change places, shuffle, fidget, and are generally restless. Immobility is very rare.

Our analysis of legitimate and illegitimate movement in and around ordinary classrooms begins with some observations from Gryll Grange, in the archetypical 'primary type' room. The pupils were doing individualized work in maths and English.

> Gryll Grange, 1H, Mrs Hind, 23rd September
> I see a boy measuring the floor, presumably as part of a maths exercise. In one direction he can use the edge of the carpet as a straight edge but in the other there is nothing and you can see him measuring rather haphazardly at about 30° from the vertical. After a short time the noise rises and Mrs Hind shouts, 'Now stop it.' She is trying to mark the English books. Some boys on the far side are playing aeroplanes with their protractors. The noise rises again, 'Yes, it's you Amy. Stop it!' shouts Mrs H and the noise drops again. One of the biggest disrupting effects is the use of felt pens. Only some children have them whereas in 1.5 at Guy Mannering most have their own. So any time anybody wants to carry out some colouring they go round the class attempting to borrow the felt pens. This can take up to three to four minutes while those concerned talk and fool around, etc. One boy, Raymond, has got the ink from felt tips all over his hands. He is sent out to wash. So far he hasn't done anything and its now 9.45.
> Another girl comes back to her place from having her work checked by Mrs Hind at the desk and she doesn't need to copy it out because it was so good. She comes back, tells her friend and then sits back and watches them copy out their work . . . I begin to watch the boy with the inky fingers, Raymond.
> 9.50 Still has not begun.
> 9.53 Gets felt tip from someone and begins to work.
> 9.55 Up again. Goes to change books. Gets out another maths book. Goes to teacher, asks question.

So far Mrs Hind's class can be seen to contain at least two kinds of pupil movement – legitimate and illegitimate. The boy measuring the floor, and the girl leaving the teacher's desk to return to her own table are meant to be moving. The playing of 'aeroplanes', and some of Raymond's moves, are *not* meant to be happening. Taking both kinds together, there is a good deal of pupil movement in the room.

> 9.57 Raymond is up again. Back in the queue for the teacher.
> 9.58 Teacher tells Raymond what to do. He is up again to borrow a pencil from a tin on the teacher's desk. During this time, Amy has been called to task and told to bring out her work for fooling.
> 10.02 Raymond is still fooling with a neighbour. Amy is being moved from her friends on to the table with Raymond. She is still adjacent to her friends, however, and can talk across the space between tables.
> 10.06 Raymond is spotted at last, fighting with a ruler.

Mrs H: 'Come out here and let me see your hands. (He had the ink on them before). What did you get on here? Go back to your place and get on with your work. You big looney!' (The class laughs at this).

10.08 Raymond is out again in the teacher's queue. Seems to have some work for marking, and it must have been yesterday's.

10.10 The book is marked. He puts it away and goes to get another one.

10.11 Raymond is fooling again. Throws his rubber on the floor and goes over to retrieve it. He starts talking to the children at the next table and stops them working.

10.13 The bright girl is beginning some maths work. (She is drawing her feet on a piece of paper.)

10.14 Raymond is up again talking at another table. He is carrying out some work whereby you have to ask everyone what they came to school on. It takes a long time and every time he stops one child he has a chat and a fool.

10.18 Raymond is working now. He is collecting the data and entering it into his book. He seems quite keen on this task. It's obvious that this suits his temperament since he is able to get up and go wherever he wants to in the class. Everywhere he goes he creates a little pocket of distraction.

10.26 Raymond has finished off his bit of the survey. Now he is chatting again. The girl who was measuring the feet is now using her diagram to measure the size of the board, to measure the cupboard, etc.

10.31 Raymond is moving around again. Mrs H dismisses them and tells them to go out and play.

The record of the lesson, focused on Raymond, contains many points which would confirm the secondary teachers studied by Stillman and Maychell (1984) in their worst suspicions, about primary and middle school teachers. Yet we found both other staff at Gryll Grange who allowed less movement, and teachers at Waverly and Melin Court who allowed as much. Freedom of movement is yet another area where each teacher draws his or her own lines, and children have to learn where each one's limits are. For example, at Gryll Grange we watched three teachers who had different attitudes to pupil movement. Mr Valentine was much less tolerant of pupil movement than Mrs Hind and Miss Tweed, and this led to confusion for the children when the teachers swapped classes. In his own room, 1V, Mr Valentine began the school year by trying to stop pupils leaving for the lavatory during classtime:

> There is a constant trickle of pupils going out to the lavatory. Mr Valentine is trying to stop it. Pupils have to ask, and he says 'Can't you wait till lunch?' and 'Did you go at break?'

Miss Tweed, on the other hand, had specifically told her class *not* to ask, but to go quickly and without a fuss, as they would at home. One day when Mr Valentine was teaching Miss Tweed's class, there was clash of regime:

> Stirling just walks out. Mr Valentine stops him, and says that he is not to

leave the room without asking. Alan says that Miss Tweed says they should just go.

Miss Tweed and Mrs Hind were the only teachers in our sample who did allow pupils free access to the lavatories during class time. In all the other schools, teachers were like Mr Valentine.

> Kenilworth, 1 zeta science Mr Pardoe
> A boy asked to go to the lavatory and Mr Pardoe said that if it was very urgent he could, but it would be highly irregular. He would rather that the boy waited if he could.
>
> Guy Mannering, 1.4 English Mr Evans
> He is reluctant to let a little girl go to the lavatory. 'You ought to go at break.'
>
> Waverly, ILE chemistry Mr Darwin
> Girl asks if she can go to the toilet. Told to wait.

Leaving the room for any other purpose was also forbidden and, this rule was established early in the school year at all the schools except Gryll Grange. For example at Maid Marion, on the first day Miss Square told her form:

> 'Don't just whip out of the room, you must always ask first.' This was prompted by a child who had raced off to his locker to fetch a pen in order to write something in his rough book.

However, apart from forbidding pupils to leave the room without permission, other teachers apart from Miss Hind and Miss Tweed actually had a good deal of movement in and around their classes, although it was not planned for, any more than Raymond's was in Mrs Hind's room. For example, one single French lesson with Mr Haydon at Melin Court showed many kinds of movement, licit and illicit. During one period the following incidents were recorded:

(1) One boy surreptitiously changed his seat several times without Mr Haydon noticing.
(2) A boy interrupts to borrow a chair to take into another room.
(3) Another master tiptoes through the room (which is a short cut to another classroom).
(4) Another master comes in and has a conversation with Mr Haydon at the front.
(5) Pupils shuffle and whisper. Lesson goes on. Mr Haydon calls for volunteers to get up, and
(6) Go over to '*Touchez la porte*'. Two boys volunteer.
(7) Rest of lesson consists of pupils getting up and going to touch things: doors (there are 3 in the room), windows, walls, chairs, books, etc.

Here we can see how there *is* movement in an ordinary lesson. In an ideal school (2) would not happen because all rooms would have enough furniture; (3) because all classrooms would be self-contained and private; (4) because all staff discussion would happen outside lessons, and only 6/7 would occur. In real schools, such movements happen in nearly every class. Interruptions and visitors were reported as frequent occurrences from primary schools by Hilsum and Cane (1971), and are equally common in the ORACLE schools: for example typical interruptions were:

> Waverly, German with Mr Mowbray and Hector (the assistant)
> Mr Bronte comes in about a lost jumper. Mr Mowbray and Mr Bronte inspect all the boys' jumpers. Don't find the missing jumper in the class.

> Guy Mannering, 1.5 geography Mr Evans
> For about a quarter of an hour Mr Evans talks to them about Australia, using his imagination to fill out the rather drab paragraphs in their geography books . . . During this time there is an interruption when Mrs Bird comes in and asks Mr Evans to go out with her to deal with two boys who have been fighting.

> Waverly, needlework Miss Bobbin
> Mr Spencer comes in with a stray girl. The class remain seated. He says 'You should be on your feet, now, girls.'

Notes that Mr Spencer not only interrupts Miss Bobbin's class physically – he also tells her class how to behave. Shuffling and fidgeting were regular features of many lessons in the six schools:

> Guy Mannering, maths Mr Apter 1.6
> As they work most of them rock on their chairs. (You wouldn't get this in 1.5.)

> Melin Court, history Mrs Newbolt
> They are not to do anything whilst she is talking and because they do she will break off from time to time to say 'Put that pencil down.' etc.

> Melin Court, geography Mr Braund
> The class is very restless. 'Will you stop moving your desks and chairs around and settle down.' Selwyn and Melvyn are sitting together and having great fun bouncing the double desk around.

Even in those classes where there were no interruptions and little shuffling or fidgeting, secondary teachers actually used movement as part of the lesson quite frequently. For example:

> Kenilworth, French 1 gamma Mrs Stockton
> Mrs Stockton arrived, said '*Bonjour, mes enfants*' – asked them all to say '*Bonjour*' to their friend and shake hands.

124

Melin Court, English Mrs Hammond
Halfway through the double period, Mrs Hammond says 'Right. Half-time.
Give your brains a shake!'

Waverly, cookery Mrs Sutcliffe
Emptying waste explained – procedure for disposing of different waste foods.
All go off outside to have a look at the dustbins.

Waverly, English Miss Lawrence
Asks one boy to open some windows, at the back. Six boys get up and have a
walk and a chat as well.

Waverly, maths Mr Jessop
'Now, no talking. Anyone with a problem come out to me.' Eight children
form a queue immediately.

Handling queuing in maths lessons was a particular problem for
all the teachers we saw. All maths teachers needed to check pupils'
work, and provide help, either by having a queue or by moving
around the class themselves. Both strategies can cause problems for
the teacher. Mrs Forrest, at Guy Mannering, began the year by
moving round the room to check the children's work, and solve
their problems. They were not allowed to leave their seats, but had
to put a hand up when stuck. By the summer term she had changed
and the observer wrote 'Mrs Forrest has given up running round the
class and now lets the children come up to her'. If the teacher moves
much of the room is not subject to her scrutiny; if she allows pupils
to come up and queue, they have an excuse to leave their seats.
Either way, disruption can follow. For the pupils, being *seen* to
move by the teacher typically results in having one's work scrutinized and/or being reprimanded. At Kenilworth, for example, in
1 zeta's maths with Mrs Lee:

> Maurice spent most of his time wandering around borrowing a ruler and
> chatting . . . Mrs Lee became aware of Maurice and his wanderings about
> and told him to stop wasting time. He must give the ruler back and sit down.

The same boy was later seen wandering in Mrs Cullen's geography
class:

> They are working on 'My route to school'. Maurice was out of his place –
> getting a pencil from another child. When she asked him what he was doing
> he gave her a very surly answer, turning his back on Mrs Cullen and walking
> away.

Mrs Cullen took this as a justification for a severe reprimand, but it
did not deter other pupils, for later in the lesson 'Several children
were wandering about. Mrs Cullen told Michael not to keep

wandering out of his place.' Similar incidents were reported from the other schools:

Melin Court, maths Mr Clift
'Selwyn, what are you doing up? There is really no need for you to be over there.' Selwyn is the one boy who sits by himself and he seems to be the only one who isn't allowed to move around freely. He goes out to the board with his book and the master explains how to do one of the sums.

Melin Court, RE Mrs Durrant
Two boys get up and walk around looking for their books. Mrs Durrant says that in future they must put up their hands: 'We must have a certain amount of order.'

In these incidents we see the staff trying to control pupil movement. However, the amount of movement which resulted depended on the degree of control the staff were able to exert, and wanted to achieve, not on the particular school. There was less movement in Mr Valentine's room at Gryll Grange than in Mr Astill's maths lesson at Waverly, because Mr Valentine both demanded, and got, less movement. There is no simple relationship between school organization and either legitimate and illegitimate pupil activity.

Conclusion

This chapter has analysed the relationship between pupil movement and teacher control in several areas of the six schools. It has shown that the transferring pupils have to learn several new kinds of movement, from the Luton Airport syndrome to specialist PE skills, as well as mastering remaining still in certain key environments. For the staff, control over the pupils' movements is one of the key elements in maintaining both their discipline and their status with colleagues. Pupils have to learn a variety of school-specific, context-specific, and teacher-specific rules about movement; and can expect a variety of movement-related punishments if they break them. This chapter has not exhausted the topics of movement and immobility in the school, but it has opened up several neglected aspects to scrutiny and analysis.

CHAPTER 6

Speed merchants and slow coaches: time in the new schools

In the morning if you get them the first two or three periods they're very docile. I think they're half asleep, some of them, and you can usually get down to it fairly quickly and quietly. In the afternoons they're jumpier. Eh, it's more difficult to read anything, it's more difficult to do anything which is silent. They're prepared to do drama, to act out and to have quizzes and things, anything which is lively but it's impossible to work. I mean, I do, I work it along these lines. They do all the hard work in the morning and they do lighter things in the afternoon. But it's unfortunate if you have the same class all the time in the afternoon.

(Corrie *et al.*, 1982, p. 18)

In this quote from a Scottish secondary teacher we see the central theme of this chapter: time as a factor in school life. Although time is a recurrent theme in medical sociology (e.g. Roth, 1963 and Zerubavel, 1979), educational researchers have been relatively uninterested in time as a factor in school life except for a chapter by Meighan (1981) and set of American studies reviewed by Karweit (1981). Here we focus on several previously under-explored aspects of school time, as well as those highlighted by Ball *et al.* (1984) in their paper 'The tyranny of the "devil's mill".' That paper draws attention to the pressures placed on teachers by the timetabling of school activities. In this chapter we examine the pressures on a teacher's management skills that time imposes, both in terms of getting the pupils through the lesson, the week, the term, the year, and in terms of managing to keep a class working together. Staff management of pacing relates to two aspects of *pupil* time: the way in which the timing allowed for tasks in school marks them as 'work' or 'pleasure', and the relationship between speed and ability. For pupils, tasks which must be completed are work, not leisure; and the relative speed at which you and your classmates complete the assignments is the best available guide to ability.

127

Time in the new schools

Zerubavel's (1979) detailed case study of how time is a significant organizational feature of hospital life provides us with a perspective for examining how teachers' and pupils' lives are temporally structured. Of course teachers are not the only occupational group to be tightly ruled by a timetable. Gamst's (1980: 34) ethnography of railway workers in the USA emphasizes the enormous impact of the rail timetable on the lives of the employees. So much importance is attached to time that when a new employee started to work on the trains, he

> purchased one of several varieties of officially authorised watches of railroad grade. The watch serves as a badge of office of a rail {way worker} and its use while on duty is required of operating employees.

Not only is a watch required, it is a dismissible offence to carry an inaccurate watch, and senior employees check the timekeeping of other workers' watches periodically. Gamst also discusses the impact of the published timetables on the men's working lives (1980: 75).

Railroad schedules are more demanding, but essentially similar to the timetables governing the teachers' daily and weekly routines. Teachers are also governed by longer cycles, of terms, years, and pupil career cycles. In these respects their lives are similar to those of construction workers studied by Applebaum (1981: 49–50), who points out that:

> Every construction project has a limited time frame. It has been estimated that for a 10- to 20-million dollar contract, it takes approximately ten years to conceive, plan, design, finance and build it . . . During the construction process, there are several crucial beginnings and endings affecting interlocking phases of the work.

Such a lengthy timetable is similar to a teacher seeing a cohort of children through their school from first to sixth form, as the staff of our six schools did during our research period and as the ORACLE project has done. This chapter examines the impact of timetabling on the classroom lives of teachers and pupils. We look in turn at the daily, weekly, termly, and annual cycles of school life, starting with the pattern of the school year.

The annual cycle
Any reader who has attended a British school will have 'recognized' the beginning of a new school year in chapter 3, when new classes meet new teachers, and the autumn term gets going. Our data on the resumption of the schools' annual cycle was overshadowed by its

Time in the new schools

novelty for our sample of pupils. In this section we show how quickly the ORACLE pupils became routine members of their new schools, caught up in the *normal* routine of the school year.

The British school year has been largely taken for granted by researchers, and is therefore 'invisible'. It is rarely even noticed that the school year in Scotland is different from many parts of England and Wales. Yet as Karweit (1981) points out, different school districts have years of varying lengths and the total time spent in lessons also varies a great deal from school to school. She reports that the length of the school year is 175 days in some states and 184 in others, *and* that the number of days when school actually functioned was further cut by: 'teachers' strikes, early school closings due to financial or fuel shortages, or a shortened term due to severe weather conditions.' The length of the school year then varies again because of the number of hours in each school day which can, over a year, produce imbalances between different states, school districts and neighbourhoods. Karweit quotes Maryland, where the elementary school day varies from 240 to 410 minutes, and the high school day from 300 to 375 minutes. Hilsum and Cane (1971) found that in one LEA the primary school day varied from 375 to 430 minutes in length, which results in a school year over four weeks shorter.

Such variations in the length of the school year are one way of forcing us to make its structure problematic. Jacquetta Burnett (1969) has focused on the rituals and ceremonial that mark the cycle of the school year for the students in an American high school (Valentine's day, junior prom, halloween, Thanksgiving) but no similar work has been done in the UK. To force ourselves to see the school year in Britain as problematic, it is instructive to compare the cycle in our six schools with that of the Lubavitcher School in Australia described by Bullivant (1978). This Orthodox Jewish school has a yearly rhythm governed by the religious and the secular events which impinge on the staff and pupils. The secular school year is punctuated by terms starting and ending, by tests, by exams, and by speech night. The religious calendar, more important than the secular at Lubavitcher School moves from *Purim*, through Passover, Tammuz, *Rosh Hashanah*, *Yom Kippur* through to *Succos* and *Simchas Torah*. Its dominance over the secular concerns of schooling, including public examinations, is chronicled by Bullivant. The rhythm of the year in a school without a religious affiliation is thrown into relief by Bullivant's account. He, as a non-Jew, was unprepared for the way in which anticipation of festivals such as *Rosh Hashanah* disrupted the secular work:

Time in the new schools

On the day before *Rosh Hashanah* work is clearly impossible. In any case, lessons finish at 1 p.m. . . . . For the sixth form, work is . . . impossible, and they say so firmly. (p. 174)

The yearly cycle in British schools has its origins in an agricultural cycle, far removed from the consciousness of today's urban teachers and pupils. Some of the holidays are attached to Christian festivals, but others have no link with them: so that the half-term break in the summer rarely coincides with the actual Whitsun dates, but is a secular holiday. It is clear from Burgess's (1983: 35–6) ethnography of a Roman Catholic comprehensive school that even in that denominational school the secular year dominated the liturgical cycle. While the headmaster tried to get his staff to emphasize the annual events in the church's year inside the school, Burgess reports that few staff obliged him, except those who taught religious knowledge. The yearly cycle of the six ORACLE schools can be seen in our fieldnotes. When the autumn term and the school year begin, the major emphasis is placed upon setting out the rules and procedures – including the weekly and daily timetables – which will govern the pupils' behaviour. Then the routine work proceeds, leading to Halloween, bonfire night and half-term. Then the build-up to Christmas intensifies, with rehearsals and carol concerts. The spring term means 'mock' exams for older pupils and is also the longest and dreariest term in British schools. The summer is characterized by its sports day, and the elongated period of public examinations. The impact of this yearly cycle on teachers' and pupils' lives and on interaction has been largely unexamined, although it is a frequent subject of conversation in staffrooms.

Zerubavel (1979) has examined the impact of the yearly cycle on hospital life and medical personnel, and his scrutiny of a cycle we normally take for granted offers us a way of highlighting yearly cycles in school. Zerubavel points out that young doctors' careers are structured in annual segments: the internship year, the junior residency, and so on, and that the yearly cycle of the American teaching hospital runs from July to July, and is out of phase with both the secular year (January to January) and the academic year (September to September). Thus hospitals, and doctors' careers, are based on an annual cycle different from the wider society. If we force ourselves to think about the school year in this way, we can see both that the cohort to which the pupil belongs is significant for him (a theme we address in chapter 7), and that at several stages in the teacher's career the specific year is significant. The probationary year, and the first year of teaching after it, are significant milestones in the teacher's career (Peterson, 1964; Hanson and Herrington,

1976; Lacey, 1977; Hannam *et al.*, 1976; Woods *et al.*, 1985). Thus for Mr Rutherford and Mrs Lake at Waverly, our sample pupils were the first to enter the school and find them already established, because they had been probationers the previous year. Mr Valentine at Gryll Grange was in his probationary year, and so the ORACLE project decided not to observe routinely in his class. Gryll Grange also had a new headmaster and deputy head (Mr Judge and Mr Forrest) and for them, too, the year of our research was a significant one – their first year as a head and as a deputy. Maid Marion, too, had a new headmaster, Mr Underwood, and all these three newcomers changed our sample schools. Mr Judge introduced a uniform at Gryll Grange, and Mr Underwood announced that he was changing Maid Marion from a primary type organization to a secondary type, based on subject rooms with the pupils moving rather than the teachers.

For other teachers the year of our fieldwork was significant as the last year of their careers. At Guy Mannering Mr LeGard was due to retire, so our sample were the last children he would introduce to the library and the bible. At Gryll Grange it was to be the last year in teaching for Mr Hogg, the head of the lower school, and senior PE master in the school. Mr Hogg actually died during the year, leaving Miss Tweed to be promoted to the head of lower school post, the advanced swimming group without its main coach, and one of those enduring school jokes analysed by Walker and Adelman (1976). The observer who visited Gryll Grange after Mr Hogg's death heard the joke, and had it explained as follows:

> Gryll Grange – Miss Tweed's class
> The atmosphere is very relaxed. When Miss Tweed comes back she tells them its mental arithmetic books. Hugh can't find his mental book. 'I'll do it in my jotter' he says and everybody laughs. Miss Tweed turns to me and says 'You won't understand this but the teacher who died last year was deaf and the children were always playing him up and coming up and saying "Should I do it in my English book, maths book, etc?" and he would always reply "Do it in your jotter." Then one day a boy came to his desk side and said "Can I go to the toilet?" and Mr Hogg replied "Do it in your jotter." '

In such ways do old teachers leave the occupation, with the school enduring and their memory lingering on.

Not only did several of the teachers in our sample schools, then, experience our fieldwork period as a significant period in their careers. For all teachers, the school year has its own rhythm, and this certainly deserves further attention along the lines Zerubavel (1979) has pioneered. Within the hospital year lie the staff rotations, and within the school year, the three terms to which we now turn.

Terms and vacations

The school and university year in Britain is divided into three terms and these are so taken for granted that it is hard to realize that they are entirely arbitrary. Stirling University's decision to adopt two American semesters is largely unknown to outsiders, and it comes as a shock to realize that the three-term system is a relatively novel one. Yet, as Dorothea Beale pointed out in 1904, the introduction of the three-term year was one of the many reforms of the mid-nineteenth century. When she became principal of Cheltenham Ladies College in 1858:

> The college had four terms in the year, and one difficulty was that some parents would give notice at Easter, because they wished to stay at the sea for part of the autumn quarter, and thus save a quarter of the fees. When the college grew more independnet, we refused to re-enter those who played this trick, and at length the three terms were introduced. In those days, holidays were very rare and the work went on from January to June, with only three or four days at Easter.
>
> (Beale, 1904: 25)

As the ORACLE fieldwork was concentrated on the first weeks of the autumn term, we have little to say on the termly cycle, except that the schools were firmly fixed into it! The shorter visits to the schools in the spring and summer terms show the pupils settling in more and more thoroughly, and the end of the summer term a relaxed atmosphere. The end of the year at Gryll Grange was marked by one activity inconceivable at the beginning:

> Gryll Grange – Miss Tweed's class
> They get out their ordinary exercise books for arithmetic and receive an amazing instruction: 'Tear up your old maths books. You are not allowed to take them home. Then you can do the same for English.'

As the observer watched the following pupil conversation was overheard:

> 'All this horrible work going to waste.'
> 'Yes but we know more than we did.'
> 'I know fractions.'

This was clearly a terminal action – destroying the year's work.

Measor and Woods (1984) who followed their pupils throughout their first year in their transfer school, argue that the start of the second term is a significant event for new pupils. In the autumn term they are still 'new', but once they return after Christmas school is 'just everyday life now really' (p. 74). For pupils a new term can be a chance to make a 'fresh start', and try to change their behaviour, friends, or work habits. One boy, Floyd, in 1 zeta at Kenilworth, catches the sense of the new term as an opportunity for a fresh start. In his essay he wrote (with his spelling retained):

> Most work we did as a class was very easy as i went throug my year at school . . . But after awhile i started to slip up on my work i started to get told off. and a ventualy i got lines and things started to get rough i had to stay in at breaks and dinners in some cases it was alright i could get on with my subjects . . . When that tearm was over i came back and started fresh again and from then until now I have worke well . . . The school motto is *Strive to succeed.*

Measor and Woods suggest that by February pupils are feeling secure enough to challenge their teachers' regimes. For the teachers, then, the spring term saw the pupils becoming more difficult to control, as their initial nervousness faded. The summer term, Measor and Woods argue, is when the pupils begin to diverge into those who will reject the school's regime and those who will conform to it. They have survived the transfer, and are 'on their way'. Measor and Woods summarize this as follows:

> (The pupils') successful negotiation of the passage is symbolized by the preparations being made for the imminent arrival of the next cohort . . . Soon they will cease to be 'first years', let alone new arrivals . . . This cycle is matched by developments in the school year . . . in the second half of the summer term, there is a general air of relaxation in the school, especially after the examination period. Sports' days, field trips, camping excursions leaven the more serious academic pursuits. (p. 109)

The three terms then have their own rhythms, as does the week, to which we now turn.

The weekly schedule

School weeks have a rhythm and tempo of their own. One of the main differences between primary schools and the middle or secondary schools to which our sample were moving was the imposition of a weekly timetable with different activities on different days. In primary schools, one day is similar to another, and it is relatively unimportant if a child thinks Monday is Tuesday or *vice versa*. At their new schools, learning the timetable and being confident about the day of the week and its consequences becomes more important. The most complicated timetable, and hence the one reproduced here (Figure 6.1), was at Melin Court, which operated a 'two-week' timetable cycle. The pupils had to learn not only which day it was, but whether it was week one or week two. As a maths teacher at

Figure 6.1 Melin Court timetable of form 1M

(a) Week One

Day	1	2	BREAK	3	4	LUNCH	5	6	7	8
Monday		PE		Music	French			Craft		Craft
Tuesday		Maths			Science			History		English
Wednesday		Craft		Craft	Science			Maths		English
Thursday	French	Music					Swimming		RE	Geography
Friday		Maths			French			English		RE

(b) Week Two

Day	1	2	BREAK	3	4	LUNCH	5	6	7	8
Monday		PE			Maths		French	Geography		English
Tuesday		Maths			Science					English
Wednesday		Art		Music	French			Craft		Craft
Thursday		History		Geography	French		Swimming		French	Art
Friday		English		RE				Maths		Music

134

Melin Court commented to one of the research team 'It's always chaos at the beginning of term with this two week timetable.' Because it was an unusual system, the staff at Melin Court warned prospective pupils and their parents about the two-week timetable before transfer. For example, at the parents' evening in the summer term before transfer:

> Mrs Hallows went on to describe the two week timetable, and here asked for some help from the parents. If they could go through the timetable the night before with their child and help them to get out the equipment necessary for the next day, this would save a lot of upset. 'We need your support to get them to take their timetables out the night before and make sure that they have the correct equipment.'

The pupils who visited Guy Mannering were told by Miss Tyree that they would 'get their timetable' as a feature of their first day. So when the children from Orton Water Lower School visited Guy Mannering Miss Tyree told them:

> They were to arrive, preferably at 8.50 a.m. on 1st September on the playground and wait until the other children had gone into the school. They would then be called to the hall where the class lists were read. Should their name not be called there was no need to worry as mistakes often occurred. Once allotted to their forms they would spend the first day being given books and writing down the timetable.

Mrs Hallows told the children entering Melin Court the same thing:

> She then continued with the first day routine. They would begin by going in straight into the hall where they would have assembly, from there they would go into their separate classes and she reminded them that they had each been shown where their class would be. In their class, with their class teacher, they would be given their timetable and shown where their locker would be. It appears that would take most of the morning.

With these statements the staff of the transfer schools communicate how important the timetable is in their schools. If merely copying it down takes 'all morning', it must be important, *and* because it covers all the new subjects the pupils will learn, it symbolizes the specialist secondary curriculum. Nor was the promise of spending a whole morning on the timetable and the distribution of exercise books an idle promise.

The first morning of the first day in all the schools but Gryll Grange was devoted to giving the pupils their timetable, as the observer at Maid Marion noted:

> On the first morning when they went into their form rooms to meet their form

teachers the first time, the first hour was devoted to handing out timetables, making sure everyone had plans of the school and other such routines. As in many of the other lessons to follow the emphasis was on speed of carrying out instructions and on low noise level.

This was Miss Square's class, and later in the morning

She reminded the children that pens, rubbers and rulers can be obtained from the tuck shop and that they were not provided by the school. On asking if anyone had lost their timetable (two children had), she immediately said, 'I hope you won't be as forgetful as this all term,' and later, 'Come on now I don't expect to have to wait five minutes every time I want to say something to you' – again the demand for prompt responses.

It is clear from such 'first mornings' that the staff are both giving the pupils a timetable on paper *and* conveying messages about the importance of speed and efficiency in the pupils' responses.

Once the pupils have grasped their timetable – and their class teachers stopped checking with them about which classes they had within the first month – the pupils begin to learn about how their staff structure the week. The data from Corrie *et al.* (1982) convey how teachers have clear views about how the rhythm of the week affects them and their teaching. As Ball *et al.* (1984) comment:

In particular these teachers attributed difficulties to those lessons situated on Monday mornings and Friday afternoons. Perhaps not to the kids but to us, yes. Monday is the day that I loathe. It takes me a long time to wind up enthusiasm. It's usually about after the morning interval before I begin to feel as though I'm with it. That might just be me.

Friday, well, you know, the next day's Saturday. The afternoon, the last couple of periods in the afternoon, tend to drag. I know this is ridiculous but this is just a subjective viewpoint. No matter how good the class is or how bad the class is you're still looking for the bell at a quarter to four. You become a clock watcher and, of course, the clocks here are not anything like accurate. I watch my watch.

Eh, Monday, when they're coming together for the first time, that's not a good day.

Not to such an extent. I think if they've had a Monday holiday then they're not very keen to work on the Tuesday, or if they're expecting a Monday holiday they're not very keen on the Friday. But normally I don't think it makes that much difference. Last two periods on a Friday are difficult.

The ORACLE pupils soon learnt about their new teachers' reactions to the different days of the week. Sometimes teachers will warn them about their state of mind. At Guy Mannering the craft master, Mr Bradshaw, warned the new pupils that

Time in the new schools

Mr Bradshaw's usually in a bad mood on Monday. Did you know that? It's a bit unfortunate for you that you are going to have me on Mondays, then, so you'll have to do what you are told.

Teachers respond to these feelings by adapting their programmes – both the lesson activities and contents – to the mood of the class and their own feelings. As Corrie *et al.*'s (1982) respondents put it:

I think to ask them to write for two whole periods, last thing on a Friday, is a bit much.

. . . I begin to become aware of time in the second period, as it gets nearer quarter to four, inevitable last period on a Friday, in that sometimes, if they've been working, we stop at say half three and I allow them to sit and talk until quarter to four.

Teachers in all schools have strategies for handling different days of the week. For example, at Kenilworth the English teacher Miss Airdale 'reserves Friday for the reading of novels because she believes this gives the children something to look forward to.' The novel for this class was called *The Silver Sword*. This was a common device in several of our schools. Mrs Hind and Miss Tweed both read aloud to their classes on Friday afternoons, and several English teachers in other schools did too.

We are so accustomed to think of Friday as the end of the school week, that it is salutory to remember that in the nineteenth and early twentieth centuries many academic schools demanded attendance on Saturday mornings. Thus Godber and Hutchins (1982: 31) writing of Bedford Girls' High School in the last quarter of the nineteenth century point out that both the girls, and the boys of Bedford School, had classes on Saturday mornings. This apart, most teachers and pupils share the view of Corrie *et al.*'s (1982) sample that Friday is not a day on which hard work can be expected. The desire to stop the same teachers facing the same pupils every Friday produced the two-week timetable at Melin Court shown in Figure 6.1.

Although a hospital is open seven days per week, many of its activities are actually planned round the same five day scheme as a school. As Zerubavel (1979: 16–17) shows, only emergency cases are admitted to hospital on Fridays or Saturdays, and Monday is the busiest day of the week. Being on duty over a weekend is not necessarily strenuous, therefore, because fewer admissions may allow staff to rest and sleep. Young doctors in the hospital Zerubavel studied were on duty either for one weeknight, or for 'the weekend', the two being seen as equally stressful. In a similar vein,

137

a teacher allocated last lesson on Friday afternoon with a difficult class will be seen as carrying a load equivalent to taking the same group for the whole of Wednesday morning.

Within the week are the individual days, each with its own cycle, and to that we now turn.

The daily grind

In summer, it is light by 6 a.m. . . . large vehicles are sifting, raking and clearing the sand, a job they began in the dead of night . . . it is now illegal to sleep on the beach between midnight and 5 a.m. . . . Most of the people on the beach in the early morning are joggers, surfers, or fishermen . . . The scene changes as the joggers and surfers leave for breakfast and work . . . By 8 or 10 a.m. the influx of daytime beachgoers begins {. . .} Beachgoers begin to leave in some numbers about 2 p.m. . . . but quite a few people will stay until sunset . . . By nightfall almost no-one remains . . .

(Edgerton, 1979: 20–27)

Edgerton's day in the life of a Californian beach may seem remote from a Coalthorpe secondary school. Yet both locations are subject to a daily *timetable*, and it is this daily routine to which we now turn. Just as the beach is occupied first by workers, so too the school is cleaned before teachers and pupils arrive. Again the beach and the school premises are both occupied by different people doing different things at varying times of the daily cycle. Yet the beach researched by Edgerton differs from a school because for most of its users (other than the employed life guards and police) it is a place of leisure, and the timetable is voluntarily adhered to. One of the distinguishing characteristics of work and schooling which separates them from unemployment, retirement and holidays is the daily timetable. Pupils and teachers are bound into a regular routine, so that for the pupil there are fixed points of arrival, registration, assembly, lessons, break, lessons, lunch, lessons, break, lessons, home, whether it is Monday or Friday. Similarly the teacher faces arrival, registration, assembly, lessons, break, lessons, lunch, lessons, break, lessons, home, every day whether it is Tuesday or Wednesday. This is true for other occupations as well, and while their daily routines may seem exotic to the teacher or pupil, they *are* routines nevertheless. For example, Daner (1976) studied the inhabitants of a Hare Krsna temple in Boston, whose daily activities are as highly structured as any teacher or pupil, though based on religious principles rather than the secular ones governing LEA schools in Britain. The Krsna devotees live by a strict timetable, punctuated by and organized around *aratrika* (greeting the Lord), and consisting of religious devotions, work and food. Daner (1976: 41–4) gives the daily timetables of several different functionaries in

138

Time in the new schools

the temple, including the *pujari*, who is the caretaker of the deities. While on the surface strange and exotic, it bears considerable similarities to secular occupations in its monotonous regularities.

Pujari's Schedule

a.m.
3.30 Rise and shower; set everything in place of mangala-aratrika
4.00 Chant japa (prayer beads)
4.30 Wake up deities by ringing a bell; say mantras; take deities out of their beds and put on their capes and crowns; set up and check to see that everything is prepared for the aratrika
4.45 Offer three trays of prasada, one for each section of the altar. The trays are left for fifteen minutes for the deities to 'eat' their fill before they are removed
5.00 Mangala-aratrika
5.30 Clean the altar
5.50 Get water for the deities' baths and get fresh clothes ready for the deities
6.10 Bathe and dress the deities during the 'Nectar of Devotion' and 'Srimad-Bhagavatam' classes
7.15 Open curtains; play tape of Srila Prabhupada; go downstairs to clean up all the articles used in bathing and dressing the deities, such as their washcloths and towels, hang up their pajamas, and so on
7.45 Set up the next aratrika; chant for two minutes
8.00 Go to the kitchen to get the breakfast prasada trays for offering, and aesthetically arrange them
8.15 Put food trays for the deities on the altar
8.30 Dhoop aratrika
8.45 Take prasada herself with the other devotees
9.15 Chant japa in the temple
10.00 Circumambulate the temple
10.15 Go to the office to see if there is any business to do there
10.30 Clean the sewing room
11.00 Sew deities' clothes with the other women
11.20 Check the altar to see if everything is ready for the next aratrika; shower
11.40 Set up lunch trays

p.m.
12.00 Offer prasada
12.15 Chant or sew in the temple
1.00 Bnog aratrika

1.30   Deities rest – take off their jewelry and crowns and put them into bed (As much quiet as possible is maintained in the temple while the deities rest so that they will not be disturbed)
1.45   Take prasada
2.15   Go out on sankirtana or have deity watch in the temple
3.30   Set up aratrika equipment; shower
3.50   Wake deities – put on their crowns and jewels
4.00   Offering prasada
4.15   Dhoop aratrika
4.30   Change deities' clothing; set up next aratrika
6.00   Talk to the deities about what she has done that day or what she should have done and didn't do; chant rounds or read 'Srimad-Bhagavatam'
6.30   Hang up deities' clothes; shower; go to kitchen to arrange trays for the deities
7.00   Offer prasada; Tulasi Devi worship in which all devotees should participate
7.15   Sunda aratrika
7.45   'Bhagavad-gita' class; clean aratrika articles and set them up again for the next aratrika
8.30   Teaching of Lord Caitanya reading
8.45   Offering to the deities
9.00   Aratrika
9.15   Devotees take milk prasada
9.30   Deities put to rest
10.10 Hang up the deities' clothes; read a few minutes in scripture
10.30 Take rest

To a non-believer this round of clothing, washing, and worshipping Hindu deities punctuated by offering them food and eating oneself may seem a pointless way of spending the day. For many disaffected pupils, what they and their teachers are doing is no less pointless. For the believer in Krsna, as for the pro-school pupil and the keen teacher, the daily activities are the main reason for living. The free school teachers studied by Ann Swidler (1979), for example, are as devoted to their lives as any Krsna follower. For many pupils and teachers, the punctuating marks in the day – the break, the lunch hour, the afternoon break – are seized on as avidly as the pauses in street-sweeping described by Martin Leighton (1981).

Leighton, a journalist, took a series of unskilled jobs including street-sweeping in Brighton, and writes vividly of the tyranny of the eight-hour day, the exhausting toil and the snatched, illicit 'breaks'. He argues that a shorter day would have produced as much productivity, because the last two hours found the men too tired to work properly. However, the bureaucrats in the cleansing department regarded the eight-hour day as sacrosanct. In the same way the school timetable can become unalterable, as at the Harold Spencer Junior High School studied by Everhart (1983: 34) where the authoritarian head, Mr Edwards, prided himself on his strong control of the school:

> For years the teachers had been trying to get him to change the schedule from a six to a seven-period day, but he firmly resisted on the basis that it would disrupt the lunch schedules.

While there are many schools in which the timetable is felt to be fixed and eternal, the length of the school day and the ways in which it can be divided are historically and culturally specific. In the great girls' day schools of the nineteenth century, lessons, and therefore the school day, ended at lunch time. This was the pattern at North London Collegiate, in the GPDST schools, at Bedford Girls' High School and at Cheltenham (Godber and Hutchins, 1982; Beale, 1904). Miss Beale had introduced the 'mornings only' pattern because of her dissatisfaction with the school day she found in 1858 which:

> had been fixed from 9.15 a.m. to 12.15 p.m., and from 2.45 p.m. to 4.15 p.m. Wednesdays and Saturdays were half holidays. Thus, four days a week girls had to dress or undress, change boots, etc. eight times a day. Parents had to send children four times and servants eight times daily over the same ground. Afternoon work had to begin immediately after the early dinner, when children and teachers were tired and sleepy, and they had to sit down in the evening to prepare lessons or correct exercises when quite worn out. (Beale, 1904: 23)

Miss Beale changed these hours in 1864 to what she considered a proper arrangement

> which made it possible for us to lengthen the morning hours, and abolish afternoon school, the number of school hours remaining unaltered. (1904: 29)

The full day of schooling, with the school dinner, only came about in these schools well into this century. Religious schools are divided by religious observances which make the daily routines of their devotees similar to that of the *Krsna* devotee (e.g. Christs Hospital Girls' School described by Louie Angus (1981). Thus Bullivant (1978) describes a school day which begins at 7.20 a.m. in the *shul*, followed by breakfast, with two hours of religious study from 8.50 a.m. A short recess at 10.50 is followed by more religious study, and secular work only starts at 11.40 p.m. Lunchtime prayers start at 1.15 p.m., then there is the ritual handwashing, then lunch, then play, then secular teaching from 2.0 p.m. till 4.0 p.m. or 5.30 p.m for the oldest boys. This is a routine quite different from any of our ORACLE schools, but one timetabled equally rigidly.

A rigidly timetabled day characterizes the teacher and pupil, the *pujari*, and the doctors and nurses in Zerubavel's (1979) hospital. The teachers in the six transfer schools spent a good deal of time explaining to the incoming pupils how their new routines worked. Thus when a handful of pupils from Stourbridge Road and Wellington Lower Schools visited Melin Court, Mrs Hallows, the head of first year, told them about their new school day:

> On the first morning they were all to come to the hall and that it was important to be on time.
> Mrs H: 'Does anyone with a brother or sister know the time we start?'
> Pupil: '9 o'clock'
> Mrs H: 'No, you'll have to get up a little earlier'
> Pupil: '7.30 a.m.'
> Mrs H: 'No, you'll be able to have a lie-in'
> Pupil: '8.50 a.m.'
> Mrs H: 'Nearer. It's actually 8.45 a.m.'
> Mrs Hallows tells them about the warning bell so that 'You won't have a row of "lates" against your name.' . . . On the first day they are to bring four things: pencil, pen, rubber and ruler, and if they forget, everything can be bought at the school shop. All equipment and items of clothing should also be labelled. She briefly described the different arrangements for lunchtime – school meals, snack bar or packed lunches, and said that after a few days parents would be asked to fill in a form stating which arrangement their child would be taking – 'in order to know where they are.'

Similarly when prospective pupils visited Kenilworth they were warned about the longer school day they faced, as well as its novel structure:

> Mrs Appleyard said after dinner they would be taken on another tour of the buildings to be reminded where the specialist rooms were and then they would go home at ten to four. She pointed out that this was rather a longer day but she said that it was all part of growing up. Having explained the first day she then invited the children to ask any questions.

The pupils are told from their first day that they have to be punctual, as for example at Waverly:

> Another point that Mr Bronte was careful to remind them about was punctuality in the mornings. He explained that there were two monitors in the entrance hall each morning who wrote down in the late book any children who came in after quarter to nine. The child then had to go and report to the teacher and explain why they were late. He said often there was a very good

excuse, may be they had had to go to the dentist or the doctor or something
like that, but if it wasn't for that kind of reason and they were late too many
times, something would be done.

In other words, the teachers and pupils are supposed to follow a
tight schedule. In this way, being at school is like being at work. The
lack of any imperatives governing time is a characteristic of unemployment (Marsden and Duff, 1975), of housework (Oakley,
1974a), and of retirement. As Jacobs (1974: 31) reports on the
elderly residents of *Fun City* (an American retirement community)
many of them had the task of producing 'the social organization of a
passive way of life.' This life is essentially *timeless*. As one respondent described it:

> In fact, down here it doesn't make any difference when you eat or when you
> sleep. Because you're not going any place. You're not doing anything. And
> uh, if I'm up all night reading and sleep all day, what's the difference?

Teachers and pupils never have this problem in term time, as we
shall see. They quickly establish a daily routine, and disruptions to it
are unpopular. The 'wet break' at Waverly, described in the previous chapter and characterized by the observer as 'a fiendish
device', is one example of such a disruption. When a 'wet break' was
signalled at Waverly the teacher of the last lesson of the day found
the pupils especially difficult because they had not had their afternoon break. However there are many other ways in which the
smooth running of the teacher's day may be disrupted by their
colleagues, their pupils or events beyond their control. Staff have
lesson plans but the best-laid plans of teachers for the efficient use
of time can go astray. Pupils can complete work too fast, and leave
the teacher with nothing to do in a lesson, or they can be too slow
and leave the teacher with lots undone. Both are equally disruptive. Equally upsetting to teacher routine are pupils who *arrive*
late:

> French Mr Haydon, Melin Court
> The lesson is delayed 15 minutes as the bus bringing the children back from
> the baths is late.

Equally disturbing are interruptions to routine such as fire drills and
the unavailability of rooms. Hilsum and Cane's (1971) study of the
primary teacher's day revealed how many such disruptions there
were in those schools, and we found several incidents where lesson
timing was thrown out by factors beyond the teacher's control. For

example, at Kenilworth (11–14) School one day in history with their form teacher Miss Stephenson:

> The first thing she had to explain for that day was about the fire drill which the whole school would be involved in later that morning.

When the class went to RE with Mr Birch,

> the lesson was very abbreviated as before the end the fire practice took place.

The same class later in the week were observed in English with Miss Airdale when:

> This should have been a library lesson but the library was not in use because of a visitation from some people from the county library services. No-one had told the form about this.

While such disruptions, like the interruptions described in the previous chapter, can upset the flow of the teacher's lesson planning, they are relatively uncommon. The commonest disruption for the teacher is the pupil who works too fast or too slowly.

Speed merchants and slow coaches

Pupils who work faster than their peers are demanding, in that the teacher has, at worst, to occupy them, and at best allocate new, sufficiently demanding tasks. Children who cannot, or will not, keep up, are equally upsetting for the smooth functioning of the class. This disruption to the teacher's lesson planning probably goes some way towards explaining the findings of Bennett *et al.* (1984) about allocation of tasks. These researchers found that above-average pupils were frequently given tasks that were too easy for them, while the slow children were often allocated work which was too hard. Both mis-allocations can be understood in part as a desire on the teacher's part to prevent both the speed merchants and the slowcoaches diverging too far ahead or behind their peers. The teacher's task is rather like the master of a wagon train, escorting wagons through Indian country, and trying to keep the convoy intact (Payne and Hustler, 1980). So, in cookery at Guy Mannering (9–13) School, Mrs Bird was doing a lesson on rules for using the kitchen, but:

> At one point she had great difficulty with Dirk because he was unable to copy down the rules. He was still doing it long after the others had finished and eventually with a shrug she just gave up. She has told me in the staffroom that

she thinks there should be a remedial form. Her last exhortation to the class is to be tidy for the visit next week to the Gas Board.

Dirk was removed to a remedial class later in the year, because he could not (or would not) keep up in any of his lessons. However, it is just as bad for children to work too fast. For example, at Maid Marion (11–14) by the third week of term the maths staff:

> are noticing which are the fast ones who need to be pumped with extra work – as Mr Taff put it – and therefore which children would probably be creamed off into the top maths set after Christmas.

That comment by Mr Taff includes two of the things teachers do to deal with speed merchants: setting extra work, and setting them in more homogeneous groups. A third response is to invent some 'make work' to fill the time, and a fourth is to reject the work as 'careless' and demand that it be repeated more carefully. When some, or all, of the class have gone too fast, 'make work' is a common strategy. At Kenilworth in geography with Mrs Cullen:

> They had been supposed to draw a map of their route to school, and some of them had done it straight into their best books instead of doing it into their rough books first. She wanted them now to transfer their maps into their best books, and to put the heading 'My Route to School'. Children who had finished their maps were then asked to draw in their rough books the route they would take if they were going into Bridgehampton.

Because some pupils had omitted a stage in their map work, Mrs Cullen's plan was thrown into confusion. Both the child who is the speed merchant, and the one who is the slowcoach, is a problem for the teacher who wants to work with the class as one unit. In nearly all classes in our six schools, the staff wanted pupils to work as a class on at least some occasions, and those who go too fast, or too slowly like Dirk, are a major problem. One speed merchant at Guy Mannering was Gavin Radice, and he revealed this trait from the beginning of the year. On September 30th a typical incident occurred. The class (1.5) were in an English lesson with Mr Evans, and when they had finished a piece of writing on their favourite TV programme, they were supposed to fill the time drawing a picture while the slow children caught up. The observer wrote:

> (Note that most of the classes are always allowed to draw a picture at the end of the written work and this seems to be the teacher's gesture towards the primary school.)
> Gavin's hand is up. 'If you are going to tell me you've not finished it, then I don't want to know," says Mr Evans.
> 'No, I have done the picture.'

'Well you shouldn't. I said that you would do that picture today, so what are you going to do? When the others are doing the picture are you going to sit and twiddle your thumbs? Your trouble is that you are always wanting to be first. I don't give a golden cup for speed. It's quality I want.'
{. . .} Some of the pupils are asked to read their stories to the class {. . .} Caitlin is next.
'You have a lovely book there,' he tells her and she talks about the *Swop Shop* and is praised profusely at the end. 'Caitlin' says Mr Evans, 'is one of these people who thinks before she writes and there are a lot of adults who don't do that. Well done.'

Indeed Gavin's career in the early weeks at Guy Mannering show all the problems that a teacher has controlling a speed merchant, and all the available management strategies. Gavin is first mentioned speeding by one observer on September 16th, in Mr Evans' English class, when the task was written comprehension.

Mr Evans goes round telling the children to get the rules right. 'Miss a line, put the date, miss a line, put the title. Come on, you must get on. Gavin is getting on like a house on fire, he has done four lines already. So get on. Mind you, I don't want scribble. I would rather you did only part than do it all and make a mess of it with a page you would be ashamed to show your father.'

In this first episode, Mr Evans is preparing the ground for rejecting untidy work, but demanding speed. As he walked round the room correcting mistakes he said:

'That's very nice . . . it's a pleasure to see, unlike one or two which we are not going to mention, are we Gavin?'

Another observer had seen Gavin in Mr Evans's geography class three days earlier, when the class were writing about the kangaroo. Then Mr Evans:

finds Gavin has started. Tells him that he has done it wrong, and he must rule if off and do it all over again. 'Do it my way.'

Later in the lesson the observer wrote:

Gavin is obviously a very fast worker. He asks if they were to go on to question 3. Mr Evans tells him that there probably isn't time. He might have time, but he mustn't forget to answer the questions (ie. he mustn't just copy the half-written answers off the board).

Here Mr Evans is hoping to stop Gavin rushing ahead with improperly completed work by issuing a warning. This can slow down a speed merchant. The next geography lesson we saw was still about kangaroos, and we noted:

> Gavin is the first to finish. It is checked out by Mr Evans. 'If it is perfect,' Mr Evans says, 'Gavin can read a book.' Gavin clearly enjoys finishing first, and ends the day on a high note. He is able to go to the bookcase and choose himself a book to read.

The observer commented that there was 'quite a gap' in working speed between the children. Gavin had finished fifteen minutes before the end of the lesson, while some people were left after the bell completing their work. Mr Evans's strategy in this lesson was unusual for Guy Mannering, but common in other schools – pupils who are finished are allowed to read.

Thus far we have shown Gavin in English and geography with Mr Evans. On September 20th we saw the same issues arise in RE. Mr LeGard had asked the pupils to copy a passage from the board, the list of the prophets except Daniel from their Bibles, and then add some notes on each prophet from the board.

> Gavin is the first to finish. He takes it out for marking.
> Mr LeGard: 'Now then, here we go.'
> But Gavin has not listened. He's only copied what was on the board and left out the list of prophets from the Bible.
> Mr LeGard: 'Oh dear! You haven't got the Bible open for fun.'

On this occasion Gavin was not alone, because all the other children had made the same mistake. After break in the library period, Mr LeGard marked the RE, and called Gavin up.

> Mr L: 'Gavin, this is good. You will get an A.
> Gavin: 'Good. I've got a credit.'
> Mr L: 'No you haven't. You've only two As for Bible study, the other one is for library. *And*, wait a minute, where's your name on the cover?'
> Gavin: 'I forgot. Sorry.'

Mr LeGard therefore withdrew the 'A' until the folder was named. The following week in the library lesson, we wrote:

> As usual, Gavin is the first to finish.
> 'I've finished' he tells Mr LeGard.
> 'I'm not surprised' says Mr LeGard looking at the book. 'You've left out a line.'

Later the same day, in Mr Evans's English class, Gavin was again the first to complete his work, but had not underlined the date.

Mr Evans: 'Do I have to tell you every time? Are you going to be a jockey?'
Gavin: 'No.'
Mr Evans: 'It's only that you like coming first. You've got 3 out of 5 right. Is that good?'
Gavin: 'No.'
Mr Evans: 'Do you know why you didn't get five?'
Gavin: 'No.'
Mr Evans: 'I do. You should be called Gavin Rush. Less haste is what you need.'

While Gavin was racing ahead of his classmates, in the 'B' band class we studied, 1.6, Dirk was falling further and further behind. By the end of September he was two lessons behind his classmates in Miss O'Hara's English course, and thus creating the other type of management problem for the staff. Similar pupil careers can be found in all our other schools. Many staff respond by setting the pupils, and the creation of a remedial form removes the slowest pupils from holding up their classmates (Smith and Geoffrey, 1968). Slow and fast children are one of the teacher's biggest problems in managing his or her timing. They are not, though, the only factor in timing lessons, for teachers sometimes mistime their teaching themselves.

Teachers and timing

Ball and his colleagues (1984) have pointed out that the teacher is caught between the social calendar (the school day, week, term, year), the 'biological time' of the pupils' working speeds, and the 'curriculum time' of the syllabus. In different classes, the three types of pressure operate differentially. As Ball *et al.* (1984) says:

> With 'good classes' the problems of curriculum knowledge predominate, 'getting through the syllabus', time usually passes too quickly; with 'poorer classes' the problems of social time predominate, 'getting through the lesson', time usually passes too slowly.

This point has also been made by Peter Woods (1978):

> There is a great deal of time passing and time-filling not as an adjunct to a larger purpose, but as an overall end in itself . . . The term, day, period is there, inevitably, and it is more necessary that it be 'got through' than it is the syllabus {sic}, especially with regard to non-examination classes.

This notion of filling the time is the educational parallel of many work environments, such as those described by Blackburn and Mann (1979) and Leighton (1981). In that sense, the lack of urgency in non-academic classes is a good preparation for the world of work. In the good classes the teacher may find time perpetually running

148

out, while in the poorer ones there is too much of it. Some teachers are late for their classes. Rutter and his collaborators (1979) argued that the lateness of teachers was a symptom of a poor secondary school. We certainly had some tardy staff in our schools. For example, at Kenilworth 1 zeta had RE with Mrs Lords in a terrapin hut:

> She was not there at 11 o'clock when the period was due to begin . . . It was ten past eleven by the time she was ready to start the lesson . . . By the time she had finished her exposition it was nearly the end of the lesson, so she said they would do the diagram next time.

Mrs Lords was not the only culprit at Kenilworth. The observer went to a 'B' band science class and found:

> Form 1 zeta were waiting glumly outside the science laboratory. As I arrived Peter Queen was just saying 'Oh dear, Mr Pardoe is going to be late again.' I asked him if Mr Pardoe had been late last time and Peter told me that they had missed 10 minutes of their lesson because Mr Pardoe had been held up. At 9 minutes past 11 Mr Pardoe arrived.

The same class suffered later the same day when they went to English with Mr Gordon and 'Mr Gordon arrived 10 minutes late saying that he was sorry.' Even though Mr Gordon had arrived late he apparently could not fill a whole lesson, for:

> There were 3 minutes to go before the bell went and Mr Gordon just stood there with the children sitting in silence until the bell did go, whereupon he dismissed them.

Later that week the observer went to a 1 zeta geography lesson with Mrs Cullen:

> The children waited for some time outside Mrs Cullen's room before she turned up . . . Neil Carpenter was looking through the door into another classroom when Mrs Cullen arrived and said 'If you are so interested in what is going on you can stand out there all lesson and come in at 12.15 to do the work.'

These children's time was, therefore, being wasted. Sometimes the teacher was not late, but was not ready to teach the next topic because books had not been marked, or some administrative task had to be done. One example of this was a lesson at Maid Marion school:

> Mr Salter with class 10 spent one entire lesson doing ink blots, which was really a time filler because he had not yet marked their homework in their

science books and he wanted the books to be marked and given back so they could write up the next experiment. The children were instructed to do one ink blot each in pairs and then do a felt tip ink blot each. However, some children finished fairly quickly, so they were told to do more and more ink blots until some had about 12 each arranged around their desk and they just went on doing this until the end of the lesson and until Mr Salter had finished marking his science books.

Similarly in 1.5 at Guy Mannering, one day Mrs Forrest said:

Because they have worked so hard she lets them off homework, but this is really an excuse because she needs to collect the books and check on their answers to the previous exercise.

In other classes pupils were left to read or play quietly while reports were written, registers made up, dinner money calculated and so on. In contrast, on some occasions, teachers allocated too much work, and even the best pupils are unable to complete it in the allocated time. Mr LeGard, who taught RE (and library practice) to most of the first year classes at Guy Mannering, relied heavily on getting the children to copy passages from the board and/or their Bibles. He put up the passages for the week on the board on Mondays, and kept them there all week, for each class that came to him. One morning 1.5 were *all* quite unable to complete the work set, and Mr LeGard told us that he had 'set too much work', but he 'needed' everything on the board for another class that afternoon, because periods after lunch were ten mintues longer than the morning ones.

Mr LeGard was in his last year of teaching, and was, presumably, getting tired of watching pupils copy paragraphs about the Bible from his blackboard. A less experienced teacher, such as the probationer, Mr Valentine at Gryll Grange, may also be unable to timetable his lessons accurately, as when we recorded:

Mr Valentine bravely attempted to get the class to draw correct pictograms of children's hair colour. However, by the time he had given the boys instructions about football practice and several children had diverted his attention there was very *little time for the actual graph*.

The observer's note that Mr Valentine was 'bravely' attempting to complete the task is an interesting judgment about his inaccurate timing of pupils' likely workrates in 1T. In contrast, the experienced craft teacher, such as Mr Quill, the technical drawing master at Waverly, could always time lessons to finish promptly, and there was always time for him to check that all the equipment was present and correct.

Time in the new schools

These are the constraints of time on the teacher. From the pupils' perspective there are three aspects of time which are important to them. These are, time as a topic on the syllabus, the idea that ability can be judged by speed of working, and the boundaries between time under the teacher's control (work) and the pupils' own time (leisure).

Time and the pupil

Time was a topic on the syllabus of most of our pupils. At Waverly, Mr Rutherford was teaching the children to measure time with a pendulum; and at Gryll Grange the Schonell books in use had several exercises on telling the time. At Maid Marion the social studies work began with evolution and an attempt to teach pupils about geological time. At Melin Court, the history mistress was teaching the pupils about the 'coming of Christianity' to Britain while in RE they learnt about Israel in the time of Jesus. Both involved pupils in conceptualizing time past. At Guy Mannering, 1.5 were taught the 24-hour clock by Mrs Forrest, and, in one 'library' lesson with Mr LeGard, how to read a timetable:

> He hands them out some red books and says that they are going to do an exercise on timetables which 'are always regarded as being complicated, that they are not once you find your way around.' A page has a timetable for a bus route from Eastbourne to Hastings. 'We have the page from the bus timetable, the first information you get is the number of the bus. That's useful. Then it tells you where it goes from Eastbourne, Pevensey, Bexhill, and Hastings. That's general, now we get to the timetable itself.'

Mr LeGard then explained how to read a bus timetable, and the children were left to work through a series of questions on this timetable. After ten minutes, Mr LeGard read out the answers for the pupils to mark their own. All the boys reported getting at least seven out of ten correct; some girls reported only getting two, three or four correct, while Mair Pryce and Leila got all ten right and a credit. Mr LeGard, however, discounts their achievement: 'Apart from Mair and Leila, the old thing has come up again, that a man can use a timetable better than a woman.' Time – musical, geological, historical, and scientific – thus figures on the pupils' curricula. However, it is likely that the two lessons about time that pupils learn most thoroughly are that the teacher controls it, and that the timing of their work is an important part of how their ability can be judged. The pupil (as Keddie, 1971, and Nash, 1973, pointed out) quickly learns to place himself when he hears a teacher like Mr Foale at Kenilworth, make an announcement in maths such as:

He began by asking whether everyone had finished their previous work as far as No.20. He said those who had not must go on until they reach No.20, and those who had reached No.20 could go on to Exercise 2.

Here the message that the best students have already done 20 sums is quite clear. Equally explicit, or blatant, is the message that time is the teacher's first, and that the pupils' time is under the teacher's control. This may be said explicitly, as when Miss Stephenson at Maid Marion, after the break bell had rung, said: 'That bell was to remind me, not you. Sit down, wait till I dismiss you.' Even when such things are not actually made explicit, pupils soon learn them.

Everyone involved in schooling takes it for granted that being released from tasks, lessons and the school buildings is a reward. Thus it is never seriously considered that a pupil or a teacher might want *more* time in school. The notorious 'wet break' at Waverly resulted in school finishing for the day ten minutes earlier. At Guy Mannering, any class who had 100 per cent attendance for a week were sent home ten minutes early on Friday afternoon. This school also sent home pupils early on the Saint's day of the Patron of their house, so on October 4th one observer wrote:

At 3.30 p.m. those in St Francis house went home – they had been given leave to do so by the head at assembly as it was St Francis' day. (I question the legality of this as children 9–11 were involved.)

The reverse of this is the way in which one punishment for pupils is to take more of their time, by keeping them in at break or lunch-time, putting them in detention or 'on report'. These would only *be* punishments if the child prefers to be out of school. The following incident only makes sense if we assume Dean wants to leave his classroom at break.

Gryll Grange – Miss Tweed's class
Since the beginning of the period Dean has been inking in pictures on his ruler and he is discovered and brought out in front of the class to be shouted at. He is made to stay in at playtime and complete the work.

Teachers can also take pupils' time by putting them 'on report', so that they have to be checked every lesson, a proceeding which only makes sense if there is a belief that the child would rather be somewhere else. Then there is the question of homework. Homework is never seen as a pleasure, but always as an unpleasant imposition on the pupils' time which they can be 'let off' if they have been good. In several of our schools homework was largely a punishment or a penalty for working too slowly or forgetting things.

Time in the new schools

The quickest pupils rarely had much homework, because they had finished their work: the laggards were told to complete their assignments for homework. Typically, when Miss Airdale had 1 gamma at Kenilworth write her an autobiography, some children did not complete it in the lesson so:

> At ten twenty-one she said that it was about time everyone finished. She said that one or two people still had difficulty in finishing off. She asked the children if they had homework tonight. If they would like to finish off their autobiography they could do it. This was an invitation rather than an instruction.

Such gentle hints from the early days of the term become more punitive inroads into the slow or forgetful pupil's time as it progresses. So when Neil, in 1 zeta, arrived at a history lesson with Miss Stephenson:

> Neil had not brought his book with him.
> Miss Stephenson gave him a plain piece of paper, and said that when he found his book he would have to copy the work up at home or at break.

Similarly when she found that Maurice, a speed merchant, had done his notes on the Bronze Age wrong, Miss Stephenson said:

> 'I'm afraid you've rushed on to No.4 before you finished No.3 . . . No you'll have to do it again I'm afraid. It's a bit of bad luck.' She tore out the page and told him to repeat the work for homework that night.

In such ways then, pupils learn that school time is under the control of the teacher, and she can overrule their own plans for spending not only the day, but some of their 'free' time as well. As pro-school pupils accept this and do homework voluntarily, their school careers begin to follow a different pattern from those anti-school pupils for whom homework is an imposed punishment, done unwillingly or not at all. Time usage is one of the key ways in which the polarization of pupil careers occurs.

Conclusions

This chapter has contrasted the school day, and the longer temporal units such as the term and the year in which it is embedded, with places and occupations which are *not* timetabled such as retirement communities, unemployment and housework. School teaching is more like being a railway worker, or even a *Krsna* priest, than at first sight would appear likely. For teachers and pupils the main divide is between those classes where the central pressure is to complete the syllabus, and those where time has just to be filled.

153

The teacher's problems in both types of class can be aggravated by pupils who 'rate-bust': that is speed merchants who complete the tasks assigned too fast, and by those who fall behind, and either have to be abandoned by their fellows or given a disproportionate amount of help. The commonest solution to this problem is to create more homogeneous groups – so that by the age of 13 all our pupils were to be in sets for maths, and in some schools for everything academic. These groupings are the focus of the next chapter, in which the product of the 'devil's mill' – sets – are examined along with other types of formal groupings.

CHAPTER 7

What group are you in?
Formal grouping arrangements
in the new schools

Pupil identities emerge from the structural arrangements that schooling imposes on young people (Lomax, 1980).

Perhaps the most startling change is the disappearance in many schools of the form, or the class unit . . . Fixed classes . . . are fast disappearing in our larger modern comprehensives, which are more likely to have staggeringly complex combinations of bands and sets, and mixed ability groups and options . . . (Hargreaves, 1982: 88).

This chapter deals with one aspect of social relations in the six transfer schools, the formal groups into which the schools divided the pupils. We also consider the way in which pupils have to learn to be solitary even in the midst of crowded classrooms, a phenomenon highlighted by Philip Jackson (1968). The formal grouping arrangements found in the six schools took a variety of shapes: we report on forms, tutor groups, streams, bands, sets, houses and teams. Our examination of the formal groupings follows a research tradition including Hargreaves (1967), Lacey (1970), Rosenbaum (1976) and Ball (1981) among others. The study of the informal groups pupils create for themselves is also a well-established research approach in school ethnography, and forms the subject of chapter 10.

Formal organization of groups in the schools

All our six transfer schools were part of comprehensive systems of local educational provision. As we have discussed elsewhere (Galton and Willcocks, 1983) some of them were based round mixed ability teaching groups, while others divided their intake into streams, bands, or ability-based subject sets. It is worth noting, therefore, that for many advocates of comprehensive education, Guy Mannering, Kenilworth and Waverly were not 'truly' comprehensive, because ability grouping was introduced for the new intake of 9-, 11- or 12-year-olds. Ball (1984) makes his point as follows:

> The public debates about comprehensive education, both at national and local levels, have been concerned almost entirely with the structure of educational provision – reorganising grammars and secondary moderns into comprehensives. However, for many teachers and educationalists the litmus test of comprehensive education requires not only the abolition of selective schooling and of streaming and banding but also a restructuring of the processes of teaching and learning. Marsden (1971: 22–3) argues that if the ideals of comprehensive education are to be achieved 'schools must exhibit a whole range of educational innovation and openness in the curriculum and teaching methods and relationships with the outside world which will bring about a new ethos and a new view of the child: only in a co-operative framework which sees children as of equal worth will equality be achieved.'

However, we know from both large surveys (e.g. Benn and Simon, 1972; Fogelman, 1976) and case studies (Burgess, 1983; Ball, 1981) that few comprehensives have lived up to that idealized pattern proposed by Holly (1972) and Marsden (1971). We do not propose here to debate the arguments for and against streaming. Rather our focus is to demonstrate the complex and perpetually shifting range and types of grouping in which new middle and secondary pupils find themselves. Pupils are constantly categorized and organized into different groups, often belonging to more than one category at the same time.

All six schools would legitimately claim that they *valued* all their children equally, but three of them had been chosen by the research team as schools which adopted streams or bands for the new intake, while the other three (Melin Court, Maid Marion and Gryll Grange) deferred grouping by ability for at least a year after the pupils entered them. As Elizabeth Richardson (1973) pointed out a decade ago, the growth of the comprehensive school has led to much more complicated grouping processes and timetabling than simple streaming in the older grammar and secondary schools did (Hargreaves, 1982; Lacey, 1982). The descriptions of how our pupils were organized in the six schools *are* complicated, especially in the three schools with mixed ability groupings.

Pupils are organized in all our six schools by ascribed rather than achieved characteristics in the formal structure (and to a large extent in the informal culture too, as chapter 9 shows). The most important organizing characteristics are age, sex and ability. The ascribed quality, race, is not much used for grouping except where it is coterminous with religion or ability.

Formal grouping arrangements in the new schools
The year group
The first organizational category to which all the transfer pupils belong is a year group – they are classified along with a large number of their fellow pupils into a cohort of 'first years'. This group has age in common, but is heterogeneous in terms of sex, race and ability. The salience of this first grouping is obvious to the pupils themselves, and may govern many aspects of their day – all first years may well have the same assembly, lunch sitting, breaktime and even a separate playground. For example at Melin Court (12–18) school there was a separate yard for the first year pupils which they were not supposed to leave except to visit the tuck shop; at Gryll Grange the three first year classes had assembly together in their area most days, and went to the same lunch sitting. Guy Mannering even taught the whole first year (six classes of 25/30 pupils each) together, for twice a week the whole year had a music lesson in the hall with two teachers.

Such occasions as assemblies are not just based on putting all the pupils in place, but are also used by staff to address the year group as a whole. Typically, they will be spoken to as 'first years'. Thus in the first year assembly at Melin Court in the third week of term when the children were talking instead of sitting in silence, the head of year, Mrs Hallows announced firmly: 'First years, I am not in the habit of saying things twice.' This utterance not only has disciplinary intention, it also stresses the category shared by all pupils, the *year*/cohort.

The form
The next grouping which dominates the pupils' lives is their form. This is again homogeneous by age, and the sexes are mixed. In four of our schools the forms were of mixed abilities (Gryll Grange, Maid Marion, Waverly and Melin Court), while at Guy Mannering and Kenilworth the form was ability-based. Whether or not the form was homogeneous by ability had a considerable influence on whether it was a teaching group or not. At Guy Mannering and Kenilworth the pupils were taught for much of their time in their forms. In the other four schools the pupils were only taught in their forms for part of the time, spending the rest of their lessons in different groups. We return to the effects of such groupings later in the chapter. The form has at least two effects on the pupils, whether it is a mixed-ability group or a homogeneous one. First, and probably most salient for the pupils, it is the place where they have to make friends. The form contains old friends and old enemies, and strangers among whom new social relationships must be developed. We address these in the second section of this chapter. Second,

157

forms get reputations, or labels, attached to them by staff and pupils. Staff labels may be public – i.e. the staff may tell a form what reputation they have or they may only be discussed inside the staffroom. Pupils, too, develop labels for other forms. Staffroom characterizations develop quite early in the school year. At Gryll Grange, by the fifth day of term Miss Tweed told one of our observers that the three classes were already getting distinct characters. Mr Valentine's class were the gigglers, she had the enthusiasts, while Mrs Hind's – and Mrs Hind broke in – 'Apathy rules OK' in 1H. Miss Tweed had divided the children according to reading scores, to create mixed ability parallel classes, yet, the two mistresses said, already they had distinct personalities.

Similarly, at Melin Court, one of the classes we observed (1M), Mrs Wordsworth's form, had been, so she told them, 'noticed' by the third week of term. In the form registration period after lunch one day, Mrs Wordsworth rehearsed with the form a problem that had arisen the previous day. Apparently, Mr Haydon had failed to appear for their French lesson, and while Eamonn's trip to the staffroom to report their lack of teacher was praised, Mrs Wordsworth told them off for the noise they had made. She then warned them that they were in danger of getting a bad reputation, and they must learn to wait quietly. Beynon and Delamont (1984) report a study from South Wales in which a mixed ability class quickly develop a bad reputation, centred on a group of boys who constantly caused disciplinary problems. This class was broken up after half-term tests, when streaming began, much to the relief of the staff.

A similar event occurred with one of the two classes we saw at Guy Mannering, where 1.6 quickly became seen by teachers as a bad class, and was broken up during the year to separate some of the most academically backward and socially disruptive pupils, such as Dirk and Annabel. Early on in the autumn when the whole first year was having singing in the hall, Mrs Tallis reprimanded one girl (Annabel) and asked her which form she was in. When Annabel said 1.6, Mrs Tallis told the whole room (180 children) that she's 'heard a lot about 1.6' and most of it not very complimentary.

Forms have a name or title to identify them, and the ways these were chosen in our six schools reveal a good deal about them. We can contrast the four schools which adopted 'neutral' nomenclature – emphasizing that all forms are equal – with two which clearly ranked its pupils. The four schools which adopted neutral labels were Gryll Grange, Maid Marion, Waverly and Melin Court. One of two common devices we used in each of these schools: calling classes either after the letters in the school's name, or the initials of the form teacher's name. Thus Maid Marion called its classes after the name of the school: 1M, 1A, 1I, 1D etc., while Gryll Grange used the teacher's initials so Miss Tweed's class was called 1T, Mr Valentine's 1V. In complete contrast, Kenilworth, a rigidly streamed school, called its classes 1 alpha, 1 beta, 1 gamma, 1 delta down to 1 theta. This was the most explicit labelling and consequently the pupils were acutely conscious of not only what form they were in, but also where it came in the hierarchy. In their end of year essays, the streaming system was clearly an important part of the pupils' experiences. For example:

> I am in a form which is the third from top called 1γ or 1 gamma.

> I am satisfied with the class I am in and I thought I would be in 1 theta, but I am in 1 gamma moved up from 1 delta so I am pleased to have got in this class.

> When I first came to this school I was a bit scared of being in a low class such as 1 epsilon or 1 theta but I got a surprise when I found I was in 1 delta . . .

> It was nearly the end of term and we had to go into the hall to see if we were moving up or if we were moving down but Kieran and I were lucky because we moved up to 1 gamma.

Even Philip, who was barely able to produce an essay, told us about the forms:

> You ofern want to go into a high fhorm e.g. Gammers, Beters, or Alfers.
> (Philip's spelling)

Form membership and consciousness of hierarchy are noticeable in the essays. We return to this issue later in the chapter.

The house system

The year and the form are made up of pupils of the same age. In two of our schools (Guy Mannering and Kenilworth) there was a third kind of formal pupil group which was heterogeneous by age – the house. The other four schools had no formal compulsory, mixed age, organized groups for pupils. The existence of houses in the two streamed schools also provided pupils in those two schools with a formal grouping of mixed ability. We return to a discussion of the house system in these two schools later in this section.

Sex-segregation

The third ascribed status which determined much of the formal divisions made between pupils is sex. (Sex is also used widely as an

informal grouping basis, but we will deal with such informal separa-
tions later in the chapter.) The pupils are grouped together with
their own sex and separated from the opposite sex throughout the
school day. Carol Buswell (1981) has argued that in one comprehensive in the north of England the pupils 'could be classified by sex
up to *twenty* times in a day – day after day.' This classification takes
many forms. All our six schools had separate lavatories, changing
rooms, cloakrooms, and games teaching. All six listed the sexes
separately on the registers and class lists, with boys first in all the
schools but Guy Mannering, which gave girls priority. Pupils are
routinely lined up separately, so that they sit apart.

These organizational arrangements are so common that they are
taken for granted, and hence invisible to staff, pupils and observers.
Most researchers do not even mention that the schools they have
studied separate the sexes in these ways, as Delamont (1980a, 1982,
1983d) has argued elsewhere. Ronald King (1978: 67–9) found that
when he attempted to interrogate teachers about such practices,
they were quite unable to account for them. Sex-segregation was
seen as 'natural' and 'convenient'.

The sex-segregation common in our six schools can be demonstrated by the organizational arrangements of the two 9–13 middle
schools in Ashburton. We might have expected that Gryll Grange
and Guy Mannering would handle gender roles differently. Yet in
terms of sex-segregation, they were identical. Both schools listed
boys and girls separately on the register, so that the children were
always called to activities separately. The nurse, photographer,
remedial teacher and so on, used the register, and so called children
separately by sex. Both schools had separate lavatories, and separate changing rooms, and both taught different games to each sex,
with a master giving boys football while a woman taught girls
netball. Neither school allowed girls to wear trousers. Both schools
separated boys from girls by lining them up by sex before and after
any activity, so that, for example, in assembly the children sat apart,
because the boys had led and the girls followed or vice versa. In
these ways the children were constantly reminded that they were
either male or female even when this was irrelevant to the activity in
which they were engaged.

Very similar sex differentiation took place in the four schools for
older pupils, Kenilworth and Maid Marion in Bridgehampton and
Melin Court and Waverly in Coalthorpe. For example, both Melin
Court and Waverly divided boys and girls for all games and PE, and
Waverly kept them separate for craft, so that only boys did wood
and metalwork, while only girls got cookery and needlework. In PE
and craft all the teachers were of the same sex as the pupils. Both

schools listed pupils in two separate lists on the register, and this had an interesting consequence when seats were allocated in class to the new 12-year-old pupils.

> In the woodwork room the new pupils are being allocated places at the benches, in alphabetical order, with the boys first. When Mr Beech found that he had 23 in the group it was girls left without bench places – about three girls left to work where someone was absent (i.e. changing seats every week/starting each lesson by trying to find a space).
>
> Melin Court (12–18) (4/9/78)

> Technical drawing – Mr Plumb
> There are more pupils than bench places so Parween and a boy are on the side bench, and three girls are down the front.
>
> Waverly (20/9/78)

> After break go to technical drawing with Mr Quill. He lines them up at back and side of the room, gives them seats in alphabetical order. Boys first – leaving spaces for absentees. There are 28 in the class list so five girls get left off proper desks and given slots in the side benches. Then they are told that they can sit in absentees' seats.
>
> Waverly (8/9/78)

Anything more calculated to make girls feel uneasy in wood and metalwork or technical drawing than to fail to give them a permanent seat is hard to imagine! Yet we are sure no master does it deliberately, rather it is an unthinking consequence of separating the sexes on the register.

Schools also divide the genders by their rules about clothing. All six schools had a uniform, which enforced different clothes for boys and girls. Boys were exhorted to look 'smart', which meant wearing tie and blazer, the clothes of the clerical worker, which numerous studies have shown to be a source of friction for working-class boys (e.g. Hargreaves, 1967; Lacey, 1970; Woods, 1979). All six schools stressed the importance of uniform at pre-transfer visits, and in the early weeks of the year. Boys were told to wear ties and blazers, and to keep their ties done up round their necks. This was not popular with many boys, as the essays written for us at the end of the year by Kenilworth and Maid Marion pupils show:

> Philip (Kenilworth):
> Uniforms for boys
> Uniforms for boys have to be warn tiys strate. If you come in arong coulard shirt you get the cane. (Spelling is Philip's)

> Richie (Kenilworth):
> Soon after the first session of lessons had fishsted we got to see each other in our uniforms this was funney. After we had stoped laffin at each outher we asked who were our teachers.

Formal grouping arrangements in the new schools

Anonymous boy (Kenilworth):
Sometimes I wish I wasn't at this school because you have to wear uniform. A boy in 1 gamma is sex mad. My best subject {is} history.

The anonymous boy's association of a classmate being sex mad and complaints about uniform may not seem connected to the reader, but in fact, as two other boys explain it, wearing a uniform is emasculating!

Irving: The things I don't like about Maid Marion . . . Having to wear school uniforms because you look a puff.

Jerome: Things I dislike about Maid Marion are . . . Having to wear a school uniform is another things (*sic*) I dislike because we look life 'BOFFS'

In these ways, then, pupils are formally divided not only into years, forms, and houses, but also by sex.

Teaching groups

The major formal groupings are the year, the form, and the separation of the sexes. However this by no means exhausts the groups into which pupils are organized formally by their schools. In all six schools there were further complicated grouping practices to produce teaching groups, both inside classrooms and to create classes for teaching. Particularly in the two biggest schools (Melin Court and Waverly) the groups for craft, science and art were smaller than the forms and involved dividing the pupils into different groups from those for maths, English and so on. Then in all six schools remedial teaching was provided, and pupils were regrouped to accommodate this. Then there were complicated arrangements in some of the schools to organize teaching, especially at Waverly. Waverly had two complex grouping patterns from the start of the first year. First, an elite group of pupils who had done French at their middle schools were started on German. They were withdrawn from some English, some maths and some French to attend German lessons. Then the double biology lesson on a Wednesday was oddly distorted by sex – one sex went swimming and missed a large part of the first period, the other sex then left early to go swimming leaving the master with a half-class to repeat the lesson.

Craft subjects, science and art were frequently taught to smaller groups than the form – often 20 pupils rather than 30. Two concrete examples will illustrate the complexities of creating and timetabling such groups. First we look at Guy Mannering. Six forms in the first year were divided into eight groups for 'craft' teaching, and worked

Formal grouping arrangements in the new schools

to the complex timetable shown in Table 7.1 from the start of term until half-term. There were six lessons scheduled for craft, in three pairs, on Mondays before break, and on Wednesdays both lessons 1 and 2 and 3 and 4. There were seven teachers involved, so one group was assigned to 'theory' – which was actually Marion Richardson handwriting exercises, in the central area around which the cookery, art and woodwork rooms were grouped. The seven teachers were:

Mr Bradshaw – Wood and metalwork
Mrs Bird – Cookery
Mrs Cherry – Cookery
Miss Miranda – Cookery
Mr Woolfe – Art
Mrs Adamson – Art
Miss Pink – Needlework

Table 7.1   Craft groups at Guy Mannering

Group	Monday 1–2	Wednesday 1–2	Wednesday 3–4
1	Cookery (Cherry)	Woodwork (Bradshaw)	Art (Adamson)
2	Cookery (Bird)	Theory (no one)	Art (Woolfe)
3	Needlework (Pink)	Cookery (Cherry)	Woodwork (Bradshaw)
4	Needlework (Miranda)	Cookery (Bird)	Theory (no one)
5	Art (Adamson)	Needlework (Pink)	Cookery (Cherry)
6	Art (Woolfe)	Needlework (Miranda)	Cookery (Bird)
7	Woodwork (Bradshaw)	Art (Adamson)	Needlework (Pink)
8	Theory (no one)	Art (Woolfe)	Needlework (Miranda)

This arrangement meant that a particular group of 20 pupils – who might come from two different forms, would experience three of the five activities for the first half-term, and meet two or three different staff. For example, most of form 1.5 were in group 4 for craft, so they had needlework with Miss Pink on a Monday, cookery with Mrs Bird on Wednesdays before break, and did 'theory' under the

163

eye of Mr Bradshaw after break. Table 7.1 shows these complex arrangements.

Our second example is Melin Court, where three of the first year classes were regrouped into four teaching groups for craft. 1M, 1E and 1L were redivided into groups A, B, C and D who spent the first double period of the morning as follows:

Group	Subject	Teacher
A	Cookery	Mrs Tyzack
B	Woodwork	Mr Steel
C	Woodwork	Mr Beech
D	Needlework	Miss Hartnell

After break the groups moved to another subject, Mrs Tyzack's class moving to Mr Steel. (This meant group B got four lessons of woodwork.) The same division operated to produce classes for science and art, which were timetabled simultaneously, so that the 'A' craft group was also the 'A' science group, who had science from Miss Fern and Mr Trelawny, and art from Mrs Madder.

Waverly based teaching on the mixed ability forms, but then created various different teaching groups. In science, history and geography the year began with the class as the teaching unit, but at the autumn half-term tests were given and the pupils reorganized into sets. In history these were to be based on six weeks teaching of the Anglo-Saxons and the Vikings – topics which had been covered by some children but not others in their middle schools. French also posed a problem in both Coalthorpe schools, because some middle schools did four years of it, some three, some two, some one and some none. Melin Court ignored this, stuck to 'mixed ability' and 'mixed experience' groups, and started French from scratch in all classes. Waverly put children into sets for French on the basis of how much they had done previously, and the top language set began German in some of their foreign language lessons, as well as missing some maths and English periods to study it. At Waverly therefore, English, maths, TD, art, music and RE were the only mixed-ability and mixed-sex subjects by Christmas.

None of our other schools had anything quite so complex as Waverly, but the fluidity of the groups was a common feature of middle and secondary school experience for all our pupils. Given the fluidity and complexity of the formal arrangements to make up teaching groups it is not surprising we found pupils unsure of which class they were meant to be in. Nor is it surprising that some enterprising boys were able to cause considerable disruption by joining the wrong class and/or claiming to be lost altogether. For example in the bottom two streams at Kenilworth, the maths was taught to two sets which mixed pupils from 1 zeta and 1 epsilon. This caused problems for some children – or allowed them space to cause a disturbance:

> Maths with Mrs Lee (1 zeta)
> Edmond came in looking very confused, and asking if Mrs Lee knew where Mr Pompey's maths set was. Mrs Lee was brusque with him, telling him that he had been in the school nearly 3 weeks now and this was the second or third time that he had appeared in her lesson. Why didn't he write down on his timetable where Mr Pompey had maths each time?

Wayne Patel at Melin Court was quickly able to maximize the disruptive potential of these complex groupings. He was extremely good at getting mileage out of both joining the wrong group and/or being 'lost' and not attending any class at all.

For example on 12/9/78 at Melin Court there was a double science lesson with Miss Fern after break for 23 of the pupils from form 1M (the rest of whom were with some pupils from 1E in a different group). Although this was the third week of term, Miss Fern could not rely on a settled group. At the opening of the class a new girl, Colette, arrived who had not been to science before. Miss Fern had to send her, with Elaine, to see Mr Trelawny the teacher who organized the groups. Then Miss Fern called the group register and found that there were some pupils present who should not be, including Wayne Douglas Patel. Colette and Elaine then returned, saying Colette was to be in group A for science. Then:

> Miss Fern gives out the pupils' science notebooks one at a time, calling the children to the front so she can learn their names. When she finds she does not have his exercise book Miss Fern sends Wayne Patel to Mr Trelawny because she is sure he is not in group A . . .
> Wayne returns, and tells Miss Fern that he is in group B. She asks him where their lesson is, and he does not know. Miss Fern asks loudly why he did not ask while he was with Mr Trelawny. She sends him back to find out where the 'B' group are.

In the notes the observer wrote after the lesson, the following comment captures Wayne's style:

> I wonder if Wayne Patel *knew* he was in the wrong group and wanted to be with his friend Eamonn, or just got muddled, or wanted to waste his time.

By this time Wayne has 'wasted' some twenty minutes of his double period of science, and impressed himself on Miss Fern as a nuisance. He has also provided entertainment for the rest of the class, and proved that Miss Fern is not going to do more than send him away. By the third week of term Wayne had established himself

Formal grouping arrangements in the new schools

with the class as a trouble maker, and as unable or unwilling to cope with the work. Nine days later an observer went to the 'B' science group (some of forms 1M and 1E) who also had Miss Fern for some of their science classes, when Wayne *was* due to have a science lesson with Miss Fern straight after break.

> The class arrived with a lot of noise and Miss Fern warns them that although she is aware they may get lost there is no need to fuss when they arrive and shout as if they are in the yard. Wayne Patel is not present. Miss Fern starts to call the register. She has reached the girls when Colin and Manji arrive. Jim says Colin *is* in this group, as the boys near him say he is not; Jim shows by grimaces that he knows and is teasing him. Miss Fern sends them off to the C group.

The observer could see Wayne Patel and two other boys in the yard wandering about:

> The books come out at 10.55 when the homework is returned . . .
> (8 minutes). Wayne and Glenn are now heading towards this laboratory . . .
> (another 7 minutes). Mrs Hallows comes in and Miss Fern and she leave together. Miss Fern returns with Glenn and Wayne. Gives out small pieces of graph paper. She asks who has not got a ruler and needless to say Wayne and Glenn haven't. Miss Fern says that those who are late also haven't got rulers, and enquires rhetorically if they have also forgotten their brains . . . When she says that one boy got 'Rubbish' written on his work several people round me say 'Wayne Patel'.

Wayne's reputation is already established with the observer ('needless to say') and with his peers. Wayne was unusually active in maximizing the disruptive potential of the complex grouping practices, but there was ample scope for such manoeuvres. As commentators on the comprehensive have pointed out, the groupings organized for teaching become more and more complex as genuine attempts are made to allow all pupils access to all subjects, maintain mixed ability teaching, and use limited specialist facilities. Two of our schools avoided much of this complexity by streaming, and we now examine its effects.

Streaming

There is a good deal of research on the effects of streaming in UK secondary schools, and at least three of the findings reported from other studies were replicated at both Guy Mannering and Kenilworth. We found that as the year progressed pupils in the lower streams became disillusioned with, or even hostile to, the school; that lower streams got worse teachers; and that the curriculum covered in the lower streams rapidly diverged from that taught in the higher ones. We also found that at Guy Mannering the alloca-

166

tion of chidren to streams by the head mistress Miss Tyree was somewhat idiosyncratic. Jackson (1964) reported that allocation to streams in primary schools was rarely based on objective test scores, but used only subjective reports from teachers. At Guy Mannering we found the headmistress used the lower school attended as her main allocation device. Children from Guy Mannering Lower School, situated near the Middle School, were more likely to be put in the top band than those from other schools. Children from Balaclava Road Lower School, in the city centre, and from Old Hill, on an estate housing over-spill families from London, were under-represented in the A band. Table 7.2 shows the stream allocation at Guy Mannering, so that the distribution of children from all the feeder schools to the two bands is displayed. Table 7.3 shows the allocation of children from Guy Mannering Lower School to the two bands compared to all the rest of the intake.

An idiosyncratic and non-test-based method of stream allocation would not matter if the allocation had no consequences. However, the literature suggests that in an hierarchical arrangement of classes, the pupils react to their allocation by living up to the label attached to them. Top streams adhere to the values of the school which has labelled them clever, and achieve academically. In

Table 7.2   Guy Mannering band placements by lower school attended

Band placements at Guy Mannering	Lower School Attended					
	OWCE	BR	CL	GM	OH	Other
A	23	9	12	21	5	9
B	25	11	13	14	9	9

Key: OWCE: Orton Water Church of England; BR: Balaclava Road;
CL: Coventry Lane; GM: Guy Mannering Lower; OH: Old Hill
(London Overspill); Other: Other local

Table 7.3   Band placements at Guy Mannering. Guy Mannering Lower School versus other schools

Band placements at Guy Mannering	Guy Mannering Lower	All other schools
A	21	53
B	14	58

contrast the lower streams reject the norms of the school which has rejected them, cease to work, to wear the uniform, to keep the rules, to play in teams, and fail academically. This showed up particularly clearly at Guy Mannering where as pupils progressed up the school, the 'B' band children became increasingly disillusioned and ceased to strive to attain the school's goals. Guy Mannering used an extrinsic reward system – merit marks which accrue to the pupil's house – and it quickly became clear that most of these were awarded in the 'A' band. If we compare the two classes we observed, it is clear that while children in 1.5 got merit points for their work quite freely and in large numbers, those in 1.6 hardly ever received any for academic tasks. Teachers did offer 'credits' for non-academic behaviours in the early weeks of the year, but here too 1.6 fared worse than 1.5. Teachers offered and even awarded 'credits' for some very unacademic 'achievements'. For example, Mrs Evans, who taught some of 1.6's English:

> She says that it is time for her to see if she can remember all their names and goes round the girls and boys trying to guess them . . . At the end of this exercise there are still four children whose names she does not know. She gives them a credit for this!

While the observer raised an eyebrow at this, it actually had some point – teachers learn the names of the most disruptive, the academically weak, and the colourful children first – and the four 'unknowns' *were* probably good.

In the massed music lesson Mrs Tallis offered 'credits' for non-academic achievement. After the class had rehearsed the hymn, the teacher checked if all the hymn books were covered. A few children had not yet covered theirs. Mrs Tallis said she would check them on Tuesday, and award a credit to every class in which *all* the hymn books were covered.

However in general credits were for academic achievement, and it was hard for 1.6 to earn any. Miss O'Hara, who was the form mistress, main English and RE teacher of 1.6 (a B band form with some of the weakest and most disruptive children in it), faced this problem. In the third week of term she was observed teaching English to 1.6.

> Miss O'Hara announces a spelling test – get out spelling book, put the date, and numbers 1–10. If they get 10/10 they'll get a credit, if they cheat or talk they'll get '0'.
> Words are:
> Because, Saturday, were, there, said, October, their, Guy Mannering, when, . . .
> After word 10, they swop books for marking, Word 1 – asks for volunteer,

word is spelled out, not written on the board. The words seem to be within the capabilities of at least some of the pupils, as there are some volunteers for each answer – and for the first six words the volunteer was correct.
Felicity spells 'said' OK
Girl volunteers 'their' wrong.
Once they all are marked Miss O'Hara tells them if they got 10 right they are to stand up. They are to write 'ONE CREDIT' on their work. (Felicity is one.) Silences dissent with a mention of counting the credits.
Done yesterday:
St Nicholas 52
St Francis 43
St Luke 36
St Michael 33
St Stephen 43
This is greeted with groans and cheers. Miss O'Hara says there is a credit for everyone for assembly next week if they could only line up straight.

Miss O'Hara's class is, in the first term, prepared to develop house loyalty and make an effort to get credits for their house. However, by the age of 13 (the fourth year) this has quite worn off, and the house system and credits have lost their power to motivate B band children. For example one observer was in the gym – used for the St Stephen's house assembly – and spotted a blackboard on which the number of credits each form had earned for the house in the previous month were shown. The results are shown in Table 7.4.

Table 7.4   Fourth year credits earned for St Stephen's by form

Form		No. of credits
A Band	4:1	56
	4:3	70
	4:5	77
B Band	4:2	27
	4:4	13
	4:6	Illegible

Such results are exactly like those reported twenty years ago by Hargreaves (1967) and Lacey (1970). At Guy Mannering and Kenilworth streaming polarized the children, and a cross-cutting house system did not mitigate the polarization.

The second feature of streamed schools reported in the literature was that the lower stream pupils are allocated to the lower-status/out-of-favour teachers: those who are new and probationary; old and tired, redeployed, incompetent and/or unable to keep order (e.g. Lacey, 1970). There were some signs of this at Guy Mannering and Kenilworth (e.g. late teachers were more common in the B streams at Kenilworth, as we showed in chapter 6). At Guy Mannering the B band forms had less continuity of instruction. They had more than one teacher for several subjects, which spread the burden of teaching them among the staff, but produced less continuity of instruction for them. Similarly at Kenilworth, where 1 zeta even had two form teachers: Mr Pompey and Mrs Monk. The B band form 1.6 at Guy Mannering, for example, had English from both Mrs Evans (the deputy head) and Miss O'Hara. In one of Mrs Evans's lessons she set an essay called 'About myself', and the observer noted:

> There are some complaints that they have already done this exercise with Miss O'Hara. Mrs Evans replies 'Well, that's the problem when you have two teachers. But you should be able to do it well this time, shouldn't you?'

The third issue where we found streaming at Kenilworth and Guy Mannering producing well-documented effects was curricula differentiation. Within the first three weeks of the first term the lower-stream children were doing a different curriculum from the top stream. Sometimes this was explicitly labelled on the timetable – so that at Kenilworth 1 alpha started Latin which no other class did. In other areas of the curriculum the subject label was the same – 'science', 'maths' – but the amount of material covered, and the type of coverage, diverged (Keddie, 1971; Furlong, 1984). The children were well aware of this. For example Gwen was promoted into 1 gamma from 1 delta and told us:

> When I moved from one class to another I was upset at having to start again. But when I settled down I enjoyed the prospect of a bit harder work. With moving up in the middle of term I didn't know some of the questions on the exam paper. I would like to go up even further but I doubt that I would love to learn 'latin'.

Similarly Thelma of 1 gamma told us:

> I am now in 1 gamma and in the second year I hope I stay in my form. If I go down I will be ahead in my work, if I go up I will be behind in my work.

The curricula divergence quickly became apparent to the ORACLE observers. For example one observer saw Mr Pardoe teach the Bunsen burner to both 1 gamma and 1 zeta and wrote after the 1 zeta lesson:

> When the children had gone I stopped for a few minutes to talk to Mr Pardoe. I complimented him (quite genuinely) on the different levels at which he had covered the same material with an A stream and a B stream class. It was very clear from what Mr Pardoe said that he is completely in favour of streaming.

170

Another observer visiting Kenilworth in the spring term wrote:

> Judging from the conversation which I overhear in the staff room it becomes
> more difficult for a child to move streams as the year progresses and it
> certainly becomes even more difficult still in the 2nd and 3rd year. The
> reasons are that the gap in the amount of work which has been covered by the
> streams gets wider and wider between streams as the children go through the
> school . . . particularly for any child to move up a stream because they would
> have missed so much . . . There is also a very big jump in moving from the
> epsilons and below as they don't do French and the deltas and above do.

One observer visited Guy Mannering in the spring term, and saw
maths in both 1.5 and 1.6. The comment was: 'Obviously, the range
of work on fractions is much more advanced here in 1.5 than with
1.6.' Note that the observer accepts that 1.6 will be doing much
simpler work, showing that s/he too has become part of the school's
taken-for-granted stratification of knowledge.

Thus far we have examined the year group, forms, houses,
sex-based groupings, streams and other teaching groups. While
mastering these groupings is a considerable task for the novice
pupil, these do not exhaust the formal groupings to which pupils
belong. Children in schools also find that they are organized by staff
into groups based on race and religion; need for remedial help,
handicaps and special talents such as musical ability or sporting
potential. Inside classrooms and labs and in games pupils are
involved in a bewildering range of groups organized by teachers.
Sometimes they have to work alone, at others they are combined
into pairs, threes, fours, sixes, rows, columns, teams or 'boys and
girls', and exhorted to co-operate with each other. Additionally, all
our six schools have officially organized, but voluntary, groups for
pupils: choirs, orchestras, hockey teams, gym clubs, chess tourna-
ments, and stamp enthusiasts' meetings. Before we turn to how the
pupils formed unoffical friendship groups, we analyse how these
remaining formal groupings impinge on their lives.

Race and religion

These two characteristics have to be considered jointly, because the
only official groupings which separated children ostensibly by religion were actually isolating them by race. All our six schools had
some pupils who were practising Roman Catholics or Jehovah's
Witnesses, and some who were Sikhs, Hindus or Muslims. Consequently, where there were Christian assemblies and RE lessons,
these children were either physically or socially absent from them.
A typical school assembly was observed at Melin Court, where
three times a month the whole first year had an assembly in the

drama hall. The majority of pupils were marched in form by form, with the Muslim and Catholic children remaining outside in the corridor. These pupils are then brought in and out whenever there is secular information proclaimed. One particular assembly we observed started with an announcement from the deputy head about elections for pupil governors, so the 'outcasts' had to be brought in at the beginning to hear him. Then they left, and the second year sang 'All things bright and beautiful', heard a homily from the senior mistress on responsibility, said the Lord's Prayer, heard another prayer, and then listened to a second homily (on litter) from the deputy head. That concluded the Christian part of the proceedings, so the 'outcasts' were ushered back to hear notices about football practice, hockey and netball.

For assembly, then, the racial/religious minority groups are physically separated. In RE lessons, such children are *socially* segregated. In all our six schools the Catholic and Muslim children were not provided with any alternative space, but were merely left to work at some other subject at the back of the classroom in which everyone else was doing RE. So, for example, at Waverly when 1BN had their first RE lesson with Mrs Attfield, the observer noted that:

> the one Muslim girl (Gita) in the class will be coming to the lessons, but using them to do extra English. As she has not brought work today the teacher gives her a book to read.

Similarly when 1E at Melin Court had a scripture lesson with Mrs Durrant, the observer noted that while the rest of the class wrote an account of 'Israel in Jesus's Time', two boys Jim (a Catholic) and Manji (a Muslim) were sitting at the back doing other work.

This is potentially a good time to give remedial help to Muslim or Hindu pupils who need it, but it is often wasted because the RE teacher is unlikely to supervise those pupils unless they are disruptive, and the conditions for working on material unrelated to lesson content are hardly ideal. In another of Mrs Durrant's lessons, the observer noted: 'We are going to learn about the life of Jesus. In the class there is one Asian boy who stares out of the window . . . he is ignored.'

There are not, to our knowledge, any studies of the effects of such social segregation, and we have no data on how pupils like Gita, Jim and Manji feel about it. We do, however, know a little about our next grouping principle – remedial teaching sessions.

Formal grouping arrangements in the new schools

Remedial groupings

Five of our six schools (all but Guy Mannering) began the autumn term by screening pupils to see who needed remedial help in reading (and sometimes maths too). Guy Mannering did not have remedial groups to begin with, but 1.6 became so impossible to teach that after Christmas the B band classes were broken up and reorganized to create a remedial form. Dirk and Caspar were both put in that form, which had nearly 20 boys and 4 girls. All the other schools used a different system, removing those pupils in need of remedial teaching from certain lessons for instruction in small groups.

At Gryll Grange Mrs Stone, the part-time remedial teacher, heard all the children read, tested them, and began to extract small groups for remedial help within the first fortnight of the school year. In some schools remedial children missed French, while in others the time was taken from English. At Maid Marion the observer commented that:

> both the English and Maths staff are very keen to pick out those who need remedial help as soon as possible. They already have lists from the junior schools as to who was receiving help there . . .

Among the new entrants to Maid Marion were two boys, Miles and Lester, who were:

> Very close buddies . . . {and} very obviously in need of remedial work and stand out amongst all the others because of their inability . . . to read even the simplest instructions.

The school organized remedial maths and English for both boys by taking them out of most French and music lessons. Both boys wanted remedial help, and were anxious at Maid Marion until their programme was settled. Lester had suffered brain damage as a baby, and neither boy had achieved a reading age of 7 by transfer to Maid Marion.

Kenilworth, the other Bridgehampton school, was equally prompt in establishing remedial groups for low-stream children. For example, early in the autumn term an observer went to 1 zeta's English lesson with Mr Gordon and found that:

> one or two of the children would be removed from the class for this lesson for a remedial session with Miss Cotton. The children arrived, and Miss Cotton came and removed a group including Ralph, Maurice, Walter, Archie, and Josie.

Mr Gordon told the observer that he found it 'amazing' how some children seemed to like being withdrawn for remedial work, although they did not appear to like being taken out for the handwriting clinic.

Remedial classes are the smallest teaching group (apart from instrumental music lessons) which any of our ORACLE children experienced. Two points are worth making about such groups concerning their location and their atmosphere. First, in all the five schools, remedial teaching took place in very unfavourable locations. At Gryll Grange, Mrs Stone's classes took place either in the first year area (effectively in a cloakroom) or in the staffroom. At Kenilworth, Miss Airdale's remedial group of six boys from 1 zeta met on a landing on the top floor of the building.

Second, the atmosphere of remedial groups was not, as one might expect, therapeutic or scholarly. Rather, those we saw were merely miniature recapitulations of the confrontations between teachers and pupils. For example, on September 6th an observer at Kenilworth found that 'Mr Gordon, the English master, had arranged for me to attend remedial groups run by Miss Cotton and Miss Airdale . . . ' Miss Airdale took six boys to their 'room' – the aforementioned landing – and the lesson began.

> Miss Airdale gave them out some reading books, and told them that she wanted them to take the books home and read them aloud . . . the children became slightly excited and over-animated . . . Kevin became quite incapable of controlling himself and was making the most ridiculous comments . . . Miss Airdale then gave them all a book of phonics, and they had to read out lists of words like cat, sad, bad, man, etc. This was far below the level at which they needed help . . . the children were being openly rude and aggressive.

This was an unhappy lesson for teacher (and observer) and had all the problems associated with a mismatch of task and child (Bennett *et al.*, 1984).

Remedial extraction is another excuse for children to avoid appearing for classes on time, or to get genuinely muddled about where they should be learning what with whom. One day at Kenilworth, 1 zeta were scheduled to have a geography lesson with Mrs Cullen and

> Six children did not turn up for Mrs Cullen's lesson. The other children said it was the remedial reading group. Mrs Cullen looked at the pink list of remedial reading groups and was very puzzled because her period was not one of those (when) the remedial reading group was supposed to absent itself.

Individual and small group music lessons, and coaching in sports, also allow pupils to avoid lessons or become muddled. On the whole those children involved in learning the trumpet or training for the

school volleyball team were either better organized or more conformist, and did not use their chances to avoid other lessons or
disrupt the school, but came and went from classes correctly. We
have not, therefore, dwelt on those other extractions, but instead
turn to groups inside classrooms.

The groups inside the groups

One of the prevailing myths about primary schools is that children
work, not alone, but co-operatively in groups. Secondary teachers
feel that learning to work alone is almost as much of a problem as
learning not to move around. We know from the ORACLE project
(Galton *et al.*, 1980; Galton and Simon, 1980; Simon and Willcocks,
1981) that very few primary teachers actually organize their pupils
in this way. Many seat them into groups, and allow talk, but few
actually set tasks which are to be done in co-operation. In this
section we look at how, if at all, teachers in our six schools
sub-divided the classes they taught for co-operative and/or practical
work.

It is clear that Gryll Grange stands out from the other schools in
the project in that it still seated children in groups around tables for
all lessons, while in the other schools seating was in desks or at
benches facing the front in all academic subjects. Gryll Grange
fitted the 'primary' pattern – the children were sitting in groups and
engaged in social interaction, but rarely co-operated on tasks. In the
other five schools, there was a clear distinction between 'academic'
and 'practical and scientific' lessons. In academic lessons, pupils
were expected to work individually even if they were allowed to talk
quietly to their neighbours; in science, craft, PE and home economics pupils were frequently required to work in pairs, threes,
fours or teams. While this is taken for granted, it has not been
studied at all – that is we know nothing about the effects of pupils
being expected sometimes to study as if there is no one else in the
room and sometimes to study co-operatively, not according to their
own desires, but subject to the *fiat* of staff.

Thus, at Melin Court, in a lesson such as geography with Mr
Braund, pupils would be told on no account to co-operate:

> I've noted that you people have been working together *COPYING*. Next
> term you will do an exam where there is no chance of copying from your
> neighbours so you've got to get used to thinking by yourselves.

Yet in the same school lessons in science, cookery and PE were
often based round enforced co-operation. Similarly at Maid Marion
in one day pupils did gym – which involved working in pairs, threes,

fours, and sixes – home economics – where Miss Devine allowed

> each group of about four to prepare a hot snack and a hot drink. The children
> were allowed to group themselves and they could then decide what they
> wanted to cook.

– and science where Mr Salter was teaching them to light the Bunsen, and 'each pair collected a Bunsen burner'. French, maths and social studies in contrast involved individual working.

Maid Marion was unusual, however, in that it was the only school where English teaching actually involved group work. We have described Mr Barrell's lessons briefly because they are quite unlike any other English lessons we saw. Mr Barrell's classroom had tables, rather than rows of desks, and he used the groups at the tables as work groups. Over a three-week period we saw Mr Barrell:

(1) Organize the children to tell each other stories in their groups.
(2) Organize the children to read to each other in the group.
(3) Organize the children to read to each other in pairs or threes to get reading practice until the end of the lesson.
(4) Organize children to tell a story to their table, and then each table had to choose the best to tell the whole class.

During all such activities Mr Barrell walked round the room, listening to the children. This was an unusual teaching arrangement in an academic subject, and it is remarkable that no other teacher used this strategy, which, as we showed in chapter 4, avoided humiliation for the pupils and a good deal of work was done.

There is one consequence of forcing children to work co-operatively on which we have some data. Some pupils do not like it at all, while others find that it highlights their social isolation in their classes, for example, Daphne and Jessica, at Maid Marion:

> Both of these girls seemed not to have any particular friends in their class.
> Jessica is with three other girls who were from Kenilworth Warden, two of
> whom are very much a pair together, and the third (Fay) is a girl whom she
> used to work with at Kenilworth Warden, but has recently fallen out with
> Daphne went to the same junior school as Jackie and Odette but they are
> such a close pair (hand in glove wherever they go) it is very difficult for
> Daphne to join in with them. Jessica and Daphne have therefore been pushed
> together by force of circumstances as they are both loners. They spent much
> of their time telling me about the problems of working together. They did not
> like each other and they did not get on. They kept pointing out all sorts of
> occasions when their different work patterns and speeds of work were very
> annoying to each other, when they were forced to work together particularly
> in science.

Similar problems of children who were put together and did not function as a team could be found in every classroom. We do not have enough detailed data on groups and their uses to expand this section, but it is worth saying that some children may have found remembering whether Miss X allows co-operation, forbids it, or insists on it, yet another burden to shoulder in their new schools.

We now turn to school clubs and societies.

Clubs and societies

All six schools had a range of official, but voluntary, clubs, teams and activities. New pupils are usually told about them, and encouraged to join, as for example, at Kenilworth:

> Mrs Blewitt turned up for this lesson telling the children that Miss Airdale . . . had been ill so she had to go home. She asked the children if they knew her name, and several of them knew that she was Mrs Blewitt. She told them that she taught biology. She then went on to tell them about the wildlife club, and urged them to come to meetings if they wanted to.

Our data show that there is no long-term effort to get pupils into clubs – the recruitment takes place in many different settings, but only for a few weeks. Thus at Maid Marion:

> Assembly, Maid Marion on September 8th
> Mr Taff took over to give an announcement about chess. The first chess club meeting would be in his room in the tower block. He would like to enter a team into a competition but he will need six first year pupils for this; at present he only has one.

Children who do not join in these early weeks are unlikely to be pursued after half-term in their first year. Recruitment is short-lived, early in the term, and not continuous. Many pupils do not join any such groups.

> Gemma (Melin Court): Knows of lots of clubs but doesn't fancy any of them.
> Bart (Waverly): Goes home to dinner so cannot go to any clubs but 'wasn't bothered about clubs anyway.' His hobby is fishing with his Dad.
> Sandra (Waverly): Hasn't joined any clubs saying 'I don't fancy any of them, Miss.'

Many of the clubs, societies and activities are sporting: hockey, netball, soccer, rugby, badminton, gymnastics, swimming, volleyball, crosscountry, weightlifting and trampolining existed in at least one of our six schools. Other activities were musical, dramatic, or more sedentary such as chess, stamp and birdwatching clubs.

There are several points about such activities worth making from our observations. First, pupils who live a long way from school or go home to lunch cannot participate in many of these activities. Miss Tyree made this point at the parents' evening at Guy Mannering, when she told them that children who went home to lunch were deprived of many valuable experiences. Josh, at Maid Marion, told our interviewer that he could not join the swimming club because it did not happen until 7.30 in the evening, and 'of course' he could not get back to Dorridge after it. Not only sports took place after school. Elmer told the interviewer that he was a very active member of the chess club, and was playing in a tournament that night. Bart, already quoted, was a typical pupil who ate lunch at home, and took no part in clubs. Some children were keen enough on an activity to change their arrangements. Alistair (Melin Court) went home to lunch most days, but brought sandwiches when he had a football practice. Malcolm (Melin Court) made an effort to get back early from lunch on one day to play table tennis, as well as staying after school for rugby practice.

Malcolm's rugby practice was because he had been chosen for a school team. Indeed in several of the schools we found that so-called 'clubs' were actually practices for the school teams. For example: Dan (Maid Marion) told the interviewer about the swimming club of which he is a keen member, and also about the football and rugby clubs, explaining that they were really teams for the school rather than clubs for anyone to join. Josh (Maid Marion) also bemoaned the fact that the football club was 'really' the school football team, and he had not made it this time and therefore could not join the club. He thought it was unfair that the football and rugby clubs were really team events only and did not give a chance to other people to join in and have practice.

Another, if somewhat different, problem is the club which was not open to first year children. For example, at Waverly Ellen described herself as a 'gymnastics fanatic' but could not join the gym club as it was only for second years and up. Delia played netball and volleyball and was in the netball team. She knew that there were also clubs for chess, birdwatching, basketball and gym – but the basketball was only for fourth and fifth years, and she 'thought you had to be asked before you could join the gym club.' At Maid Marion Nathan mentioned to the interviewer a lot of the clubs like chess, rugby, football and gym, adding that there were quite a few other clubs which the first years could not join (e.g. badminton). Indeed this was a common complaint at Maid Marion, where both badminton and dancing clubs were not open to the first years.

We should not, however, assume that if all clubs were open to everyone that all pupils would join. Some children never joined a club at all; others tried one briefly and left it. Vaudine and Merle, at

Maid Marion, had visited the drama club, but left it because it did not seem very interesting, it was mainly preparing for the Christmas concert, it seemed rather chaotic, and they 'did not really know what it was about'. Other pupils had left other societies and activities equally unimpressed.

For those pupils who were activists and joiners, school clubs often competed with out-of-school bodies for their time. Davina, Miss Tweed's prize pupil, was an activist – singing, playing an instrument, swimming, running. We found parallels in all our other schools. For example, Juliette at Melin Court goes swimming, likes school dances, and does cross-country every Wednesday night after school. Ellis at Melin Court is in the soccer team and practised on Wednesday lunchtimes and Thursday nights, and was planning to play in a Sunday League team too. Norman (Melin Court) plays badminton, table tennis and trampolining. Three boys at Maid Marion, Rolf, Madoc and Dermot, all played in the school soccer and rugby teams; Dermot had joined the drama group, and Madoc and Dermot were both Scouts and went rowing out of school. Two other boys in their class, John and Richard, belonged to the drama club and the choir – which exhausted Richard so much that on those nights he had to go to bed early to make up for the extra strain. Neil, in contrast, was slightly aggrieved that he could not join any more clubs at Maid Marion because of his Sunday league soccer club, Scouts, and Kenilworth Warden Community Centre swimming club. Similarly Avril at Waverly had joined the netball and volleyball clubs, was in an amateur dramatic society outside school but could not act at school because drama clashed with volleyball.

The problem of clubs, teams and societies in our six schools can be summarized as follows: recruiting drives for new pupils stop quite early in the term; many pupils join nothing; the activists belong to several things; some children are unable to participate because of living a long way from school; or going home to lunch; and clubs unavailable to first years strike them as especially desirable. We have already seen in chapter 6 that many children find breaks and lunchtimes boring; even activists are bored on days when they have no engagements. Overall our data suggest that for the majority, school clubs are not a salient part of school life. Our last comment before moving on to informal groups in schools comes from an 11-year-old cynic – Nathan from Maid Marion. Nathan 'complained' to the interviewer that in the little booklets which they had been given, Maid Marion had listed lots of clubs and he had not heard of most of them since he started as a pupil, and did not think they really existed at all.

Nathan's cynicism about the existence of school clubs is clearly related to their relatively unofficial and voluntary nature. Nathan could not doubt the existence of most of the other groups he had been assigned to: his year, his sex, his form, his craft group, and, later in the year, his sets for maths and English. These were all too real. Sometimes the pupils' allocations to multiple groups produced conflicts between their different interests, and that issue concludes the chapter.

Conflicts of interest?

Pupils belong to so many groups that merely remembering them is a considerable task. Then, as Lomax (1980) has pointed out at the opening of this chapter, the structural arrangements the school makes have consequences for the pupil identities. Pupils have to find friends in each teaching group they are allocated to, because their closest companions in their class may not be in the same remedial group, craft group, maths set or whatever. This is one of the central themes in chapter 9, but the data on Wayne in this chapter showed him aligning himself with Glenn when his normal buddy, Eamonn, was in a different group. When the teacher wants co-operation, the social composition of the group may become very important, and the interests of the different groups pupils belong to may conflict.

One of the most obvious examples of two different allegiances conflicting with educational purposes is that between sex and small group work. Tann (1981), drawing on ORACLE work done in the lower schools, argues that 10- and 11-year-old pupils are unwilling to form mixed sex small groups to work co-operatively, and if they are forced to form them, the two sexes do not actually share the task. Failures of boys and girls to combine for academic or practical operations have been reported from the transfer schools earlier in this volume (e.g. chapter 4). This is, in part, the result of pupils being assigned to two groups: sex and a small working group. As Buswell (1981) has pointed out, pupils can be divided by sex twenty times per day (when the register is called, seating in assembly, for a PE lesson, at dinner, when a teacher says 'Right, girls, line up first and so on) by the school authorities. The rare assignments which involve forgetting the sexual divide are unlikely to succeed in overcoming the conditioning of the sexual division. This is not the place to discuss the merits and demerits of co-operative working (Galton, forthcoming; Bennett, 1985) but it is clear that mixed groups have little chance of functioning against the tide of sexual segregation that normally characterizes pupils' lives.

There are potential conflicts between the relative demands of the various groups to which pupils are assigned. The child may be needed by the choir master and the remedial reading teacher at the same time; attending a house assembly may involve being late for cookery; and being left to work alone in an RE lesson is a visible stigma that can vitiate any attempts at multi-racial group work. It is possible that as schools become more complex, understanding how the various overlapping and separate groups function is a major task for research. The complexities do not end with the formal groups, however, because there are two sets of informal groups to which pupils have important allegiances which cross-cut the formal groupings. These groups – the pupils' families and their cliques – are the subjects of the next two chapters.

CHAPTER 8

One big family?
The home and the school

The custom of holding family prayers for the whole household spread
gradually from the 1830s until it was a practice widespread throughout the
upper and middle class . . . All segregated categories of the household, e.g.
servants, children, adults and visitors, were gathered together . . . the
occasion reinforced the idea of community . . . Private family worship,
believed to be the prime duty of the Master/Father of this small hierarchical
kingdom, was seen as one of the keystones of the social fabric.

(Davidoff, 1973: 35)

Davidoff's analysis of family prayers in the Victorian home is a
prime example of the imagery of the family superimposed upon the
actual family. In this chapter we examine the two themes in relation
to the ORACLE schools: that is the impact of the real family upon
everday life in schools *and* the invocation of the 'ideal-type' family
in school rhetoric. The home-school relationship is scrutinized first.

The home and the school

The teacher and school are always working in the shadow of the
children's families. Parents are expected to perform certain duties,
may become hostile to school events, and are always a potential
audience for the teacher's work. Siblings, too, are often present in
the classroom in a shadowy, distant manner. In this section we
examine the parents as audience, as a group with specified duties to
the school, as an enemy force, and as a potential source of 'problems' for the teacher.

Parents as audience
Parents are not present physically in the classroom, but the work

done in the school is often visible to the parents. Teachers sometimes refer explicitly to this, as in the following example from Maid
Marion.

> Mrs York is the fabric teacher. The children were told that they were going to
> make some stuffed soft toys. She showed them some examples of what had
> been made in earlier years and told them the range of patterns which they
> could use. Seals, 'Snoopies', elephants and mice were the main ones. She said
> that the task was very simple and they had probably done something rather
> like this before in their junior schools. The idea was again something that
> they could make fairly easily, fairly quickly so that they could take it home
> and show it off to their mums and dads and in order for them to get used to
> using these particular machines.

The pressure on craft teachers may be particularly strong, but
similar comments were made in academic lessons as well. There is,
for example, little functional difference between the next two
extracts. At Kenilworth Mrs Stockton had given the pupils a list of
75 words which were the same in French and English:

> Kenilworth – French, Mrs Stockton
> She said they could tell their parents that they learned 75 French words today.
> 'They'll think you are a genius,' she said.

This is not very different from the first woodwork lesson at Maid
Marion:

> Mr Moore explained they would be making something 'quite simple' and that
> they would finish quickly so that they felt they had achieved something and
> could really take something home to show it off to their parents.

The 'something' in woodwork was a keyring decorated with shaped
and polished pieces of wood. When parents are actually coming up
to visit the school, a special effort may be made. Thus one day at
Kenilworth, Miss Stephenson tried to enthuse 1 gamma to be neater
by the threat of a parental visit to the school:

> She warned them that there was a parents' evening tomorrow, and she
> wanted to be able to tell their parents that their work was getting *neater*.

> Gryll Grange – October 10th
> There will be a parents' evening after half-term when an assessment will take
> place of children's work. There is an appointment system for the parents.
> One consequence is that staff are aiming to cover the walls with displayed
> work as the school has a good reputation for this.

Occasionally the passive audience of parents turns into an active
participant in the school's life. Usually this happens when a parent is

unhappy with what they think is going on at the school, as in the 'case of Benedict Kortright' which erupted at Guy Mannering. Benedict was in 1.6 at Guy Mannering, the most 'difficult' lower-band class who were quickly unpopular in the staffroom. One of our observers was in the staffroom when it was announced that Mrs Powlett, his mother, had written to the head saying that Benedict's work was not being marked and his teacher had left spellings wrong.

> Mrs Evans, the deputy head, reads out the letter to us when we are having coffee after lunch. There is much laughter because Mrs Powlett has spelt unhappily with two Lls.

Mrs Evans went on to explain why she had not corrected all Benedict's spelling mistakes:

> If I marked every spelling wrong with Benedict he would be permanently discouraged. So I had Benedict in and asked him, 'Where does your mother teach, Benedict?'
> Benedict: 'She doesn't.'
> Mrs Evans: 'Oh I thought she was an expert' {said very sarcastically}
> Benedict: 'No, Miss. She works in a shop.'

Later in the lunch hour there was a further development when:

> Another staff member comes in and says Mrs Powlett was on the phone to Miss Tyree {the head} for half an hour today. The staff teaching Benedict go through his books very carefully before Mrs Powlett comes up for her visit.

It seems especially unfortunate that the school and the home should have fallen out over Benedict, because his problems were such that he urgently needed all the adults in his world cooperating. The ORACLE interview with his parents reveals the difficulties in Benedict's life. The interviewer reported on his meeting as follows:

> I saw Mr and Mrs Powlett at Guy Mannering Middle School. Mr Powlett is Benedict's step-father, and did most of the talking. He told me that Mrs Powlett had been divorced from Ben's father because he used to beat her up and generally ill treat her. He thinks that Ben is very like his father in many ways, and gave me a short lecture on the importance of heredity as opposed to environment in the development of the young human. Ben has been seen by the Child Guidance Clinic in Ashburton because of a variety of behaviour problems. Mr Powlett outlined this in some detail, and dwelled at some length on Ben's earlier habit of urinating on his bedroom carpet. Whereas Mrs Powlett tried several times to indicate that there is a sensitive side to Ben, Mr Powlett would have none of this. He repeatedly said that there is no point in talking to Ben because he does not have any of the normal human feelings of affection, remorse, etc.
> It was very clear that this child is causing his mother and step-father a good deal of worry, and that they are finding it very difficult to find in him qualities which they can like.

One big family? The home and the school

In the light of this, the failure of the school and the parents to work together is sad. The interview with Benedict himself was not a 'confessional', unlike those with some other children, but revealed Benedict as 'impassive'. The longer-term relationship of Benedict and Guy Mannering was not happy, for by the July of his first year he was 'on report'. The case of Benedict Kortright shows the kind of parental involvement the ORACLE schools did not want. Presumably it is because of a desire to avoid such parental involvement that Gryll Grange adopted the following policy. An observer went to the school on July 10th and visited Miss Tweed's class:

> Then Miss Tweed issued an amazing instruction. 'Tear up your old maths books. You are not allowed to take them home. And then you can do the same for English.'

Parents are expected to be an *appreciative* audience; admiring the stuffed toy, applauding the French vocabulary, and looking at homework. If, however, they start to involve themselves in criticizing the teacher's work they have probably 'overstepped' the boundaries of their role. One way in which parents were seen as 'going too far' was also reported from Guy Mannering. In the staffroom one of the PE teachers:

> said she was fed up with parents wanting their children to be in sports teams, and even some of the children got very stroppy because they were not in the team. One case concerned a girl who was half a length behind the child who was picked in the trials for the swimming team and the mother came up and demanded that her daughter should be in the team because she had practised.

Many of the occasions where the family impinged on the school during the autumn term concerned parents who were failing in their duties – for example:

> Melin Court
> Mrs Hallows (head of year) told me about a child who had been absent for a week. The staff thought it was because her father had stolen her sponsored walk money for drink and she was too scared/embarrassed to come in and admit this.
>
> Waverly – 1st and 2nd year assembly
> Mr Parkin reminded the 2nd years to bring in their sponsored walk money. This was the last week – 'If you haven't brought it in this week we will be visiting your homes to ask your parents where it is and to hand it over. That money is legally the school's . . .'

These parents had failed in their duties to the school either by being officious or by defaulting. It is worth examining what the schools think the parents' duties are, and how they communicate them.

The duties of the parents

The clearest statement of what role parents were to play in their children's schooling came from Guy Mannering, when Miss Tyree addressed a parents' evening. An examination of her address reveals what every parent needs to know:

> Miss Tyree says the school gives a 'moderate' amount of homework. Most parents are in favour of this, and they should encourage children to do the small amount given conscientiously.
>
> Children will be allocated to a house, and they become loyal to their house. Parents should encourage this loyalty to the house and its colour. The school's disciplinary system is based on duty to the form teacher, to the house, and to parents, and so parents should encourage this.
>
> On the first day of the autumn parents should *send* their children, not bring them. 'Please don't *bring* your child on September 1st' because she has no time to see parents. When they want to see her they should make an appointment.
>
> Parents should make sure all the children's belongings are labelled with their name . . . and provide children with a satchel – or some kind of a bag, but please not a hard attaché case.

This speech covers the main duties the six schools required of parents: overseeing homework, labelling belongings, supporting the school, and not turning up to see teachers except by appointment. Miss Tyree's emphasis on the house system was unusual, but the rest of her injunctions were not. She also asked parents to recognize that initially the incoming pupils would find Guy Mannering tiring so parents should 'give them nourishing food and make sure they get plenty of rest.' Miss Tyree also announced that parents are expected, having chosen a school with a uniform, to make sure their children wear it. Finally, they are not to mollycoddle children (see Prendergast and Prout, 1986) by stopping them doing PE even in winter – and ideally should ensure they have school dinners, because most of the school clubs meet at lunchtime. There is one other duty parents have which becomes apparent early in the autumn term, and that is completing a form giving basic information about child, home and family for the school files. This form was a significant event in the early weeks of all our schools.

> Gryll Grange, 1T
> Miss Tweed goes through the form that their parents have to fill in, and return to the school. It includes questions on allergies to elastoplast and penicillin, and requires 'mother's phone number at work'.

One big family? The home and the school

Waverly, Mr Bronte's class
Told there are two letters to take home. Letter one asks parents about dinner arrangements. 'Take it home, get your parents to sign it, and bring it back! Do it neatly!'
Second letter requests information about where parents can be contacted, etc.

Guy Mannering, 27th Sepember, Miss O'Hara 1.6
3.35 The period ends. Those children who haven't brought their phone nos. are told not to forget. There are still children therefore who have not named a place where their parents can be contacted in working hours.

Melin Court, Mrs Wordsworth's class
Mrs Wordsworth explains there is a letter to take home – about how lunchtime is to be occupied. Parents have to complete it.

Melin Court, Assembly
Mrs Marks the senior mistress gives a homily about the two forms their parents have to sign.
A Importance of form one (re dinner hour). Children are *not* to leave the school in the dinner hour unless their parents have signed the form saying they are going home to lunch.
B. A second form coming on which they must put the phone number of where their mother works.

In all six schools, the parents were responsible for providing the basic information these forms demanded, and their efficiency or dilatoriness in doing so reflects on the child in his classroom. In such ways the parents are under scrutiny by the school from the first day.

One duty which Miss Tyree did not mention, but which was stressed at some of our other schools, was ensuring that children *attended*. That is, parents were responsible for ensuring that the children came rather than played truant, and that when they were legitimately absent, a parental note signifying this was received. For example:

Waverly – 1st year assembly
Mr Bronte warned the whole year group that anyone thinking of playing truant should know that there were two attendance officers who were sent to visit their homes if anything suspected – so in the case of genuine absence parents should phone or send a letter.

Waverly also provided a 'compensation' for parents who failed to encourage or supervise homework. They had a quiet room set aside for homework at lunchtime so that children could do prep even if their homes were too crowded, noisy or disruptive. The other schools expected *parents* to ensure that homework is done, and a suitable location to do the task provided:

One big family? The home and the school

Kenilworth – Mr Barrell's English class
Mr Barrell said that to do written work 'we have to have quiet'. The same thing applies at home. It is no good trying to do homework with the television on.

Maid Marion – social studies 3rd week of term
Mr Welsh said that by now they should all have finished evolution, volcanoes, and two short pieces of written work. Some hadn't finished. They had to plan their own homework, to spread it out and 'not leave it all to the last night' when their mothers would 'start ringing up and saying how their little Jimmy had been working till 11 o'clock at night' because he had so much work to do.

The parents' role in overseeing homework can sometimes lead to active intervention in the classroom.

Gryll Grange 1T
Friday afternoon means PE. Miss Tweed told me at breaktime that Dean had been in tears all morning. He had been told that if he did not know his 4x table he would not be allowed to play soccer in his PE lesson. That day he had brought a note saying that his father had heard his 4x table and he knew it at home – but that morning in class he couldn't get past 4x3.

Miss Tweed accepted his father's account and said to the observer that Dean had 'poor retention'. Other teachers discovered that parents were getting involved with their children's homework during teacher-pupil interaction. For example at Guy Mannering in Mrs Forrest's maths class, she had been talking quietly to Lawrence, and was so surprised by something he told her that she commented aloud 'Your mum watches you do all your homework? To see you do it properly? She must be very busy then.' On another occasion when 1.5 had English with Mr Evans, and he had them speaking to the class for one minute, Lawrence spoke on 'My Bedroom' and the observer wrote 'We learn that Lawrence's mother takes all his work for which he got a star and hangs it on his bedroom wall.' Another example of active involvement in school work from Guy Mannering parents also appeared in Mr Evans' English class with 1.5:

The task this morning is to finish off the piece that they were given for homework. They had to write an essay on 'My Favourite TV Programme' and this morning they are to colour in a picture about it . . . Some of them are to come out to the front and read their essays. Mirelle, Howard and Caitlin read their pieces. Then Terence is next. He says that his favourite programme is 'The World About Us'. 'Is it really?' says Mr Evans. 'Well actually it's not my first choice,' says Terry. Apparently, he chose Benny Hill but his mother wouldn't let him do that because she didn't like it. He has written quite a large chunk from the *Radio Times*. Mr Evans spots this and makes a joke of it.

Terence's parents were not the only ones to intervene in that particular homework test. Gavin Radice's had also taken a hand in his essay. Once the class were drawing their pictures Mr Evans called Gavin to bring his book out for marking.

'Look here' (takes Gavin to the board and writes field and then crosses it out heavily). 'What do you think of that?' Gavin: 'It's messy.' Mr Evans: 'Well that's what I think of your work.' He gives me Gavin's book to read. His favourite programme is *Hackett* because it's violent. He says that he likes the violence and the killing but not the bad language. At one point he has written about a girl in bed in the nude and 'in the nude' has been crossed out by his parents.

Guy Mannering parents were not the only ones to check homework, and involve themselves in the tasks. At least one parent at Gryll Grange did, incurring Miss Tweed's wrath.

Gryll Grange 1T
Marcia was really shouted at by Miss Tweed. Her father had torn a page out of her homework book because it was untidy.

Some teachers suggested that children should involve their parents in their homework, although it is not clear how seriously the following proposals were made:

Kenilworth
In 1 zeta Mr Pompey and Mrs Monk were talking about homework. Mr Pompey said if it was something extremely simple perhaps their parents would be able to help.

Gryll Grange
Mr Lyons said that they must practise French at home and with their friends.

Kenilworth
Mrs Cullen gave them a worksheet with questions about Bridgehampton. She explained that it was to be completed for homework, and that the answers to all the questions except no.8 were on the paper. If the pupils did not know the answers to no.8 they should 'ask your mum and dad.'

In these ways, the classroom teachers reinforce to the children what their parents were told by the head before transfer. Miss Tyree's message already quoted was like Mr Stackpole's, the head of Melin Court, who had told parents in answer to a question on homework:

In the 1st year this would consist of finishing off tasks set in class, and in the 2nd year they would have a homework timetable. If they were working as they should in the 4th and 5th they would have quite a lot of work to do.

He wanted the parents to support the school in ensuring this was done. As parents were enjoined to ensure that homework was done, so too they were expected to be active in sending pupils properly dressed.

Uniform

If a school has a uniform, one of the parental duties is to ensure that children are wearing it to school. Miss Tyree was particularly strong in this, as the Pilchs found out when they tried to enrol their son, Carter, and his sister at Guy Mannering. The story began on October 4th.

> A boy (Carter Pilch) had been admitted to 1.5 the day before and his sister was brought this morning. As she was wearing earrings Miss Tyree made some comment. After consultation with her husband in their car the mother returned to the school and withdrew both children.
> Miss Tyree reported this to the staff at break, by saying she'd seen them off. Seeing me, she added 'But you see – last week we accepted a child whose parents wanted a school with discipline – that is what we have at this school, – ' This incident was the predominant staffroom topic for the rest of the day.
> P.S. Carter Pilch and sister are to be readmitted on Monday. Apparently, according to a triumphant Miss Tyree, their mother had visited Banbury Middle School and decided Guy Mannering was preferable, and had rung, in tears, asking if the children could be readmitted.

In general, Miss Tyree succeeded in getting her whole school into uniform, as the observer noted early in the field work when he wrote:

> Unlike those at Gryll Grange the boys have all had haircuts and new uniforms, while the girls with long hair now have short hair or tied back in plaits.

The incident with Carter Pilch was such a topic of staffroom conversation that the next observer to visit the school was immediately regaled with an account of events:

> Carter is a new boy who has been admitted into the school late and whose sister created the fuss because she wouldn't take off her earrings. Apparently the parents tried every other school in the area and then had to come back and ask Miss Tyree to take the children back in, having said they would never allow them to enter the school! Naturally Miss Tyree is rejoicing in her triumph.

However, at the end of October the issue of earrings had not been finally resolved:

> Guy Mannering, October 31st – home economics flat
> There is a new crisis over the wearing of earrings in that another boy has

come in having had his ears pierced over the half-term holiday. Miss Tyree
has sent him off home and the parent is ringing up to try and get him back into
the school. Some of the girls in the same year say that they were waiting to see
what the reaction would be before having theirs done . . .

Apart from these few incidents – and the excitement over two boys
and a girl shows how rare breaches of the rules at Guy Mannering
were – Miss Tyree succeeded in enforcing her uniform rules. All the
other schools tried to persuade parents to keep their children in
line. Thus on parents' evenings at Melin Court, Waverly, and Gryll
Grange, Mr Stackpole, Mr Parkin, and Mr Washbrook (the retiring
head) all told the parents their duties:

Melin Court
Mr Stackpole told parents that what he wanted was 'children suitably dressed
for the job in neat, tidy clothing.' He thought that the vast majority saw the
point of this. 'I've been through it and I know every trick that children can
play,' he said, 'I know you will give firm and proper guidance on this.'

Waverly
Mr Parkin warned parents against children bringing expensive clothing to
school. He wants the pupils to be proud of their school and the uniform . . .
He has brought along a number of pupils . . . to show the children what they
can wear and what they can't wear . . . Most interesting is that he has asked
one girl to come along whose mother had made the whole uniform and this is
singled out for special praise. In the nicest possible way he informs some
parents that if they can't afford the shop prices then it is possible to have
home-made garments. Girls can wear trousers, and one 'model' has trousers
on.

In a similar vein, the retiring head of Gryll Grange (9–13) school
told his parents that:

they had already had a note on school uniform. They were told not to buy a
blazer if they didn't want to – the children don't wear blazers in school, and
not to worry about expensive uniforms 'my own children always had "hand-
me-downs"'!'

At those schools where many children did not wear uniform, an
interesting situation can arise concerning the pupils who do not live
with their families but come from local authority children's homes.
Such pupils actually have a complete, smart, new uniform with all
the extras like PE kit. Thus, at Waverly, Denzil, the only West
Indian boy in 1 LE, was the smartest boy with the most complete
and immaculate uniform, proper football kit, clean gym shoes, and
the 'correct' type of craft apron. Gordon Wilde in 1 BN, who came
from a large, loving and cheerful family, had an imcomplete,
secondhand and scruffy set of school clothes. In such cases the local

authority has behaved as an impeccable parent, who obeys the rules suggested by the heads for getting children into uniform. While these remarks make it clear what the parents' duties are, the children are sometimes reminded of their role.

> Gryll Grange – assembly
> Mr Judge takes the new children's first-ever assembly. He began by telling them how their 'parents had turned them out smartly – the smartest in Ashburton.' They are to keep it up.

Here the parents' duty is to ensure that children wear the uniform, and the children's to keep themselves looking smart. Some children are explicitly told that parents can supply cheaper substitutes for uniform items and use their labour and skill to perform their role, as their parents were told by Mr Parkin at Waverly. For example, at Melin court:

> Melin Court – girls' PE
> PE teachers explain what clothes are needed for PE. Included is a skirt for hockey and dance. 'If your mum's quite handy at needlework there's no reason why you shouldn't make your own.' Later when they are examining the kit the girls already have, one teacher says to one girl 'Your mum made this?' Girl nods. 'Right, that's fine.'

Special clothes also have to be provided for craft and art, as in the following:

> Waverly annex – metalwork with Mr Pewter
> Gordon hasn't got an apron. Told where to buy one in the army surplus shop in Ashwood Bank.

Sometimes the protective clothing for craft has to be bought, but more frequently the parents are asked to send the children with an 'old shirt' or 'old apron' from home. Mr Mauss, the pottery teacher at Kenilworth, had insisted that pupils bring an old garment to protect their uniforms from the clay. The next lesson he planned to write the children's names in a washable ink, on their 'cover-ups' in large letters to help him learn their names. As he began to carry out this labelling, however, he hit a snag:

> One of the girls had a very fancy apron, and he decided he would not mark it, in case her mother was angry. When Maurice brought a shirt to him Mr Mauss made a big fuss over whether he should write 'Maurice' on it, because it was such a good shirt.

It appears that at least two sets of parents in 1 zeta had provided art aprons that were too good for their purpose.

When parents have done their duty and provided children with the correct clothing and equipment, properly labelled, they can be understandably annoyed when the clothing or equipment go missing. Searches for lost property sometimes interrupted lessons, and certainly made teachers conscious of parental wrath.

Lost property

One pretext on which parents feel able to intervene is lost property. Several times in all our six schools the smooth running of lessons was interrupted by searches for lost property. For example at Guy Mannering:

> Mirelle's mother is on the phone, because Mirelle has lost her brand new leotard and skirt.

Later that morning, in Mirelle's form-room

> Two older girls come in to tell Mrs Forrest that Mirelle's gym kit – or at least the leotard – has turned up.

Similarly at Gryll Grange the teaching was interrupted when:

> Raymond Lynn had lost his tie after PE. He was wearing a tie which was not his, but belonged to a fourth year girl! They were all asked to look at their ties to see if they had Raymond's. His tie has V. Lynn in it, because it was his sister's when she attended Gryll Grange.

There are other examples of such incursions in chapter 5. Parents are warned before transfer to mark everything, and not send expensive items to school with their children. Thus at the parents' evening in Maid Marion (11–14) School, Mr Seed told the mothers and fathers that:

> it was very important for children to have the right uniform and particularly for mothers to see that every article was marked as all the items being the same they were hard to identify.

At Waverly, Mr Parkin told the pupils on their pre-transfer visit about labelling things:

> He made quite a point of the need to mark all the property which they had and told again lurid stories about people who have lost things, lost their trousers, he couldn't understand how they could go home without their trousers on.
> One boy asked if there was any thieving at the school. Mr Parkin said 'I am sure there isn't' but then began to modify that by saying that he would be wrong to say there wasn't any thieving after all things did get lost in many

different places. It could not be helped but there was the lost property box they could always go and look for things there. If they had things marked they will be sure to find them.

The relationships between labelling property, losing it and theft were explained to parents at Melin Court by Mrs Hallows:

> Quite interestingly, unlike Waverly where they came clean about the thieving, here at Melin Court they mask it but at the same time try to warn parents about likely loss. 'Don't waste money on a gold pen. Label equipment since it is amazing how many watches are stolen (always stolen) only to be found elsewhere.'

Parents are duly warned about the negative consequences of failing to label things, and their duty to provide things. As well as uniform, PE kit and various aprons or overalls, parents are expected to supply things and to have certain resources at home children can use:

> Maid Marion, Mrs York – fabric teacher
> At the end of the lesson they were asked to bring their own little boxes with pins, needles and matching cotton for the materials they had chosen and next week they would begin the actual machining.

> Kenilworth, Mrs Stockton – French
> Mrs Stockton told the children that it was very nice to have a small French dictionary, and that Christmas would be a good time for them to get one. If their grannies ask them what they would like, perhaps they would think it sensible to ask for a French dictionary

> Waverly, Mrs Bobbin – girls' needlework
> Girls are to bring money to pay for the material for the apron, and a polythene bag to keep their work in. Next week they are to bring three long pieces of wool.

Some of these things cost money, others involve only time and trouble. Mr Bradshaw, the craft teacher at Guy Mannering, asked children to bring in to school any old exhausted ball-point pens, which were useful for marking cardboard and other materials. Miss Tweed at Gryll Grange wanted pupils to bring in the empty box of a Toblerone chocolate bar, because being triangular it was a useful illustration of a solid shape for doing one of the *Oxford Middle School Maths* exercises. At Melin Court, Mrs Zeldin asked pupils to provide some magazine cuttings or posters of 'things French' to display on her boards. Sometimes the parents' duties are to perform some small service for the child, such as:

> Kenilworth
> Miss Stephenson gave out new rulers to the class. Told the children when they got home they should ask their father to scratch their name on the back.

Frequently parents are expected to provide the wherewithal to cover, or in Coalthorpe, 'back' books. For example, Kenilworth children were told that they must cover their art folders, dictionaries, and their English books. Those who did so were rewarded, and so, vicariously, were their parents. For example the French teacher, Mrs Stockton, gave a house point to 'the fourteen children who had covered their books.' Sometimes the covering seems unnecessary, as when Miss Airdale told the children that:

> the dictionaries are new, or nearly new, and they must be covered properly. If one's dictionary is covered already, one must take off the old cover and put on a new one.

Sometimes children complained that their parents could not provide the materials or services that the school required of them, such as paper to cover books. In a science lesson of Mr Pardoe's with 1 zeta at Kenilworth:

> Master suggests that they could do the gluing at home. Somebody said they had *no glue at home*. Master suggests perhaps they could cut it out at home. One girl said they had *no scissors at home*. {Emphases ours}

Of course the children may well be teasing their teacher, but they may not have been. When the Guy Mannering children did their first cooking, chocolate crispies, they had to supply ingredients from home. The week before the lesson in which cooking was to take place:

> Mrs Bird explained that they had to bring all the ingredients except the golden syrup. Mrs Bird tells the class to tell their mothers to save margarine tubs and similar containers for bringing ingredients to school.

The following week we saw the cookery lesson and noted that:

> Several of the children buttonhole Mrs Bird to tell her that something is wrong. They have brought cocoa instead of drinking chocolate, or they have brought their own treacle, and *most common* 'Mum hasn't any scales' so things they have brought are not weighed . . .

Here the 'inadequate' parent is contrasted with the adequate one, such as Lauretta's:

> Lauretta has been sent with a tupperware box, and all her ingredients carefully packed in plastic bags, double-wrapped, but has left her syrup money (2p) somewhere.

By such classroom incidents, teachers come to judge the children's homes. They also, in the course of lessons, learn things about the families from what the pupils say.

Finding out about the families

Whether or not teachers want to investigate what their pupils' home lives are like, many happenings in the classroom reveal facets of the children's worlds beyond the school. Sometimes we felt that the teacher was deliberately 'researching' the home circumstances of their charges. The cookery lesson at Maid Marion which follows shows this:

> Each group of about four had to prepare a hot snack and a hot drink. The children were allowed to group themselves and they could then decide what they wanted to cook. Most of them choose such things as scrambled egg, paoched egg, cheese on toast and they could have a variety of drinks including tea, coffee and hot chocolate. Miss Devine explained that the first practical lesson was going to give the children an opportunity to show her how much they knew as well as to familiarize themselves with the equipment. When it actually came to the practical lesson she expected the children to lay a table with a tablecloth and to set out plates, knives, forks and everything else in the correct way which she first demonstrated. I feel she was also on the lookout for such things as table manners and how they went about the general preparation of the meal. She was not very amused when some of the boys did not bother to use their knives and forks to eat their cheese on toast. However it was very clear that she certainly did want the children to show her what their approach to cookery as well as eating was and that this method of getting them to provide themselves with a hot snack did just that.

This lesson revealed many things about how the children have been reared by their parents to *eat*: one important social skill. In fact one of the classes we observed at Maid Marion included a boy for whom the cookery lesson could have been particularly revealing about home and family circumstances. The observer was invited to share the hot drink and snack of one group of boys which included Earl, a boy whose mother had recently died.

> While we had coffee Earl confided that he never ate breakfast at home and did not each much at all ever since his mother died because he never felt hungry.

Sometimes the teachers requested information about the children's families, as in the following incidents. At Guy Mannering, we observed Mr Evans ask class 1.5 if their parents took *The Observer*, and Miss Miranda enquire 'Who's been to the Costa Brava?' Frequently, lesson topics require pupils to use material on their homes to write their essays, to answer questions, or in public speaking. For example:

196

One big family? The home and the school

Guy Mannering – 1.6 English Miss O'Hara
Puts Crispin up in front of the class to talk for one minute on 'My favourite
dinner'. His choice is 'Fish and chips, pancakes and butterscotch Angel
Delight'. This is greeted with groans and cheers. Felicity is next on her
siblings: she has three brothers aged 14, 16 and 18.

Maid Marion – home economics, Miss Devine
Miss Devine asked if any of the children had either very young or very old
people in their homes. Two girls said they had young children, one boy that
he had an old person in his home. Miss Devine asked 'How old, who is it?'
Boy: 'My sister, she is 20.'

Waverly – English, Miss Lawrence
Cherie reads out her essay about her earliest memories . . . (she fell
downstairs)
{Later}
Miss Lawrence asks: 'What do your parents do in order to frighten you? In
order to get you to do what they want? Laurence – what does your mother
do?'
Laurence: 'Threatens me with a knife, Miss'.
Coralie tells how she burnt her fingers aged 2.

These extracts show pupils using such enquiries to make jokes – but
Laurence's remark might be true. Essays are frequently set on 'my
family' and as in Miss Lawrence's class, the family comes into the
classroom. For example at Guy Mannering in both 1.5 and 1.6 we
saw the English teachers ask the pupils to write about their families.

1.5 English, Mr Evans
They have to write an account of their own family . . . One of the pieces of
information they are asked for is their father's occupation. Many of the
children don't know this and are told to leave it blank. Some call out and it is
clear that most of these are in the middle class group of 'Accountants',
'Scientists' and 'Sales Managers'. Dominico is an exception – his parents run a
fish and chip shop.

When the 'B' band class did the same exercise for Mrs Evans, the
result was rather different.

1.6 do the same exercise on their families including father's occupation. Most
of them volunteer the information very quickly and do not say they don't
know. Here occupations are lower SES: Policeman/works at Simkins/
manageress of Golden Egg/works at Plessey/works at shoe factory.

The observer wondered whether the jobs done by 1.6's parents
were easier to describe to chidren, or whether it was something else
about 1.5's parents that kept pupils ignorant about the nature of
their work. Dominico Grillo's family background was out of line
with most of the other occupations mentioned by his classmates. In

197

fact his father's chip shop became an important factor of the oral culture of the form. Early on in the autumn term, they had to write an essay on 'My Old School' for Mr Evans while he was at a funeral. A needlework teacher, Miss Pink, was sitting with them, and:

> The children write their essays, and are told that when they have finished writing they should draw their old school. Dominico Grillo says he wants to draw an aerial view – Miss Pink says that is 'ingenious' and asks after the fish and chips. Asks the class if they know Dominico's family have a fish and chip shop. They all say 'yes'.

As the term progressed it became clear that Mr Evans was not going to let anyone forget Dominico's background. He made a point of telling one of the ORACLE researchers about the Grillos' shop, and stressed that Dominico was a prime example of a boy who could use the education system to better himself. He obviously found Dominico a pleasure to teach, and revealed this by making a series of jovial comments about him. In one English lesson the children were supposed to be learning how to write a set of instructions:

> Mr Evans told them to write down three tasks – frying an egg, making toast and cleaning a pair of muddy shoes. They were to find out how to do these tasks, and write an explanation – a set of instructions so someone else could do it. Then he added 'Dominico knows how to fry an egg – he knows about frying.'

In another:

> Children are being chosen to address the whole class for one minute on a topic chosen by Mr Evans. 'Well Dominico, now's your big chance.' By a strange coincidence Dominico Grillo picks 'My Favourite Meal'. He begins: 'My favourite meal is fish and chips' and easily makes a minute.

In a third lesson Mr Evans read a passage on hobbies, and:

> used this to lecture to the class on the virtues of reading a good book or indulging in other hobbies rather than watching the TV. Dominico was in prominence and comments such as 'I know Dominico's hobby is fish and chips, but I am sure that he does not watch TV everyday, do you Nico?'

Lest the reader feel that Dominico resented Mr Evans' teasing, when interviewed he told us he rather liked English and geography (as he liked Mr Evans). The project team also interviewed Mr Grillo, who gave us more detailed information about his family:

> Mr Grillo told me that since he and his wife came to England they have had a

variety of occupations. First they were in service; subsequently Mr Grillo has
been a waiter, a bus conductor and an ice-cream man as well as a fish and chip
shop owner.
    Dominico had some trouble at school when the other children called him
'chippy'. Mr Grillo told him that he must not be upset by this; on the contrary
he must think himself fortunate that whenever he wants a bag of chips he can
have one without having to fork out any of his pocket money.

Mr Grillo's suggestion, that Dominico should be pleased to live in
a chip shop, seems to have worked, as Dominico's interview did not
include any mention of being taunted by his father's occupation.
Dominico's background had not, incidentally, given him a detailed
knowledge of cookery. In his home economics class, when Mrs Bird
was supervising the production of chocolate crispies, we noted:

Mrs Bird asked 'What do you get if you boil sugar?'
One boy says it would stick to the pan.
Dominico says 'salt.'
Another boy says 'water.'

Dominico's subsequent school career is outlined in appendix 2.
    A parallel example of a pupil's parent intruding into the class-
room concerned Sebastian Gunn in 1.5 at Guy Mannering. In July,
at the end of their first year in the school, an observer was present in
a maths lesson with Mrs Forrest. The topic was Roman and Egyptian numbers.

Mrs Forrest asked Sebastian 'How many players in a rugby team?' which is
one of the questions. They have to write the answer in Egyptian numerals.
Sebastian: '30'.
Mrs Forrest: (raises her eyebrows) 'You ought to know better.'
Sebastian: '15 each side.'
Mrs Forrest: (to the other children) 'Why should he know?'
Class: 'Because his dad plays rugby for England.'

Thus far we have concentrated on the ways in which parents, and
the home, can impinge on classroom life. There is a second aspect of
the pupils' homes and families which is important in the school –
their siblings – and it is to this we now turn.

Sibling rivalries

In this second section of the chapter we turn from relations between
the school and the parents to a further aspect of family relationships
– siblings. Many of our sample were *not* the first member of the
family to pass through their schools, and had to contend with
teachers' commenting upon whether or not they resembled older
brothers and sisters in appearance, ability, demeanour or be-

haviour. A few examples of what is typically said are given first:

Melin Court, girls' PE
Teacher takes the register. Recognizes a surname: 'Have you got a sister? Are you Suzanne's sister?' Girl says she has got a sister, but Suzanne in the second year is her cousin.

Waverly, biology Mr Darwin
Asks Ellen Farley is she 'Christine's sister?'

Waverly, physics Mr Rutherford
Asks Laura Eggleston 'Are you any relation of Julie Eggleston?'

Melin Court, RE Mrs Durrant
Tamara Fields comes late from room 11. Mrs Durrant says 'I've forgotten your name, but you're Sally Fields' sister.'

Guy Mannering, English 1.5 Mr Evans
Mr Evans finds several siblings as he goes over the names. 'You're a Pryce – you must be Eluned's sister.'
Mair Pryce admits she is.

Melin Court, music Mrs Altham 1E
As she takes the register she 'recognizes Vincent Delgardo because he looks like his brother.'

Waverly, home economics
Mrs Sutcliffe takes register. A couple of girls are recognized as having sisters in the school.

Gryll Grange
Mrs Stone takes the girls from 1V on a tour of the school. In the domestic science area they meet the teacher. She and Mrs Stone ask who likes sewing and who likes cooking? The cookery teacher looked at the girls and spotted about six who had brothers and sisters in the school. 'You're Nicky Tate's sister – what's your name?'
'Veronica.'

At break the observer was told that Nicky Tate was an odd child – 'not with us' – and the staff hoped Veronica would be better.

A good example of the interpenetration of the home and the school took place when Miss Pink, a needlework teacher, sat with 1.5 at Guy Mannering because Mr Evans had to attend a funeral. The children were supposed to be writing an essay 'My old school'.

Miss Pink explained who she was, and starts by going over the siblings in the room: 'You're David's brother.' 'You live in Partridge Street.' 'You must be Beverly's sister.' 'And you must be Eluned Price's sister.'

Later in the lesson when most of the class had written their essay and were drawing their old schools –

Another boy is stuck. Miss Pink says 'You're not quiet like your brother' and gives him some ideas for finishing his essay such as any school visits he went on.

Here we see the simple identification of children ('You must be Jonathan's sister') turning into something more complex and intimate – public comparisons of siblings ('You're not quiet like your brother'). Such comparisons were quite frequent in our six schools, for example:

Melin Court, music Mrs Altham 1M
Goes through the register, and asks them which Middle School they have come from. Whenever she gets to a pupil who resembles someone already in the school she enquires: 'Are you Stephen's brother?' 'Are you any relation of Darren's?'
'Warren White's brother – you must be'
When she reaches Danielle Draper she just looks and says 'Martin?' and Danielle nods . . . When they are asked to take notes Eamonn O'Malley has nothing to write with, and Mrs Altham says 'Don't get like your brother and forget it every lesson.'

Waverly, maths Mr Astill
A boy arrives late. 'Got lost sir.'
Mr Astill looks at him and says: 'Oh no! Diane Wilde, and Beverly Wilde and Philip Wilde – we do know your family, don't we?'

Gryll Grange, French in 1T
Mr Lyons arrives in 1T for their first ever French lesson. Does siblings, and finds seven or so. Tells some of them that their siblings will help them with French, for example: 'Your brother – when he's here – when he's with us that is – is quite good at French . . . '
Kenneth is lambasted for the behaviour of his brother.

Gryll Grange, 1T
One boy says he doesn't like acting. Miss Tweed says his brother said he couldn't act, but he played the Artful Dodger in *Oliver*, and was very good.

Melin Court, science Miss Fern
Melvyn Pym is asked if he is Gavin's brother – when he says he is, she asks whether she is meant to sympathize with him or Gavin.
Eamonn O'Malley is told she doesn't need to see his face – she can tell from his crew cut that he is Shaun's brother.

Why do teachers make these identifications and how do children feel about them? Only one teacher mentioned the topic to an observer, Miss Stephenson at Kenilworth.

Miss Stephenson told me that she knows lots of the brothers and sisters of her new form (1 gamma). She has even taught some of their uncles and aunts. She thought it was a big help for the new children if they realized the teachers at the school already knew members of the family.

However there is no evidence that pupils actually want such reassurance. The sample children who talked to the ORACLE researchers about the issue actually disliked such references. For example, a researcher at Maid Marion was talking to Gareth Williams:

> He ruefully told me 'Everybody seems to know me!' He was well-known from his elder brother who was quite a trouble maker.

A similar case was that of the Waverly boy, Rex Mackie, whom we have written up elsewhere (Galton and Willcocks, 1983: 146–51). Rex was following an older brother to Waverly who had told him 'it was rubbish here.' The brother had been disruptive, disaffected and disliked by teachers, but Rex was determined *not* to follow in his footsteps. (His career is in appendix 2.) Given his wish to break away from his brother, he did not enjoy staff's explicit comparisons between them. For example:

> Metalwork, Mr Pewter – Waverly annex
> Mr Pewter looks at Rex's work. 'Is that the best you can do, Mackie?' Rex nods. 'Well, I'll tell you something. It's fifty per cent better than your brother can.'

> Waverly staffroom
> Am talking to Mr Darwin and another young master, when we are joined by the French master. He says that he went down to Ashwood Bank Middle School last year to teach some French, so he knows something about the Ashwood Bank children, including Rex Mackie . . . (*Now* I understand his comment in the class about Rex having had 'a good teacher last year'!) I say Rex is easy to spot in lessons because he answers a lot. Mr Darwin says he was keen in biology and there is a discussion of his older brother, Donovan, who is 'a nuisance'. They say Rex has a brain.

Another pupil, again a boy, with a 'bad' older brother was Mitchell Gardiner at Guy Mannering. He too seemed to be working hard to overcome his brother's reputation. One of the ORACLE team discussed him with Mrs Forrest, his form teacher.

> I ask her at the end of the lesson about Mitchell. She says that his brother has a terrible reputation in the fourth year but that Mitchell is an adopted child. He is clearly trying very hard as the children have told Mrs Forrest that he was terrible at his last school.

(This is the boy whose intimidation was punished in chapter 4.)

Siblings rarely become directly involved in school work, but there were a few occasions on which they impinged on academic classroom life. At Maid Marion, in Mrs Rumsey's science lesson:

> Rolf said that he had already seen the experiment in his sister's book (and so

knew what the results and conclusions were going to be). Mrs Rumsey said that perhaps they ought to do different experiments each year to stop people like Rolf.

(This is a nice example of how guided discovery science lessons can easily be spoiled as discussed in Atkinson and Delamont, 1977.) Sometimes, too, siblings can be useful. During the first term at Gryll Grange, Miss Tweed had a pupil, Lucy, who was in hospital with a broken leg. School work was despatched to Lucy via her brother who was in a senior class.

In these ways, then, the pupils, parents and their siblings were sometimes explicitly mentioned in the class, and when they were not, they were always in the background, as audience, potential interferers, providers, and comparisons. It is far less common for the teacher's family to be mentioned, but it does happen, as we describe in the next section.

Teachers as family members

Occasionally teachers reveal to children that they, too, have families. As Delamont (1983a) has pointed out, the balance of power here is one-sided. Teachers have the right to demand information about pupils' families 'Who's been to the Cheddar Gorge?' 'Who's got a double garage?' 'Who lives in a flat?' but on the rare occasions when children ask teachers about their families, teachers are free to refuse the information. However some teachers do use their family relationships inside the classroom – although *not* in the ways described by Ann Swidler (1979) for Californian free schools.

The teacher who most frequently discussed her own family with her pupils was Mrs Forrest. She lived near Guy Mannering in the same neighbourhood as many of her pupils, her daughter was a pupil at the school, her son was a friend of children in 1.5 and her husband was deputy head of Gryll Grange, so she had little chance of privacy. However, she often used her family as a conversational topic:

> 1.5 return to their classroom after art with Mr Woolfe, to maths with Mrs Forrest. She checks their hands (as they have been fingerpainting). 'If I was your mother, Shelly, I'd go mad at the state of your uniform. I washed a uniform this weekend and I know I'd be furious if I had to do it again today.' {Monday}

In one science lesson with 1.5 Mrs Forrest told the class how her family went to Scotland so her son could see an eagle, but they did not manage to see one. In an earlier science lesson she had revealed her family network to the class as follows:

Sonia is talking; Mrs Forrest says 'That will do Sonia. A little bird told me
before you came to this school that you were inclined to chatter.' She explains
that her little boy knows what they were like at Guy Mannering Lower
School.

Later Mrs Forrest explained to the observer that:

the boy third along on the front bench is her son's best friend at junior school,
and was very embarrassed to have her as a teacher.

It transpired that the lower school had vertical grouping and her son
was still there, but many of his former classmates were in 1.5.

The only example we have of a pupil directly asking a teacher
about his or her family circumstances occurred in 1 zeta at Kenilworth, in Mr Birch's RE class.

Terry asked Mr Birch if he had a wife in the infant school. Mr Birch said yes,
he had, and asked if she had had to suffer Terry.

One other incident was interesting on this point. At Melin Court
two women PE teachers were oberved during the first double lesson
with all the girls from two classes. Kit was inspected, feet checked,
and the syllabus outlined. As part of this long lesson, the question of
showers was discussed. The teachers explained:

They keep a record of who has showers and who goes swimming. Girls are
told to tell her if they cannot shower because they are 'on period', and they
must tell the swimming master they are 'on period'. 'He won't be
embarrassed, he's a married man.'

This is the only incident we have in which one teacher told children
about another's marital status – except when the Miss/Mrs distinction was emphasized to children who had got a woman's title wrong.

In these ways, then, the children's families are present in the
classroom more frequently than the teachers' families, and the
latter are rarely invoked as part of the curriculum. This is one way in
which the six ORACLE schools are quite different from the two
free schools in California studied by Swidler (1979) where the staff
routinely invoked their personal and family lives in the school. (See
the extract from Swidler reprinted in Delamont, 1984, pp. 160–82.)

There are, however, at least two other evocations of 'the family'
in the schools, and it is to these we now turn.

The symbolic families

Thus far we have been discussing the interrelationships between the children's actual families and their schools. However, just as in the hymn 'I vow to thee my country' we are presented with *two* realms: a real one on earth to which we owe a patriotic duty and a symbolic one in heaven to which we owe a religious duty; school children have two types of family held out to them. Most have their real families, but they are also offered two symbolic, idealized families to belong to. Pupils are frequently told *both* that they now belonged to a 'new family' in their school which was 'one big family'; and that their lives are part of an idealized family which bears strong relationships to a cereal commerical or a Patience Strong poem. That is, the image of 'the family' is frequently invoked as part of the rhetoric of the school. In the following examples we see these two types of invocation in our six schools.

The image of the school as a family
The six schools we studied were rather keen on the image of a school being like a family. For example:

> Maid Marion assembly week one
> Taken by Mr Seed (acting head) and Mr Welsh (head of 1st year). The children were warmly welcomed into the Maid Marion *family*.

> Waverly Assembly
> Mr Spencer (deputy head) mentioned the school rules. Families had rules and 'as we are a big family' it was important to have them at Waverly.

> Kenilworth assembly
> Mr Leach (deputy head) gave a talk – the theme was the family and the need for tolerance within it. He drew a parallel between the children's families at home and the larger family which they belong to at Kenilworth School.

This image is frequently invoked, but whether it actually makes sense to pupils is unclear. For those, like Denzil at Waverly, who live in Children's Homes, or those like Benedict Kortright whose experience of family life has been disrupted and disturbing, it cannot be reassuring. There is considerable scope for a study of the metaphors used in school rhetoric, and their impact and effectiveness.

Assemblies, of the whole school or some segment of it, are a frequent source of homilies and invocations of the symbolic family. For example, at Melin Court, the senior mistress, Mrs Marks, told the whole first year what would happen if they were taken ill in school hours, and in doing so created an imaginary, idealized family:

> If they are ill or have an accident the school tries to get hold of their mothers.

One big family? The home and the school

School tries not to bother father – because he is the head of the family, his
wage keeps the family, while mother's is only for luxuries – so school tries to
contact mother. If they are ill they are not to go home alone. Must report to
the deputy heads and they will probably be taken home – escorted – they are
too young to decide. If there is no one at home – mum, granny, aunty – they
will be put to bed at school.

As Delamont (1980a: 50) has commented on this homily elsewhere,
this image of the children's families is decidedly odd. Apart from
the pupils who live in Children's Homes and those whose fathers are
unemployed (not unheard of in Coalthorpe), many of those in the
hall know perfectly well that their mothers work for necessities, like
their school uniforms, PE kit and dinner money. Even odder, the
person saying that women's work is not important is a mother
herself, whose own career is clearly important, for she is running
assembly. It is even arguable that the comments on the family
confuse the real point of the homily, which is that they are *not* to go
home alone. Some senior teachers combined the symbolic family
the child belonged to with an explicitly religious message. For
example when Mr Judge the head of Gryll Grange took an assembly
he told the children:

that some men are good at some jobs and some at others. Some women are
good at cooking and some at washing. When you are housewives you have to
do both – school children are like housewives – Moral is: what you have to do,
do well.

Waverly assembly
Mr Parkin tells the first and second years about Martha and Mary. 'I suspect
that Martha was like most of us, good with her hands, like your mums. But
Mary was a thinker, and so when Martha was annoyed and said to Jesus
"Send her into the kitchen to help", Jesus said "No, better stay here and
think". The message of this assembly is that there is room for all of us in our
families and in the school, and with Jesus.'

The idealized family, with its moral and even religious overtones, is
invoked in lessons, as well as in assembly. This was made particularly clear in a home economics lesson with Miss Devine at Maid
Marion:

Miss Devine asked 'What is home economics?' Didn't get any coherent
answers so she asks: 'What is the difference between a house and a home?'
This also daunted the children, and Miss Devine had to supply her own
answer: 'A house is just a building while a home is a house with a family . . . '
When she asked 'What do you do at home when you look after a family?'
Children made suggestions: cooking, cleaning, shopping . . .

As Delamont (1980a: 54–6) has argued elsewhere it is when

206

teachers try to humanize the content of their lessons, and make it relate to pupils' home lives in explicit ways, that they evoke the most sexist stereotypes about adult roles. Ironically, the same teacher who explicitly rejects the pupils' idea that singing is a 'sissy' occupation by telling them about the great male choral tradition in mining areas, is likely, when relating some other feature of music to the pupils' everyday lives, to imply that mothers never work, spend all day cooking and never think about sport, politics, cars or anything scientific. Typical examples of teachers' comments are:

'When your mum wants to put liquid in her cake mixture.' (Miss Fern)

'Your mum sends you shopping. Where would you go for meat?' (Mr Huxley)

'How does your mother cut a birthday cake?' (Mr Quill)

'If you were sent by your mother to buy half a dozen eggs, how many would you bring her?' (Miss Tweed)

'When you are grown up, you boys may have to go up into the attic and get rid of the birds' nests in it.' (Mr Evans)

'The girls will know what's special about *Pyrex*.' (Mr Darwin)

From examples such as these the pupils are offered an idealized family in which 'Mother' is always baking cakes and is obsessed with shopping, while men occasionally do some hazardous task. These themes were brought together in the first girls' PE lesson at Melin Court, when their kit was inspected. The girls were told they needed a leotard for dance and gymnastics, plus a short skirt.

If you don't wear a leotard you must buy decent knickers for hockey because there are boys on the top pitch . . . Jewellery must all come off for PE except sleepers. One girls says her ring won't come off. She is told that tight rings are dangerous when you get swelling in pregnancy. If they have a ring that is too tight they should get it cut off . . . Teacher asks what can go into socks to protect your legs when playing hockey?
'Shin pads,' 'foam rubber,' 'Miss, Newspaper.' 'Yes, borrow your dad's page three from *The Mirror*.' . . . (Later) if the girls buy a skirt with an adjustable waist . . . it will last them throughout their school life, and when they leave school, if they work in an office and want to play in the badminton team, it will do for that.

While the whole tone of this lesson was supportive and friendly, the image of the girls' families, where 'Mum' was handy with a needle and 'Dad' looks at nudes in the paper, being reproduced by the girls themselves when they leave work in their offices to become swollen with pregnancy, is terribly stereotyped. Invoking the family seems to involve stereotyped sexist images, even when the subject matter is, theoretically, impersonal. Thus at Kenilworth, in a music lesson Mr Tippett was introducing the stringed instruments:

> Mr Tippett gave out a large number of broken and derelict violins. He said they were not all complete but they would do for drawing . . . He began by saying that violins were like young ladies: they are fairly big at the top, they are small-waisted, and they have got . . . err
> 'Big bums' says a child.
> 'Yes, that is right, large bottoms' says Mr Tippett. Then he asked what the *family* the violin belonged to was called. Luella said 'The strings.'

Equally blatant was Guy Mannering's Mr LeGard when teaching 1.5 about 'The Book':

> He tells them on the title page there will be the author's name, and that tells you something about the book. You may recognize the author and therefore know he is a good one. 'If you get a chemistry book by a senior master at a big school he ought to know what he is talking about but if it is by someone who is just a housewife, *well*!'

Clearly the housewife must stick to her real job, and not branch out.

This is not the place to discuss all the ways in which the curriculum, and lessons are sexist, or offer stereotyped images of the family, a theme explored in Whyld (1983). For the purpose of this chapter, the point has been sufficiently made that a sexually-stereotyped idealized family is present, in a shadowy way, in many areas of the school. Its relations to the pupils' real families – or its impact on those pupils who do not have families – is unclear, and deserves further examination.

Conclusions

Miriam David (1980) has offered one of the few theoretically sophisticated analyses of the triangular relationship between the family, the state and education. The data in this chapter illuminate two sides of that triangle, at the empirical and at the symbolic level. They might also be interpreted as a contribution to the debate on 'cultural capital' (Bourdieu and Passeron, 1977) and educational success. The ORACLE project was not planned with such themes in mind, and it would be inappropriate to overstate the extent to which the data can now address such themes. However, this chapter has shown how far the family – real and symbolic – penetrates into everyday life in the school.

CHAPTER 9

Help from my friends? The staffroom and the peer groups

> The free peer group activity of children is by its very nature a privileged realm in which adults are alien intruders, especially so insofar as much of the children's folklore repertoire violates what children understand to be adult standards of decorum. (Bauman, 1982: 178)

> I do not know why I am so terrified of the staffroom which is a very large one. Two contributory factors are, I think, that the rest of my department are older and sit in a large clique in one corner of the room so that I cannot talk to any of them about the work and secondly, that the younger set of teachers are all married and sit in the corner with the 'middle-aged mums' and talk house-shop. (Hannam *et al.*, 1976: 216)

One of the most significant features of schooling for the pupils is their friends and enemies among the other pupils; for teachers having congenial colleagues is an important factor in enjoying, surviving, or being swamped by, their demanding job. In this chapter we examine how the pupils in our six schools formed and reformed their friendship groups and how they fell out with other children; and how the staffrooms in the six schools functioned. Analyses of pupils' friendship patterns and hostilities are fairly common, so we begin with the less usual topic, the staff and their relationships.

In teaching, as in other occupations which involve groups of people, or take place in institutions, workplace friendships are important. This is true of both white-collar and manual occupations. Blackburn and Mann (1979: 154–5) asked manual workers in Peterborough what they enjoyed about their present job, and had enjoyed about the best job they had ever had. Social relationships were the second most important reason for liking the respondents' 'best ever' job, and the most significant reason for liking their present job, 360 of 796 responses (45 per cent) gave social relations as the best part of their present occupation. Blackburn and Mann point out that these social relationships are out of the employer's control, and are 'largely created by the workers themselves'. The importance of social relations at work are not confined to men. Ann Oakley's (1974a, 1974b) housewives mention friends as the main attraction of the workplace and the feature they missed on leaving for full-time child-rearing. For teachers, the staffroom is an important place to see friends and share problems. It is also a place where staff, especially newcomers, are judged. Thus one of the probationers studied by Hannam *et al.* (1976), quoted at the head of this chapter, was suspended because her peculiar behaviour in the staffroom showed she was not coping with the job. Staffroom life is, therefore, an important performance arena for the teachers as well as a social space. The data presented in this chapter on pupils' friendship groups parallel that found in such works as Cusick (1973), Larkin (1979), Fuller (1980), Llewellyn (1980), Meyenn (1980), Bauman (1982), Everhart (1983) and Macpherson (1983). Staffroom groupings are less frequently studied, but the material in this chapter can be compared with McPherson (1973), Ginsburg *et al.* (1977), Woods (1979), Ball and Lacey (1980), Riseborough (1981), Hammersley (1984), A. Hargreaves (1984) and Pajak and Blase (1984). The social relations of staff among themselves, and with the observer, in that archetypal 'backstage' region, the staffroom, are the focus of the first half of the chapter.

The staffroom

As participant observers, we naturally spent a good deal of time in the staffrooms of the six schools. The informal relations among the teachers were not a focus of the ORACLE programme, but to understand the pupils' lives in the six schools, some data on the staffroom are useful. Unfortunately, there are few data on staffroom relationships in other British schools which can be used for comparative purposes. As Hargreaves and Woods (1984) make clear in the introduction to their collection *Classrooms and Staffrooms*, despite the growth of ethnographic research on education in Britain since 1965, teachers have received less attention than pupils. What follows is therefore a small contribution to a sparse field, as well as bearing upon the lives of the ORACLE pupils. We do not claim to have data of the depth of Hargreaves (1984), Hammersley (1984) and Woods (1979), and the data collected by Ginsburg *et al.* (1977) on *The Role of the Middle School Teacher* in five middle schools in Hereford and Worcestershire are much more extensive, and deal with multiple aspects of the teachers' lives. Here we are merely reporting the material from the initial fieldwork in order to throw light on the transfer issue. There are three themes about the staffrooms of the six schools which seem relevant here: the use of the staffroom, the conversational topics, and the educational problems discussed there. These are discussed in turn, with the emphasis on their implications for pupil transfer.

The use of the staffroom(s)

The use made of the staffroom or rooms in our six schools varied quite considerably. The most extreme contrast was between the two 9–13 Middle Schools in Ashburton, Gryll Grange and Guy Mannering. There was a considerable difference between the two schools in the use made of the staffroom. At Gryll Grange all the teachers and the ancillary staff, used the one staffroom. The headmaster and his deputy both came there for tea and coffee on occasions, and the rest of the staff were all frequently found there when not on duty. Guy Mannering was very different, as this extract from the fieldwork diary shows:

> Diary (19. 9. 77)
> The second issue at Guy Mannering is staff cliques. It is much more like a secondary school, with the art and craft staff brewing up in the domestic science flat and the scientists in the preparation room. This came up in conversation on Tuesday when someone asked Mr Black if they had a coffee club in the science area. He said everyone brought their own coffee – and then made a joke about real teachers being too busy to leave their working areas and come to the staffroom. This was recognized as a great joke – both because he is a leg-puller and because the science laboratories are nearer the staffroom than any of the other classrooms. Someone said the staffroom is too big now {i.e. the school has too many teachers, not the room was too large}.

Ginsburg *et al.* say (1977: 35) that each of the five middle schools in their sample had a staffroom, which was large enough to hold all the staff, and this differentiated middle schools from most primary schools which lack a 'real' staffroom, or large comprehensives which have several. This is partially true of both Gryll Grange and Guy Mannering, but the one at Gryll Grange was too small, while that at Guy Mannering was not used by several cliques of staff. Some used it at break and not at lunch, while others could be found there at lunchtimes and not at break.

Physically the two rooms were very different. Gryll Grange was a purpose-built middle school, and the staffroom was open-plan. It was up a short flight of stairs above the school library, with no door, and only a waist high wall. Anyone standing at the end of the

211

staffroom nearest the stairs was visible from the library, as was anyone using the sink and kettle. Only by retreating to the far end of the staffroom, where a table for marking was behind a large bookcase, could be a teacher be private; and conversations in the staffroom could be heard in the library. This was not a popular arrangement:

> In the staffroom at Gryll Grange I hear a long lament about the lack of privacy in the staffroom. Because it has no doors staff are always in danger of being overheard, things are stolen, and teachers need somewhere to go and kick the furniture. And the headmaster who was in favour of the open-plan staffroom had his own office.

In important ways, this staffroom did not function as a proper 'backstage' area (Goffman, 1971) where performers (teachers) could truly relax, 'switch off' and become people again. Gryll Grange also lacked enough backstage space for pupils, in that the changing rooms for PE were too small and the younger pupils often had to change in their classroom. Goffman (1971) argued that performance teams need backstage regions to gather themselves together and discuss things and the lack of both sound and sight insulation destroyed this function for the staffroom at Gryll Grange. These problems were confounded by the overcrowding of the school, for Mrs Stone had to do remedial reading classes in the staffroom, which destroyed any privacy for teachers during free periods.

Guy Mannering's staffroom was set away from the main thoroughfares of the school, and was a self-contained room in a corridor which included the school secretary and the head and deputy's offices. This was also true at Waverly, where there was also a *cordon sanitaire* around the staffroom, which had a door that could be shut. Melin Court's position was more complex, because Melin Court has two staffrooms, one in the original building and one in the extension. Neither was large enough to hold the entire staff in comfort. The room in the original building had 30 easy chairs arranged in groups and six working spaces – that is upright chairs at tables or desks. At Waverly the staff facilities were all centred in one part of the school:

> There is a centre behind a door with staffroom, loos, small offices, Mr Parkin's room, etc. Much more civilized than Gryll Grange . . .

Waverly's main staffroom was also too small, and we never saw *all* the teachers there at once. As one of us wrote:

The staffroom and the peer groups

I counted 68 staff on the notices in the staffroom – but I haven't seen more than 25 people use it at any time. I suspect that the English staff are not alone in having a cupboard to lurk in.

One important aspect of the staffroom or rooms for an observer is whether it is possible to get a cup of tea or coffee at break times. In most staffrooms it is possible to join whatever shared system operates, and by contributing a small sum of money, an observer can share the refreshment. This was possible at five of the six schools, whether we stayed in English cupboards and science prep rooms or went to the main staffroom, we could pay and join. Guy Mannering, however, had no 'coffee club' to join. As one of us wrote:

During the break I go to the staffroom for coffee. In this school everyone brings their own. On the Monday no-one thought to offer me a cup but today I have come armed with my Thermos. Quite a few of the staff do not come in for coffee and I only find out later that they go off and have theirs in the science lab. This is very much what one would find in most secondary schools where the science staff always tend to brew up in the prep room.

The availability of tea and coffee can also divide two staffrooms, as at Maid Marion:

Staffrooms
At Maid Marion there are two staffrooms. The one upstairs is used by the rowdies as they are referred to. The upstairs room is where tea and coffee can be made. In the lunch hour it is here that mostly older members of staff go and particularly the men. Here, almost as a matter of principle, school matters are never discussed. Downstairs there is the quiet room and this is where many of the younger female members of the staff collect. In this room there is supposed to be almost a silence so that those who want to work and correct books can do so. It is during the correcting of these books that there is often considerable comment and discussion about individual children.

From these extracts it is clear that the physical facilities are not the only thing that varies between the schools. Different schools have different arrangements about noise or work, about smoking or not, about food and drink, and about whether the room is for recreation or toil. Larger schools are more likely to have more than one staffroom, and subject departments are more likely to produce colleague groups who socialize in their area. That is, if all the English teachers are based in a terrapin hut, which also includes the 'English cupboard', then the English staff may well spend some or all their breaks there. Of the six ORACLE schools only Gryll Grange had one staffroom which everyone used where work was discussed and a coffee fund existed. It was the smallest school, with

213

the simplest internal organization. In the other five there were either several rooms, or groups who stayed in their areas, and the staffrooms were divided into places for recreation and places for work in some way. This separation leads to the differentiation in teachers' use of them, and talk in them, to which the chapter now turns.

Staffroom conversations and jokes

Martyn Hammersley (1984), drawing on his research in an inner city boys' secondary modern school he calls Downtown, points out that in the staffroom:

> Talk was undoubtedly the major activity, ranging in focus from football to classical music. However most staffroom conversation was shop talk, and usually about Downtown and its pupils.

Hammersley presents material on how teachers, who work *alone*, spend much of their communal time telling each other news – about pupils, other staff, and school events. Much of what we have in our ORACLE notes falls into these categories, augmented with jokes. We have dealt with jokes first, and our data are essentially similar to those of Woods (1979). This account is less tolerant of the essentially sexist and racist nature of many of the jokes than Woods' interpretation: a feature of his analysis one of us had queried elsewhere (Delamont, 1980a).

There is no doubt that the richest vein of staffroom humour we tapped was Guy Mannering's because of the uneasy relationship between Miss Tyree and her staff. Among the jokes were:

> Staffroom at lunch-time . . . the main discussion was the *Times Ed. Supp.* which had gone missing the day it appeared and someone joked that maybe Miss Tyree (the headmistress) was job-hunting.

Similar mirth was occasioned by a factual notice about a day's holiday:

> The staff noticeboard stated today:
> *Occasional Day's Holiday*
> I am asking for Friday October 21st. Please do not take for granted just yet, but I am presuming (*sic*) the plan will go through unopposed.
> HM

> This caused several comments. The staff were pleasantly surprised at the date being the same as other schools, as usually Guy Mannering were given odd days – 'the coronation' or 'when "her" cat had to go to the vet's!'

These are similar jokes to those recorded by Woods (1979) against the head of Lowood, and serve to reinforce the solidarity of the staff. Sometimes the teachers at Guy Mannering used Miss Tyree's idiosyncrasies as the starting point for jokes on other topics, as in the 'Trousers' conversation. Miss Tyree, like several of the infant school heads studied by King (1978), forbade her female staff to wear trousers. On September 27th 1977 we recorded a discussion about this ban in the staffroom:

> There was also a discussion about whether the women teachers could wear trousers. Apparently Miss Tyree won't have the staff wear them and when she was asked by the deputy before she said, 'No!' and then 'Are they all transvestites?' The deputy now says 'I'll not put my head on the chopping block alone this time' (This must refer to another occasion when she did something which Miss Tryee disapproved of).
> 'Anyway' says one young male teacher, 'she would soon let you wear trousers if she knew the boys stand at the bottom of the stairs looking up your dresses!' 'I bet they keep a book on the colour of our knickers' says the deputy.
> This is quite a good illustration of the staffroom banter which on the whole is usually directed against Miss Tyree. Miss Tyree seems to frequent the staffroom less and less and the staff obviously get a sense of comradeship by ganging up against her in this way.

This long extract shows both the *camaraderie* of a group of colleagues, and the strain between the classroom teacher and the head. Typical of the situation at Guy Mannering was the following extract from the 'Out of the field' notes.

> On Wednesday there was to be a meeting of the 'homework committee' and Mrs Forrest was in the staffroom after lunch waiting for it to begin. She did not expect to get out in time for afternoon school and I said I'd count her class and send them to PE. Other staff near then began to tease her – asking if she had her speech ready, etc. The idea was obviously that Miss Tyree would launch into a monologue and no one else would get a word in edgeways.

The only other head who was the subject of staffroom humour to anything like the same extent as Miss Tyree was Mr Parkin at Waverly. There were two jokes about him told to the observers, who recorded that:

> Even amongst the typical union representatives he invites a fair degree of affection if not respect for some of his 'democratic' methods. For example, there has been a jumble sale and he sold off a stereo. When the buyer asked him whether it worked Mr Parkin replied 'You're not allowed to ask that question.' This story is told briefly during coffee break.

The other joke concerned the 'fiendish device' of afternoon 'wet break', when school finished ten minutes early but the last class was full of 'stale, tired and very fidgety children'. Staff at Waverly

215

believed, in one of those staffroom jokes so necessary for teacher survival (Woods, 1979) that Mr Parkin (the head) instituted a wet break when he had a golf game arranged so he could leave school earlier.

Jokes against a head are more likely to arise when he or she has been in the school for a long time. As the heads of Gryll Grange and Maid Marion were newly appointed, their role as 'folk heroes' or otherwise had not yet become established. Miss Tyree and Mr Parkin were heads of many years standing, who had therefore become legends in their own staffrooms.

Humour in the staffroom is not only sparked off by, or directed at, the head. Other teachers, and an ethnographic observer, can also be the source of endless amusement. Woods (1979) reports a series of jokes about the senior mistress at Lowood who was caricatured as a bossy old maid. At Guy Mannering the elderly RE master who ran the school library was a source of amusement to his colleagues. During a hard winter he took to wearing plus-fours to school, to his colleagues' delight; and when he was due to retire the refusal of some pupils to contribute to his present was gaily relayed to the visiting researcher. Mr LeGard was stigmatized by his colleagues for his attitude to pupils. One day an observer found Miss O'Hara had been receiving complaints from Mr LeGard about her form, 1.6, and spent the afternoon break:

> trying to reassure her that it wasn't her fault. (I even hinted that it had to do with the way Mr LeGard organized his teaching.) Mr LeGard is in trouble at the moment and clearly unpopular. He has offended the other teachers by insisting that he is going to do the Christmas play himself using only his class and school librarians. There was strong comment about Mr L's sex life in that one of the younger male teachers commented that 'only the pretty boys' were picked to be librarians. This is clearly a slander because it could not be said that Terence in 1.5 who Mr L picked as librarian on the first day is in any way pretty. In fact he is rather fat and jovial.

This extract shows as much distasteful sexism as anything collected by Woods (1979), except that the object here is a man rather than a woman. It is also revealing about the observer, and the observer's presence both as an audience for corny staffroom jokes and as the butt of new ones, cannot be underestimated. John Beynon's (1983) relationship with the PE master and their joke about cross-country running has been quoted in chapter 5. Such interactions can provide light relief as well as establishing teacher-observer *rapport*. There were jokes about the observer in several of our schools. For example when one of the male observers visited Melin Court he was taken by Mrs Hallows up to the staffroom:

216

The staffroom and the peer groups

As we enter the commonroom Mrs Hallows says to Mrs Wordsworth 'I've brought a man to see you.' Mrs Wordsworth expresses pleasure as long as I am not there to observe her.

Then at Kenilworth:

At break I had to go to the school secretary to collect the change from my dinner money, and as I was walking into the staffroom I was tucking four £1 notes into my wallet. Mrs Stockton saw this and cheerily said: 'Don't flash your money about in here, you'll never get out alive!'

In the same vein is the reaction to one of the observers when s/he returned to Guy Mannering in July after a long absence:

As I enter the staffroom I am greeted with some sarcasm by Mr Evans who said he thought I had died!

At Gryll Grange one observer took parties of children out to count passing traffic for an exercise from *Oxford Middle School Maths*. This allowed for a staffroom joke.

The traffic survey was interesting – I took two groups down hill to major dual-carriageway to count traffic – some did both lanes, some only one. There were so many cars that I'm sure most lost count – lorries and vans were easier, motor cycles rarer – but in one lot we had a boat and in another a caravan. Miss Tweed made fun of the boat in the staffroom at lunchtime – saying that when these expert observers and researchers come they cause problems – who would believe they could take a group out to count traffic and see a boat! Staff around laughed. I said I was sorry, and joined the laughter.

Jokes at the researcher's expense can be linked to staffroom questions and discussions about the research. For example at Kenilworth one of the researchers was 'grilled' by the staff about ORACLE. First, Miss Stephenson queried the whole comparative basis of the transfer study in Bridgehampton.

During another lunchtime I had quite a lengthy discussion with several staff who were all very keen to find out all about the project. 'What we were actually doing' and 'what it was proving'. Miss Stephenson felt that it would be a very false comparison if Kenilworth and Maid Marion were compared without taking into account the different kinds of social catchment areas. She wanted to know how much background information about each child and its family we had already collected and how it was going to be used. {. . .}

Then Mrs Lee joined the conversation from the perspective of her specialist subject (PE), wanting information from the researcher about the children.

Mrs Lee was very keen to know if I felt that children behaved differently in

different classes because she commented that very often PE department
thought that a child that other people never had a good word for did
extremely well for them and worked hard and that in their experience it was
often the only place the baddies could prove themselves good. {. . .}

Sometimes, too, teachers are able to catch researchers on the
wrong foot, as Mr Arrow does in the following incident.

Later Mr Arrow bounded up to me in the corridor and asked me if I knew
Gump's work. He explained that this was an American who had done a lot of
work on child behaviour in different environments. When I confessed that I
did not know it he then looked very surprised and said 'You do work for
Brian Simon's project don't you?' I had to admit that I did and he then
explained that this Gump had examined children's behaviour in school, in
home, at play and in the summer camp and found very different responses in
different environments. He then asked me 'Have you noticed changes in
response?'

Mr Arrow must have derived great pleasure from this interaction!
Sometimes the observer could share the staff's *camaraderi*, and join
in their activities. Sometimes the observer can be useful to the staff.
At Melin Court, one of the observers had lunch with some of the
staff:

Lunchtime is fairly short (12 noon to 1 p.m.) and the staff have lunch by
themselves in a classroom served by some of the older pupils. There are only
four of us. The head is one and we both struggle through a revolting meat loaf
with chips and tinned tomatoes. He gives me the philosophy of the school.
We have general chat about the politics of education and the other staff seem
quite happy to have someone who will make conversation to him and so
relieve them of the problem. He leaves me to go and play in the band while I
go into the playground.

Here the observer seemed to be a useful ally to the other staff,
because the head was occupied and they did not have to talk to him.
At Guy Mannering 'avoiding the head' was a staff preoccupation,
which the observers were encouraged to share. Thus one observer
noted:

It is also noticeable that many staff try to avoid her – if she sits at their dinner
table they finish and go and if she comes to sit in the staffroom they make
excuses and leave.

And another wrote:

I lunch with Mrs Forrest. She tells me that we must sit on a table which has no
other free places because otherwise Miss Tyree will come in and we will get
caught. 'Haven't you seen how all the staff do this?' she asks me. I feel very
much the conspirator.

The staffroom and the peer groups

Lest the reader decides that the humour in the Guy Mannering staffroom was all directed at Miss Tyree and Mr LeGard, it is worth quoting one further example of their jokes which could have occurred in any staffroom in Britain:

> At break, the staff were very jolly and much of the talk was how to get through the term without having to do much teaching. Some of this was clearly for my benefit but it started naturally enough with a number of the teachers asking the deputy if they could go on the trip to see *Mother Goose* at Coventry which one of the teachers had organized. This led to a discussion of how some of the classes could be put together to allow some teachers to be free to go and the suggestion was that they should get someone in from the outside to talk about First Aid and show a film. Someone else then said, 'Isn't it about time we had the Police back in?' to which the deputy head replied, 'Don't worry, they're coming in in the following week.' The conversation went on like this and more and more bizarre suggestions were made as to how the children were to be kept occupied so that the staff would be free.

Of course not all staffroom talk is humourous, or aimed at the researching visitor. In the next section we turn to educational talk in the staffroom.

News from the front

In all our six schools much of the staffroom talk took the form of 'news' from the classrooms and corridors which individual teachers brought back to their colleagues. Hammersley (1984) points out that such news is exchanged in staffrooms because:

> While the information acquired by one {teacher} in the course of his work is likely to be different from that acquired by others, it is nevertheless of potential relevance to the whole staff . . . the teachers all face the same pupils at one time or another.

Even if a staff member does not teach a pupil, she may come across them on dinner duty, in a corridor or when covering for a colleague. It is as well to be prepared. Typical of the large secondary school staffroom was Waverly's. One day's account will show how acute Hammersley's concept of 'news' is.

> The staffroom were organizing their football pool syndicates at lunchtime. One teacher who is a fanatical Coalthorpe United supporter sells bingo cards to raise funds for them. Two teachers discussed a very fat fifth year girl called Moira. The male teacher said he was recording the class's height and weight, and Moira refused to get on the scales – he said he would have asked for her wasit measurement but he was afraid Moira would thump him! {He had apparently said this out loud to the class}. The head of the fifth year said that when Moira misbehaved like that she should be sent to sit and work outside his office.

This offensive commentary on a fat girl is typical 'news'. Much of the 'news' centres on pupils, and indeed typical staff conversations consist of swapping information, opinions or remarks about the pupils, and sorting out their reputations. For example, at Guy Mannering we observed:

> Today in RE Gavin Radice told Mr LeGard that he was pronouncing his name wrong. Mr LeGard was calling him 'Radish' instead of 'Radiche'. In the staffroom at break a small number of teachers were talking about the weather, a gifted child called Camilla and the names new pupils have. Mrs Evans said she had spotted Camilla as the brightest girl in the first year. The other staff were more interested in making fun of the foreign names among the new pupils, such as the Asian names like Mahesh and Dilip, and also Gavin Radice. They all agreed that his name was really 'Radish' and compared him with an older pupil whose name was 'Bucket' but tried to insist on being called 'Bookay'.

Similarly, later in the fieldwork:

> Today in the staffroom talk centred on form 1.6. The troublemaker is seen to be Dirk, but already the whole form is not popular. Several teachers, including Miss Kroll, have said they are not a very nice class. Their personalities are not nice and they do not mix well. Dirk and Annabel are unpopular already.

And again on another day:

> During the lunch break the conversation turned to a boy (Gerald D in 1.4) in the first year who has brothers and sisters already in the school. Everyone agreed that the new boy came from a problem family.

And again later in the term:

> At coffee break, all the talk is of the difficult pupils such as Gerald and Dirk who are in 1.2, now called the remedial form. Mr Evans comments, there is nothing but trouble from these Old Hill children (how is this for labelling?) 'I was talking to a Garden Centre chap the other day and he said he had never had any trouble with the local people until these new ones came.' One of the other teachers says defensively as if in disagreement 'Trouble is that the naughty ones give the good ones a bad name,' and she refers to a boy who is in 1.3 who is 'very good and sensible'. (This is rapidly becoming the favourite word around here).

Similar conversations took place at Waverly where one observer wrote:

> During conversation in the lunch break, members of the English department mention Simone as being a good student and Jake as being a chatterbox and nuisance (these were both targets last year at Ashwood Bank Middle School).

Also several children have been asking for homework – it seems that homework timetables are not published until a couple of weeks after the beginning of term.

At Maid Marion, in the staffroom where work was discussed, an observer wrote:

There is very little of the type 'not that awful family again' but there is often detailed constructive comment on the specific children and their problems and how to get over them. However it is fairly noticeable that the patience of the earlier comments about children's difficulties are beginning to wear through and give way to exasperation over their persistence. In the staffroom I am often asked for comments about some of the children and they freely discuss problems with me which they have discovered about certain individuals not only in the two classes which we are observing.

Stories about the clientele can also serve to challenge or reinforce points about appropriate staff behaviour. For example, at Guy Mannering some younger teachers were discussing the older ones:

The PE teacher next enters the conversation and takes up the point about Mrs Bird.
PE teacher: 'You know Bagshaw wouldn't come into school on the first day? I was told to carry him to the class and he was fighting and kicking. Eventually I got him there and my shins were black and blue. He eventually calmed down and I told him he could come back and see me at the break for a chat. He did. But, when I got back to the staffroom, Mrs Bird said "I hope you gave that child a smack every time he kicked you." So I told her, "Yes, of course." '
Teacher 1: 'It does not say much for us if someone who knows what it is like in here doesn't want to come in.'

The 'point' of this story is both that the PE teacher had different beliefs from Mrs Bird, *and* that Bagshaw is the son of the school's groundsman. The observer noted:

This exchange seems to me to illustrate some of the ethos of the staffroom rather well. There are a set of rules which are observed to the letter by the older staff. New rules or alterations appear on the blackboard at regular intervals. The younger ones observe the rules also, particularly when the older staff are present, but they laugh at their conformity and there is much irreverent banter between them.

One topic on which staff in comprehensives are commonly in disagreement is grouping policies (Ball, 1981; Evans, 1985). Stories about the pupils and about other staff are frequently also contributions to on-going school-wide debates about how the pupils are grouped, and how they should be organized. Thus during a break at Gryll Grange:

221

Break. Discussion: problems of classes being too big. Ideal is 27 for Mr
Valentine, Mrs Hind and Mrs Tench. There is talk of 'nice ones' versus
'yobbos' from Mrs Tench. Discussion of Oxfordshire, where teachers are
sending home excess children in rotation. Problems of mixed ability in maths.
The third year top set maths master says the range is too wide. He wants to
class teach and can't. Mrs Tench has the remedial third year maths set. 'Very
difficult to motivate.' 'Not interested in maths.' Mrs Hind says that the
Oxford LEA middle schools 'don't have supernumeraries – run like primary
schools.' Mrs Tench says 'They're not proper middle schools, then.'

This conversation about class sizes, supernumeraries, and grouping, could be the basis for what A. Hargreaves (1984) has called
contrastive rhetoric. Ashburton's schools are being compared with
Oxfordshire's rather as Hargreaves' staff referred to Countesthorpe
College. In general, the ORACLE fieldnotes do not record much
educationalist conversation from the staffrooms, except about
grouping arrangements which was a frequent topic in the staffroom
at Guy Mannering:

At lunchtime I have a long talk with Mrs Forrest about the organization of
school time. She says that a lot of the staff are unhappy about the special
treatment which the craft teachers get. 'They get a far better staff-pupil ratio.'

Guy Mannering had banding, and, as we showed in chapter 7, the
basis for the allocation was idiosyncratic. Teachers thus discussed
placement:

There is also quite a bit of a conversation about children needing to be
separated and what a good idea it would be if they were moved up and down
to different classes. (Miss Tyree has told us that she refuses most of these
requests.) Clearly this is a bone of contention particularly among the older
staff who believe that they should segregate the bad children and produce
'good' classes. (No doubt which they keep for themselves.)

Setting was controversial at Waverly, and figured in staffroom
conversations:

At lunch I met the history teacher who thinks that the eleven year olds waste
their time in the middle school and that he no longer can get them into shape
for the academic work. Later Mr Bronte tells me that they have been
attempting to destream in the second year and although there has been some
opposition the department that have done it have reported much better social
integration and less discipline problems. History and geography however
have claimed they can't cope and have gone back to streaming (*sic*).

On another occasion at Waverly the observer wrote:

At lunchtime some of the English staff were complaining about some

222

disruption of their lessons with the (more able?) children taken out for
German.

These topics occupy some of the conversations in the staffrooms of
our schools. Another issue in several of the staffrooms was teacher
unionism, and its role in the school.

Union men? (and women?)

Our six schools varied a great deal in the amount of union activity
and union-related talk in the staffroom. Waverly had the most overt
activity, and discussion, including a considerable rivalry for membership between the NUT and the NAS/UWT. This showed up in
all the observers' reports:

> Over break all the talk is of union matters. The English cupboard in the
> second year annexe is a hot bed of revolution and they are planning to oust
> one of the older teachers as their representative on the board of governors.
> The results are due that day and there is also some negotiation going on
> between union representatives over the question of time (i.e. when teachers
> should be in the school and how long they must stay after the last period,
> etc.). The union representative is the one who has been put up for the board
> of governors and clearly is unpopular with the head who one assumes believes
> that teachers should just do their duty and not worry about all this rights and
> duty nonsenses.
> At coffee time there is a great triumph because the NUT representative has
> been elected to the governors and displaced the older member of staff. One
> of the women tells us that for the women's position there has been
> intimidation as the deputy head has got one of the younger members of staff
> on one side and tried to persuade her to withdraw her nomination because
> she says it would just be wasteful to have the election.

At Waverly, there was a sharp differentiation between members
of two different teacher unions, the NUT and the NAS/UWT.
Competition was keen to recruit the newest staff member, a woman
home economics teacher based at the Annexe. She was the only
woman based at the Annexe (apart from the dinner ladies). The
men based there all belonged to the NUT, and NAS/UWT staff at
the main site complained that she had been 'forced' into the NUT
because as a lone female she could not resist the pressures of the
male craft teachers there. Certainly she was expected to make their
tea and coffee, and wash up after them, and her life would have
been very isolated if she were not on good terms with them. The first
year pupils were based in the 'English area' of the school, so all the
ORACLE researchers often had coffee in the English cupboard.
The English staff were all NAS/UWT activists, and so it was their
view of these issues we collected:

The staffroom and the peer groups

In the English cupboard at the early part of the day there was more discussion
of teacher politics – governors/holiday ballot, etc. The English staff are very
angry about the way the new teacher at the Annexe is being 'forced' into the
NUT.

As far as we could ascertain the NAS/UWT was the largest union,
with about 40 members, while the NUT only had 16. The staffroom
noticeboards at Waverly for each union were full of information,
and the unions were very visible. In contrast, the other large school,
Melin Court, was quite different, despite, or because, the headmaster, Mr Stackpole, was on the national executive of one of the
unions. So we were told:

Melin Court
The teacher on duty in the yard, a maths master, tells me that he has been
here for six years and really liked it because it was a very happy school.

They were under-unionized, no posters or information about the
unions were visible in the staffroom, and no observers recorded any
conversations about union matters. At Guy Mannering, union
issues were rarely mentioned, but on one occasion they became a
subject for another joke:

I get in at 8.40ish and sit in the staffroom till the bell, chatting to Mrs Bird.
Mrs Evans comes in with a letter for 'the NUT rep. Guy Mannering School'.
Mr Evans says '*No one* belongs to the NUT,' which causes laughter. Actually
Mr Beldham is the rep. and several staff, including Mrs Bird belong to the
NUT.

However, though the teacher unions were rarely mentioned at Guy
Mannering, issues relevant to trade unionism, such as the staff's
working conditions, repeatedly caused heated controversy in the
staffroom and were aired in front of all three observers. Thus one of
the team wrote in an 'out of the field diary' in the second week of
term:

I have now spent two days in Guy Mannering and I cannot honestly say that
they have been very enjoyable. The staffroom is either an unhappier place
than Gryll Grange OR they do not care about letting outsiders hear the
school's problems. As I was leaving yesterday something happened which
epitomized this. When I went in to collect my coffee mug Mrs Hargreaves was
expostulating to one of the young men. Miss Tyree had just told them that
they were to give up a free period the next morning to see a parent who
wasn't happy about a child's progress/last term's report. Mrs Hargreaves went
off, but the man exploded – as far as I could see the child wasn't in their
forms, they were not particularly involved and Miss Tyree had done it
because they both happened to have a free period at the time. The man was
very angry – complaining that he wasn't prepared to have his free periods

given away without prior consultation – and went on at some length about it.
There were supportive murmurs, but not a sign of supportive action.

The loss of free periods, often at short notice, was a frequent
occurrence at Guy Mannering, although usually the reason was a
colleague's absence rather than a parent coming, and it always
caused angry comments. As an observer noted:

> Another point is the staff absence and emergency timetable issue. At Guy
> Mannering an absent member of staff is covered by using up the free periods
> of other staff – Mrs Evans makes up an emergency list, and puts it on the
> board.

Later in the year, a different observer in the school wrote:

> I ask the staff by way of conversation what would happen if they needed to go
> to the doctors. Could they take time off during lessons? The answer is 'only in
> an emergency,' 'except for Miss Tyree' adds one of the staff. 'You see,' says
> Mrs Bird, 'We know that if we go then someone else has to do our turn.'
>   In fact substitution is a very big problem here. Unlike Gryll Grange there
> always seems to be someone off and everyday a note will go up on the board
> saying who has to cover for that form's timetables. People come in,
> automatically look at it, and groan because they have been caught again. It's
> very like a secondary school in this respect with constant grumbles at having
> to take over from someone else.

The relationship between Miss Tyree and her staff went through
several 'purple patches' during our fieldwork, which, ironically
served to integrate the researchers into the social system of the
staffroom. One observer was present during the following dramatic
incident:

> During break there are lots of conversations in the staffroom. The staff are
> very angry about the treatment of one of the boys on the desk. Apparently,
> Miss Tyree wanted to take her foster daughter out of the class for a dental
> appointment and sent the boy to Mrs Hargreaves to ask for the girl to come
> down to her room. Mrs Hargreaves was not teaching in her room (a fact
> which could have been checked by Miss T) and the deputy, Mrs Evans, who
> was did not feel it was right for her to open the note, and so left it there. In point
> of fact Mrs Evans could have sent the messenger off to where Mrs Hargreaves
> was teaching. Anyway when her foster daughter did not come Miss T blew up
> the boy, called him an incompetent and dismissed him off the desk. She then
> later rounded on Mrs Hargreaves and accused her of not being where she
> should be. Apparently the interview ended with Mrs Hargreaves in tears and
> the staff were quite naturally on her side. The master in charge of the B form
> which was supplying children on the desk that week refused to send anyone else
> down to replace the dismissed boy.

This row was still alive at lunchtime:

The staffroom and the peer groups

During the lunch break the staffroom is still angry about Miss Tyree and Mrs Hargreaves. 'Has she apologised yet?' asks one.
'Not her,' replies another.

Incidents of this type were not uncommon at Guy Mannering. When one of the ORACLE observers fell foul of Miss Tyree, her relationship with the remaining staff immediately became much warmer:

Tuesday, January 24th.

I am somewhat apprehensive about coming this morning. An observer, X, rang on Thursday to say that she had arrived at the school to find everything in chaos. Many of the staff hadn't been able to get in because of the snow and when she asked Miss Tyree if she could help, Miss Tyree became very abusive. I decided to leave it until Monday and then to ring and ask the office if it was convenient for me to come in. While the office staff had gone off to ask Mrs Forrest, Miss Tyree came on the line and was very apologetic about her behaviour. I laughed it off and said that I had been just like that on Thursday over the M.Ed. students who kept on ringing me up and asking if the course was still on.

On arrival it is singing so I chat to the deputy head. She expresses her sympathy about what happened and tells a lovely story of Miss Tyree in the last snow. Apparently she had rung for a taxi to take her home and no-one would come and in the end, much to her annoyance, she had had to walk down into town and get a bus. One good thing to come out of the episode is that X has, as it were, become one of the club. All the teachers asked me if X was coming in again, and when I said 'Yes of course,' they all apologised for what Miss Tyree had done and added that they had all been through it too.

There were similar disputes and conflicts in the other five schools, but they occurred more rarely and were less dramatic. Waverly was riven by a quarrel when someone crashed their car into the senior mistress's vehicle in the car park and failed to 'own up'. Maid Marion saw a conflict between the new headmaster, Mr Underwood, and Mr Salter, when the former wrote to the parents of two boys in Mr Salter's form without consulting him first. In general, however, the staffrooms of our schools were places where colleagues relaxed, joked, relayed the news, heard what their union was doing, and fought their battles with each other and their Heads. While each teacher is 'alone' in the classroom, and the staffroom is the place for friendship with peers, for the pupils both classroom and playground are arenas for peergroup activities to which the chapter now turns.

Pupils and their peers

The social relationships of pupils have been the subject of a good deal of research attention by a variety of methods. Although

Macpherson (1983: 1) claims that these studies 'have been theoretically and methodologically limited,' most commentators (e.g.
Hammersley and Woods, 1984) are more confident about the work
on pupils than that on teachers, and feel convinced it has made a
significant contribution to our knowledge of schooling processes. In
this section some of the material on pupils' informal groupings is
presented, to complement the material in Delamont (1983b: 137–
46).

In the previous volume we described briefly how the two main
anxieties pupils had about their peers were resolved. The first
anxiety concerned friends, and pupils were worried both about
losing their existing friends and failing to make new ones. The
second focused on bullying, and some pupils were frightened that
they would be victims at their transfer schools. Our data showed
that those children who had these anxieties soon lost them. Most
pupils reported that both these fears were soon dispelled. If they
were separated from old friends they made new ones, and most
found there was little bullying. The material on bullying has been
rehearsed in chapter 4 on 'Dangers in the School', and here we
concentrate on how the pupils' friendship groups are formed and
dissolved, with the emphasis on the impact of these on classroom
interactions.

Off with the old and on with the new?

Measor and Woods (1984: 30–31) describe how their sample were
allowed to see the class lists of their transfer school during the
pre-transfer programme and these 'told them whether their friends
from middle school would be in a class with them', which was
'probably their major concern'. Measor and Woods contrast the
reactions of two girls, one who is to be separated from her best
friend and is in tears; and another who is elated because she is
allocated to the same form as hers. Both responses are to be found
in our data, in the essays pupils wrote, and the interviews they gave
us. For example, one girl who transferred to Kenilworth, Inge, had
been placed in 1 gamma, and she wrote 'When I first came I got split
up from my two best friends who are now in 1 alpha . . . ' This had,
initially distressed her, but she soon made new ones. In contrast,
Denzil, transferring to Waverly, told our interviewer that:

> He had made a lot of new friends, but from the beginning he has sat next to
> Bart, also from Ashwood Bank. They are usually in each other's company –
> so his best friend is still the same as before. These two see each other out of
> school, as Denzil goes fishing with Bart and his dad at weekends.

Denzil, a British West Indian boy, lived in a local authority children's home, and so these out-of-school contacts were particularly precious to him. Thus some pupils are separated from their friends, and some transfer with them.

Measor and Woods (1984: 31) point out that their sample did not understand why they had been separated from their friends, and explain that the reasons were usually to do with allocating children to the same 'house' as an older sibling, the exigencies of the mixed ability grouping, or a policy decision to separate people for disciplinary reasons. Thus although the middle schools gathered information on friendship choices, and supplied it to the transfer school, it was not always used in drawing up the new class lists. Our six schools also operated in this way, and some of them explained to the pupils, or parents, or both, *why* children might be separated from friends. For example when Mr Seed and Mr Welsh visited Kenilworth Warden Lower School before transfer, they explained to the children how their new classes were made up.

> Mr Seed then handed over to Mr Welsh explaining that now he must come to the exciting part of actually telling the children which classes they were going to be in. This was obviously what the children really wanted to hear . . . Mr Welsh first of all explained that there would be children from quite a few other junior schools and they all had to be mixed together so that the children would find new friendships as this was part of life, i.e. learning to cope with people.

Mr Welsh stressed that all the classes were equal, and all mixed ability and why this was fair.

> He explained that he had acted very much on the advice of the junior school teachers who { . . . } also gave advice on any particular friendships which help work and also of particular friendships which hinder it. He pointed out to the children that although they might like to sit near a particular person it was not always best for them that they did so, and he warned them not to be too disappointed if any particular child did not find themselves with their special buddy.
>
> He softened the blow by explaining that classes which were adjacent often joined together for things like PE and also went to dinner together. So although particular friends might not be in the same class they would still have plenty of opportunity to see each other.

These pupils were, therefore forewarned that if they were separated from their friends it was 'for their own good' and due either to the exigencies of the organization or their previous misdeeds. Similar points were made at other pre-transfer events. During the pre-transfer parents' evening at Melin Court Mr Stackpole told the parents that: 'Every effort had been made to put some children from the same middle school into the same class.' Then Mrs

Hallows amplified this by saying that in making up the class lists they had ensured there would be familiar faces, but Melin Court might separate friends:

> Their child would be in a class with pupils from their old middle school, and whether they will be with their best friend will depend on whether they waste their time.

Parents visiting Gryll Grange were told the same thing about grouping 'that the only time random selection was not practised was in separating the livelier children through recommendation of the lower school'. These arrangements were more readily accepted by those pupils who ended up with their friends, than those who had been separated. For example, Lucinda, who transferred from Burton Upton to Melin Court, told the project interviewer:

> The only thing she was worried about was being split up from her friends, but before leaving Burton Upton they had had to write down the names of their friends, so she knew she would be in the same class as some of them.

Similarly two boys moving from Mitchell Butler to Maid Marion, Nathan and Errol, had always been friends, and Nathan told the researcher:

> He always stays with his particular friend Errol, who is also from the same school. He very rarely mixes with other children. He knew he was coming up with his particular friend, Errol, who is in the same class, and he felt no worries of any kind.

Thus, students who knew they were going to be in the same class as a friend – especially their 'best friend' – face transfer with great equanimity. This applied to Jackie and Odette moving to Maid Marion who were quoted in chapter 2. Pupils who had been separated from a close friend 'for their own good' could accept that as long as someone they knew would be with them. The interview with Vaudine and Merle illustrates this point about their transfer to Maid Marion:

> Both the girls had been a bit perturbed that they were being split from some of their other friends on coming to Maid Marion. However, they had been warned about this and it had been explained to them that they were being split because they tended to chatter too much and that it was for their own good. This they seemed to accept and in fact they found they got on quite well with the other children who were in their class.

In contrast, pupils who did not have anyone else from their school transferring were especially anxious about being lonely. Althea and Trudie:

> were both the sole representatives of their junior school coming up to Maid Marion. Althea had only just moved to this area of Bridgehampton and Trudie had been in London before. Both of them said they had been very worried about finding new friends.

A similar situation faced Luke and Josh transferring to Maid Marion, who were worried they would not have any friends because they were the only children from their school at Maid Marion. Josh's sister had told him 'not to worry as he would soon make friends', and in fact, the two boys: 'on the very first day both seemed to pair up together and have been together ever since'.

Overall then, the ORACLE data show that continuity of friendship eases transfer, but even children who start a new school 'cold' soon make friends. However, keeping them, and the positive and negative consequences of peer groups, are a slightly different story.

Making and breaking friendships

Commentators on the age range with which ORACLE is concerned (9–12) frequently stress the importance of peer relationships in children's lives. Our data reinforce this. The sample pupils' interviews and essays show a preoccupation with making friendships, and breaking them. Insofar as pupils are expected to co-operate in their work, or at least not disturb each other, their abilities in maintaining friendships have consequences for school work – just as in working life a network of friends and contacts is a prerequisite for finding and keeping employment in many occupations. As Applebaum (1981: 27) argues in his study of construction workers:

> Each foreman or superintendent tends to set up a circle of friends or relatives who become a labour pool from which he hires. Tests for hiring are personal ones. {. . .} Construction work is based on teams and gangs and without sociability there is often no cooperation. Dissension can wreck a project, so men who foment dissension are avoided.

Dissension can also wreck classroom work, and we observed lessons fail because of the quarrels which disrupted the peer groups in them. Thus, at Gryll Grange in 1T, Miss Tweed's class, there was a group of girls who sat and worked together, and were nominally friends. This group included Davina (a girl we have described in Galton and Delamont, 1980), Nanette, Jaquetta, and, when she was able to come to school after breaking her leg, Lucy. The following incident took place in July, nine months after transfer, and shows how peer relations can disrupt work. Miss Tweed had got the pupils, as a class, to construct a large matrix of the 7 times table up to 900 x 7. The observer wrote:

> The main task of the morning is then to use these tables to do more complex multiplications. For example, 174 x 7 can be obtained by adding the result of a 100, 70 and 4 x 7, from the corrected table. There has clearly been some tightening up of rules. At one point Miss Tweed shouted out at the pupils 'Don't write on the cover of the folder. This is something that makes Mr Judge furious.' The approach is class teaching but there is a discovery type strategy employed. For example they are never shown how to work out 174 x 7 other than being told they are not to do it by the usual multiplication method.
>   An argument develops between some of the girls about the method. Lucy, is putting the numbers in a row and trying to add them up. 'You'll do it alright if you do it in columns with units and tens,' say the others. 'I do know. I've been shown,' replies Lucy. {. . .}

The group of girls, Davina, Nanette, Jaquetta, Sheila and Lucy, are working cooperatively on this maths task, but because they disagree among themselves, their disagreement comes to overshadow the arithmetic.

> The group of girls have got very argumentative and at the beginning of playtime they are checking off their answers. Nanette is the odd one out in that her answers do not agree with the others! They try to persuade her that it is better to write down their answers than hers, but she keeps on saying 'I want to show you my way.' Sheila says 'She always thinks she's right.' 'No I don't, but I want to show you my way' says Nanette and then rushes out. 'She's crying,' says Lucy smartly 'She'll tell Miss Tweed, let's get there' – they all rush out.
>   After break they continue with the maths. The atmosphere is so relaxed that occasionally there is a sharp shaft of angry sarcasm by Miss Tweed. The argument between the girls is still going on. Nanette has been accused of being stuck-up. Miss Tweed arrives and makes light of Nanette's tears, 'Yes Miss, sniff' says Miss Tweed. But now that she is crying there are others on the table trying to make up; they shake hands, that's because of fear what Miss Tweed is going to say when she comes back having been interrupted by Mr Valentine. After about ten minutes nearly 60% of the class are distracted in one way or the other and are only working spasmodically. Miss Tweed goes back to the girls' table and jollies Nanette out of her tears. 'I've never met such a group, one minute you are the friendliest, next you are scratching each others' eyes out. Then you are kissing each other better. Don't take any notice of Lucy,' she tells Nanette.

Such quarrels are highly disruptive of the work-rate of the group of girls, and may even disturb the rest of the room. They also pre-occupy the pupils themselves. Lee Anne transferred to Kenilworth, and was in 1 gamma. In the June following transfer she wrote us an essay on her first year, most of which is concerned with her friendships. The extract below includes all the comment on friends:

> I can make friends easily and soon knew every girl in the class. I like to work hard and please the teachers. When I first came to this school my best friend was Deanna, but I hate her. My best friend now is Verity. I play always with Verity. We both play with two funny boys (the names I will not mention). I like Verity because she can be trusted, she never falls out, and she will help people and comfort people. Above that she is funny. We started being great friends when I moved up a set in maths to let room for Bethany and Inge (her best friend then) had fell out with her. I sat next to her and we did everything together. If we ever fall out we just laugh our heads off and fall in again.
> I used to like all of 1 gamma but I don't now, because some are cheeky, included April, Leonora, and Emily.

This essay's remarks about friendship show the major themes in adolescent girls' sociability rehearsed in the literature (e.g. Ball, 1981; Davies, 1984; Fuller, 1980; Meyenn, 1980; Measor and Woods, 1984; Llewellyn, 1980; Pollard, 1985; and Macpherson, 1983). There is a divide between cliques who want to please teachers (Lee Anne and her friends) and those who are 'cheeky' (Emily and hers). The changing patterns of allegiance are reported as Lee Anne falls out with Deanna and becomes close to Verity. An embryonic interest in boys is present ('the names I will not mention'). Also, because Kenilworth was streamed, the impact of teaching groups on friendship is apparent ('I moved up a set in maths').

Verity's essay contains the same themes, plus some new ones. Again the material on friendship has been extracted from the essay:

> On the first day . . . I walked to school with Inge and a lot of others. I like Kenilworth because there are a lot of children to play with. My best friend is Lee Anne. We sit together in every lesson. Our term marks are nearly the same. Lee Anne has been my best friend since just after the Easter holidays. At dinner Lee Anne and I play with two boys (I won't tell you their names). I like Lee Anne best because she makes a good friend and always helps people when they need help.
> We both like dogs and Lee Anne owns one. When we did maths we were in different sets but she moved up after Christmas. Sometimes Lee Anne goes mardy and pretends to fall out with me and we both start laughing.
> Some of 1 gamma are very naughty. April cheeked Miss Airdale. . . .
> Kieran is always asking me to ask Lee Anne some private questions. . . .

('Mardy' is a dialect word for being bad-tempered, or temperamental.) Verity's essay shows the same concerns as Lee Anne's, but also adds the information that the two girls *get similar marks*, and have at least one out of school interest (dogs) in common. Verity, too, distances herself from the cheeky girls. The group of 'naughty' girls are identified by other females in the class, for Luella wrote: 'The people who spoil the class are Emily, Leonora, and April.'

Similar differentiations were taking place at Maid Marion, and can be seen in both our target class 1O and 1I. The peer groups that formed in 1I were considered so disruptive to good teaching that the staff intervened to try and change it during the school year. Before we examine the cliques in 1I, those among the girls in 1O are worth a brief description. Some of these girls have already been quoted in this and earlier chapters (Merle, Vaudine, Jessamine, Lavinia, Althea and Trudie). The 'fallings out' and 'fallings in' among these girls were chronicled by the researcher from observation and interviews. The influences of the junior schools the girls had previously attended, attitudes to school work, and preferred playground activities can all be seen in the cliques formed and dissolved. Inside the classroom, the pupils sat in groups, which were largely based on the junior school attended. Thus the girls from Kenilworth Warden sat together, as did those from Mitchell Butler. However the friendships were more complex than this. The girls from Kenilworth Warden, though seated together, did not form an harmonious group. Merle and Vaudine had been split from their previous friends 'for their own good', and although they shared a table with Jessamine and Lavinia:

> they frequently fall out with these other two and there are often quarrels between them although of a fairly short lived nature. Merle and Vaudine do not mix with any of the other girls. . . .

These four did not spend any time together in the classroom, and had different pastimes. Jessamine and Lavinia were the pair who described Maid Marion as having a lot of bullying (Delamont, 1983b: 143). They regarded the other girls as childish, and Jessamine told the interviewer:

> They play such immature games it is about time they learned to be a bit more sensible and grown up. They play all this hide and seek stuff. I do not want to do silly immature things like that.

The exclusive friendships of each of these pairs created feelings of isolation for Althea and Trudie who had each come to the suburb from elsewhere. Trudie had met four girls during the summer holidays who were transferring to Maid Marion from Mitchell Butler, and began the year sitting with them. Althea had met Merle during the holidays, and started the year sitting with Merle, Vaudine, Jessamine and Lavinia. These four were so exclusive that Althea was an unwanted extra and early in the research the obser-

The staffroom and the peer groups

ver 'found her, on about the third day, in tears, because, she said, the others were all talking about her behind her back.' Althea moved from that table and joined Trudie's, but there was not room for her 'on a bench designed for four', and Althea had to sit on her own. The researcher commented 'She has certainly fallen out with Merle, as have quite a few others in the form.' Such convulsions can disrupt not only the girls' happiness, but also the academic work of the form. The staff of Maid Marion were convinced that the clique structured of 1I was causing academic problems. The friendship groups of both boys and girls were causing problems, the teachers believed, so both are described. The problem with the boys was highlighted by the observer's notes during the spring term:

> The major problem of this term – in fact of the whole year – has been a particular group of boys in 1I, which includes Harry, Sinclair, Greg and Dickon. They had been spotted from the very beginning, particularly by Mr Salter, their form master who takes them for science, as general troublemakers. They were always messing about with apparatus and fiddling with it, and playing around, and generally not concentrating. Mr Salter is a great one for what he calls 'discipline in the lab' because he feels that the children's lack of control can be a serious hazard. He was, therefore, very quick to pounce on this group, and to try and suppress their misbehaviour from the start.

Mr Salter's displeasure with this group of boys had been noted by one of the observers within the first two weeks of the autumn term. The notes on a science lesson include:

> During the setting up of the experiment Harry, Dickon, Greg and Sinclair had become the group who were always labelled as troublemakers. They often tend to fiddle around with equipment and fidget with it. { . . . . } They often come in late for the lesson and Mr Salter generally characterized them as 'A group that needs to be checked'.

The group of boys had been noticed by the head of first year, Mr Welsh, by September 25th. An observer had the following interaction with him:

> Mr Welsh keeps a much tighter eye on some children for many different reasons all of which he gave to me. One particular group in 1I had been causing a lot of difficulty in all their lessons. This includes Harry, Dickon, Greg and Sinclair. They are often quarrelling among themselves and sometimes involved in punch-ups, not only in the playground but in the classroom as well.

The disruptive behaviour of these four boys was visible to staff and observers from the first fortnight of the autumn term. The school's

234

reactions to them will be described, but first, the head of first year's views on the whole class are given. In the spring term the observer was told:

> Mr Welsh is very concerned about the whole class which he says has not 'jelled'. It is difficult to understand quite what he means by this. I think the main issue which he has in mind is that the class is very 'cliquey', and they are therefore not a united class and don't have any class loyalty.
> Mr Welsh feels there is very little willingness between the different cliques ever to break up and work in different patterns, and thus, in his terms, to be a 'class'.

Mr Welsh had devised a plan to try and tackle what he perceived as this 'cliqueyness' and failure to operate as a class, including a camping trip and an inter-class quiz. One boy in 1I, Craig had noticed the exclusive cliques, and told us in his essay:

> When I came to Maid Marion and saw the kids in my class I noticed people sticking together. Saul, Russ and I stuck together. Luke, Dan, and Josh stuck together; Errol and Nathan; Eunice and Fay; Josephine, Gail and Antonia; Meriel, Daphne, Odette and Jackie; Heather and Fern; Wanda and Petunia; Greg, Harry, Sinclair and Dickon; and Jessica stuck with Fay.

Craig's list is a bit confusing, but outlines several of the cliques we found. The closeness of some of the pairs of girls (Odette and Jackie, for example) caused problems in lessons, some of which we outlined in chapter 7, especially for Jessica and Daphne who had been 'forced' into working together when their styles did not match. Craig had taken the girls' seating pattern as evidence of friendship, when the girls reported that the two did not necessarily coincide.

The friendships and quarrels among the girls may not have helped their work – it is unlikely that Daphne and Jessica produced as much as they could have done – but it was the boys who worried the staff.

On September 25th one observer noted Mr Welsh's concern for the four boys (Harry, Greg, Sinclair and Dickon) and the disruption they were causing:

> They are all football mad and Dickon is for ever mimicking football commentary and team accents, and deriding the teams which the others in the group support. I think this is often part of the cause of the uproar which ensues. In every single lesson they have caused trouble and it ended with a real punch-up between Harry and Dickon in an English class with Mrs Gaskell. She therefore sent all four of them to see Mr Welsh . . . and he gave them a severe talking to.

Mr Welsh's first strategy was to separate the boys within the class. This worked for a few days, as the observer wrote:

Greg now works on his own. Sinclair has moved in with another group and refuses to join his old mates at playtime. Harry, who would like to get on with his work, is under Dickon's spell and is far too weak-willed to say no.

However Mr Welsh's action did not solve the problem, for on October 22nd in an English lesson with Mrs Gaskell, the observer wrote:

> The classroom is L-shaped and at the table round the corner Josh, Sinclair, Greg, Harry and Dickon were indulging in a great deal of very noisy chatter, silly yawning, etc. . . . Harry was sitting next to Dickon and chatting a lot with him. Dickon began a very audible and silly wailing 'Oh, I've got constipation. . . . ' . . . . Right at the end of the lesson Mrs Gaskell became aware of Dickon's performance and asked him what was the matter. He said the other boys kept telling him he couldn't go to school football.

Mrs Gaskell then spent some time trying to sort out the quarrel and get the boys back to working. at this period the researcher interviewed Harry and Greg, noting that they, with Sinclair and Dickon 'Have become the "black four" of the first year.'

The boys told the interviewer that they felt victimized:

> They both felt that they were being picked on a great deal and very unfairly. They blamed the trouble on one particular boy they nicknamed Dix (Dickon).

The researcher commented that:

> When I watched in class it is always Dix who pulls the faces, mimics the football commentators, and generally causes some kind of distraction and makes the others laugh. It is then the others who get into trouble and get seen, or rather heard, laughing. Dix has a lovely straight face, and an innocent look in his eye, and always gets away with murder.

These boys did not only fight amongst themselves. Greg also had a fight with Gail, and gave her a black eye. The interviewer reported that while both Greg and Harry agreed that Dickon caused the trouble, and that they should avoid him; but:

> When we went back into the science lesson Dickon had been working on his own. There was a golden opportunity for Harry and Greg to start work together on their own away from Dickon (as they were asked to work in pairs). Dickon immediately called Harry over to join him, and Harry meekly agreed. Greg protested and said: 'Come on, he's already started on his own. You come and work with me.'

Harry went to work with Dickon.

The staff decided at Christmas to move Dickon to another class, and Sinclair stopped associating with Greg and Harry. However in the spring term 'Greg and Harry remained the main troublemakers'. There was a special staff meeting about them, and they were put 'on report' for a month. This worked for that month, but did not change the boys' longer-term behaviour. The staff therefore tried a different approach. They adopted a strategy of pupils reporting on their work to their classmates instead of 'intensely individualized work', and Mrs Gaskell and Mr Salter both tried to give them responsibilities. Mrs Gaskell gave them parts in a play, and Mr Salter 'sends them on special errands'.

Mr Welsh, the head of year, worried about the 'cliqueyness' of 1I, set out to foster class spirit. The staff ran an inter-form quiz, and:

> this apparently generated a great deal of enthusiasm among 1I who, when there was a competition and something to win, really pulled out their stops. Luckily, from the staff's point of view, 1I actually won the quiz without any cheating. This was thought to have been a great success.

To reinforce this success, the staff decided to take the whole class on a weekend camping trip to a youth centre with many activities. The staff had taken pupils there quite often, but only volunteers. To deal with 1I, they planned to make it 'almost compulsory' for the class. The observer was told:

> In the evenings, at this camp place, they all sing songs around the fireside, etc. There is a great emphasis on the 'community spirit' and 'united action'. This it is hoped will make the class 'jell' and feel themselves to be a class rather than a group of disparate individuals.

Here we see an extreme example of how the pupils' peer groups can affect the staff. Several teachers become involved in giving up a whole weekend to take a whole class camping to try and create a more wholesome atmosphere. It worked, in that the teachers were pleased with the class's social adjustment by the end of the summer term. The pupils also seem to have found the camping trip rewarding because out of twenty-three essays from 1I, thirteen mentioned enjoying the camping, and no one said they had disliked it. Jessica wrote that 'The best part of the year was the camp,' Josephine that 'The other outing that I really enjoyed was when we went camping for the weekend.' Jackie wrote that:

> The camp that was organized by Mr Salter was most enjoyable, it was great fun playing in the woods, at football and rounders, cooking sausages outside in the middle of the night and putting up our tents. It was very nice of Mr Salter to go to the trouble of getting all the trip organized for us.

Meriel perhaps captures the staff's hopes best when she wrote for us:

> But if I had to chose my really best thing. I'd chose outings because you really learn something. Camping weekends are fun because you make your own food, play games, go for walks and lots more things. Also you sleep in tents and you can have a lot of fun at nights. . . . On the camp I liked cooking our own dinners. It was really great fun. I think the camp is the very best outing I have been on.

The boys were less fulsome about it, with typical comments being Luke's, 'Mr Welsh and Mr Salter took us for a weekend to Pemberton Hall. I enjoyed that.' and Nathan's 'I licked the outin to pembertonhall.'

One boy, Royston, joined 1I in the middle of the year. He wrote that:

> My thoughts about the children in my class were that they were nutters (especially Russell) except Saul who looked like a wide-eyed frog. (This was only my first impression.)

However by the end of the year Royston had decided that the best thing about 'the school is that it is good fun and has a friendly atmosphere.' This was what Mr Welsh and Mr Salter wanted, and the camping trip *had* changed the social climate.

Conclusions

Mary Metz (1984) has argued that:

> Teachers' life experiences and the cultural and structural demands of their work settings shape their behaviour – with fateful consequences for their students.

Similarly, research has repeatedly shown an interaction between the social structures of schools and their pupils' social relationships. This chapter has discussed the teachers' 'backstage' area – the staffroom – with particular attention paid to an unhappy one at Guy Mannering. The relatively poor social relations in one class at Maid Marion have also been featured at some length. These disrupted social relations are highlighted to throw into relief the more peaceful colleagueship in the other schools' staffrooms, and the newly established friendships in the freshly created classes of pupils. Underlying the pupils' informal groups is the complex set of formal groups (discussed in chapter 7) to which every child belongs, and the ways in which schools organize pupils is also felt in the staffroom. The two sets of social relations are interrelated in that what the pupils do forms a major topic of staffroom talk, and the quality of social life in the staffroom is carried back into the classrooms. The presence of the observer can affect both spheres, for s/he is both a source of humour and 'news', and a witness when things go right or wrong. This chapter has presented the ORACLE data on social relations in staffroom and classroom, to add to the available material on everyday life in school.

CHAPTER 10

Conclusions

'You're not in Baby School – in Lower School. You're big boys and big girls. I've asked you to do a simple thing – do it.' (Miss Miranda to class 1.5 at Guy Mannering)

Case studies have as a primary purpose the illumination of a small set of social phenomena and hence by their very nature cannot be comprehensive. (Borman, 1981)

The material in this volume has been concerned primarily with the nature of the six institutions to which our ORACLE pupils transferred. In the previous volume (Galton and Willcocks, 1983: 102–18) we demonstrated that despite their different rhetorics and social organizations, the six schools had essentially similar curricula. This similarity in course content will have been apparent in this book too, as the extracts from notes taken in the six schools have shown pupils copying very similar things from similar blackboards in similar rooms. Alongside the common curriculum we have argued in that earlier volume, and demonstrated here, that school transfer produces only very temporary problems for nearly all children. Within a very few weeks the difficulties pupils are having are schooling problems, *not* transfer problems.

This volume had four main objectives. It was designed to highlight some generally neglected aspects of school life (such as danger); to cover the ways in which initial encounters are transformed into routine ones, to report an unusual exercise in team-based, comparative, 'hired-hand' (Roth, 1966) ethnography, and to cover the whole spectrum of the curriculum. Each of these aims has been achieved, and the material presented adds to the body of ethnographic material on middle and upper schools in the state sector.

Conclusions

The ORACLE ethnography was intended to focus on many previously taken-for-granted, familiar, aspects of schooling, and treat them as anthropologically 'strange'. This has been done by highlighting, for example, the extent to which schools are differentiated environments in terms of physical and social dangers (chapter 4), the arbitrary divisions of school time (chapter 6) and the omnipresence of the family in the school (chapter 8).

The importance, for understanding school life, of observing initial encounters has been made in chapter 3. This book provides the richest selection of initial encounters published in Britain, and also, by presenting material gathered later in the school year, also shows how the honeymoon phase passes. In the case histories of individual pupils, such as Jessamine and Lavinia, Yvette (Horace), Dominico, Rex and Wayne, their immediate reactions to the transfer schools are shown shading into the longer-term pupil-careers. Combined with the follow-up data in Appendix 1, the ORACLE transfer study provides a rich portrait of pupils' lives in several different schools.

The ORACLE transfer ethnographies were also an unusual example of a comparative, team-based, 'hired-hand' ethnography, with all the benefits and problems that brings (Galton and Delamont, 1985). Many of the school ethnographies done in Britain have been single-handed analyses of single schools. For this research, the different perspectives and insights of six people were deployed. The data are thus richer and more varied, as each observer deployed different skills around their two schools.

The ORACLE ethnography included all areas of the curriculum, in a deliberate attempt to break the pattern of studying only English, maths, science and other humanities subjects. This volume has therefore included material on PE and drama, woodwork and cookery, 'topics' and swimming, alongside the central academic subjects. It is in the area of the curriculum that recent debates about the future of comprehensive schooling are most interesting, and where the contradictions in mass secondary education are most painfully visible. As Resnick and Resnick (1985) have argued for the USA, and Lawton (1972), Hargreaves (1982) and Lacey (1982) for the UK, have argued, the problems of offering a core curriculum of high-status knowledge to all teenagers have yet to be thought through, far less solved.

Resnick and Resnick have argued that in the USA an elite minority have always been taught to criticize what they are taught, to engage in manipulation of knowledge, and thence, ultimately to create it, while the majority have only been expected to regurgitate it, uncritically. Lawton pointed out that only in 1944 was the

241

high-status curriculum opened to anyone who was 'able' to benefit from it, and only with Circular 10/65 was the dream of opening it to everyone even properly formulated. Achieving the dream of a whole population who are educated as critical manipulators of knowledge has proved far more difficult than educational reformers of the late nineteenth and early twentieth centuries ever imagined.

Hargreaves' (1982) controversial proposal involved abandoning the dream. Resnick and Resnick, in contrast, argue that America can afford to try and produce 'a fully educated citizenry – not just a long-schooled one.' To achieve this they want a programme that sets 'strong intellectual standards in a core' curriculum for all students, using the research on teaching to change classroom instruction. That is, they believe that there is now research on how to teach, and how to teach pupils to think and learn effectively, which if used properly could involve the whole ability range, all ethnic groups, both sexes, and all social classes, becoming 'successfully engaged' in the solidly intellectual programme. (The research on teaching to which they refer can be found in Doyle and Good, 1982, and Fisher and Berliner, 1985.)

The Resnicks' vision is an inspiring one. However, as Lacey (1982) argued, such a vision can create intolerable pressures on the teachers. He claims that British teachers found themselves caught between demands for giving a wide ability and social range of pupils the high status curriculum; and the unpleasantness of classroom disorder and stress which result from trying to do this to an unwilling clientele. The teachers' solutions to the containment problem have resulted, Lacey argues, in creating new types of grouping (e.g. mixed ability forms and sets rather than streams); new curricula (e.g. discovery science or Diene maths); and individualized learning (no public grading) which conceal from outsiders, including parents, who is succeeding and failing in conventional ways.

All six ORACLE schools were facing this dilemma, with pressure for exam success from outside (parents with influence, the upper schools) and a need to create working conditions which were bearable for teachers. The resolution of this dilemma adopted by the six schools has been seen in this book. If the reader has found the portraits of the teachers, pupils and lessons depressing or negative, this was not our intention. All six schools, all the staff, and most of the 300+ pupils were managing some extremely difficult tasks. The schools had worked hard to ease the pupils' transfer, most of the staff were conscientious and hard-working, most of the pupils were relatively cheerful and cooperative. If the portrait of British schooling which results is not a uniformly optimistic one, this is because the comprehensive dream is such an exalted one it is not

Conclusions

surprising that it exceeds the grasp of some schools, some teachers and some pupils on some occasions.

APPENDIX I

Lists of participants

This appendix provides the pseudonyms of all the schools, teachers and pupils described in the book.

Local Authority A – Ashburton

(5–9 Lower Schools, 9–13 Middle Schools, 13–18 Upper Schools)

5–9 Lower Schools attended by ORACLE children:

Banbury Lower
Orton Water Lower
Enville Lower
Solihull Street Lower
Coventry Lane Lower
Balaclava Road Lower

Guy Mannering Lower
Blossomfield Lower
Shawfield Lower
Ashburton Saints Lower
Old Hill Lower

9–13 Middle Schools in study:

Guy Mannering – called AST (A Secondary Type) in Galton and Willcocks (1983)
Gryll Grange – called APT (A Primary Type) in Galton and Willcocks (1983)

Other Middle Schools mentioned in the text:

St Bridget's
Banbury
Hinckley Road

13–18 Upper Schools:

Woodhouse Upper School (formerly Woodhouse Secondary Modern)
Ashburton Boys' School (formerly Ashburton Boys' Grammar School)
Ashburton Girls' School (formerly Ashburton Girls' Grammar School)
Dashwood Upper School (formerly Ashburton Technical High School)
Morland Upper School (new school built on new estate)

244

Appendix 1

Names of classes inside 9–13 Middle Schools:

Guy Mannering: 1.1, 1.3, 1.5 (A Band)
1.2, 1.4, 1.6 (B Band)
Classes observed,
1.5 and 1.6

Gryll Grange: 1T – Miss Tweed's class
1H – Mrs Hind's class
1V – Mr Valentine's class

Teachers at Ashburton Schools:

Banbury Lower headteacher: Mr Jolly
Guy Mannering

Miss Tyree	Headmistress	Mr Sturgess-Jones	PE
Mrs Evans	Deputy head, English	Mr Beldham	NUT rep.
Mr Evans	Senior master, English and geography	**Gryll Grange:**	
		Mr Judge	Headteacher
Mrs Forrest	Form teacher of 1.5, science and maths	Mr Forrest	Deputy head (husband of Mrs Forrest at Guy Mannering)
Miss O'Hara	Form teacher of 1.6, English and RE	Mr Washbrook	Previous headteacher
		Miss Tweed	Teacher of 1T
Mr Black	Science	Mrs Hind	Teacher of 1H
Mrs Bird	Cookery	Mr Valentine	Probationary teacher of 1V
Mrs Cherry	Cookery		
Miss Pink	Needlework	Mrs Stone	Remedial teacher
Miss Miranda	Cookery and 'topics'	Mr Lyons	French
		Mr Vaughan	Music
Mr Bradshaw	Wood and metalwork	Mr Hogg	Head of Lower School (first and second years)
Miss Kroll	PE		
Mr Macauley	History	Mrs Tench	
Mr LeGard	RE and the library		
Mr Woolfe	Art		
Mr Apter	Maths		
Mrs Tallis	Music		
Mrs Maplin	Home economics		
Mrs Hargreaves			
Mrs Adamson			

Local Authority B – Bridgehampton

(5–11 Lower Schools, 11–14 Middle Schools, 14–18 Upper Schools)

5–11 Lower Schools attended by ORACLE children:

Mitchell Butler Lower	Whitteck Lower
Kenilworth Warden Lower	Knowle Park Lower
Dorridge Lower	Lichfield Lane Lower
King's Heath Lower	

Appendix 1

11–14 Middle Schools in study:

Kenilworth – called BST (B Secondary Type) in Galton and Willcocks (1983)

Maid Marion – called BPT (B Primary Type) in Galton and Willcocks (1983)

14–18 Upper Schools:
Sanditon Community College

Classes in the 11–14 Middle Schools:

Kenilworth: 1 alpha, 1 beta, 1 gamma, 1 delta, 1 epsilon, 1 zeta, 1 eta, 1 theta.

Classes observed, 1 gamma, and 1 zeta

Maid Marion: 1M, 1A, 1I, 1D, 1R, 1O, 1N

Classes observed, 1I and 1O

·Teachers at Bridgehampton Schools:

Kenilworth:		Maid Marion:	
Mr Arrow	Headteacher	Mr Underwood	New headteacher from Xmas
Mr Leach	Deputy head		
Miss Chichester	Head of first year	Mr Blundell	Retiring headteacher
Miss Stephenson	Form mistress of 1 gamma (history)	Mr Seed	Acting head in first term
Mr Pompey	Joint form master of 1 zeta (PE)	Mr Welsh	Head of first year
Mrs Monk	Joint form mistress of 1 zeta	Mr Salter	Science, form teacher of 1I
Mr Flanigan	Craft, design and technology	Miss Square	PE, form teacher of 1O
Mr Mauss	Pottery	Mr Barrell	English and drama
Mr Pardoe	Science	Mrs Gaskell	English
Miss Airdale	English	Mrs Edwards	Maths
Mr Foale	Maths	Mr Taff	Maths
Mrs Stockton	French	Mrs Rumsey	Maths and some science
Mr Gordon	English		
Mrs Lords	RE	Mr Nailsea	Music
Mr Birch	RE	Mr Brett	Head of CDT, metalwork
Mrs Lee	Maths		
Mrs Cullen	Geography	Mr Penzance	Art
Miss Cotton	Remedial	Mrs Elmhirst	Pottery
Mr Tippett	Music	Mr Moore	Woodwork
Mrs Appleyard		Miss Devine	Cookery
Mr Southern		Mrs York	Needlework
Mr Cowell	PE	Mr Weir	PE
Mr Hutchinson		Mr Stoller	
Mrs Forsyth		Mr Griffiths	
Mrs Blewitt	Biology	Mr Butler	
		Mr Rhys	Remedial maths
		Mr Quaife	Head of science
		Mr Tracey	PE

Appendix 1

Local Authority C – Coalthorpe

(5–8 Lower Schools, 8–12 Middle Schools, 12–18 Comprehensive Upper Schools)

8–12 Middle Schools attended by ORACLE children:

Ashwood Bank Middle
Burton Upton Middle
Villebourne Middle
Pickwick Middle
Stourbridge Road Middle

Eglinton Middle
Fordhouses Middle
Shrewsbury Avenue Middle
Wellington Middle

12–18 Upper Schools in study:

Waverly – called CST (C Secondary Type) in Galton and Willcocks (1983)
Melin Court – called CPT (C Primary Type) in Galton and Willcocks (1983)

Names of classes inside 12–18 schools:

Waverly:
There were 8 parallel classes identified by the teachers' initials.
We studied Miss Lawrence's form, 1LE, and Mrs Bobbin's form, 1BN

Melin Court:
There were 9 parallel forms, identified by the letters of the school's name – 1M, 1E,
1L, 1I, 1N, 1C, 1O, 1U, 1R. We studied 1M and 1E

Teachers at Coalthorpe Schools:

Waverly:		Melin Court:	
Mr Parkin	Headmaster	Mr Stackpole	Headmaster
Miss Lawrence	Form teacher of 1LE, English	Mrs Hallows	Science, head of first year
Mrs Bobbin	Form teacher of 1BN, needlework	Mrs Wordsworth	Form teacher of 1M, English
Mr Bronte	Head of first year, English	Mrs Zeldin	Form teacher of 1E, French
Mr Plumb	Technical drawing	Miss Fern	Science
Mr Quill	Technical drawing	Mr Trelawny	Science
Mr Darwin	Science	Mr Steele	Craft
Mr Rutherford	Science	Mr Beech	Craft
Mr Huxley	Science	Miss Hartnell	Needlework
Mr Baden	French and German	Mrs Madder	Art
		Mrs Marks	Senior mistress
Mr Mowbray	French and German	Mr Haydon	French
		Mr Clift	
Mr Pewter	Metalwork	Mr Griffin	
Mr Brearly	Art	Mrs Huntley	Maths
Mr Palet	Art	Mrs Hammond	
Mrs Lake	Geography	Mr Braund	Geography
Mr Spencer	Deputy head	Mrs Durrant	RE
Mrs Wheel	Science	Mrs Tyzack	Cookery
Mrs Southey	English	Mr Yardley	
Mr Fawlty	Music	Mrs Altham	Music
Mr Jessop		Mrs Newbolt	History
Mrs Attfield	RE	Mr Eggleston	Music

Mr Winterton	English	Mr Waterworth
Mr Astill	Maths	
Mrs Sutcliffe	Cookery	
Mr Oakley	Woodwork	
Mrs Osbaldeston	Senior mistress	
Mr Harpole		

The Pupils

Pupils are generally known by first names only, but where a surname is needed, that too is a pseudonym.

1 – Ashburton

Guy Mannering:

Form 1.5 (A Band)		Form 1.6 (B Band)	
Audrey	Barny	Adela	Aidan
Caitlin	Barry	Annabel	Angus
Coral	Carter Pilch	Bonita	Austin
Gabrielle	Derrick	Cynthia	Benedict Kortright
Lauretta	Dominico Grillo	Dionne	Brendon
Leila	Eric	Felicity	Caspar
Lillian	Gavin Radice	Fleur	Conrad
Mair Pryce	(later Radley)	Janet	Crispin
Martina	Gene	Paula	Dirk
Mirelle	Howard	Sian	Hamish
Rhoda	Lawrence	Tessa	Joel
Rowena	Marvin	Zelda	Lionel (later Joe)
Shelly	Mitchell Gardiner		Mahomed
Sonia	Norris		Nitim
	Sebastian Gunn		Randal
	Terence		Roger
			Vernon
			Victor
			Wallace

Children in other classes mentioned in text:

Camilla	Alvin
Arlene (Annabel's sister)	Amos
Eluned (Mair's sister)	Gerald
	Magnus
	Bagshaw – the groundsman's son

Appendix 1

Gryll Grange:
1T – Miss Tweed's class

Alan Bewes	Angela	Quentin	Nanette
Alfred	Cecilia	Roy	Philippa
Daniel	Davina	Sammy	Priscilla
Dean	Fatima	Stirling	Rosalie
Duncan	Hazel	Tom	Sheila
Hugh	Jacquetta		Stacey
Jeremy	Judith		Stephanie
Kenneth	Lucy		Sybil
Malcolm	Marcia		Tammy
Morris	Melissa		Yvette

Other children mentioned: Rhodri – Davina's brother

1H – Mrs Hind's class

Adrian	Amy	Raymond Lynn	Louisa
Charles	Candy	Robin	Melody
Cliff	Claudia	Shane	Monica
Darryl	Cordelia	Toby	Morag
Dominic	Dolores		Nicola
Dudley	Evaline		Rebecca
Justin	Ianthe		Ruth
Len	Janice		Selina
Murray	Kathleen		Sheena Bewes
Noel	Kirsty		(Alan's twin)
Oliver	Lois		Tina

1V – Mr Valentine's class

Blaise	Anita	Maxwell	Parween Khalid
Clive	Bijou	Nigel	Paulette
Cole	Deirdre	Patrick	Petra
Curtis	Elvira	Piers	Polly
Fergus	Faith	Rupert	Renate
Grant	Justine		Rosamund
Hedley	Karel		Sheryl
Jack	Madeline		Theresa
Karl	Marilyn		Veronica Tate
Leslie	Nadine		Zoe

Appendix 1

2 – Bridgehampton

Maid Marion:
Form 1O – Miss Square's form

Althea	Dermot	Merle	John
Chantel	Earl	Myra	Lester
Fida	Edward	Sally	Madoc
Jessamine*	Elmer	Trudie	Miles
Julia	Gerard	Vaudine	Rolf
Karena	Irving		Richard
Lavinia	Jerome		

Form 1I – Mr Salter's form

Antonia	Craig	Heather	Josh
Daphne	Dan	Jackie	Luke
Donna	Dickon	Jessica	Nathan
Eunice	Errol†	Josephine	Royston
Fay	Gareth Williams	Meriel	Russell
Fern	Greg	Odette	Saul
Gail	Harry**	Petunia	Sinclair
		Wanda	

Kenilworth:
Form 1 gamma – Miss Stephenson's class

April	Bruce	Jenny	Thelma
Alvina	Clyde	Lee Anne	Verna
Deanna	Fenton	Leonora	Verity
Dorinda	Frank	Luella	Ted
Emily	George	Lydia	
Estelle	Gilbert	Marsha	
Gwen	Hunter	Melanie	
Inge	Kieran	Naomi	
Jean	Lance	Noelle	

Form 1 zeta – form of Mr Pompey and Mrs Monk

Bronwen	Archie	Oonagh	Ralph
Gaynor	Arnold	Paige	Richie
Hester	Brett		Ryan
Holly	Christian	Maurice	Terry
Josie	Edmond	Michael	
Krystyna	Emlyn	Neil	
Lyndall	Floyd	Peter Queen	
Meade	Kevin	Philip	

(After Christmas Blair and Walter joined this form)
Other pupils mentioned: Bethany

---

* (mistakenly called Jasmine in Galton and Willcocks, 1983)
† (mistakenly called Amos in Galton and Willcocks, 1983)
** (mistakenly called Jacky in Galton and Willcocks, 1983)

3 – Coalthorpe

Melin Court:

1M – Mrs Wordsworth's form

Alistair	Alison	Ninian	Glenys
Allen	Colette	Norman	Juliette
Eamonn O'Malley	Danielle Draper	Selwyn	Leonie
Francis	Delma	Simon	Petula
Glenn	Dorothy	Theo	Tiffanie
Lloyd	Elaine	Thomas	Yvonne
Melvyn Pym	Gemma	Wayne Douglas	
Neal	Gerda	Patel*	

1E – Mrs Zeldin's class

Alec	Byrony	Jim	Lucinda
Carl	Corrine	Liam	Natalie
Colin	Crystal	Malcolm	Rita
Damian	Darlene	Manji	Sophie
Douglas	Evelyn	Max	Stella
Dylan	Fenella	Mervyn	Tamara Fields
Ellis	Janey	Ramsay	
Jasper	Joscelin	Vincent Delgardo	

Waverly:

1LE – Miss Lawrence's form

Andrew	Avril	James	Serena
Bart	Bernadine	Neville	Vanessa
Cameron	Delia	Phil	Vera
Chandra	Francine	Warren	Vivienne
Denzil	Heidi	William	
Dick	Jasmine	Winston	
Donald	Peggy	Zak	
Ivor	Sandra		

1BN – Mrs Bobbin's class

Clifford	Adele	Lewis	Gita
Connor	Belinda	Martyn	Joyce
Dale	Carys	Rex Mackie	Laura Eggleston
Gordon Wilde	Cherie	Rob	Tanya
Jason	Coralie	Scott	Zillah
Jeffery	Dawn	Stuart	
Keith	Ellen Farley	Wilfred	
Laurence	Giselle		

Rex Mackie's older brother – Donovan
Pupil who transferred from Melin Court to Waverly after one week – Brent
Pupils in Mr Bronte's class: Simone, Jake, Royce, Pamela

---

* (called only Wayne Douglas in Galton and Willcocks, 1983)

APPENDIX 2

Follow-up data

The ORACLE project was funded by the ESRC from 1975 to 1980. The transfer ethnographies took place in Ashburton in 1977/78, and in Bridgehampton and Coalthorpe in 1978/79. The pupils we observed in those two years have now all left school, although they were quite young when we watched them. The books from the ORACLE project began to appear in 1980, and while the time-lag between data-collection and publication of the transfer studies is not excessive in educational research, this volume has taken longer to produce than originally planned. It was decided, in 1983, that an (unfunded) follow-up of as many of the pupils as possible should be undertaken. In this appendix, the stories of those pupils we could trace are brought up to 1983/84. Sara Delamont visited the three towns, and, thanks to the cooperation of the Upper Schools in each LEA, traced a substantial proportion of the ORACLE pupils.

The Ashburton pupils were traced at the age of 15, in the fourth year of secondary schooling. The Coalthorpe pupils were traced when they were 17, and most had left Melin Court and Waverly. The Bridgehampton pupils were followed up when they were 17, in 1984. It was not possible to find out what had happened to every single pupil, and those who had moved away from the areas were not pursued. The tracing was relatively straightforward in Bridgehampton, where almost all the pupils from Kenilworth and Maid Marion moved at 14 to Sanditon Community College, the upper school on the same campus. In Coalthorpe, the transfer described in this book to Waverly and Melin Court, was the pupils' last move, and it was these schools which were revisited for the follow-up. The Ashburton pupils had moved at 13 out of Gryll Grange and Guy Mannering to a variety of Upper Schools, and five of these were visited. Table A2.1 shows the Upper Schools visited in this follow-up phase of the ORACLE work:

Before presenting the data on how the pupils fared in their upper schools, it is necessary to say something about the different schools in Ashburton, to amplify the material in chapter 1.

252

Table A2.1   Upper Schools visited in follow-up phase

Town	Name of School	
Ashburton	Woodhouse	(13–18 Upper School)
	Ashburton Boys'	"
	Ashburton Girls'	"
	Dashwood	",'
	Morland	"
Bridgehampton	Sanditon	(14–18 Upper School)
Coalthorpe	Waverly	(12–18 Upper School)
	Melin Court	"

The Ashburton upper schools

The Ashburton pupils were the hardest to trace, in that more of them had moved out of the area, or transferred to schools we could not identify. Even those who could be found had transferred from Gryll Grange and Guy Mannering to a wide range of different upper schools. We only visited the schools shown in Table A2.1, which had received several of our pupils.

Most of our sample moved at 13 to Woodhouse Upper School. This school is on the same site as Gryll Grange Middle School, Banbury Lower School, and a technical college. Thus it is in the middle of an expanding residential area, with both council and private housing, and was in easy walking distance for most of the Gryll Grange pupils *and* many of the Guy Mannering ones. It was also near the Hinckley Road Middle School, and pupils who had been there were a noticeable presence at Woodhouse. The staff of the other upper schools in Ashburton told us that Woodhouse was the upper school that they all had to live up to: it was a parental favourite, and received favourable press coverage at frequent intervals from the *Ashburton Evening Argus*. Woodhouse had been a secondary modern school, and was upgraded by extra facilities when re-designated as an upper school after comprehensive reorganization. The staff were young and enthusiastic, the facilities were good, the exam results pleased parents, and the majority of the pupils wore uniform. Among the 'events' at Woodhouse were science enrichment courses for all the gifted science pupils from the whole town, and a craft exhibition sponsored by the town's leading jewellers. Cynical staff in other schools claimed that Woodhouse was successful because all the potentially disruptive pupils were allocated to Morland Upper School, which was sited in a major shopping complex the other side of the urban ring road which passed in earshot of the campus.

Morland Upper School was a purpose-built institution, planned to serve the burgeoning population of the new London and Birmingham overspill estates. It was built alongside the Morland shopping centre, and had all the facilities that an upper school could use. However it was not as popular with parents as the other schools to which our sample had transferred: that is, it was not a parental 'first-choice' school. A small number of our sample went to Morland, and all but one of those was reported as presenting problems for the school.

Ashburton Girls' Upper School was also in new, purpose-built facilities, on open ground as far to the west of the Woodhouse/Gryll Grange campus as Morland was to the east. This single-sex upper school was based on the institution of the nineteenth-century girls' grammar school, which had premises in the city centre. Thus it was a new type of school in an outlying suburb, and the only link with the girls' grammar school was that it was the only non-Catholic *girls* upper school in Ashburton. Given its origins in a grammar school, Ashburton Girls' Upper School might have become the most oversubscribed choice for girls. However, according to the head of the fourth year, the new site had led to the school acquiring a reputation for being 'rough', and full of Muslim girls, from which it was only beginning to recover when the ORACLE pupils chose their upper school. Some of our female pupils *had* opted for Ashburton Girls', mostly from Guy Mannering.

Ashburton Boys' Upper School was chosen by several of the boys from Guy Mannering, and it, too, had lost much of its once proud reputation with the change from grammar to comprehensive. The boys' grammar school had moved to its present site in 1911, and these were quite near Guy Mannering. This school had, as a grammar school, a sixth form of 400 boys, and the change to a comprehensive upper school with a relatively small sixth form had perplexed some teachers, but unlike Ashburton Girls' School, the grammar school staff had not resigned, but still taught there. It is probable that parents who had deliberately chosen Guy Mannering, the formal middle school, were those who would prefer single-sex education when available.

There was one other upper school to which a group of Guy Mannering pupils had moved at 13: Dashwood. This upper school lies across Dashwood Park from Balaclava Road, the original site of Guy Mannering. Thus its immediate catchment area included the inner city red brick terraces from which some Guy Mannering pupils came. Dashwood had been created from the old Technical High School for Boys (founded in 1881) and St Bridget's Secondary Modern School for Girls (see chapter 1).

Ashburton also has an independent girls' school, established in the nineteenth century, which has a highly academic reputation, and at least two of our sample went there. More, however were lost to the follow-up because they had left Ashburton altogether – for Italy, Canada, Bahrain and for villages in the county.

Bridgehampton and Coalthorpe were much easier to conduct the follow-up in, as Table A2.1 showed. The information gathered is now presented.

Following our sample

The data available in the various upper schools, and those parts of it we were allowed to see, varied considerably. When possible, we examined the academic, attendance, health, and behavioural records kept on our sample. These data allow us to report what happened to some of the specific individuals who have featured in our publications (e.g. Galton and Delamont, 1980), and to provide some quantitative material on our sample's school careers. This appendix presents some pen portraits of pupils who have figured as individual 'personalities', and some of the numerical data. There are pleasures and sadnesses in following a cohort of pupils for six or seven years. It is satisfying to discover that a particular pupil has proceeded happily through their upper school and achieved some scholastic success. It is unpleasant to find out that other pupils have suffered unhappy adolescences, with truancy, failures, court hearings, pregnancies and unemployment. Some of the follow-up material shows patterns which are consistent with the ethnographic data from the transfer period; other parts reveal a sharp break from what seemed set for promising school careers. The *vignettes* will show both continuities and ruptures.

Table A2.2 shows the names of those pupils spotlighted in earlier publications whose pupil careers are summarized here. The first boy we feature is Dominico Grillo.

Dominico Grillo

Dominico, the middle son of a fish and chip shop owner (Delamont, 1983b: 141; and pages 197–9 above), was in 1.5 at Guy Mannering. He was a particular favourite of their English teacher, Mr Evans, who saw him as a bright boy who could be academically successful. He transferred from Guy

Table A2.2   Pen portraits of pupils followed up

Name	Middle School	Upper School	Page nos
Dominico Grillo	Guy Mannering	Ashburton Boys'	
Gavin Radice	Guy Mannering	Ashburton Boys'	
Barry	Guy Mannering	Ashburton Boys'	
Lionel	Guy Mannering	Dashwood	
Alvin	Guy Mannering	Morland	
Dawn	Eglinton	Waverly	
Nanette	Gryll Grange	Woodhouse	
Audrey	Guy Mannering	Woodhouse	
Tanya	Wellington	Waverly	
Pamela	—	Waverly	
Vanessa	—	Waverly	
Francine	—	Waverly	
Annabel	Guy Mannering	Woodhouse	
Fida	Maid Marion	Sanditon	
Karena	Maid Marion	Sanditon	
Harry	Maid Marion	Sanditon	
Sinclair	Maid Marion	Sanditon	
Greg	Maid Marion	Sanditon	
Rex Mackie	Ashwood Bank	Waverly	
Wayne Douglas Patel	—	Melin Court	

Mannering to Ashburton Boys' School, where he was very successful. The school expected him to pass 9 GCE 'O' levels and one CSE (with a science bias), and a senior master at the school described him as:

> A very able boy with an easy social grace. He is good humoured, and very popular with his peers. He is polite and well-mannered with teaching staff. He should do well in the sixth form.

Dominico was following his elder brother through both Guy Mannering and Ashburton Boys', and the brother had been vice-captain of the school, a member of the 1st XV, and entered medical school. Dominico was following his brother's successes, and the academic and social achievements will have given great pleasure to his father, who had ambitions for his sons. Dominico had gained the kind of school achievements that Mr Evans had hoped for, and could be seen as a success for Guy Mannering as well as his family.

In contrast to Dominico's successful career at Guy Mannering and Ashburton Boys', his classmate at 9, Gavin Radice, had a less conformist response to the same schools.

Gavin Radice

Gavin featured in our accounts of class 1.5 at Guy Mannering, both because he usually worked too fast for his teacher's comfort (Delamont, 1983b: 118; pages 145–8 above) and because the staff refused to pronounce his name Radiche and persisted in calling him Radish (Delamont, 1983b: 141–3; pages 219–20 above). The distress caused to Gavin by the teachers', and some other pupils', persistence in calling him Radish led his parents to change his surname to Radley until he was 18. His career at Ashburton Boys' had not been academically successful, for although the school thought he should have done 'O' levels, he had underachieved and only took CSEs. The deputy head described him as 'a lovable punk', and he had chosen to dye his hair, sport many earrings, and reject the standards of Ashburton Boys'. He was also reported as disruptive in class, although not malicious.

Somewhere between the first form at Guy Mannering, where apart from being a speed merchant Gavin was keeping abreast of the work, and seemed pro-school, his relations to both work and authority had soured. His reported ambition was to attend an art school, but the school did not feel he was capable of such a course.

While dealing with boys from Guy Mannering, three others are worth a briefer mention, Barry, Lionel and Alvin, all of whom have rather sad stories.

Barry

Barry started off in 1.5 at Guy Mannering by being elected Boy Form Captain. In our early notes he is not very prominent either academically or in the disciplinary area. He appeared to settle in to Guy Mannering without problems. When he transferred to Ashburton Boys' something went wrong, for he became a 'school-refuser'. The staff were convinced that Barry was an intelligent boy with university potential, but that this promise had been blighted by the school refusal. Barry was under the care of the school psychological service, and had spent a period in a hostel. The school felt that Barry's behaviour was directed at his parents, and when the follow-up took place Barry was at home again, having some private tutoring.

Lionel

Lionel was a pupil in 1.6 at Guy Mannering and had transferred to Dashwood (the old Technical School). His academic record was adequate there, but two things had happened to him. Firstly he had changed his name – apparently because other boys had been calling him 'Nelly', he had gone over to his other name, Joe. Secondly, he had been involved in several extremely violent incidents at school. He was not a problem in class, and was not rude to teachers. However in his 3rd year he had often been late and in his 4th year had 2 suspensions both for severe violence in the play-ground: attacks on other boys – 1 head kicking, 1 pushed through a glass window. Nothing in his record at Guy Mannering explained these out-bursts, and we have no evidence of such violence in our data from Guy Mannering.

In contrast to Barry and Lionel, who did not reveal signs of their subsequent problems at 9, Alvin's unhappy career at Morland can be predestined in his time at Guy Mannering.

Alvin

Alvin was a target pupil at his lower school, but because he was placed in 1.4 at Guy Mannering he was not observed there. He and his mother were both interviewed there, because he was seen by the staff as having adjustment problems. The interviewer (who did not know this) wrote – 'I found myself wondering whether he might have difficulty in getting on well with other children.' In his interview Alvin revealed a distaste for PE ('Actually I don't think football is good for you'), claimed to be good at art and craft, and to be fond of reading ('I've got a very good vocabulary') books such as *The Hobbit*. He told the interviewer that Guy Mannering had 'a good repre-sentative' (meaning reputation) and played with words (joking that his brother 'at ABS had joined the ASC' – i.e. that the brother at Ashburton Boys' School had joined the Ashburton Town Soccer Club).

Alvin's mother told the interviewer that he had been premature, was badly co-ordinated, left-handed, and had difficulty in relating to other pupils. She was worried about him, though she thought the school and its staff were doing the best that could be done with him.

At 13 Alvin transferred to Morland Upper School, on the rough estate. Here he had developed into the archetypal 1980s 'loner' – the computer addict. His year tutor told us that he was teased and derided by his peers as a 'Nelly' and so became more and more of a loner. Alvin hated all sport, and all craft subjects which reinforced his low status with his peers. All his time and enthusiasm was spent on the school computer, and reading science-fiction. His academic achievement was CSE standard, and he annoyed the

Appendix 2

teachers by being 'absent-minded', forgetting things, being late and so on. Morland has an open sixth form, and the school expected Alvin to stay on after 16 – but they knew they had been unable to solve any of his social problems.

In these five boys, Dominico, Gavin, Barry, Lionel and Alvin, we have seen a variety of male pupil careers. Dominico epitomizes the academically successful boy, Gavin the popular adherent of a 'youth culture', and the other three examples of boys developing 'problems' the schools feel powerless to solve. Similar female pupil careers can be found among the girls described in this volume, and, as Table A2.2 shows, we examine first the career of Dawn, a pupil at Waverly.

Dawn

Dawn was one of our targets at Waverly, and she had not wanted to attend that school. Dawn's parents had asked for an upper school that was refused, and by the time that refusal came through all her friends had been allocated to Melin Court which was full, so she had been sent to Waverly. It is nice to report that she made a success of Waverly, getting 9 'O' levels and 1 CSE (home economics which was not available as an 'O' level at the school). Her parents had not been reconciled to Waverly sufficiently to leave her there for her 'A' levels, however, but had transferred her to a private sixth form college in the city. Her record card was uniformly positive about her – she had good attendance, was well-behaved, and so forth. Dawn was one of Waverly's academic successes. The signs of this were there in our early fieldnotes, and in her interview, where among other things she told us that she liked maths.

> I like maths, Miss, because you can go in front if you work faster, but its boring in a lot of others, Miss, because you have to wait for the others.

Dawn had riding as her main hobby at 12, and also wrote to several penfriends. She was reasonably happy at Waverly but 'I think I would have preferred to go with my friends to Melin Court, Miss.' Given this rather tepid start to her Waverly career, Dawn's achievements there come as a pleasant case history. A similarly heartening story is that of Nanette, in Miss Tweed's class at Gryll Grange.

Nanette

Nanette was one of the group of girls in Miss Tweed's class at Gryll Grange who were friends of Davina's (Delamont, 1983b; pp.230–1 above). She was a tiny 9-year-old, with spectacles, who like Davina sang, swam, ran, played the violin, and worked hard at all her lessons. On leaving Gryll Grange she went to Woodhouse, and was described to me by the head of year as one of the star pupils of that school. She was doing well academically, and was active in all the musical activities of the school. Her timetable was all 'O' level, and all academic (physics, geography, music, chemistry, French and German as her options) with none of the typing and child development that many of her peers had chosen. Her mother was an

Appendix 2

active parent-governor, and the head of year spoke warmly of her as one of Woodhouse's staunchest supporters and most energetic parents.

Woodhouse had been an equally successful upper school for Audrey, a girl in 1.5 at Guy Mannering when we observed there, who was doing well academically and had won the top award at the school's craft fair. Pupil careers like Dawn's, Nanette's and Audrey's have to be contrasted with those of girls like Tanya, Pamela, Vanessa and Francine at Waverly and Annabel at Guy Mannering. Tanya, a pupil at Waverly, managed only one CSE 'pass' (in commercial studies) and in 1981 was absent from school for a week because she had no shoes and there was no money to buy any. Pamela had a baby at 15 and was taken away from the school to a hostel. Vanessa's adolescence had consisted of a series of drugs charges, under-age sex and attempted suicide, and she left school without any qualifications. So too did Francine, who was late starting at Waverly because she had chicken pox. She had begun to truant in her second year, and from the age of 14 hardly attended school at all. Her report in 1983 showed she had missed *all* of 346 possible attendances.

Waverly was not alone in having such pupils, and in mentioning Tanya, Pamela and Vanessa we are not meaning to condemn that school for 'failing' its girls. The other upper schools had pupils whose adolescents were equally distressing to hear about. Even Ashburton's Woodhouse, the 'show' upper school, had female pupils it could neither teach nor control – particularly Annabel.

Annabel

Annabel followed her sister Arlene to Guy Mannering from Orton Water, and was placed in 1.6, the 'B' band class which we observed, and which quickly became labelled as hard to teach, and was broken up at Christmas (see pp. 59–62 above). At Guy Mannering she was the most disruptive girl in the first year – and arguably the most disruptive pupil in 1.6. Her interviewer, who did not know this, wrote: 'It was clear to me that Annabel does not really like the school very much.' Annabel spent much of her interview telling us how she disliked all her lessons, PE, the older pupils, and that Miss Tyree was frightening. She also recounted all the possible punishments, including 'the slipper and the cane', which most 9-year-olds had never heard of. At 9, she appeared to dislike the school, the work, and the staff.

At 13 Annabel transferred to Woodhouse, which had not been her family's first choice. They had opted for the Catholic girls' school, but were refused because Annabel had not been to the Catholic Middle School. Woodhouse found her one of the most difficult girls they had ever tried to educate. She was academically weak, and rebellious, symbolized by her persistent refusal to wear the uniform. The year tutor added that refusing to come in uniform was understandable in girls if they had good clothes sense, and wanted to wear feminine, fashionable clothes, but Annabel did not do this – she came to school dirty. (A parallel case can be found in Llewellyn's (1980) work, and in Lambart (1982).) It apears that a 'feminine' objection to uniform can be understood, but a scruffy, dirty girl is inexplicable.

Appendix 2

Annabel's behaviour at Woodhouse had been so bad that when she signed up for a school trip to Spain, the staff in charge of the trip refused to take her. This was, according to the head of year, the 'last straw' for Annabel, who subsequently refused to cooperate with any of the school's wishes.

The school found Annabel's intransigence puzzling because she had a conventional 'feminine' adolescent side out of school. Annabel at 14 had won a competition run through a chain of hairdressers, sponsored by one of the big cosmetic companies. Her prize was to be photographed by one of the top photographers, and the resultant portrait of Annabel, clean, smart, and unrecognizable to her teachers, smiled down at the women staff from the walls of the town's leading hairdressers. Annabel was a paradox they could not come to terms with at all.

Of course many of the girls in our sample had school careers like Dawn's rather than like Annabel's. Among the conformist, academically successful girls were two of our targets at Maid Marion, Fida and Karena. These two girls had been unwilling pupils at Maid Marion (Kenilworth had been their parents' choice) and had been frightened of the school (Delamont, 1983b; pp. 22, 25–6 above). Fida had been particularly scared of the showers, and Karena of the 'tower block' at Maid Marion. Fida's mother had visited the school to try and get her exempted from showers, but the PE staff's argument that once with her new friends Fida would not mind showering had prevailed and been proved correct. Karena had been apprehensive about the tower block, and about PE, because she thought she would have to climb ropes and high apparatus. Both girls were quiet in class, disliked having to speak, and were in ORACLE terms quiet collaborators.

These two girls had transferred to Sanditon at 14, and had continued to be conformist, quiet pupils. Both had passed sufficient 'O' levels to go into

Table A2.3   Fida and Karena's fifth year reports

	Fida	Karena
Attendance	Good	Good
Health	OK	Good
Appearance	Good. Uniform neat and tidy	Very good – Uniform
Punctuality	Very good	Very good
Conduct	Excellent	Very good
Attitude to staff	Good	Very good
Attitude to peers	Quiet – Has small group of friends	Does not mix well
School participation	Little	None
Out of school interests	None	None

Appendix 2

the sixth form, and their reports at the end of their fifth year were extremely favourable as Table A2.3 shows. Karena had decided to go on to a secretarial course from the sixth form, Fida had still to finalize her future plans, but both had passed successfully through Maid Marion and two years at Sanditon. Their careers at Maid Marion can usefully be compared with those of three of the four boys in class 1I at that school who caused the staff such anxiety (pp. 234–8 above). Harry, Sinclair and Greg. (Their fourth classmate, Dickon, was not traced in 1984.)

Harry, Sinclair and Greg

At 11 these three boys were separated within their class, and the subject of considerable anxiety among the staff. When we left them, Sinclair appeared to have detached himself from Dickon, Greg and Harry and begun to work hard rather than disrupt lessons. All three left school at 16, but Greg, who left at Easter, had obviously had the least successful career at Sanditon. Table A2.4 shows their final fifth year reports. This table encapsulates three different male responses to schooling. Greg, considered highly successful with his peers, took no part in school activities, refused to conform to the dress code, and truanted so often in his final year that he effectively left at Christmas. The headmaster had written him a bad leaving report, saying that Greg could not be recommended as honest, punctual or industrious. This is a classic anti-school, rebellious pupil career.

Sinclair, in contrast, appears to have adopted the pro-school role. He joined school clubs, wore the uniform, and had a small group of friends. Not enough of an academic success to go into the sixth form, he clearly was regarded highly by the staff at Sanditon, who hoped he would get an

Table A2.4 Leaving reports of Harry, Sinclair and Greg

	Harry	Sinclair	Greg
Attendance	Frequent short absences	Good	Good when not truanting
Health	Tonsilitis	Good	Good
Appearance	Fair to good	Uniform, neat and tidy	Rarely in uniform, scruffy
Punctuality	Poor	Very good	Frequently late
Conduct	Never in trouble, often near it	Good	Negative attitude
Attitude to staff	Ignores them	Very good	Negative
Attitude to peers	Gets on well – can be a bully	Has own circle	Fits in well
School activities	Railway Club	Railway Club, Cross country	None
Out of school	Cricket	Soccer	None

apprenticeship. Harry's school life seems to have been poised somewhat uneasily between being a lad and being an earhole (Willis, 1977). More conformist to the school's regime than Greg, he has clearly not been prepared to adapt himself to it totally.

As a conclusion to these follow-ups, two boys who were featured in Galton and Willcocks (1983) are compared. Rex Mackie, at Waverly, was shown trying hard to be a good pupil, while Wayne Douglas Patel seemed to be striving to be a bad one.

Rex and Wayne

Rex had transferred to Waverly from Ashwood Bank Middle School, apprehensive because his older brother, Donovan, had hated the place and done very badly there. In his early weeks we showed him deliberately setting out to build a different reputation from Donovan's (pp. 202–3 above). In this he triumphantly succeeded, having passed nine subjects at 'O' level or grade one CSE, gone into the sixth form, and played leading parts in two school plays. Rex was one of Waverly's most successful pupils, and one of the nicest follow-up stories we found.

In contrast, the discovery that Wayne Douglas Patel had truanted consistently throughout his fourth and fifth years, failed to turn up for one of his leaving exams (English) and failed the other (social studies), and was unemployed, has a certain inevitability about it. As our descriptions of Wayne's reaction to Melin Court (Delamont, 1983b: 146–51: pp. 165–6 above) showed, he began the school year challenging the rules, the staff and his peers on every possible occasion, and rarely made any attempt to work. The staff member who talked to us said he had become the type of pupil who staff preferred to truant, because he caused such trouble in class when he did attend. If Rex was a success for Waverly, Wayne was one of Melin Court's failures.

This concludes the pen portraits of particular pupils, and in the next section we present some of the numerical material from the follow up.

Part two: aggregate data from the follow-up study

In this second part of the appendix, some aggregate data on the ORACLE pupils are presented. They are fragmentary and not suitable for statistical analysis. Some schools provided follow-up data only on the ORACLE target pupils, others open the books on the whole year. Sometimes a class who had been observed at transfer, such as 1M at Melin Court, could be traced through to 16; in other cases, such as 1.5 at Guy Mannering, there were several pupils entirely lost to the study. (For example from 1.5 Lauretta and Shelly left Britain, Gabrielle, Coral, Lillian and Barny moved away from Ashburton.) This fragmentation was not due to the schools, who were unfailingly tolerant and cooperative, but to differences in record-keeping, access, and the energy of the researcher. Some of the findings which follow refer only to target pupils, some to all pupils in the classes observed after transfer, and some to a whole year cohort. The information we have presented concerns a variety of issues of interest to educationalists,

Table A2.5   *Number of girls doing science 14–16*

Town and school	Doing science	Not doing science	Total no. traced
Ashburton			
Woodhouse	25	37	62
Ashburton Girls'	—	8	8
Dashwood	—	1	1
Morland	—	2	2
Bridgehampton			
Sanditon	3	10	13
Coalthorpe			
Melin Court	6	17	23

including subject choice at 14–16; youth unemployment and the proportion reaching the sixth forms of our upper schools.

Subject specialization at 14–16

Two issues have become controversial here: girls and science/technology, and its converse, boys doing modern languages. The schools we studied had different policies about compulsory subjects and the amount of choice pupils had (for example, at Woodhouse, all pupils had to take one science and one craft subject). However, all schools allowed pupils to specialize to the extent of either dropping all or most science, or escaping languages. Table A2.5 shows the numbers of girls specializing in science (i.e. taking more than one compulsory science subject) in six of our schools. This table shows that very few of the girls we observed start science were still doing it voluntarily by 16, even Woodhouse Upper School had hardly any girls

Table A2.6   *Number of boys doing a foreign langage at 14–16*

Town and school	Doing languages	Not doing languages	Total no. traced
Ashburton			
Ashburton Boys'	3	7	10
Woodhouse	33	22	58
Dashwood	—	2	2
Morland	—	3	3
Bridgehampton			
Sanditon	—	15	15
Coalthorpe			
Melin Court	1	29	30

taking physics and most science specialist girls were only doing chemistry and biology. Only one girl in our Ashburton sample was doing a 'male' craft subject by 14, a Woodhouse pupil doing design technology. (Ashburton Girls' School did not have any facilities for 'male' craft subjects.) Despite the co-educational introduction to craft at 9, 11 and 12 they had become sex-segregated by 14. The number of boys still doing a foreign language (or French studies) by 14–16 is shown in Table A2.6. This table shows that very few boys are still studying any language after the age of 14 except at Woodhouse. An analysis of the boys' craft choices shows only one boy taking a 'girls'' craft (home economics). The overall subject specialization pattern then, is conventionally sex-stereotyped.

School leavers and stayers
In Bridgehampton and Coalthorpe the ORACLE pupils were already over 16 when the follow-up took place. In Table A2.7 the numbers of pupils who stayed on into the sixth forms of the three relevant schools are shown, and in Table A2.8 the destinations of those fifth form leavers known to the schools are displayed. These two tables suggest that neither of the two Coalthorpe schools was very successful at producing sixth formers compared to the Bridgehampton one, and that the destinations of many of the fifth year leavers are not known to the schools (or not recorded). Thus at Waverly the destinations of 46 leavers from our two classes are not recorded and at Melin Court the destinations of 32 of the 59 people in our two classes were unknown or unrecorded. However, what is clear is that very few of the Coalthorpe leavers had been known to get jobs.

Table A2.7   Number of pupils staying into the sixth forms

School	Stayers	Leavers	Total traced
Sanditon	21	71	92
Melin Court	32	240	272
Waverly	7	58	65

Table A2.8   Destinations of fifth year leavers from observed classes known to schools

School	Job	MSC Scheme	FE College	Unemployment	Full-time motherhood	Total known
Melin Court	8	7	7	3	—	25
Waverly	5	2	2	1	2	12

Appendix 2

One reason for the relatively low attainments of many of our pupils was their hostile reaction to schooling represented by their truancy. A number of our sample had histories of truancy by the age of 16, as shown in Table A2.9. This table shows that Waverly had the largest truancy problem of these three schools, despite the strenuous efforts to stop it made by the staff, which have been outlined in this volume.

Our final topic is the actual exam successes of our sample pupils.

Table A2.9   Number of 16-year-olds recorded as truants

School	No. with truancy record	Total no. traced
Sanditon	5	92
Melin Court	10	59
Waverly	15	53

Exam results

It is hard to decide how to present the data we were able to collect on exam results. We have chosen to summarize the 'O' levels and CSE results in the following way. We have listed the number of pupils who got 5 'O' levels or grade 1 CSE, the number who got less than 5 but passed some 'O' levels or grade 1 CSE, those who got some CSEs at grades 2 and 3, and those who achieved only CSEs at grade 4 or less, or nothing. This is extremely crude, but the numbers are so small a more subtle classification would be tendentious. Ouston and Maughan (1985) have pointed out how difficult it is to produce meaningful analyses of exam results, and we have only presented our data for their interest value. Table A2.10 shows the exam results in the three relevant schools broken down into the broad categories explained above, for those pupils we were able to trace, including the Easter leavers in the 'Nothing' category. For Sanditon, the results of all the target pupils from Maid Marion and Kenilworth; for Melin Court the results are of all pupils from classes 1M and 1E; and for Waverly, all pupils from classes 1LE and 1BN; all pupils, that is, who were traced in those three schools. Coalthorpe LEA has a certificate for 16+ leavers who are not up to CSE standard, and where passes have been obtained in this exam at Waverly they have been counted as equal to CSEs at grades 4 and 5.

Table A2.10 shows that Waverly had the highest number of unqualified school leavers, and many of the fifteen habitual truants shown in Table A2.9 were unqualified leavers.

Conclusion

These brief and fragmentary data give some indication of what happened to our target pupils and their classmates between the school transfer described in this book and reaching 15 or leaving school. Taken with the pen portraits in the first part of this appendix, a flavour of growing up in the early 1980s in England will have been conveyed.

Appendix 2

Table A2.10   Number of pupils gaining categories of qualifications at 16+, from Sanditon, Melin Court and Waverly

Exam qualifications obtained	Sanditon	Melin Court	Waverly
5 or more 'O' levels or grade 1 CSEs	4	9	3
1–4 'O' levels or grade 1 CSEs	11	11	9
One or more CSEs at grades 2 or 3	15	17	12
One or more CSEs at grades 4 or 5 (or LEA 16+ Certificate)	—	7	4
Unqualified leaver	4	12	25
Total traced	34	56	53

Bibliography of publications from the ORACLE project

This bibliography lists the publications up to September 1985 about the ORACLE project, or using the data from the study, by the key research workers from the ORACLE project team. Defining a publication, and deciding whose publications to include, are both somewhat arbitrary matters. For the purposes of this bibliography 'publications' do not include reports of the findings in the popular or the educational press (e.g. *TES*), or the 'end of grant reports' to the SSRC. The publications of the researchers on projects which served as pilot work for ORACLE, especially those by Deanne Boydell (née Bealing) are also excluded, but can be traced from Boydell (1978). Those authors whose work is included are: Brian Simon, Maurice Galton, John Willcocks, Paul Croll, Anne Jasman, Pat Ashton, Deanne Boydell, Sara Delamont and Sarah Tann. The bibliography was compiled by Sara Delamont who apologizes for any omissions, errors or misjudgments.

The books directly reporting the ORACLE project are:

Galton, Maurice, Simon, Brian (eds) (1980), *Progress and Performance Classroom*, London, Routledge & Kegan Paul.

Galton, Maurice and Simon, Brian (eds) (1980), *Progress and Performance in the Primary Classroom*, London, Routledge & Kegan Paul.

Galton, Maurice and Willcocks, John (eds) (1983), *Moving from the Primary Classroom*, London, Routledge & Kegan Paul.

Simon, Brian and Willcocks, John (eds) (1981), *Research and Practice in the Primary Classroom*, London, Routledge & Kegan Paul.

Galton, Maurice (forthcoming), *Group Work in the Primary Classroom*, London, Routledge & Kegan Paul.

The articles, and books which use some of the material from the project are:

Ashton, Patricia (1981a), 'Primary teachers' aims 1969–77', in Simon and Willcocks (eds), see above.

Ashton, Patricia (1981b), 'Primary teachers' approaches to personal and social behaviour', in Simon and Willcocks (eds), see above.

Bibliography of publications from the ORACLE project

Boydell, Deanne (1978), *The Primary Teacher in Action*, London, Open Books.

Boydell, Deanne (1980) 'The organization of junior school classrooms: a follow up survey', *Educational Research*, 23.

Boydell, Deanne (1981), 'Classroom organization 1970–77', in Simon and Willcocks (eds), see above.

Croll, Paul (1980a), 'Data presentation, analysis and statistical methods', Appendix 2 of Galton, Simon and Croll, (1980).

Croll, Paul (1980b), 'Replicating the observational data', Appendix B of Galton and Simon, (1980).

Croll, Paul (1981), 'Social class, pupil achievement and classroom interaction', in Simon and Willcocks (eds), see above.

Croll, Paul (1983), 'Transfer and pupil performance', in Galton and Willcocks (eds), see above.

Croll, Paul and Willcocks, John (1980), 'Pupil behaviour and progress', in Galton and Simon (eds), see above.

Delamont, Sara (1980a), *Sex Roles and the School*, London, Methuen.

Delamont, Sara (1982), 'Sex differences in classroom interaction', *EOC Research Bulletin*, 6 (Spring), pp. 30–37.

Delamont, Sara (1983a), *Interaction in the Classroom* (2nd edition), London, Methuen.

Delamont, Sara (1983b), 'The ethnography of transfer', in Galton and Willcocks (eds), see above.

Delamont, Sara (1983d), 'The conservative school?', in S. Walker and L. Barton (eds), *Gender, Class and Education*, Lewes, Falmer Books.

Galton, Maurice (1979), 'Strategies and tactics in junior school classrooms', *British Education Research Journal*, vol. 5, no. 2, pp. 197–210.

Galton, Maurice (1983a), 'Problems of transition', in Galton and Willcocks (eds), see above.

Galton, Maurice (1983b), 'Teaching and learning in the classroom', in Galton and Willcocks (eds), see above.

Galton, Maurice (1983c), 'Classroom research and the teacher', in M. Galton and B. Moon (eds), *Changing Schools . . . Changing Curriculum*, London, Harper & Row.

Galton, Maurice and Croll, Paul (1978), 'A question of style', *Research Intelligence*, vol. 3, no.2, pp. 20–21.

Galton, Maurice and Croll, Paul (1980), 'Pupil progress in basic skills', in Simon and Galton (eds), see above.

Galton, Maurice and Delafield, Angela (1981), 'Expectancy effects in primary classrooms', in Simon and Willcocks (eds), see above.

Galton, Maurice and Delamont, Sara (1980), 'The first weeks of middle school', in A. Hargreaves and L. Tickle (eds), *Middle Schools*, London, Harper & Row.

Galton, Maurice and Delamont, Sara (1985), 'Speaking with forked tongue? Two styles of observation in the ORACLE project', in R.G. Burgess (ed.), *Field Methods in the Study of Education*, London, Falmer Press.

Galton, Maurice and Simon, Brian (1980), 'Effective teaching in the primary classroom', in Galton and Simon (eds), see above.

Galton, Maurice and Simon, Brian (1981), 'ORACLE: its implications for teacher training' in Simon and Willcocks (eds), see above.

Jasman, Anne (1980), 'Training observers in the use of systematic observation techniques', Appendix 1 in Galton, Simon and Croll (1980).

Jasman, Anne (1981), 'Teachers' assessments in classroom research', in Simon and Willcocks (eds), see above.

Simon, Brian (1976), 'ORACLE – Research note', *Education 3–13*, vol. 4, p. 117.

Simon, Brian (1981), 'The primary school revolution: myth or reality?', in Simon and Willcocks (eds), see above.

Simon, Brian (1980), 'Inside the primary classroom', *Forum*, vol. 22, no. 3, pp. 68–9.

Simon, Brian (1983), 'Education in theory; schooling in practice: the experience of the last hundred years' (The Fink Memorial Lecture, 1981), in Stephen Murray Smith (ed.), *Melbourne Studies in Education*, 1982, Melbourne, The University Press. Reprinted in B. Simon (1985), *Does Education Matter*? London, Lawrence & Wishart.

Simon, Brian and Galton, Maurice (1980), 'Research in the primary classroom', in Galton and Simon (eds), see above.

Tann, Sarah (1981), 'Grouping and group work', in Simon and Willcocks (eds), see above.

Willcocks, John (1980), 'The primary curriculum and the Bullock Report', Appendix 4 of Galton, Simon and Croll.

Willcocks, John (1981), 'Teachers' perceptions of their pupils' anxiety', in Simon and Willcocks (eds), see above.

Willcocks, John (1983), 'Pupils in transition', in Galton and Willcocks (eds) see above.

Willcocks, John and Jasman, Anne (1980), 'Study skills and pupil performance', in Galton and Simon (eds), see above.

One of the project team also published anonymously the following:

Anonymous (1982), 'Primary School' Digest, *Education*, 5th March 1982, pp. 1–1V (this is a separate pull-out of the journal).

Bibliography of works cited in the text

Angus, Louie (1981), *Blue Skirts into Blue Stockings*, London, Ian Allan.

Applebaum, Herbert A. (1981), *Royal Blue: The Culture of Construction Workers*, New York, Holt, Rinehart & Winston.

Atkinson, Paul (1978), 'Fitness, feminism and schooling', in S. Delamont and L. Duffin (eds), *The Nineteenth Century Woman*, London, Croom Helm.

Atkinson, Paul (1981), *The Clinical Experience*, Aldershot, Gower.

Atkinson, Paul (1983), 'The reproduction of professional community', in R. Dingwall and P. Lewis (eds), *The Sociology of the Professions*, London, Macmillan.

Atkinson, Paul (1985), 'Strong minds and weak bodies', *British Journal of Sports History*, vol. 2, no. 1 (May), pp. 62–71.

Atkinson, Paul and Delamont, Sara (1977), 'Mock-ups and cock-ups', in M. Hammersley and P. Woods (eds), *School Experience*, London, Croom Helm.

Atkinson, Paul and Delamont, Sara (1980), 'The two traditions in educational ethnography', *British Journal of Sociology of Education*, vol. 1, no. 2, pp. 139–52.

Atkinson, Paul and Shone, David (1982), *Everyday Life in Two Industrial Training Units*, Cologne, IFAPLAN.

Ball, Stephen (1980), 'Initial encounters in the classroom', in P. Woods (ed.), *Pupil Strategies*, London, Croom Helm.

Ball, Stephen (1981), *Beachside Comprehensive*, Cambridge, The University Press.

Ball, Stephen (1984), 'Inside the School', Units 8/9 of Block 2, Course E205 Conflict and Change in Education, Milton Keynes, The Open University Press.

Ball, Stephen and Lacey, Colin (1980), 'Subject disciplines as the opportunity for action', in P. Woods (ed.), *Teacher Strategies*, London, Croom Helm.

Ball, Stephen, Hull, Robert, Skelton, Martin and Tudor, Richard (1984),

Bibliography of works cited in the text

'The tyranny of the "devil's mill" ', in S. Delamont (ed.), *Readings on Interaction in the Classroom*, London, Methuen.

Bauman, R. (1982), 'Ethnography of children's folklore', in P. Gilmore and A.A. Glatthorn (eds), *Children in and out of School*, Washington, D.C., Centre for Applied Linguistics.

Beale, Dorothea (1904), *History of the Cheltenham Ladies' College 1853–1904*, Cheltenham, Looker-On Printing Works.

Becker, Howard, S. (1971), Footnote, p.10 of M. Wax and R. Wax's paper 'Great tradition, little tradition and formal education', in M. Wax, S. Diamond and F. Gearing (eds), *Anthropological Perspectives on Education*, New York, Basic Books.

Becker, Howard, S. *et al.* (1961), *Boys in White*, Chicago, The University Press.

Benn, C. and Simon, B. (1972), *Halfway-There* (2nd edition), Harmondsworth, Penguin.

Bennett, S.N. (1976), *Teaching Styles and Pupil Progress*, London, Open, Books.

Bennett, S.N. (1985), 'Interaction and achievement in classroom groups', in S.N. Bennett and C. Desforges (eds), *Recent Advances in Classroom Research*, Edinburgh, Scottish Academic Press.

Bennett, S.N. *et al.* (1980), *Open-Plan Schools*, Slough, NFER-Nelson.

Bennett, S.N., Desforges, C., Cockburn, A. and Wilkinson, B. (1984), *The Quality of Pupil Learning Experiences*, London, Earlbaum.

Berlak, Ann and Berlak, Harold (1981), *Dilemmas of Schooling*, London, Methuen.

Bernstein, Basil (1971), 'On the classification and framing of educational knowledge', in M.F.D. Young (ed.), *Knowledge and Control*, London, Macmillan.

Bernstein, Basil (1974), 'Class and pedagogies', in B. Bernstein (ed.), *Class, Codes and Control*, vol. 3, London, Routledge & Kegan Paul.

Beynon, John (1983), 'Ways-in and staying-in', in M. Hammersley (ed.), *The Ethnography of Schooling*, Driffield, Yorkshire, Nafferton Books.

Beynon, John (1985), *Initial Encounters in a Comprehensive School*, London, Falmer Books.

Beynon, John and Atkinson, Paul (1984), 'Pupils as data-gatherers', in S. Delamont (ed.), *Readings on Interaction in the Classroom*, London, Methuen.

Beynon, John and Delamont, Sara (1984), 'The sound and the fury', in N. Frude and H. Gault (eds), *Disruptive Behaviour in Schools*, Chichester, Wiley.

Blackburn, R.M. and Mann, M. (1979), *The Working Class in the Labour Market*, London, Macmillan.

Blatchford, Peter *et al.* (1982), *The First Transition*, Windsor, NFER-Nelson.

Borman, Kathryn (1981), 'Review of recent case studies on equity and schooling', in R.G. Corwin (ed.), *Research on Educational Organizations*, Greenwich, Conn., JAI Press.

Bourdieu, P. and Passeron, J.-C. (1977), *Reproduction in Education, Society*

271

and Culture, London, Sage.

Bream, F. (1970), *Chalk Dust and Chewing Gum*, London, Collins.

Bryant, K.A. (1980), 'Pupil perceptions of transfer', in A. Hargreaves and L. Tickle (eds), *Middle Schools*, London, Harper & Row.

Bullivant, B.M. (1978), *The Way of Tradition*, Victoria, ACER.

Burgess, R.G. (ed.) (1982), *Field Research*, London, Allen & Unwin.

Burgess, R.G. (1983), *Experiencing Comprehensive Education*, London, Methuen.

Burgess, R.G. (ed.) (1985), *Field Methods in the Study of Education*, London, Falmer Books.

Burnett, Jacquetta Hill (1969), 'Ceremony, rites, and economy in the student system of an American High School', *Human Organization*, vol. 28, no. 1, pp. 1–10.

Burnett, Jacquetta Hill (1973), 'Event description and analysis in the microethnography of urban classrooms', in F. Ianni and E. Storey (eds), *Cultural Relevance and Educational Issues*, Boston, Little, Brown & Co.

Buswell, Carol (1981), 'Sexism in school routine and classroom practices', *Durham and Newcastle Research Review*, vol. 9, no. 4, pp. 195–200.

Chanan, G. and Delamont S. (eds) (1975), *Frontiers of Classroom Research*, Slough, NFER.

Clarricoates, Katherine (1980), 'The importance of being Ernest, Tom, Jane', in R. Deem (ed.), *Schooling for Women's Work*, London, Routledge & Kegan Paul.

Cleave, Shirley *et al.* (1982), *And So To School*, Windsor, NFER-Nelson.

Cohen, Peter (1973), *The Gospel According to the Harvard Business School*, New York, Penguin.

Coombs, R.H. (1978), *Mastering Medicine: Professional Socialization in Medical School*, New York, Free Press.

Corrie, M., Haystead, J. and Zaklukiewicz, S. (1978), *The Classroom Situation*, Edinburgh, Scottish Council for Research in Education.

Corrie, M., Haystead, J. and Zaklukiewicz, S. (1982), *Classroom Management Strategies*, London, Hodder & Stoughton.

Cusick, Philip (1973), *Inside High School*, New York, Holt, Rinehart & Winston.

Daner, F.J. (1976), *The American Children of Krsna*, New York, Holt, Rinehart & Winston.

David, M. (1980), *The State, the Family and Education*, London, Routledge & Kegan Paul.

Davidoff, Leonore (1973), *The Best Circles*, London, Croom Helm.

Davies, Brian, Corbishley, Peter, Evans, John and Kenrick, Catherine (1985), 'Integrating methodologies', in R.G. Burgess (ed.), *Strategies of Educational Research*, Brighton, Falmer.

Davies, Lynn (1984), *Pupil Power*, London, Falmer.

Delamont, Sara (1980a), *Sex Roles and the School*, London, Methuen.

Delamont, Sara (1980b), *The Sociology of Women*, London, Allen & Unwin.

Delamont, Sara (1981), 'All too familiar?', *Educational Analysis*, vol. 3, no. 1, pp. 69–83.

Bibliography of works cited in the text

Delamont, Sara (1982), 'Sex differences in classroom interaction', *EOC Bulletin*, 6, pp. 30–7.

Delamont, Sara (1983a), *Interaction in the Classroom* (2nd edition), London, Methuen.

Delamont, Sara (1983b), 'The ethnography of transfer', in M. Galton and J. Willcocks (eds), *Moving from the Primary Classroom*, London, Routledge & Kegan Paul.

Delamont, Sara (1983c), 'Salmon, chicken, cake and tears', in A. Murcott (ed.), *The Sociology of Food and Eating*, Aldershot, Gower.

Delamont, Sara (1983d), 'The conservative school?', in S. Walker and L. Barton (eds), *Gender, Class and Education*, Lewes, Falmer.

Delamont, Sara (ed.) (1984), *Readings on Interaction in the Classroom*, London, Methuen.

Denham, Carolyn and Leiberman, Ann (eds) (1980), *Time to Learn*, Washington D.C., NIE (DHEW).

Denscombe, Martyn (1980), 'Keeping 'em quiet', in P. Woods (ed.), *Teacher Strategies*, London, Croom Helm.

Doyle, W. and Good, T. (eds) (1982), *Focus on Teaching*, Chicago, The University Press.

Edgerton, R.B. (1979), *Alone Together*, Berkeley, University of California Press.

Eickelman, Dale (1978), 'The art of memory', *Comparative Studies in Society and History*, vol. 20, no. 4, pp. 485–516.

Evans, John (1985), *Teaching in Transition*, Milton Keynes, The Open University Press.

Everhart, R.B. (1983), *Reading, Writing and Resistance*, London, Routledge & Kegan Paul.

Finnan, C. (1982), 'The ethnography of children's spontaneous play', in G. Spindler (ed.), *Doing the Ethnography of Schooling*, New York, Holt, Rinehart & Winston.

Fisher, C. and Berliner, D. (eds) (1985), *Perspectives on Instructional Time*, New York, Longmans.

Fogelman, K. (1976), *Britain's Sixteen Year Olds*, London, NCB.

Fuller, Mary (1980), 'Black girls in a London comprehensive school', in R. Deem (ed.), *Schooling for Women's Work*, London, Routledge & Kegan Paul.

Furlong, V. John (1976), 'Interaction sets in the classroom', in M. Stubbs and S. Delamont (eds), *Explorations in Classroom Observation*, Chichester, Wiley.

Furlong, V. John (1984), 'Black resistance in the liberal comprehensive', in S. Delamont (ed.), *Readings on Interaction in the Classroom*, London, Methuen.

Galton, Maurice (1979), 'Strategies and tactics in junior school classrooms', *British Educational Research Journal*, vol. 8, no. 2, pp. 197–210.

Galton, Maurice, Simon, Brian and Croll, Paul (1980), *Inside the Primary Classroom*, London, Routledge & Kegan Paul.

Galton, Maurice and Simon, Brian (1980), *Progress and Performance in the Primary Classroom*, London, Routledge & Kegan Paul.

Bibliography of works cited in the text

Galton, Maurice and Delafield, Angela (1981), 'Expectancy effects in the primary classroom', in B. Simon and J. Willcocks (eds), *Research and Practice in the Primary Classroom*, London, Routledge & Kegan Paul.

Galton, Maurice and Willcocks, John (1983), *Moving from the Primary Classroom*, London, Routledge & Kegan Paul.

Gamst, F.G. (1980), *The Hoghead*, New York, Holt, Rinehart & Winston.

Gannaway, H. (1976), 'Making sense of school', in M. Stubbs and S. Delamont (eds), *Explorations in Classroom Observation*, Chichester, Wiley.

Ginsburg, Mark., Meyenn, R.J., Miller, H.D.R. and Ranceford-Hadley, C. (1977), 'The role of the middle school teacher', Aston Educational Enquiry Monographs 7, Birmingham, University of Aston in Birmingham.

GIST, (1984), 'The final report of the GIST project' (by A. Kelly, B. Smail and J. Whyte), Manchester, The Sociology Department, The University.

Glaser, B. and Strauss, A. (1965), *Awareness of Dying*, Chicago, Aldine.

Godber, Joyce and Hutchins, Isabel (1982), *A Century of Challenge: Bedford High School 1882 to 1982*, Biggleswade, Beds, privately printed for Bedford High School by C. Elphick Ltd.

Goffman, E. (1971), *The Presentation of Self in Everyday Life*, Harmondsworth, Penguin.

Guttentag, M. and Bray, H. (eds) (1976), *Undoing Sex Stereotypes*, New York, McGraw Hill.

Hamblin, D.H. (1978), *The Teacher and Pastoral Care*, Oxford, Blackwell.

Hammersley, Martyn (1980), 'Classroom ethnography', *Educational Analysis*, vol. 2, no. 2, pp. 47–74.

Hammersley, Martyn (1982), 'The sociology of classrooms', in A. Harnett (ed.), *The Social Sciences in Educational Studies*, London, Heinemann.

Hammersley, Martyn (ed.) (1983), *The Ethnography of Schooling*, Driffield, Yorks, Nafferton Books.

Hammersley, Martyn (1984), 'Staffroom news', in A. Hargreaves and P. Woods (eds), *Classrooms and Staffrooms*, Milton Keynes, The Open University Press.

Hammersley, Martyn and Atkinson, Paul (1983), *Ethnography*, London, Tavistock.

Hammersley, Martyn and Woods, Peter (eds) (1984), *Life in School*, Milton Keynes, Open University Press.

Hamilton, David (1977), *In Search of Structure*, London, Hodder & Stoughton.

Hanna, Judith (1982), 'Social policy and the children's world', in G. Spindler (ed.), *Doing the Ethnography of Schooling*, New York, Holt, Rinehart & Winston.

Hannam, C., Smyth, P. and Stephenson, N. (1976), *The First Year of Teaching*, Hardmondsworth, Penguin.

Hanson, Derek and Herrington, Margaret (1976), 'Please miss, you're supposed to stop her', *New Society*, 10/6/76, pp. 568–9.

Hargreaves, A. (1984), 'Contrastive rhetoric and extremist talk', in A.

Hargreaves and P. Woods (eds), *Classrooms and Staffrooms*, Milton Keynes, The Open University Press.

Hargreaves, A. and Woods, P. (eds) (1984), *Classrooms and Staffrooms*, Milton Keynes, The Open University Press.

Hargreaves, David (1967), *Social Relations in a Secondary School*, London, Routledge & Kegan Paul.

Hargreaves, David (1972), *Interpersonal Relations and Education*, London, Routledge & Kegan Paul.

Hargreaves, David (ed.) (1980), 'Classroom Studies', *Educational Analysis*, vol. 2, no. 2 (Winter).

Hargreaves, David (1982), *The Challenge for the Comprehensive School*, London, Routledge & Kegan Paul.

Hargreaves, D., Hester, S. and Mellor, F. (1975), *Deviance in Classrooms*, London, Routledge & Kegan Paul.

Hart, N. (1976), *When Marriage Ends*, London, Tavistock.

Hart, R.A. (1979), *Children's Play Experience*, New York, Irvington.

Hilsum, S. and Cane, B. (1971), *The Primary Teacher's Day*, Slough, NFER.

Holly, Douglas (1972), *Society, Schools and Hunanity*, London, Paladin.

Jackson, Brian (1964), *Streaming*, London, Routledge & Kegan Paul.

Jackson, P.W. (1968), *Life in Classrooms*, New York, Holt, Rinehart & Winston.

Jacobs, J. (1974), *Fun City*, New York, Holt, Rinehart & Winston.

Karkau, Kevin (1976), 'A student teacher in the 4th grade', in M. Guttentag and H. Bray (eds), *Undoing Sex Stereotypes*, New York, McGraw-Hill.

Karweit, N.L. (1981), 'Time in school', in R.G. Corwin (ed.), *Research on Educational Organizations*, Greenwich, Conn., JAI Press.

Keddie, Nell (1971), 'Classroom knowledge', in M.F.D. Young (ed.), *Knowledge and Control*, London, Collier-Macmillan.

Kelly, Alison (ed.) (1981), *The Missing Half*, Manchester, The University Press.

Kelly, Alison (1985), 'The construction of masculine science', *British Journal of Sociology of Education*, vol. 6, no. 2, pp. 133–54.

King, R. (1978), *All Things Bright and Beautiful*, Chichester, Wiley.

Kounin, J.S. (1967), *Discipline and Group Management in Classrooms*, New York, Holt, Rinehart & Winston.

Lacey, Colin (1970), *Hightown Grammar*, Manchester, The University Press.

Lacey, Colin (1977), *The Socialization of Teachers*, London, Methuen.

Lacey, Colin (1982), 'Freedom and constraints in British education', in R. Frankenberg (ed.), *Custom and Conflict in British Society*, Manchester, The University Press.

Lambart, Audrey (1977), 'The sisterhood', in M. Hammersley and P. Woods (eds.), *The Process of Schooling*, London, Routledge & Kegan Paul.

Lambart, Audrey (1982), 'Expulsion in context', in R. Frankenberg (ed.), *Custom and Conflict in British Society*, Manchester, The University Press.

Bibliography of works cited in the text

Larkin, R.W. (1979), *Suburban Youth in Cultural Crisis*, New York, Oxford University Press.

Lawton, D. (1972), *Class, Culture and the Curriculum*, London, Routledge & Kegan Paul.

Leighton, M. (1981), *Men at Work*, London, Jill Norman.

Leonard, D. (1980), *Sex and Generation*, London, Tavistock.

Lightfoot, Sara Lawrence (1983), *The Good High School*, Harvard, The University Press.

Llewellyn, Mandy (1980), 'Studying girls at school', in R. Deem (ed.), *Schooling for Women's Work*, London, Routledge & Kegan Paul.

Lomax, Pamela (1980), 'Progression through school', *British Educational Research Journal*, vol. 6, no. 2, pp. 127–40.

MacNamara, D. (1980), 'The outsider's arrogance', *British Educational Research Journal*, vol. 6, no. 2, pp. 113–25.

McPherson, G.A. (1973), *Small Town Teacher*, Harvard, The University Press.

MacPherson, James (1983), *The Feral Classroom*, London, Routledge & Kegan Paul.

Mahony, Pat (1985), *Schools for the Boys?*, London, Hutchinson.

Marsden, D. (1971), *Politicians, Equality and Comprehensives*, London, The Fabian Society.

Marsden, D. and Duff, E. (1975), *Workless*, Harmondsworth, Penguin.

Measor, Lynda (1984), 'Gender and the sciences', in M. Hammersley and P. Woods (eds), *Life in School*, Milton Keyenes, The Open University Press.

Measor, Lynda and Woods, Peter (1983), 'The interpretation of pupil myths', in M. Hammersley (ed.), *The Ethnography of Schooling*, Drifield, Yorks, Nafferton Books.

Measor, Lynda and Woods, Peter (1984), *Changing Schools*, Milton Keynes, The Open University Press.

Meighan, Roland (1981), *A Sociology of Educating*, London, Holt Saunders.

Metz, Mary H. (1978), *Classrooms and Corridors*, Berkeley, University of California Press.

Metz, Mary H. (1984), Editorial, *Sociology of Education*, vol. 57, no. 4, p. 199.

Meyenn, Robert J. (1980), 'School girls' peer groups', in P. Woods (ed.), *Pupil Strategies*, London, Croom Helm.

Nash, Roy (1973), *Classrooms Observed*, London, Routledge & Kegan Paul.

Newbold, D. (1977), *Ability Grouping – The Banbury Enquiry*, Slough NFER.

Nixon, Jon (ed.) (1980), *A Teacher's Guide to Action Research*, London, Grant McIntyre.

Oakley, Ann (1974a), *The Sociology of Housework*, London, Martin Robertson.

Oakley, Ann (1974b), *Housewife*, London, Allen Lane.

Oakley, Ann (1979), *Becoming a Mother*, Oxford, Martin Robertson.

Bibliography of works cited in the text

Orbach, M.K. (1977), *Hunters, Seamen and Entrepreneurs: The Tuna Seinermen of San Diego*, Berkeley, University of California Press.

Ouston, Janet and Maughan, B. (1985), 'Issues in the assessment of school outcomes', in D. Reynolds (ed.), *Studying School Effectiveness*, London, Falmer.

Pajak, E.F. and Blase, J.J. (1984), 'Teachers in bars', *Sociology of Education*, vol. 57, no. 3, pp. 164–73.

Payne, G. and Hustler, D. (1980), 'Teaching the class', *British Journal of Sociology of Education*, vol. 1, no. 1, pp. 49–66.

Peterson, Warren, A. (1964), 'Age, teacher's role and the institutional setting', in S. Delamont (ed.) (1984), *Readings on Interaction in the Classroom*, London, Methuen.

Pollard, A. (1984), 'Goodies, jokers and gangs', in M. Hammersley and P. Woods (eds), *Life in School*, Milton Keynes, The Open University Press.

Pollard, A. (1985), *The Social World of the Primary School*, London, Holt, Rhinehart & Winston.

Prendergast, S. and Prout, A. (1986), 'The school and the sick child', *Sociology of Health and Illness*, vol. 8, no. 3.

Rees, T.L. and Atkinson, P. (eds) (1982), *Youth Unemployment and State Intervention*, London, Routledge & Kegan Paul.

Resnick, D. and Resnick, L. (1985), 'Standards, curriculum and performance', *Educational Researcher*, vol. 14, no. 4, pp. 5–21.

Richardson, E. (1973), *The Teacher, the School, and the Task of Management*, London, Heinemann.

Riseborough, G.F. (1981), 'Teachers, careers, and comprehensive schooling', *Sociology*, vol. 15, no. 3, pp. 355–81.

Rosenbaum, J.E. (1976), *Making Inequality*, New York, Wiley.

Roth, Julius (1963), *Timetables*, Indianapolis, Bobbs-Merrill.

Roth, Julius (1966), 'Hired hand research', *American Sociologist*, 1, pp. 190–6.

Roth, Julius (1978), 'Ritual and magic in the control of contagion', in R. Dingwall and J. McIntosh (eds), *Readings in the Sociology of Nursing*, Edinburgh, Churchill Livingstone.

Rutter, Michael *et al.* (1979), *Fifteen Thousand Hours*, London, Open Books.

Shone, David and Atkinson, Paul (1981), 'Industrial training for slow learners', *Education for Development*, vol. 6, no. 3, pp. 25–30.

Simon, B. and Willcocks, J. (eds) (1981), *Research and Practice in the Primary Classroom*, London, Routledge & Kegan Paul.

Smith, L.M. and Geoffrey, W. (1968), *Complexities of an Urban Classroom*, New York, Holt, Rinehart & Winston.

Spencer, Herbert (1911), *Essays on Education*, London, Dent.

Spindler, G. (ed.) (1982), *Doing the Ethnography of Schooling*, New York, Holt, Rineheart & Winston.

Stillman, A. and Maychell, K. (1984), *School to School*, Windsor, NFER-Nelson.

Stubbs, M. and Delamont, S. (eds) (1976), *Explorations in Classroom Observation*, Chichester, Wiley.

Bibliography of works cited in the text

Sussman, Leila (1977), *Tales out of School*, Philadelphia, Temple University Press.

Swidler, Ann (1979), *Organization without Authority*, Harvard, The University Press.

Tann, S. (1981), 'Grouping and group work', in B. Simon and J. Willcocks (eds). *Research and Practice in the Primary Classroom*, London, Routlege & Kegan Paul.

Turner, Glen (1983), *The Social World of the Comprehensive School*, London, Croom Helm.

Walker, R. and Adelman, C. (1976), 'Strawberries', in M. Stubbs and S. Delamont (eds), *Explorations in Classroom Observation*, Chichester, Wiley.

Walker, R. and Goodson, I. (1977), 'Humour in the classroom', in P. Woods and M. Hammersley (eds), *School Experience*, London, Croom Helm.

Wax, Murray and Wax, Rosalie (1971), 'Great tradition, little tradition and formal education', in M. Wax, S. Diamond and F. Gearing (eds), *Anthropological Perspectives on Education*, New York, Basic Books.

Whiteside, M.T. and Mathieson, M. (1971), 'The secondary modern school in fiction', *British Journal of Educational Studies*, vol. xix, no. 3, pp. 283–92.

Whyld, Janie (ed.) (1983), *Sexism in the Secondary Curriculum*, London, Harper & Row.

Willes, Mary (1981), 'Learning to take part in classroom interaction', in P. French and M. Maclure (eds), *Adult-Child Conversation*, London, Croom Helm.

Willis, Paul (1977), *Learning to Labour*, Farnborough, Saxon House.

Wolpe, Ann Marie (1977), *Some Processes in Sexist Education*, London, WRRC.

Woods, Peter (1975), 'Showing them up in secondary school', in G. Chanan and S. Delamont (eds), *Frontiers of Classroom Research*, Slough, NFER.

Woods, Peter (1978), 'Negotiating the demands of schoolwork', *Journal of Curriculum Studies*, vol. 10, no. 4, pp. 309–27.

Woods, Peter (1979), *The Divided School*, London, Routledge & Kegan Paul.

Woods, Peter (ed.) (1980a), *Teacher Strategies*, London, Croom Helm.

Woods, Peter (ed.) (1980b), *Pupil Strategies*, London, Croom Helm.

Woods, Peter, Sykes, P. and Measor, L. (1985), *Oral Histories of Teachers*, Milton Keynes, The Open University Press.

Wragg, E.C. and Dooley, P.A. (1984), 'Class Management during teaching practice', in E.C. Wragg (ed.), *Classroom Teaching Skills*, London, Croom Helm.

Wragg, E.C. and Wood, E.K. (1984), 'Teachers' first encounters with their classes', in E.C. Wragg (ed.), *Classroom Teaching Skills*, London, Croom Helm.

Wylie L. (1974), *Village in the Vaucluse* (3rd edition), Harvard, The University Press.

Bibliography of works cited in the text

Young, M.F.D. (ed.) (1971), *Knowledge and Control*, London, Collier-Macmillan.

Youngman, M. and Lunzer, E. (1977), *Adjustment to Secondary Schooling*, Nottingham, The School of Education.

Zeldin, T. (1983), *The French*, Harmondsworth, Penguin.

Zerubavel, Eviator (1979), *Patterns of Time in Hospital Life*, Chicago, The University Press.

Index of authors

Adelman, Clem, 36, 44, 47, 62, 131, 278
Angus, Louie, 141, 270
Applebaum, H.A., 65, 75, 128, 230, 270
Ashton, Patricia, 267
Atkinson, Paul A., 16, 17, 46, 57, 65–6, 70, 75, 87, 99, 203, 270

Ball, Stephen, 2, 3, 45–6, 55, 57, 127, 136, 148, 155, 156, 210, 221, 232, 270
Barton, L., 268
Bauman, R., 19, 209, 210, 271
Beale, Dorothea, 132, 141, 271
Bealing, D., see Boydell
Becker, H.S., 6, 17, 271
Benn, C., 156, 271
Bennett, S. Neville, 2, 144, 174, 180, 271
Berliner, D., 242, 273
Bernstein, Basil, 5, 271
Beynon, John, 3, 24, 44, 51–2, 57–9, 67, 68, 76, 87, 113, 116–17, 153, 216, 271
Blackburn, R.M., 75, 148, 209, 271
Blase, J.J., 210, 277
Blatchford, Peter, 16, 26, 271
Borman, K., 240, 271
Bourdieu, P., 208, 271

Boydell, Deanne, 267, 268
Bream, F., 45, 271
Bryant, K.A., 18, 21, 22, 26, 107, 272
Bullivant, B.M., 17, 95, 120, 129–30, 141–2, 272
Burgess, R.G., 130, 156, 268, 272
Burnett, Jaquetta Hill, 80, 129, 272
Buswell, Carol, 160, 180, 272

Cane, B., 124, 129, 143, 275
Cleave, Shirley, 17, 26, 272
Cohen, P., 26, 48, 272
Coombs, R.H., 17, 272
Corrie, Malcolm, 127, 136–7, 272
Croll, Paul, 1, 267
Cusick, P., 210, 272

Daner, F.J., 138–40, 272
David, Miriam, 208, 272
Davidoff, Leonore, 182, 272
Davies, Brian, 3, 272
Davies, Lynn, 2, 232, 272
Delafield, Angela, 268
Delamont, S., 2, 3, 4, 5, 6, 7, 17, 24, 44, 45, 46, 47, 51–2, 27–9, 86, 87, 89, 106, 117, 119, 120, 156, 160, 203, 206, 210, 230, 232, 241, 254, 256, 258, 260, 262, 268, 272–3

Index of authors

Denscombe, Martyn, 53, 76, 273
Dooley, P., 46–7
Doyle, W., 242, 273
Duff, E., 143, 276

Edgerton, R.B., 80, 138, 273
Eickelman, Dale, 120, 273
Evans, John, 221, 273
Everhart, R.B., 100, 210, 273

Finnan, C., 99, 273
Fisher, C., 242, 273
Flecker, J.E., 43
Fogelman, K., 156, 273
Fuller, Mary, 210, 232, 273
Furlong, V. John, 58, 75, 170, 273

Galton, Maurice, 1, 2, 3, 4, 5, 6,
   7, 8, 26, 41, 44, 51, 59, 67,
   155, 175, 180, 202, 230, 240,
   241, 254, 262, 267–9, 273
Gamst, F.G., 75, 128, 274
Geoffrey, W., 148, 277
Ginsburg, M., 210, 211, 274
GIST, 71, 274
Glaser, B., 16, 274
Godber, J., 137, 141, 274
Goffman, E., 212, 274
Good, T.L., 242, 273
Goodson, I., 36, 278
Greig, M., 2

Hamblin, D.H., 35, 274
Hamilton, D., 45, 274
Hammersley, Martyn, 2, 210,
   214, 219, 227, 274
Hanna, Judith L., 24, 73, 88, 99,
   274
Hannam, C., 131, 209, 210, 274
Hanson, D., 130, 274
Hargreaves, Andy, 210, 222, 268,
   274
Hargreaves, David, 2, 45, 79–80,
   92–3, 106, 108, 155, 156, 161,
   169, 241–2, 275
Hart, R.A., 98, 275
Herrington, M., 130, 274
Hilsum, S., 124, 129, 143, 275

Holly, D., 156, 275
Hustler, D., 144, 277
Hutchins, I., 137, 141, 274

Jackson, B., 167, 275
Jackson, P., 55, 155, 275
Jacobs, J., 92, 143, 275
Jasman, Anne, 269

Karweit, N., 127, 129, 275
Keddie, N., 151, 170, 275
Kelly, Alison, 70, 71, 275
King, R., 160, 215, 275
Kounin, J.S., 115, 275

Lacey, Colin, 2, 131, 155, 156,
   161, 169, 210, 241–2, 275
Lambart, Audrey, 259, 275
Larkin, R.W., 210, 275
Lawton, D., 241, 276
Lea, Janice, 2
Leighton, Martin, 140–41, 148,
   276
Leonard, D., 17, 276
Lightfoot, Sara L., 93, 276
Llewellyn, Mandy, 117, 210, 232,
   259, 276
Lomax, Pamela, 155, 180, 276
Lunzer, E., 26, 279

MacNamara, David, 80, 276
McPherson, Gertrude, 210, 276
MacPherson, James, 8, 210, 227,
   232, 276
Mahony, P., 98, 276
Marsden, D., 143, 156, 276
Mann, M., 75, 148, 209, 271
Mathieson, M., 45, 278
Maughan, B., 265, 277
Maychell, K., 35, 118, 120, 122,
   277
Measor, Linda, 18, 19, 20, 21, 23,
   24, 35, 37, 42, 46, 55, 57, 71,
   85, 107, 116, 132–3, 227–8,
   232, 276
Meighan, R., 127, 276
Metz, Mary H., 73, 88, 91, 93, 99,
   103, 238, 276

Meyenn, R., 97, 210, 232, 276
Moon, B., 268

Nash, Roy, 151, 276
Newbold, D., 3, 276
Nixon, J., 45, 276

Oakley, Ann, 17, 143, 210, 276
Orbach, M.K., 65, 75, 276
Ouston, Janet, 265, 277

Pajak, E.F., 210, 277
Payne, George, 144, 277
Peterson, Warren A., 130, 277
Pollard, Andrew, 5, 232, 277
Prendergast, S., 186, 277
Prout, A., 186, 277

Rees, Teresa L., 16, 277
Resnick, D., 241–2, 277
Resnick, Lauren, 241–2, 277
Richardson, Elizabeth, 156, 277
Riseborough, G.F., 210, 277
Rosenbaum, J.E., 155, 277
Roth, Julius, 68, 127, 240, 277
Rutter, Michael, 2, 149, 277

Shone, David, 65–6, 70, 270, 277
Simon, Brian, 1, 156, 176, 267–9,
271, 273, 277
Smith, Louis, M., 148, 277
Spencer, Herbert, 98, 277
Spindler, George, 273, 274, 277

Stillman, Andrew, 35, 118, 120,
122, 277
Strauss, Anselm, L., 16, 274
Sussman, Leila, 89, 277
Swidler, Anne, 140, 203, 204, 278

Tann, Sarah, 2, 180, 278
Tickle, L., 268
Turner, Glenn, 2, 278

Walker, R., 36, 44, 47, 62, 131,
278
Walker, S., 268, 273
Whiteside, M.T., 45, 278
Whyld, J., 208, 278
Willcocks, John, 1, 2, 3, 4, 7, 8,
26, 41, 47, 67, 155, 175, 202,
240, 262, 267–9
Willes, Mary, 45, 278
Willis, P., 76, 262, 278
Wolpe, A.M., 98, 278
Wood, E.K., 44, 47, 278
Woods, Peter, 2, 18, 19, 20, 21,
23, 24, 35, 36, 37, 42, 44, 46,
53, 55, 57, 76, 80, 85, 107,
116, 131, 132–3, 148, 161, 210,
214, 216, 227–8, 232, 278
Wragg, E.C., 44, 46–7, 278
Wylie, L., 119, 278

Youngman, M., 26, 279

Zeldin, T., 119, 279
Zerubavel, E., 127, 128, 130, 131,
137, 142, 279

Index of participants

The teachers

Miss Airdale, 105, 137, 144, 153, 174, 177, 195, 232, 246
Mrs Altham, 101, 200, 201, 248
Mrs Appleyard, 27–8, 38, 72, 142, 246
Mr Apter, 124, 245
Mr Arrow, 218, 246
Mr Astill, 106, 126, 201, 248
Mrs Attfield, 172, 248

Mr Baden, 81, 247
Mr Barrell, 54, 85–6, 109–10, 120, 176, 188, 246
Mr Beech, 161, 164, 247
Mr Beldham, 224, 245
Mr Birch, 144, 204, 246
Mrs Bird, 61–2, 66, 73, 83, 114, 124, 144–5, 163, 195, 199, 221, 224, 225, 245
Mr Black, 211, 245
Mrs Blewitt, 177, 246
Mrs Bobbin, 49, 124, 194, 247
Mr Bradshaw, 137, 163–4, 194, 245
Mr Braund, 124, 175, 247
Mr Brearly, 105, 247
Mr Brett, 67, 246
Mr Bronte, 37, 48–51, 101, 104, 124, 142–3, 187, 222, 247

Mr Blundell, 29, 37, 246

Miss Chichester, 37–8, 246
Mr Clift, 126, 247
Miss Cotton, 173, 174, 246
Mr Cowell, 110–11, 246
Mrs Cullen, 125, 145, 149, 174, 189, 246

Mr Darwin, 69, 123, 200, 202, 207, 247
Miss Devine, 176, 196, 197, 206, 246
Mrs Durrant, 95–6, 103, 126, 172, 200, 247

Mr Eggleston, 76–7, 248
Mr Evans, 78, 86–7, 118, 123, 124, 145–8, 188–9, 196, 197, 198, 200, 207, 217, 220, 224, 245, 255–6
Mrs Evans, 60, 118, 168, 170, 184, 197, 220, 224, 225, 245

Mr Fawlty, 84–5, 248
Miss Fern, 53, 103, 106, 164, 165–6, 201, 207, 247
Mr Flanigan, 72, 246
Mr Foale, 151–2, 246
Mrs Forrest, 53, 78–9, 82–3, 115, 125, 150, 188, 199, 202, 203–4,

215, 218, 222, 226, 245
Mr Forrest, 131, 245

Mrs Gaskell, 235–37, 246
Mr Gordon, 115, 149, 173–4, 246

Mrs Hallows, 29, 32–4, 36, 39, 72,
    89, 135, 142, 157, 166, 185,
    194, 217, 247
Mrs Hammond, 125, 247
Mrs Hargreaves, 224, 225, 226, 245
Mr Harpole, 50, 248
Mr Haydon, 80–1, 105, 114, 123,
    143, 158, 247
Mrs Hind, 11, 121–3, 137, 158,
    222, 245
Mr Hogg, 131, 245
Mr Huxley, 207, 247

Mr Jessop, 125, 248
Mr Judge, 11, 36, 98, 131, 192,
    206, 231, 245

Miss Kroll, 220, 245

Mrs Lake, 131, 247
Miss Lawrence, 49, 51, 82, 115,
    125, 197, 247
Mr Leach, 72, 205, 246
Mrs Lee, 125, 165, 217–18, 246
Mr LeGard, 131, 147, 150, 208,
    216, 219, 220, 245
Mrs Lords, 149, 246
Mr Lyons, 189, 201, 245

Mrs Madder, 106, 164, 247
Mrs Marks, 105, 187, 205–6, 247
Mr Mauss, 67, 192, 246
Miss Miranda, 163, 196, 240, 245
Mrs Monk, 170, 189, 246
Mr Moore, 67, 183, 246
Mr Mowbray, 81, 104, 124, 247

Mrs Newbolt, 114, 124, 248

Mr Oakley, 51, 248
Miss O'Hara, 60–1, 102, 115, 148,
    168–9, 170, 187, 197, 216, 245

Mrs Osbaldeston, 48, 248
Mr Palet, 101, 247
Mr Pardoe, 54, 123, 149, 170,
    195, 247
Mr Parkin, 50, 95, 185, 191, 192,
    193–4, 206, 212, 215–16, 247
Mr Pewter, 192, 202, 247
Miss Pink, 103, 163, 198, 200, 245
Mr Plumb, 161, 247
Mr Pompey, 110–11, 165, 170,
    189, 246

Mr Quill, 150, 161, 207, 247

Mrs Rumsey, 68, 69, 113, 202–3,
    246
Mr Rutherford, 51, 69, 83, 104,
    131, 151, 200, 247

Mr Salter, 52, 68–9, 113, 118, 149,
    176, 226, 234, 237, 238, 247
Mr Seed, 28–9, 37, 73–4, 94, 101,
    193, 205, 228, 246
Mr Southern, 28, 36, 246
Mrs Southey, 85, 104, 248
Mr Spencer, 48, 124, 205, 247
Miss Square, 57, 123, 136, 246
Mr Stackpole, 32–4, 189, 191,
    224, 228, 247
Mr Steele, 104, 247
Miss Stephenson, 72, 114, 152,
    153, 183, 194, 201, 217, 246
Mrs Stockton, 84, 124, 183, 194,
    195, 217, 246
Mrs Stone, 173, 174, 200, 245
Mr Sturgess-Jones, 112, 116, 245
Mrs Sutcliffe, 66, 125, 200, 248

Mr Taff, 145, 177, 246
Mrs Tallis, 158, 168, 245
Mrs Tench, 222, 245
Mr Tippett, 208, 246
Mr Trelawny, 164, 165, 247
Miss Tweed, 11, 62–3, 83, 97,
    112, 117, 122–3, 131, 132, 137,
    158, 159, 185, 188, 189, 194,
    201, 203, 207, 217, 230–31,
    245, 258

Index of participants

Miss Tyree, 30, 61, 96, 135, 178, 186, 187, 189, 190–91, 214–16, 218, 219, 222, 224, 225, 226, 245, 259

Mrs Tyzack, 164, 247

Mr Underwood, 131, 226, 246

Mr Valentine, 11, 112, 114, 122–23, 126, 131, 150, 158, 159, 222, 231, 245

Mr Vaughan, 84, 245

Mr Washbrook, 36, 191, 245
Mr Weir, 67, 117, 246
Mr Welsh, 29, 74, 188, 205, 228, 234–8, 246,
Mrs Wheel, 69, 247
Mr Woolfe, 53–4, 73, 77–9, 163, 203, 245
Mrs Wordsworth, 84, 101, 104, 158, 187, 217, 247

Mrs York, 183, 194, 246

Mrs Zeldin, 81, 94, 101, 106, 114, 194, 247

The pupils

Alan Bewes, 123, 249
Alistair, 178, 251
Althea, 57, 71, 81, 230, 233–4, 250
Alvin, 248, 255, 256, 257–8
Amos, 116, 248, 250
Amy, 121, 249
Annabel, 59–62, 96, 115, 158, 220, 248, 255, 259–60
Antonia, 235, 250
April, 232–3, 250
Archie, 173, 250
Arnold, 111, 115, 250
Audrey, 255, 259
Avril, 179, 251

Bagshaw, 221, 248

Barny, 248, 262
Barry, 78, 248, 255, 256–7, 258
Bart, 20, 21, 177, 178, 227, 251
Benedict Kortright, 185–6, 205, 248
Bethany, 232, 250
Blair, 110, 250
Brent, 102, 251
Brett, 110, 250
Bryony, 25, 251

Caitlin, 146, 188, 248
Camilla, 220, 248
Carter Pilch, 82, 190, 248
Caspar, 173, 248
Chantel, 109, 250
Cherie, 82, 197, 251
Clyde, 23, 250
Colette, 71, 165, 251
Colin, 166, 251
Coral, 248, 262
Coralie, 197, 251
Craig, 235, 250
Crispin, 118, 197, 248

Dan, 15, 69, 94, 101, 178, 235, 250
Danielle Draper, 201, 251
Daphne, 22, 57, 176, 235, 250
Davina, 8, 44, 117, 179, 230–1, 249, 258
Dawn, 21, 25–6, 71, 251, 255, 258, 259, 260
Dean, 152, 188, 249
Deanna, 232, 250
Delia, 25, 40, 71, 178, 251
Denzil, 20, 24, 191, 205, 227–8, 251
Dermot, 96, 109, 179, 250
Derrick, 82–3, 248
Dickon, 234–37, 250, 261
Dirk, 60–2, 115, 144–5, 148, 158, 173, 220, 248
Dominico Grillo, 197–9, 241, 248, 255–6, 258
Donald, 115, 251
Dudley, 44, 59, 62, 249

Eamonn O'Malley, 114, 158, 165, 180, 201, 251
Earl, 196, 250
Edmond, 110–11, 165, 250
Edward, 109, 250
Elaine, 84, 165, 251
Ellen Farley, 20, 71, 178, 200, 251
Ellis, 19, 179, 251
Elmer, 25, 88, 178, 250
Emily, 41, 232–3, 250
Errol, 229, 235, 250
Eunice, 21, 22, 23, 57, 235, 250

Fay, 57, 176, 235, 250
Felicity, 169, 197, 248
Fenella, 40, 71, 251
Fern, 69, 235, 250
Fida, 22, 25, 81, 109, 250, 255, 260–61
Floyd, 133, 250
Francine, 251, 255, 259

Gabrielle, 248, 262
Gail, 235, 236, 250
Gareth Williams, 202, 250
Gavin Radice (Radley), 118, 145–8, 189, 220, 248, 255, 256, 258
Gemma, 177, 251
Gerard, 88, 108, 117, 250
Gerald, 220, 248
George, 22, 95, 250
Gilbert, 23, 41, 250
Gita, 83, 172, 251
Glenn, 166, 180, 251
Gordon Wilde, 19, 20, 40, 191, 192, 201, 251
Greg, 22, 118, 234–7, 250, 255, 261–2
Gwen, 170, 250

Harry, 15, 118, 234–7, 250, 255, 261–2
Heather, 22, 69, 235, 250
Howard, 77, 188, 248
Hugh, 131, 249

Inge, 227, 232, 250

Irving, 25, 162, 250
Ivor, 115, 251

Jackie, 176, 229, 235, 237, 250
Jake, 220, 251
Jaquetta, 230–1, 249
Jasmine, 8, 250, 251
Jerome, 25, 109, 162, 250
Jessamine, 8, 89, 96, 108, 233–4, 241, 250
Jessica, 15, 176, 235, 237, 250
Jim, 166, 172, 251
John, 85, 109, 179, 250
Joscelin, 20, 21, 251
Josephine, 235, 237, 250
Josh, 21, 94, 178, 230, 235, 236, 250
Josie, 173, 250
Julia, 117, 250
Julietta, 179, 251

Karel, 97, 249
Karena, 22, 25, 108, 109, 250, 255, 260–1
Keith, 19, 251
Kenneth, 83, 85, 97, 201, 249
Kevin, 110, 115, 174, 250
Kieran, 232, 250

Laura Eggleston, 71, 200, 251
Lauretta, 195, 248, 262
Laurence, 197, 251
Lavinia, 89, 96, 233–4, 241, 250
Lawrence, 188, 248
LeeAnne, 231–32, 250
Leila, 151, 248
Leonora, 232–3, 250
Lester, 57, 109–10, 117, 173, 250
Liam, 114, 251
Lillian, 248, 262
Lionel (Joe), 61, 115, 248, 255, 256, 257, 258
Lloyd, 114, 251
Lucinda, 229, 251
Lucy, 203, 230–31, 249
Luella, 232, 250
Luke, 21, 94, 230, 235, 238, 250

Madoc, 96, 179, 250
Magnus, 108, 248
Mair Pryce, 151, 200, 248
Malcolm, 178, 249
Manji, 166, 172, 251
Marcia, 189, 249
Maurice, 125, 153, 173, 192, 250
Melvyn Pym, 114, 124, 201, 251
Meriel, 235, 238, 250
Merle, 20, 71, 178–9, 229, 233–4,
     250
Mervyn, 20, 114, 251
Michael, 125, 250
Miles, 57, 109, 173, 250
Mirelle, 188, 193, 248
Mitchell Gardiner, 87, 90, 202,
     248
Myra, 109, 250

Nanette, 230–1, 249, 255, 258–9
Natalie, 71, 251
Nathan, 39, 113, 178, 179–80,
     229, 235, 238, 250
Neil Carpenter, 149, 153, 179,
     250
Nigel, 97, 249
Norman, 179, 251

Odette, 15, 176, 229, 235, 250
Oliver, 97, 249

Pamela, 251, 255, 259
Paula, 60, 96, 115, 248
Peggy, 19, 40, 251
Peter Queen, 149, 250
Petunia, 96–7, 108, 235, 250
Philip, 110, 159, 161, 250
Priscilla, 97, 249

Ralph, 173, 250
Raymond Lynn, 112, 121–3, 193,
     249
Rex Mackie, 44, 62, 202, 241,
     251, 255, 262
Rhoda, 82–3, 86, 115, 248

Richard, 108, 109, 179, 250
Richie, 161, 250
Rolf, 96, 179, 202–3, 250
Royce, 50, 251
Royston, 22, 238, 250
Russell, 235, 238, 250

Sally, 108, 250
Sandra, 40, 177, 251
Saul, 235, 238, 250
Sebastian Gunn, 199, 248
Selwyn, 81, 114, 124, 126, 251
Sheila, 231, 249
Shelly, 82, 203, 248, 262
Simone, 49, 220, 251
Sinclair, 234–7, 250, 255, 261–2
Sonia, 204, 248
Stephanie, 83, 249
Stirling, 122–3, 249

Tamara Fields, 200, 251
Tammy, 83, 249
Tanya, 251, 259
Terence, 188–9, 216, 248
Terry, 204, 250
Thelma, 170, 250
Trudie, 57, 71, 81, 95, 108, 230,
     233–4, 250

Vanessa, 251, 255, 259
Vaudine, 71, 178–9, 229, 233–4,
     250
Verity, 232, 250
Veronica Tate, 200, 249
Vincent Delgardo, 40, 200, 251

Walter, 173, 250
Wanda, 96–7, 108, 235, 250
Wayne Douglas Patel, 44, 58–9,
     62, 84, 114, 165–6, 180, 241,
     251, 255, 262

Yvette (Horace), 62–3, 83, 241,
     251
Yvonne, 71, 251

Index of subjects

annual cycle, 128–33
anxieties, 17–26, 35, 41, 227, 229, 230
art, 53, 73, 77–9, 102, 105–6, 162, 163, 164, 256
Ashburton Boys' School, 244, 253, 254, 255, 256, 263
Ashburton Girls' School, 244, 253, 254, 263
Ashwood Bank Middle School, 20, 30, 40, 49, 71, 192, 202, 220, 247
assembly, 12, 27, 49, 50, 73, 102, 104, 152, 157, 160, 169, 171–2, 181, 185, 187, 192, 205–6
attendance *see* truancy

backstage region, 212, 238
Balaclava Road Lower School, 167, 244, 254
Banbury Lower School, 36, 244
Banbury Middle School, 190, 244
banding, 12, 13, 155, 156, 168–70; *see also* streaming and setting
biology, 71, 162, 177, 200, 202
Black *see* Negro
'boffs' *see* Homosexuality
breaktime, 49, 50, 73, 92, 93–9, 107, 140, 143, 152, 153, 157, 179, 190, 211, 215, 216
British West Indian *see* Negro

bullying, 20, 21, 29, 30, 39, 40, 41, 50, 86–90, 96–7, 227, 233
Burton Upton Middle School, 40, 71, 229, 247

careers, of pupils; 153, 255–62; of teachers, 128, 130–31, 150
changing rooms, 37, 38, 59, 110–11, 116, 160, 212
chemistry, 71, 123, 208
Chicanos, 80, 93–4
choirs, 55, 171, 179
classification, 5
cliques of teachers, 57, 209, 211–14
cloakrooms, 86, 160, 174
clubs, 55, 177–80, 186, 261
Coalthorpe High School, 25
'coffee clubs', 211, 213
computer addict, 257
construction workers, 65–6, 128, 230
contrastive rhetoric, 22
cookery classes, 23, 27, 61–2, 65, 66–7, 71, 73, 83, 125, 144, 160, 163–4, 181, 195, 196, 199, 200, 206
coping strategy, 5, 210
corridors, 22, 55, 73–4, 86, 88, 91–2, 99–109, 219

Coventry Lane Lower School, 167, 244
craft, 23, 36, 56, 70, 76, 136–7, 150, 160, 162, 163–4, 175, 183, 191, 194, 220, 223, 253, 257, 264
cross country running, 24, 32, 59, 78, 97, 116–17
cynicism, 29, 31, 34, 179–80

daily routine, 138–44
danger, 4, 13, 14, 24, 51–4, 64–90, 240, 241
Dashwood Upper School, 244, 253, 254, 255, 257, 263
design *see* craft
detention, 152–3
developing sexuality, 24–5, 96–7, 232
dinners and dinnertime, 15, 29, 30, 33, 49, 50, 87, 92, 93–9, 100, 141, 142, 157, 177–9, 186–7, 211, 214, 215, 218, 219, 228
dinner ladies, 87, 97
discipline, 28, 47, 84, 86, 91, 158, 186, 190, 234
dissection, 24, 28, 31
domestic science *see* home economics
Dorridge Lower School, 57, 178, 245
drama, 55, 76, 91, 105, 109–10, 113, 127, 172, 179

earrings *see* jewellery
English, 3, 13, 20, 23, 27, 49, 56, 60, 82, 85, 86, 101, 104, 105, 115, 118, 121, 123, 125, 132, 145–8, 149, 162, 168, 170, 173–5, 176, 185, 188, 197–9, 200, 213, 223, 235, 236
entries, 102–6
errands, 117–18, 237
establishing order, 44–7
ethnography, 2, 4–6, 75, 88, 89, 117, 128, 155, 210, 240–41
exits, 102–6

familiarity, 2, 6, 241
families, real, 56–7, 181, 182–204, 217; *see also* parents; symbolic, 56–7, 182, 204–8
favouritism, 117, 179, 255
fighting, 87–90, 95, 98, 121, 124; *see also* violence
firedrill, 72–3, 144
fisherman, 65, 138, 177, 227
folklore, 19, 20, 23, 32, 209, 216
Fordhouses Middle School, 71, 247
foreshadowed problems, 5, 55
framing, 5
friendships of pupils, 20–1, 57, 86, 89–90, 157, 176–7, 226–39
French, 3, 18, 23, 27, 31, 41, 49, 71, 76, 80–2, 84, 96, 104, 105, 106, 114, 119, 123, 124, 162, 164, 171, 173, 183, 185, 189, 194, 195, 201, 202, 264

games, 27, 55, 110–12, 116, 204; *see also* PE
games kit, 28, 37, 93, 110, 112, 191, 192, 193, 206, 207
geography, 13, 101, 124, 125, 145, 146, 149, 164, 174, 175, 198, 22
German, 49, 124, 162, 164, 223
girls and science, 70–2, 263–64
golf, 92, 216
groups, formal, 55–6, 155–81; *see also* cliques and friendship
Guy Mannering Lower School, 167, 244
gym *see* PE

Hinckley Road Middle School, 244, 253
history, 13, 114, 124, 151, 153, 162, 164, 222
home economics, 34, 96, 175, 176, 190, 197, 200, 206, 211, 223, 258
homosexuality, 23, 24–5, 161–62, 216

homework, 33–4, 149, 152–3, 166, 185, 186, 187–90, 220
hospitals, 128, 130, 131, 137, 142, 203
house system, 9, 12, 13, 152, 155, 159, 168–70, 186, 228
housework and housewives, 143, 206, 210
humiliation, 76–86
humour, 28, 36, 62–3, 117, 131, 214–19, 257

immobility, 54–5, 91–126
industrial training units, 65–6, 70
initial encounters, 3, 44–51, 57–62, 240, 241
Islamic schooling and pupils, 120, 171–2, 254

jewellery, 27, 50, 72, 190–91, 207, 253, 256
Jewish schooling, 95, 120, 129–30, 141–2
jokes *see* humour

Kenilworth Warden Lower School, 27, 28, 37, 57, 228, 233, 245
King's Heath Lower School, 57, 245
Knowle Park Lower School, 57, 245
Krsna devotees, 138–40

labelling, 5, 53, 60, 158, 159, 167; of property, 142, 186, 192–4
laboratories, 31, 34, 52, 66, 67–8, 70, 104, 105, 113, 118, 234
lateness of pupils, 48, 55, 78, 107, 142–3, 165–6; of teachers, 149
Latin, 13, 27, 170
lavatories, 20, 23–4, 29, 32, 38, 54–5, 78, 88, 96, 122–3, 131, 160
library, 85, 131, 144, 147, 150, 211–12, 216
lifeguards, 80, 138
lost property, 28, 93, 124, 193–4

lunch and lunchtime *see* dinner
Luton Airport Syndrome, 91, 92–3, 106–9, 126

maths, 3, 13, 31, 56, 69, 71, 77, 82–3, 85, 106, 115, 121, 124, 125, 126, 132, 133, 152–3, 154, 162, 164, 165, 173, 185, 188, 194, 199, 201, 222, 224, 231, 232, 258
medical school, 17, 256
medical sociology, 127
metalwork, 13, 40, 64, 67, 75, 160, 163–4, 192, 202
mixed ability teaching, 3, 9, 155, 157, 158, 164, 222, 242
Mitchell Butler Lower School, 27, 28, 36, 57, 229, 233, 245
Morland Upper School, 244, 253, 255, 257–8, 263
movement, 49, 54–5, 91–126
music, 76–7, 84–5, 101, 109, 158, 164, 168, 173, 174, 200, 201, 207, 208, 258
mythology, 20, 23–4, 35, 38

needlework, 65, 124, 160, 163–4, 183, 194, 200
negro pupils, 80, 88, 93–4, 99, 191, 227
neighbourhoods, 92–4

Old Hill Lower School, 167, 220, 240, 244
Orton Water Church of England Lower School, 167, 244

Paddington Station effect, 92–3, 106–9
parents, 15, 30, 32–4, 48, 49, 50, 63, 135, 142, 182–99, 224, 226, 256, 257, 258, 260; *see also* families
parents' evenings, 18, 26, 32–4, 135, 183, 186, 229–9
PE, 4, 22, 23, 26, 31, 37, 55, 67, 71, 72, 79, 92, 105, 109, 110–13, 114, 117, 126, 160, 172,

175, 186, 188, 192, 200, 204, 207, 217–18, 221, 228, 257, *see also* games
PE kit *see* games kit
physics, 51, 83, 104, 200
Pickwick Middle School, 40, 247
playgrounds, 12, 31, 55, 73, 86, 87, 88, 89–90, 91, 93–9, 101, 103, 135, 137, 157, 166, 218, 224, 233, 257
pottery, 67, 119, 192
pregnancy, 17, 207, 255, 259
pre-transfer programme, 17–18, 26–42, 135, 142, 161, 193, 228
pseudonyms, 6–8
punishment, 28, 82–3, 91, 114–18, 259

race, 85, 99, 156, 157, 171–2, 181, 220, 242
railway workers, 128
religion of pupils, 156, 171–2
religious education, 95–6, 103, 126, 144, 147, 149, 150, 151, 168, 171–72, 200, 204, 206, 220
remedial teaching, 28, 148, 172, 173–5, 180–81, 212, 220
retirement, 92, 138, 143
Roman Catholics, 130, 171–2, 254, 259
rules, 44, 45, 47, 48, 58, 73, 93–9, 144, 231

St Bridget's School, 9, 244, 254
sanatoria, 68
Sanditon Community College, 10, 246, 252, 253, 255, 260, 261, 263, 265, 266
science, 3, 23, 24, 28, 31, 54, 68–70, 71–2, 97, 103, 106, 123, 149, 150, 162, 164, 165–6, 175, 176, 195, 201, 202–03, 211, 213, 234, 236, 253, 256; *see also* biology, chemistry, physics
sets, 154, 155, 222, 232, 242
sex differentiation, 51, 80–2, 83–

5, 88–9, 96, 103, 104, 105–6, 109–10, 112, 116–17, 118, 151, 156, 157, 159–62, 171, 180, 206–7
showers, 22, 26, 32, 38, 111, 204, 260
siblings, 5, 51, 56–7, 182, 197, 199–203, 220, 262; *see also* families
social studies, 56, 151, 176, 188
speed of work, 144–51
sports teams, 28, 41, 55, 155, 168, 171, 174–5, 177–80, 185, 199, 256
staffrooms, 50, 130, 144, 171, 174, 184, 185, 190–1, 202, 209, 210–26, 238–9
status passage, 16–17
Stourbridge Road Middle School, 29, 30, 39, 40, 247
streaming, 9, 12, 13, 28, 155–6, 158, 159, 166–71, 232
swimming, 30, 62, 71, 131, 162, 178–9, 185, 204

teachers' families, 203–4
technical drawing, 150, 161, 164
termly cycle, 123–33
theft, 28, 73, 193–4
time, 4, 14, 48, 55, 82, 127–54, 241
timetables, 49, 55, 92, 133–44, 151, 224–5
trade unions, 223–6
transitions, 16–17, 132–3
trips and excursions, 28, 61–2, 114, 132, 235, 237–7, 260
truancy, 48, 187, 255, 259, 261, 262, 264–5

unemployment, 11, 33, 138, 143, 206, 255, 262, 264
uniform, 9, 11, 13, 25, 28, 30, 48, 50, 72, 131, 161–2, 168, 186, 90–3, 203, 206, 259, 260, 261

Vietnamese, 99

Villebourne Middle School, 25, 245

violence, 46, 52–3, 58–62, 73, 87–90, 257

visible pedagogies, 5

Wellington Middle School, 29, 39, 247

West Indian *see* negro

whistle-stop tours, 29, 50, 142

Whitteck Lower School, 22, 57, 245

Woodhouse Upper School, 244, 253, 255, 258, 259, 263

woodwork, 4, 13, 40, 67, 71, 79, 114, 161, 163–4, 183

workplaces, 75, 148, 209–10

yards *see* playgrounds